Tennessee Valley Beach

"The inland we found to be a goodly country, stored with many blessings for man, and a multitude of creatures. The people are of a tractable nature, free and loving, without guile and treachery; their bows and arrows they use with great skill, yet not to do any great harm with them. They are so strong of body that two or three of our men could hardly carry what they could pick up and carry an English mile; they are swift in running for long periods, and seldom walk but for the most part run."

Diary of Chaplain Francis Fletcher
Aboard the Golden Hind, Drake's Bay, 1579

"It was westward they ran. Hunger, you would have thought, came out of the east like the sun, and the evening was made edible of gold."

Robert Louis Stevenson, 1879

GOLDEN GATE TRAILBLAZER
Where to Hike, Stroll, Bike, Jog, Roll
In San Francisco and Marin

first edition
text by Jerry Sprout
photographs, design, production by Janine Sprout

For Carina Dove, Richard, Michael and Cynthia, Matthew and Amy, Gail and Brian

ISBN 0-9670072-2-4
Library of Congress Catalog Card Number: 00-103722

Diamond Valley Company, Publisher
89 Lower Manzanita Drive
Markleeville, CA 96120
www.trailblazertravelbooks.com
trailblazer@gbis.com

Printed in the United States of America

Thanks to: Georgia Sagues; Christina Cliff; Chet Carlisle; Carl "Red" Brown; Michael Sagues; Thomas M. Sagues; Amy Vogel; Matt Sagues; Sam Scott; Laura Gotz; Joseph Stroud; Elsa Kendall; John and Suzanne Barr; Spencer Rogers; Christine Evans Clark; Patty Brissenden, Joan Green and Betty Dietz of the Canal Community Alliance; Kim Sulkirk, Archives and Records, GGNRA; Meiya at Green Gulch; Jerry Lott, WildCare; Amy Dawson, Randall Museum; Casey May and others, Marin Municipal Water District; Tammy Jernigan, S.F. Mayors Office; Georgette Quan Dahlka and Frank Quan, China Camp; Chris Lang and Nancy at Marin Bicycle Coalition; Eric Chase, Samuel P. Taylor State Park; Jeff Hays, Bay Audubon Center & Sanctuary; France Laud; Bob Holloway, Michael Feinstein and many others at the Golden Gate National Recreation Area; docents at the California Legion of Honor; Sherry Sweet, Marin County Convention and Visitors Bureau; William Cox, Friends of China Camp; Nancy Chan, San Francisco Zoo; Joan at Town of Tiburon; Carlene McCort, Bob Hess and Maradel Rowlands, San Rafael Community Services; Golden Gate Transit; Edward Zelinsky, Musee Mecanique; Dara Schwarzchild, S.F. Recreation & Parks; Jeff Goodwin, Postmaster, San Quentin; Laurie Armstrong, S.F. Convention and Visitors Bureau; Jim Swanson, State Fish and Game Department; Kay McCord, Larkspur Library; Steve Petterle, Marin Department of Parks; Jem Graphics; Larry Perkins, China Camp State Park; Jackie Branch, Celine Calahorro, Corte Madera Parks and Recreation; Karin Urquhart; Marin Conservation League staff; Lori Simpkins, City of Novato; Maureen Larson, Jeff Price, California State Parks, Marin Office; Lynn Skillings, Marin History Museum; numerous staff at Bear Valley Visitors Center, Point Reyes National Seashore; Peter Tanin, San Francisco S.F. Department of Parking and Traffic; Nancy Botkin, S.F. Bike Coalition; Dan Winkelman, Angel Island State Park; Ron Sonenshine, Presidio Trust; Verna Smith, Marin Museum of the American Indian; Danny Dann, San Francisco Giants; staff at Senator John Burton's office; David Hansen at Marin Department of Parks and Open Space; and many others who provided information along the way—keep up the good work!

Proofreaders: Cynthia Sprout, Greg Hayes

Old St. Hilarys Preserve

GOLDEN GATE TRAILBLAZER

is published with respect for the natural wonders
bestowed upon these lands, for its plants and animals,
and for all people who have worked to put parks in our
cities and preserve wild lands for future generations.

The Presidio

GOLDEN GATE

Trailblazer

WHERE TO
HIKE, STROLL, BIKE, JOG, ROLL
IN SAN FRANCISCO AND MARIN

JERRY AND JANINE SPROUT

DIAMOND VALLEY COMPANY

MARKLEEVILLE, CALIFORNIA

PUBLISHERS

TABLE OF CONTENTS

INTRODUCING THE GOLDEN GATE

Midway along the Coast Range of California is a single opening one-mile wide called the Golden Gate. The rainwater that falls on half the state meets the Pacific Ocean at this opening, a constant ebb and flow, creating a vast system of rivers, streams, bays, marshes and lagoons. To the north and south of the Golden Gate are the Marin and San Francisco peninsulas. Prior to the building of the Golden Gate Bridge in 1937, land travelers needed to make a trip of some 200 miles around the bays to get across the strait.

Making this spot more dynamic is what lies beneath the surface: Under water just offshore from San Francisco and running through the western part of Marin County is the San Andreas Fault, where the two largest of the earth's twelve continental plates come together. Occasionally the plates move. In 1906 the entire spring-loaded land-mass of the Point Reyes Peninsula lurched 20 feet in a matter of seconds. So, inherent in the awe of all that is wonderful about San Francisco is the knowledge that it can all come down like a house of cards.

The Golden Gate's physical dynamic, as incredible as it is, has been matched by its human history. In the mid-1800s, the region was part of Mexico, and had been for 70 years. Mexico was preparing for a showdown with the Russians, who were settling the lands north of Marin County. But when gold was discovered, the Americans sailed a superior force through the Golden Gate and claimed California for the United States.

Into the Golden Gate during the decades following 1850 rushed the largest voluntary human migration in recorded history. And going out the gate during those same years, not coincidentally, was the gold and silver dug from the mines of the Mother Lode and Comstock Lode in the Sierra Nevada, to this day the richest deposits ever discovered. In a single generation, San Francisco morphed from being a fishing village to one of the largest cities in America.

Coyote Ridge, Crissy Field

Near Fort Scott overlook

During the following century it has become one of the world's most beloved cities, ranking up there with Paris and Rome on visitor surveys. Although most of the gold is gone, the rush is still on. At the turn of the 21st century, if real estate and rental prices in Marin and San Francisco can be used as a yardstick, no other place in the world beckons like the Golden Gate.

Since the Gold Rush, new population booms have followed, one upon the other, each leaving its own layer on the region's historical landscape. In the early 1900s, post-earthquake San Francisco was rebuilt in grand fashion, as the shanties that had been erected in haste were replaced with Victorians and artful civic buildings. After the Golden Gate Bridge was completed in 1937, an exodus to Marin began in earnest, and that was accelerated by the post-World War II exodus that affected all of California. In the 1960s and 70s, Flower Power brought young people to the city from all over the world. In the 1970s and 1980s, the Hippies were followed by the migration of Hollywood-north, New York-west and multi-national money from everywhere, as those-in-the-know selected Marin and San Francisco as the place to Be. From the 1970s to present—thanks to engineers at Cal and Stanford, universities with Gold-Rush roots—the region has seen booms in aerospace, high-tech and dot-com. And from the 1980s to the present, the Mexicans and other working-class immigrants from countries south of the border have returned to the Golden Gate.

Attracting all of these migrations of people has been new gold in California: scenic beauty and quality of life. Although nature provided these riches, recent generations can be credited with taking steps to see that the wealth has not been squandered.

In Marin and San Francisco are some 150,000 acres of parklands—more than six times the area of the city, and over 40 percent of the two land areas combined. Nature lovers will find the Golden Gate National Recreation Area, the largest urban park anywhere, which extends to both sides of the bridge. Marin's crown jewel, the Point Reyes National Seashore, was signed into being as one of John F. Kennedy's last official acts.

San Francisco has a number of large parks, including Golden Gate Park, which dates from the philanthropy following the Gold Rush. In Marin is Muir Woods National Monument, also created by philanthropy at the end of the 19th century. The entire Mount Tamalpais Watershed, some 20,000 acres, is public land owning to the establishment of California's first water district in the early 1900s. Tamalpais is also the site of the first California State Park, thanks to the individuals who had established historic hiking clubs on the mountain. When the post-World War II rush was on, other state parks were established, including Angel Island, China Camp and Tomales Bay. In the 1970s, Marin voters established an open space district, which has since created dozens of large preserves, purchasing lands that would have otherwise been

Ferry Building, Loma Alta, Pt. Reyes Lighthouse

Golden Gate Bridge, Ocean Beach, Sleepy Hollow Divide

converted to housing tracts. These public lands have been preserved through both the grand gestures of wealthy individuals, and the life-long efforts of thousands of every-day people.

But, perhaps the biggest step in this preservation was provided by accident. In an effort to protect the land from invasions, military forces for the last two centuries have constructed a system of defenses on the coastal bluffs and islands of the Golden Gate. It started with the Spanish in 1790, when they installed cannons near today's Fort Mason. And the building continued, with new batteries placed during the Civil War, Spanish American War, both World Wars, and right on up to the Cold War with Nike Missile pads. Each generation of weapons became obsolete, thankfully, before it was ever put to use. In the 1970s, these old military sites became the basis for Golden Gate National Recreation Area. Ironically, in an effort to protect these lands from invaders we had preserved them for ourselves.

HOW TO USE THIS BOOK

Use the INDEX to locate a trail or place that you've already heard about. Use the TABLE OF CONTENTS and MASTER MAP to find a region you'd like to explore. Then use the TRAILHEAD MAP to focus on a trailhead number in that region, and go the description to pick out a hike or other adventure that looks good to you. Each trailhead contains hikes of varying lengths.

Use the Activities Banner in the TRAILHEAD DIRECTORY to look for specific recreational activities. Use the BEST OF section to find something to suit the day and your mood.

CALCULATING HIKING TIMES: Average walkers will cover about 2 miles per hour, including stops. Exercise walkers can figure 3 miles per hour. Strollers and larger groups may average only 1 to 1.5 miles per hour.

DRIVING TIMES: When there is no traffic, ha, ha, you can drive from San Rafael south to San Francisco or north to Novato in less than a half-hour. From central Marin to West Marin takes 30-to-40 minutes, and to the far reaches of the Point Reyes Peninsula a little more than one hour. MAPS: You'll probably want to get a street map; see *Resource Links* for sources.

KEY TO READING TRAILHEAD DESCRIPTIONS

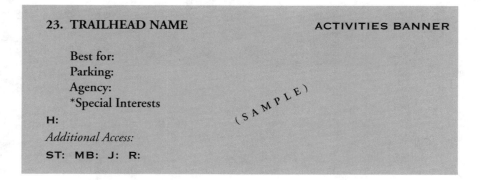

"23." Trailhead Number: These correspond to the numbers shown on the six Trailhead Maps. Numbering begins with Map 1, San Francisco, and ends at the northern end of Marin, Map 6. Within each region, trailheads that are close together numerically will also be close together geographically. Within the text of the book, trailhead numbers are listed sequentially, starting at 1 and ending at 102. When looking for a particular trailhead, "TH65" for example, you may find it easier to leaf through the text rather than look up the page number in the Trailhead Directory.

Trailhead Name: This is where you park for hiking, strolling, biking, jogging and rolling. Each trailhead has numerous activities. Each trailhead may also have several access points, that is, different places to begin activities.

Activities Banner: This shows which of the five recreational activities are available at this trailhead. Activities include one or more of the following, always listed the same order.

H = Hike. Hikes in natural settings, from short walks for a picnic to all-day treks.

ST = Stroll. Around-town strolls, and walks around cultural attractions.

MB = Mountain and Road Bikes. Paths for off-road adventure rides and practical ways of getting across town on bike routes.

J = Jogging. Paths and trails, for both runners in training and recreational joggers.

R = Roll: Skates, scooters, baby strollers, and wheelchairs. Details are given in descriptions for each trailhead. *Best Of* section also offers a directory for each of these rolling modes.

Best for: Tells you, in a nutshell, what to expect when visiting this trailhead's primary attractions.

Parking: Gives you specific directions, usually from the nearest freeway, to the primary parking area. If trailheads have secondary parking areas nearby they will be noted in this paragraph, and then detailed in the hiking descriptions. Ferry and bus information, if appropriate, is also provided. GGT = Golden Gate Transit.

Agency: The public agency that oversees the park in which the activities take place. Phone numbers are listed in *Resource Links*. **Abbreviations:** GGNRA = Golden gate National Recreation Area; PRNS = Point Reyes National Seashore; MMWD = Marin Municipal Water District; MCOSD= Marin County Open Space District.

*Special Interest: Notes other activities, other than those listed in the *Activities Banner*, that are popular at this trailhead. These interests include activities for Kids, Kayaks and Camping. Further information is provided in the last paragraph for the trailhead. Summaries can be found in *Best Of* section.

H: The first paragraph after the **H:** symbol lists each hike destination available at this trailhead, followed by the (distance in parentheses) for that destination. *All hiking distances in parentheses are round trip, unless otherwise noted for car shuttles.* A variety of hiking lengths is offered for each trailhead. We try to include all of the best hikes without exhausting you with hikes that are less likely to be enjoyed. Hiking distances are given to the nearest .25-mile. Loop hikes use a different return route from a hike destination back to trailhead parking.

The second paragraph following the **H:** symbol contains background information and history for the trailhead. The first reference for a **Hike Destination** is boldfaced. Trail descriptions follow. Descriptions include trail distances and junctions, as well as changes in elevation. Destinations are described in the same order as listed in the first **H:** paragraph. The first hike begins at the primary parking area. If a **Second Destination** begins at a different access point, then driving directions precede the trail description.

Additional Access may follow a trail description. This sentence or paragraph notes other trails that branch off from a hike destination. Different access points for this trailhead may also be noted. Additional access destinations are less popular, meaning usually that they are less aesthetic and often more secluded.

ST: The first paragraph following the **ST:** symbol gives the areas to be strolled and sometimes the (length of the stroll in parentheses).

The second paragraph following the **ST:** symbol gives the history and highlights for the stroll. The first reference for a **Stroll Area** is boldfaced. Often times, the strolling area is a building or grounds. Other strolls are of cities and towns, in which cases specific directions are provided.

MB: The first reference to a **Bike Trip** is boldfaced. The distance and elevation changes for each trip are usually noted. Sometimes, cyclists are referred to a hike destination that is the same as the bike trip. Other trips are a variation on hikes, or entirely new trails; in these cases, the street and trail connections are described. Most trailheads also contain directions to connect with other trailheads via paths and surface streets. Cyclists, therefore, can then "connect the dots" to travel by bike anywhere within San Francisco and Marin.

J: Most often, a jogging route is also a hike destination. Runners will refer to the hike paragraphs for distances and descriptions. Jogs are suggested for all skill levels. Additional jogging routes are also provided. In these cases, new parking and trail descriptions are given.

R: Most often **Skates and Scooters** are grouped together, as are **Wheelchairs and Baby Strollers.** Rolls are the same routes as one of the hikes, or a variation of a hiking route. Special destinations are also described.

*Special Interest: A *special interest* will be italicized. Different directions and descriptions provided as needed.

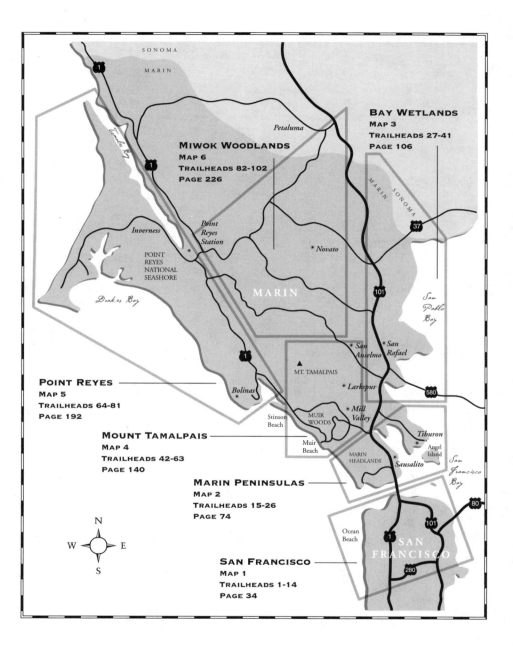

SONOMA

MARIN

Petaluma

BAY WETLANDS
MAP 3
TRAILHEADS 27-41
PAGE 106

MIWOK WOODLANDS
MAP 6
TRAILHEADS 82-102
PAGE 226

Tomales Bay

MARIN

SONOMA

37

Inverness

Point
Reyes
Station

POINT
REYES
NATIONAL
SEASHORE

* *Novato*

101

San
Pablo
Bay

Drakes Bay

MARIN

* *San*
Anselmo
* *San*
Rafael

▲
MT. TAMALPAIS

580

POINT REYES
MAP 5
TRAILHEADS 64-81
PAGE 192

Bolinas
*

* *Larkspur*

* *Mill*
Valley

Stinson
Beach

MUIR
WOODS

MOUNT TAMALPAIS
MAP 4
TRAILHEADS 42-63
PAGE 140

Muir
Beach

Tiburon
* Angel
Island

San
Francisco
Bay

MARIN
HEADLANDS

* *Sausalito*

MARIN PENINSULAS
MAP 2
TRAILHEADS 15-26
PAGE 74

80

101

N
W ⊕ E
S

Ocean
Beach

1
SAN
FRANCISCO

SAN FRANCISCO
MAP 1
TRAILHEADS 1-14
PAGE 34

280

TRAILHEAD DIRECTORY

H: HIKES
ST: STROLLS
MB: MOUNTAIN AND ROAD BIKES
J: JOGGING
R: ROLL: SKATES, SCOOTERS, BABY STROLLERS AND WHEELCHAIRS

SAN FRANCISCO Trailheads 1-14

MARIN PENINSULAS Trailheads 15-26

BAY WETLANDS Trailheads 27 through 41

MOUNT TAMALPAIS Trailheads 42 through 63

POINT REYES Trailheads 64 through 81

MIWOK WOODLANDS Trailheads 82 through 102

The Best of

San Francisco

and Marin

Crissy Field, Ridgecrest Boulevard

What do you want to do today?

Find an adventure to suit your needs. Within each *Best Of* category, trailheads are arranged by trailhead number. Leaf through the text to find page numbers, or consult *Trailhead Directory*. Then go to the trailhead and read activity description. Also see *Doggie Trails* for places to take your pet.

TH = Trailhead

HIKES

Short Walks to High Places
Buena Vista, TH2
Hawk Hill, TH15
Ring Mountain, TH26
Azalea Hill, TH42
Mount Tam, TH60
O'Rourkes Bench, TH61
Mt. Vision, TH72

Summits to See It All
Hill 88, TH20
Mount Livermore, TH24
Pine Mountain, TH42
Bald Hill, TH46
Mount Tam, TH60
Mount Wittenberg, TH67
Point Reyes Hill, TH68
Barnabe Peak, TH84
White Hill, TH89-90
Loma Alta, TH91
Big Rock Ridge, TH94-95
Mount Burdell, TH101-102

Long Beach Walks
Fort Funston, TH6
Ocean Beach, TH7
Stinson Beach, TH62
Limantour, TH69
Point Reyes Beaches, TH76
Kehoe Beach, TH78

A Day at the Beach
Baker Beach, TH9
Rodeo Beach, TH16
Muir Beach, TH55
Stinson Beach, TH62
Bolinas Beach, TH64
Limantour Beach, TH69
Hearts Desire, TH70
Drakes Beach, TH74
Kehoe Beach, TH78

HIKE-TO BEACHES AND COVES
Sand Ladder Trail, TH6
China Beach, TH9
Kirby Cove, TH15
Tennessee Valley Beach, TH20
Pirates Cove, TH55
Sculptured Beach, TH67
Shell Beach, TH70
McClures Beach, TH79

BAY SIDE STROLLS
Fort Mason, TH12
Crissy Field, TH13
Sausalito, TH18
Blackies Pasture, TH22
Tiburon, TH23
Angel Island, TH24
Shoreline Park, TH30
Millerton Point, TH81

DOCKS, PIERS, JETTIES
Pier 7, North Beach Stroll, TH1
Aquatic Park, Pier 39, Hyde Street Pier,
 Golden Gate Yacht Harbor, TH12
Crissy Field, TH13
Fort Baker, TH17
Sausalito, TH18
Marinship Pier, TH19
Paradise Cove, Tiburon, TH23

COASTAL BLUFFS AND CLIFFS
Sunset Loop, TH6
Fort Scott Overlook, TH14
Sutro Ruins, Coastal Trail, TH8
Coastal Trail, TH16, TH20, TH55
Palomarin, TH65

TIDE POOLS AND WAVE WATCHING
Sutro Bath Ruins, TH8
Duxberry Reef, TH64
Santa Maria Beach, TH69
Lifeboat Station, TH75
McClures Beach, TH79
Tomales Point, TH79

OCEAN SUNSET VIEW
Sutro Heights Park, TH8
Hawk Hill, TH15
Point Bonita, Battery Townsley, TH16
Coyote Ridge, TH20
Muir Beach Overlook, TH55
Ridgecrest Boulevard, TH61
Mount Vision, TH72
Chimney Rock, TH75

SAN FRANCISCO POSTCARD VIEWS
Coit Tower, TH1
Alcatraz, TH11
Golden Gate Bridge, TH14-15
Sausalito, TH18
SCA Trail, TH18
Tiburon, TH23
Angel Island, TH24

VIEWING THE GOLDEN GATE BRIDGE
Eagles Point, TH8
Baker Beach, TH9
Fort Point, TH13
Battery East, TH14
Bridge Walkway, TH14-15
Battery Spencer, Kirby Cove, TH15
Horseshoe Bay, TH17

PLACES TO WOW
THE HOUSEGUESTS
The City, TH1
Golden Gate Park, TH3
Lands End, TH8
Alcatraz, TH11
Fort Mason, TH12
Crissy Field, TH13
Tiburon, Angel Island, TH23-24
Muir Woods, TH55
Mount Tam, TH59-60
Point Reyes Head, TH75

SCENIC DRIVES WITH SHORT HIKES
Lands End to Fort Funston, TH6-8
Golden Gate North, Headlands,
   TH15-16
Peacock Gap, China Camp,
   Civic Center, TH32-33, TH35
Ridgecrest Boulevard, TH61
Audubon Canyon Ranch to
   Muir Beach, TH63, TH55
East Tomales Bay, TH81

SHOREBIRD WATCHING
Rodeo Lagoon, TH16
Richardson Bay, TH21, TH22
Shorebird Marsh, TH27
Shoreline Park, TH30
WildCare, TH31
Audubon Canyon, TH63
Bolinas Lagoon, TH64
The Esteros, TH73
Abbotts Lagoon, TH77

RAPTORS AND WOODLAND BIRDS
Hawk Hill, TH15
Deer Island, TH40
Audubon Canyon Ranch, TH63
Point Reyes Bird Observatory, TH65
Devils Gulch, TH83
Village Valleys, TH97

WILDFLOWERS
Old St. Hilarys, TH25
Ring Mountain, TH26
Easy Grade loop, TH58
Portrero Meadows, TH59
Chimney Rock, TH75
Nicasio Hill, TH88
Mont Marin, TH95
Verissimo Hills, TH100

LAKES AND LAGOONS
Bon Tempe and Lagunitas lakes, TH43
Phoenix Lake, TH47
Bolinas Lagoon, TH64
Bass, Crystal, Pelican lakes, TH65
Drakes Estero, TH73
Abbotts Lagoon, TH77

WATERFALLS *(best during rainy season)*
Cataract Creek, TH42, TH59
Cascade Falls, Fairfax, TH44
Dawn Falls, TH49
Warner Canyon Cataract, TH52
Cascade Falls, Mill Valley, TH53
Alamere Falls, TH65
Stairstep Falls, TH83
Waterfall Trail, TH98

FORESTED CREEKS
Cataract Creek, TH42, TH59
Cascade Canyon, TH44
Deer Park, TH45
Dawn Falls, TH49
Mill Valley, TH53
Bootjack, TH57
Devils Gulch, TH83
Papermill Creek, TH85-87

MARSH AND WETLANDS
Bothin Marsh, TH21
Corte Madera and Muzzi marsh, TH27
Shoreline Park, TH30
Turtle Back loop, TH33
McInnis Park, TH36
Bel Marin Keys, TH38
Rush Creek, TH41

SPECIAL TREES
Stern Grove, TH5
Sargent cypress, TH42, TH44
Muir Woods, TH54
Jepson Grove, TH70
Esteros Bishop Pines, TH73
Samuel P. Taylor, TH85
Roys Redwoods, TH88
Indian Trees, TH99

ARBORETUMS & MIXED CONIFERS
Strybing Arboretum, TH3
Golden Gate Park West, TH4
The Presidio, TH10
Angel Island, TH24
Bootjack, TH57
Five Brooks, TH66
Bear Valley, TH67
Devils Gulch, TH83

OAK SAVANNAH
Loma Alta, TH91
Sleepy Hollow Divide, TH92
Lucas Valley, TH95
Pacheco Creek, TH97
Deer Camp loop, TH101

AFTER WORK VIEW HIKES
Fort Funston, TH6
The Presidio, TH10
Alta Trail, Rodeo Avenue, TH18-19
Ring Mountain, TH26
San Rafael Hill, TH30
Deer Island, TH40
Bald Hill, TH46
Blithedale Summit, TH52
Terra Linda Ridge, TH92
San Rafael Ridge, TH93
Mont Marin, TH95

STROLLS
*Also see Resource Links, Museums and Attractions,
as well as Family Outings, below.*

GARDENS
Pioneer Park, North Beach Stroll, TH1
AIDS Memorial Grove, Rose Garden,
    Japanese Tea Garden, and
    Conservatory of Flowers, TH3
Queen Wilhelmina Tulip Garden, TH4
Marin Art and Garden Center, TH47
Green Gulch Farm, TH55

OF HISTORICAL SIGNIFICANCE
Golden Gate Park East, TH3
Lands End, TH8
The Presidio, TH10
Alcatraz, TH11
Marinship, TH19
San Rafael, TH31
China Camp Village, TH33
Marin Civic Center, TH35
Pierce Ranch, TH79
Miwok Park, TH100
Olompali, TH102

CITY LIFE & NEIGHBORHOODS
The City, TH1
Chestnut Street, TH13
San Rafael, TH31
San Anselmo, TH46
Larkspur, TH50

TOURIST TOWNS
The City, TH1
Sausalito, TH18
Tiburon, TH23
Mill Valley, TH53

FUNKADELIC
Haight-Ashbury, TH2
Fairfax, TH45
Bolinas, TH64

NATURE LEARNING
Golden Gate Park East, TH3
San Francisco Zoo, TH6
Gulf of the Farallones Center, TH13
Marin Headlands Visitors Center, TH16
Bay Model, TH19
WildCare, TH31
Point Reyes Bird Observatory, TH65
Bear Valley Headquarters, TH67

Filbert Steps

BIKE RIDES

See trailhead for specific rides.

CENTRAL TRAILHEADS WITH MANY CROSS-TOWN OPTIONS
Golden Gate Bridge,
 South and North, TH14-15
Richardson Bayfront, TH21
Shorebird Marsh, TH27
Corte Madera Creek, TH28
Larkspur Landing, TH29
Larkspur, TH50
Sleepy Hollow Divide, TH92

FORESTED LOOPS
The Presidio, TH10
Angel Island, TH24
China Camp, TH33
Pine Mountain, TH42
Sky Oaks Lakes, TH43
Phoenix Lake, TH47
Mountain Home Inn, TH56
Five Brooks, TH66
Bolinas Ridge, TH82
Samuel P. Taylor, TH83-86
Marinwood, Lucas Valley TH94-95

OCEAN VIEW, COASTAL BLUFFS
Golden Gate Bridge,
 South and North, TH14-15
Marin Headlands, TH16
Tennessee Valley, TH20
Muir Beach, TH55
Ridgecrest Boulevard, TH61
Limantour High Trails, TH68
Mount Vision, TH72

OCEAN AND BAY
Fort Funston, TH6
Ocean Beach, TH7
Lands End, TH8
Fort Mason, Crissy Field, TH12-13
Marinship, TH19
Blackies Pasture, TH22
Shoreline Park, TH30
Limantour Beach, TH69
Point Reyes Station, TH80

CREEK AND MARSH
Corte Madera Creek, TH28
Larkspur Landing, TH29
McInnis Park, TH36
Bel Marin Keys, TH38
Rush Creek, TH41

FAMILY RIDES
Golden Gate Park, TH3-4
Lake Merced, TH6
Ocean Beach, TH7
Crissy Field, TH13
Angel Island, TH24
Shoreline Park, TH30
McInnis Park, TH36
Baltimore Canyon, TH48
Bear Valley Headquarters, TH67
Marshall Beach, TH71
Samuel P. Taylor Park, TH85-86
Miwok Park, TH100

BIG TIME MOUNTAIN RIDES
Marin Headlands, TH16
San Pedro Mountain, TH32-34
Pine Mountain, TH42
Sky Oaks Lakes, TH43
Phoenix Lake, TH47
Baltimore Canyon, TH48
Blithedale Summit, TH52
Pantoll Ranger Station, TH58
Rock Springs, TH59
Mount Tam Peak, TH60
Five Brooks, TH66
Bolinas Ridge, TH82
Kent Lake, TH87
San Geronimo Ridge, TH89
Marinwood, Lucas Valley, TH94-95

ROLLING HILLS, BIG HILLS
Ring Mountain, TH26
Marshall Beach, TH71
The Esteros, TH73
Barnabe Peak, TH84
Loma Alta, TH91
Sleepy Hollow Divide, TH92
Indian Tree Hills, TH99
Mount Burdell, TH101

TOWN & COUNTRY COMBOS
Sausalito, TH18
Blackies Pasture, Tiburon, TH22-23
Ring Mountain, TH26
Corte Madera Creek, TH28
Fairfax, TH45
Larkspur, TH50
Blithedale-Mill Valley, TH52-53

FERRY 'N' RIDE
The City, TH1
Fort Mason, TH12
Sausalito, TH18
Tiburon, TH23
Angel Island, TH24

JOGS

PAVED FOREST AND PARK
Golden Gate Park, TH3-4
Stern Grove, TH5
The Presidio, TH10
Angel Island, TH24
Tam Peak, TH60
Cross Marin Trail, TH85-86
Stafford Lake Path, TH99

PAVED OCEAN, BAY, LAKE
Lake Merced, TH6
Ocean Beach, TH7
Fort Mason, TH12
Crissy Field, TH13
Tennessee Valley, TH20
Richardson Bay, TH19, TH21
Blackies Pasture, TH22
Shoreline Park, TH30

MARSH AND CREEK PATHS
Shorebird Marsh, TH27
Corte Madera Creek, TH28
Santa Venetia Marsh, TH35
McInnis Park, TH36
Bel Marin Keys, TH38
Rush Creek, TH41

BEACH RUNS
Ocean Beach, TH7
Stinson Beach, TH62
Limantour Beach, TH69
Point Reyes Beaches, TH76
Kehoe Beach, TH78

OCEAN AND BAY VIEW
Fort Funston, TH6
Lands End, TH8
Coastal Trail, TH14
Palomarin, TH65
Limantour High Trails, TH68
Chimney Rock, TH75
Tomales Point, TH79
Millerton Point, TH81

FOREST AND WOODLAND TRAILS
Golden Gate Park West, TH4
Deer Island, TH40
Lake Lagunitas, TH43
South Marin Line, TH48
King Mountain, TH49
Five Brooks, TH66
Bear Valley Trail, TH67
Devils Gulch, TH83
Indian Valley, TH98

ROLLING HILLS
Marshall Beach, TH71
The Esteros, TH73
Sleepy Hollow Divide, TH92
San Rafael Ridge, TH93
Marinwood, TH94
Mont Marin, TH95
Mount Burdell, TH101

San Francisco skyline

ADVENTURE TRAINING
Marin Headlands, TH16
Angel Island, TH24
San Pedro Mountain, TH32-34
Sky Oaks Lakes, TH43
Blithedale Summit, TH52
Muir Woods, TH54
Coastal Trail, TH61
Palomarin, TH65
Five Brooks, TH66
Tomales Point, TH79
Bolinas Ridge, TH82
Mount Burdell, TH101

BABY STROLLERS
Also see Family Outings

AROUND BIG PARKS
Mothers Meadow, Strybing
  Arboretum, Stow Lake, TH3
North Lake, Lloyd Lake, TH4
San Francisco Zoo, TH6
Sutro Heights Park, TH8
Civic Center Lagoon, TH35
Marin Art and Garden Center, TH47
Piper Park, TH50
Bear Valley Headquarters, TH67
Quietwood Park, TH94
Miwok Park, TH100

WOODED TRAILS
Arguello Gate, TH10
Lake Lagunitas, TH43
Phoenix Lake, TH47
Southern Marin Line, TH48
Blithedale Park, TH52
Muir Woods, TH54
Gravity Car Grade, TH56
Mountain Theater, TH59
Five Brooks, TH66
Devils Gulch, TH83
Kent Lake, TH87
Indian Valley Road, TH98

SEA AIR
Sunset Trail, TH6
Fort Mason, TH12
Tennessee Valley, TH20
Tiburon, TH23
Limantour Beach, TH69
Drakes Beach, TH74
Point Reyes Head, TH75

UNPAVED LAGOON AND MARSH
Shorebird Marsh, TH27
Santa Venetia, Santa Margarita, TH35
McInnis Park, TH36
Bel Marin Keys, TH38
Abbotts Lagoon, TH77

RIDGES AND PEAKS
Ring Mountain, TH26
Tam Peak, TH60
Mount Vision, TH72
Sleepy Hollow Divide, TH92
San Rafael Ridge, TH93

MULTI-USE ALONG THE WATER
The Esplanade, TH7
Golden Gate Promenade, TH13
Mill Valley-Sausalito Path,
  TH19, TH21
Blackies Pasture, TH22
Corte Madera Creek, TH28-29
Shoreline Park, TH30

PAVED WOODSY
Stern Grove, Pine Lake, TH5
Angel Island, TH24
Cross Marin Trail, TH85-86
Peters Dam Road, TH87
Old Lucas Valley Road, TH95

Crissy Field

WHEELCHAIRS

PARKS AND GARDENS
Golden Gate East, TH3
Sutro Heights Park, TH8
Palace of Fine Arts, TH13
Civic Center Lagoon, TH35
Marin Art and Garden Center, TH47
Piper Park, TH50
Quietwood Park, TH94
Miwok Park, TH100

WOODSY
Windmills, TH4
Presidio, TH10
Angel Island, TH24
Phoenix Lake, TH47
Southern Marin Line, TH48
Muir Woods, TH54
Gravity Car Grade, TH56
Mountain Theater, TH59
Five Brooks Pond, TH66
Bear Valley Headquarters, TH67
Kent Lake Spillway, TH87
Russom Park, TH95
Indian Valley, TH98

ALONG THE WATER
Lake Merced, TH6
The Esplanade, TH7
Aquatic Park, TH12
Golden Gate Promenade, TH13
Blackies Pasture, TH22
Angel Island, TH24
Corte Madera Creek, TH28-29
Shoreline Park, TH30
Abbotts Lagoon, TH77

AROUND TOWN
Justin Herman Plaza, TH1
Sausalito, TH18
Tiburon, TH23
Bolinas, TH64
Point Reyes Station, TH80

OCEAN AND BLUE WATER VIEW
Sunset Trail, TH6
Golden Gate Bridge, TH14-15
Point Bonita, TH16
Tennessee Valley, TH20
Limantour Beach, TH69
Peter Behr Overlook, TH74
Point Reyes Lighthouse, TH75

*Marin
Headlands*

HIGH PLACES
Ring Mountain, TH26
Mount Tam Peak, TH60
Mount Vision, TH72
Mission Pass, Sleepy Hollow, TH92
San Rafael Ridge, TH93

MARSH AND BAY TRAILS
Shorebird Marsh, TH27
Santa Margarita, TH35
McInnis Park, TH36
Bel Marin Keys, TH38

TREE-LINED
Cross Marin Trail, TH85-86
Old Lucas Valley Road, TH95
Stafford Lake Path, TH99-100

SKATES AND SCOOTERS

PEOPLE-WATCHING PATHS
Kennedy Drive, TH3
Middle Drive West, TH4
The Esplanade, TH7
Fort Mason, TH12
Golden Gate Promenade, TH13

LAKE AND BAY SIDE
Lake Merced, TH6
Sausalito-Mill Valley Path, TH19, TH21
Blackies Pasture, TH22
Corte Madera Creek, TH28-29
Shoreline Park, TH30

FAMILY OUTINGS
See also Family Bike Rides and Baby Strollers.

MUSEUMS AND ATTRACTIONS
Randall Museum, TH2
Steinhart Aquarium, Planetarium,
    California Academy of Sciences, TH3
Musee Mecanique, TH8
Exploratorium, TH13
Bay Area Discovery Museum, TH17
Bay Model, TH19
WildCare, TH31
Point Reyes Bird Observatory, TH65
Marin Museum of the American
    Indian, TH100

Golden Gate Park East

FAMILY VARIETY PACK
Golden Gate Park, TH3-4
Fort Mason, TH12
Marin Headlands, TH16
Fort Baker, TH17
Angel Island, TH24
China Camp, TH33
Bolinas, Palomarin, TH64-65
Bear Valley Headquarters, TH67
The Esteros, TH73
Miwok Park, TH100

PLAYGROUNDS
Buena Vista Park, TH2
Childrens Playground, TH3
South View Park, TH18
Bayfront Park, TH21
South-of-the-Knoll Park, TH22
Creekside Park, TH28
Boyd Park, TH31
Peacock Gap Park, TH32
Civic Center Lagoon, TH35
Dolliver Park, TH50
Old Mill, Boyle parks, TH53
Santa Margarita Valley Park, TH92
Quietwood Park, TH94
Westgate Park, TH95
Hoog Community Park, TH98

MINI WALKS
Stow Lake, TH3
Sutro Bath Ruins, TH8
Alcatraz, TH11
Aquatic Park Pier, TH12
Santa Margarita, TH35
Deer Island, TH40
Lake Lagunitas loop, TH43
King Mountain, TH49
Mountain Theater, TH59
Mount Tam Peak, TH60
Audubon Canyon Ranch, TH63
Fox Hollow, TH91
Indian Valley, TH98
Olompali, TH102

KAYAKING

BAY
Crissy Field, TH13
Fort Baker, TH17
Sausalito, TH18
Marinship, TH19
Richardson Bayfront, TH21
Angel Island, TH24
Larkspur Landing, TH29
China Camp, TH33
Tomales Bay, TH70
East Tomales Bay, TH81

CREEKS
Larkspur Landing, TH29
Larkspur, TH50
Marin Civic Center, TH35
McInnis Park, TH36
Black Point, TH39

LAKES, LAGOONS
Lake Merced, TH6
Bel Marin Keys, TH38
Bolinas Lagoon, TH64
Drakes Estero, TH73

OCEAN — You're on your own

Shoreline Park

San Francisco

Palace of Fine Arts lagoon

To exercise a cliché born for the occasion: You could spend a lifetime exploring San Francisco and never feel like you've done the same thing twice. With nearly 30 miles of scenic shore and city panoramas that keep postcard companies in business, San Francisco offers a world-class blend of urban strolling and enjoyment of the outdoors.

About one-third of the northern San Francisco peninsula—some 8,400 acres—is parkland, including Golden Gate National Recreation Area, which runs along the Pacific coast and most of the San Francisco Bay. Also in the GGNRA is the Presidio, a 1,500-acre National Historic Monument that lies on the forested bluff at the south end of the Golden Gate Bridge. Some well-known attractions are within GGNRA, including Alcatraz, Hyde Street Pier, the Cliff House, and Sutro Baths.

Running through the heart of the city is Golden Gate Park, San Francisco's answer to Central Park—with forests, fields, museums, statuary, arboretums, gardens and fountains. The city-run park stretches westward from midtown to the coast, an urban playland for San Franciscans and visitors from all over the globe. On the southwest coast of San Francisco is a large park frequented mostly by locals—Fort Funston, with historic bluffs and miles of beach, next to placid Lake Merced.

In San Francisco, parks are not the only drawing card. People come from around the world to see Chinatown, Fishermans Wharf, Union Square, old Victorians near Haight-Ashbury, cable cars, and Nob Hill. Other attractiois may not draw visitors from afar, but they keep them coming back: North Beach, Coit Tower, Transamerica Pyramid, Palace of Fine Arts, Legion of Honor, and Grace Cathedral. Urban hikers will find the city's landmarks as advertised—and separated by walking distances. Return visitors begin to find the places that hold for them a special appeal, like Steinhart Aquarium, DeYoung Museum, the Exploratorium, Fort Point, Baker Beach, St. Francis Hotel, Portsmouth Square, Ocean Beach, and Crissy Field.

The city's attractions begin to read like a shopping list. But the allure of San Francisco is not just the considerable length of the list, but the dynamic sum of its parts—fitted cohesively together upon the famous hills, rolling seamlessly from the ocean to bay. Knitting all of it together is the Golden Gate Bridge, among the world's elite attractions not only as a engineering marvel and work of art, but also as a symbol of all that is California.

Just three average lifetimes ago, the land on which the city now sits was a windswept and fog-shrouded peninsula, largely uninhabited. Its native people, the Ohlone, are thought to have been drawn here to partake of food that was abundant in the bay wetlands and then to retreat south to villages in the leeward hills. Mountainous sand dunes crept up the west side of the peninsula, ever-growing in an onshore wind, thwarted midway by weirdly shaped igneous outcroppings. To the east, these rocky hills fell to bay marshlands, just six miles from the sea, a shoreline scalloped by creeks, mudflats and lagoons. On the north side of the peninsula were cliffs ending at a mile-wide straight, with deep water and strong current.

In 1775, Juan Bautista de Anza led a band of immigrants and livestock on a thousand-plus mile pilgrimage up from Mexico to Alta California, reaching the cliffs of the peninsula and setting up camp. Their journey was the northernmost expansion of the Spanish Empire that had begun 200 years earlier when Cortez and others set sail for the New World. By 1821, a garrison had been established at the Presidio, and Mission Delores was spreading Christianity. Down the hill from the mission was Yerba Buena Cove—named for the fresh aroma of mint that grew there. In 1835, William Richardson camped above the cove, building a tent house from spars and sails for the mission's Don Francisco de Haro. The camp was located where today's Grant Avenue meets Clay Street. At this time the Spaniards held a wary eye on the north coast of California, where Russian ships encroached upon the empire. No Americans, save a few trappers, had been to the California coast until John C. Fremont's expedition, led by Kit Carson, came through in a small party in the early 1840s.

In 1849, the Mother Lode was struck about 150 miles east in the Sierra Nevada foothills, followed 11 years later by the Comstock Lode just over the crest; combined,

Chinatown, Crissy Field, Conservatory of Flowers, Kennedy Drive

Transamerica Pyramid,
North Beach, Victorians,
Palace of Fine Arts,
Fishermans Wharf,
Ocean Beach, Ft. Funston

these strikes are by far the largest deposits of gold and silver ever dug out of the earth. The Mexicans were swept aside by a strong-arm treaty, as California became a state. By 1870, Yerba Buena was San Francisco, with a population of 150,000, with people coming literally as fast as humanly possible, the largest migration in history, over land on wagons and around the Horn on ships. By 1890, with railways firmly established, the population doubled to 300,000, at a time when Los Angeles residents numbered about 10,000. In 50 years, the city had gone from virtually zero to the nation's eighth largest.

The precious metals made millionaires of many—among them, engineer Adolph Sutro and the railroad's Big Four of Charles Crocker, Leland Stanford, Mark Hopkins and Collis Huntington. Smitten as they were by fine scenery and a Mediterranean climate—not to mention an infusion of money by the boatload—the new millionaires and a host of civic leaders laid the groundwork that made San Francisco one of the world's most desirable places—a development only delayed by the horrific quake of 1906. Today, American travelers consistently rank San Francisco with Paris and Rome as top destinations.

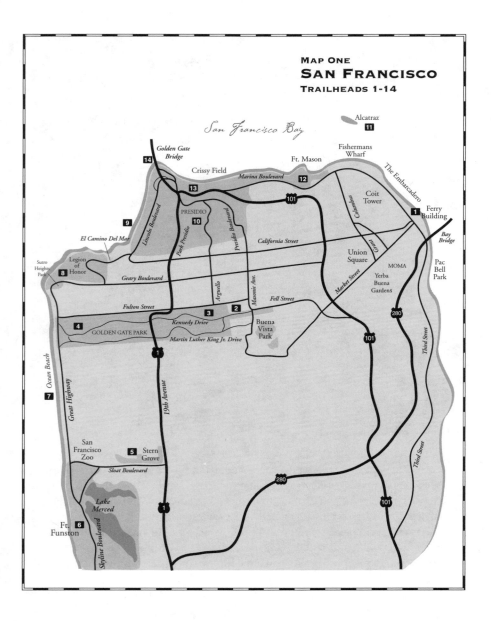

MAP ONE
SAN FRANCISCO
TRAILHEADS 1-14

San Francisco Bay

Alcatraz **11**

Golden Gate Bridge **14**

Fishermans Wharf

Ft. Mason

Crissy Field

The Embarcadero

Marina Boulevard **12**

13

101

Coit Tower

Columbus

Ferry Building **1**

PRESIDIO **10**

Park Presidio

Presidio Boulevard

Lincoln Boulevard

9

California Street

Union Square

Grant

Bay Bridge

El Camino Del Mar

MOMA

Pac Bell Park

Sutro Heights Park

Legion of Honor **8**

Geary Boulevard

Arguello

Masonic Ave.

Market Street

Yerba Buena Gardens

Fulton Street

Fell Street

3 **2**

280

Third Street

4

Kennedy Drive

GOLDEN GATE PARK

Martin Luther King Jr. Drive

Buena Vista Park

1

101

Ocean Beach

Great Highway

19th Avenue

7

San Francisco Zoo

Stern Grove **5**

Sloat Boulevard

280

Third Street

101

Lake Merced

Ft. Funston **6**

Skyline Boulevard

1

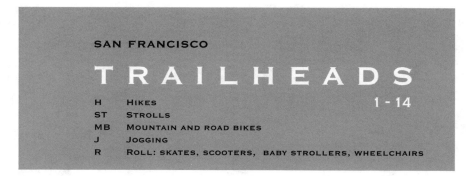

SAN FRANCISCO

T R A I L H E A D S

1 - 14

H	HIKES
ST	STROLLS
MB	MOUNTAIN AND ROAD BIKES
J	JOGGING
R	ROLL: SKATES, SCOOTERS, BABY STROLLERS, WHEELCHAIRS

All hike and stroll distances are ROUND TRIP except as noted for shuttles.
Please contact Agency to obtain current rules and regulations. See Resource Links for all telephone numbers.
See also special Doggie Trails section.

1.   THE CITY   ST, MB

Best for: Three urban hikes along the streets and waterfront of downtown San Francisco, amid the landmarks and curiosities that make this one of the most beloved cities in the world.

Parking: For all three strolls, begin at the Ferry Building, located on The Embarcadero at Market Street. On-street and garage parking available in the vicinity, but taking a ferry, streetcar or bus is recommended. *Ferries:* Golden Gate Ferry from Larkspur or Sausalito; Blue & Gold Fleet from Tiburon, Vallejo, Alameda, Oakland; Red & White Fleet from Richmond. *Note:* In front of the Ferry Building—between the deco Millennium Light Towers—is a streetcar terminal. For cable car rides, head up Market two blocks to California Street.

Agency: City of San Francisco Recreation and Park Department

ST: **Downtown (2.5 mi.); North Beach (3 mi.); SoMa (South of Market) (3.5 mi.)**

San Francisco—known locally as The City—ranks at the top, or near it, among surveyed travelers asked for their wish list of worldwide vacation destinations. The Downtown stroll takes you through the heart of the financial district, into Chinatown, up to Nob Hill hotels and then down to the hubbub of Union Square, with its designer fashion stores. The North Beach stroll goes along The Embarcadero waterfront, over historic Coit Tower, featuring bay views, down into bohemian North Beach, followed by a walk through Chinatown on the homestretch. The SoMa stroll goes south on The Embarcadero to the Giants' new Pac Bell Park, then through the gritty-arty neighborhoods comparable to New York's SoHo, and winds up at the Museum of Modern Art and Yerba Buena Gardens, featuring outdoor art, hip shops and restaurants.

Millenium Light Towers, Yerba Buena Gardens

The Ferry Building, which opened in 1898, is known for its 240-foot clock tower that survived the earthquake. For the **Downtown stroll** cross The Embarcadero in front of the Ferry Building and veer right into Justin Herman Plaza. You'll see cubist Vaillancourt Fountain to your right. To your left midway in the plaza, enter the Embarcadero Center, a three-level shopping complex that stretches from the plaza four blocks up to Battery Street. Maritime Plaza, a greenbelt, parallels the center to your right, connected by above-street walkways. Continue through Embarcadero Center and descend stairs, coming out at the corner of Battery and Sacramento streets. Head up Sacramento, passing the columns of the old Federal Reserve Bank, and then turn right on narrow Leidesdorff Street, which leads to the huge Transamerica Pyramid. In the Transamerica plaza, you'll find Redwood Park, a favorite among office workers taking respite among the large trees and fountain.

In front of the Pyramid, go right on white-collar Montgomery Street and turn left on Washington. Here you'll see a plaque marking the headquarters of the Pony Express, begun in 1861. Continue up Washington to Portsmouth Square, a gathering place for the city's thriving Chinese neighborhoods—and the site where John Montgomery planted the flag and claimed the area as part of the United States in 1846. Meander to your left through the square, and cross Kearny Street, and head up Clay. After a block you reach Grant Avenue, the heart of Chinatown. Turn left, or south, on Grant. Wander around on side streets to get the full multi-sensory impact. Near the south end of Chinatown, at Grant Avenue and California, is Old Saint Mary's, the first cathedral built in California, in 1853.

Turn right on California Street and walk up the steep hill alongside humming cable car tracks. You're headed to Nob Hill, site of San Francisco's posh hotels. At Stockton Street is the Ritz Carlton, where you may enjoy high tea in its fabulously ornate dining room. A block farther up are the Mark Hopkins and Fairmont hotels, with smashing city views that can be enhanced by taking afternoon rides up their elevators. In the 1880s, Nob Hill was the site of the mansions of the Big Four—railroad and mining industrialists Charles Crocker, Leland Stanford, Mark Hopkins and Collis Huntington. Nearby Huntington Park is an excellent rest or picnic stop. Across from Huntington Park is Grace Cathedral. The cathedral, with recently restored stained glass windows, is a smaller replica of Notre Dame in Paris.

Head back down California and turn right on Powell Street, a downhill cable car route. At the bottom of the hill, at 450 Powell, is the Sir Francis Drake Hotel, featuring the Starlight Room on top, one of Herb Caen's favorite watering holes. A block farther, at Post Street, is Union Square, the heart of downtown's designer stores. Most department stores and boutiques are within a two-block radius. On the Post Street corner of Union Square is the St. Francis Hotel, which features perhaps the best glass elevator of all, a breathtaking jolt from the lobby to a city panorama toward the Bay Bridge. Walk through Union Square, away from Post Street; cross Stockton Street and head down quaint Maiden Lane, featuring the Folk Art International Gallery and sidewalk cafes. You pop out of Maiden Lane at Kearny Street, where, at 49 Kearny, are several prominent photography galleries. Turn left on Kearny to California Street; go right on California to Market, where you turn left back to the Ferry Building.

For the **North Beach stroll**, turn right on The Embarcadero as you leave the Ferry Building. Docked two piers to the north is the ferry Santa Rosa, built in 1927 and now open weekdays and Saturdays, free to the public. Next you'll come to Pier 7, a walk over the water on planks lined by iron railing and old street lamps. If you're taking this stroll on a Saturday, cross over The Embarcadero near Pier 9 and visit the Ferry Plaza Farmer's Market for a sprawling assortment of organic veggies and specialty foods.

Cross The Embarcadero near Pier 23, on Greenwich Street. You pass Sansome Street and then ascend the Greenwich Steps, through hidden gardens, reaching Coit Tower, which sits upon Telegraph Hill. *Note:* You can also jog left on Sansome and then turn right up the Filbert Steps, also reaching Coit Tower. Telegraph Hill, with its commanding bay view, was named in the Gold Rush when it was the site of a marine telegraph and semaphore station. Pioneer Park, which surrounds the tower, was established in 1875 by citizens alarmed at growing commercial development. Coit Tower was built in 1933—you can take an elevator to the top. The murals in the foyer artfully depict San Francisco history.

From the west side of Coit Tower, take stairs from Telegraph Hill Boulevard to Telegraph Place. At the bottom, jog left to Greenwich Street and walk right to Stockton. Go left for a block to Washington Square, a grassy piazza off which is the Church of

Saints Peter & Paul. You're now in North Beach, the city's Italian neighborhood that has been compared to Paris' Left Bank. The neighborhood was birthplace of the Beat Generation, the Beatniks of the late 1950s and early 1960s. Walk through Washington Square and go left on Columbus Avenue, featuring cafes, clubs, and hip boutiques. Poet Lawrence Ferlinghetti's City Lights bookstore is on Columbus near Jack Kerouac Street. Nearby is Café Trieste, a favorite of Allen Ginsberg and other poets. But don't let a literary quest keep you from finding Stella pastries, Molonari salami, Lucca ravioli, or a foamy cappuccino. At Columbus and Grant, you may wish to double back left on Grant—the Upper Grant area—to soak in some more bohemian atmosphere.

Then head up Grant Street, San Francisco's oldest street, which will bring you immediately into Chinatown. Chinatown was established during the Gold Rush and grew as the demand for railroad workers increased. It is one of the largest Chinese settlements on this side of the Pacific, with 24 blocks of thriving shops and restaurants. The action is to either side of Grant. One good side trip is to turn right at Jackson Street and visit the fortune cookie factory on Ross Alley. Or, go left one block on Clay Street to Portsmouth Square, the center of leisure-time life for the community. The Chinese Cultural Center, at 750 Kearny, has exhibits of arts and crafts. At 650 Commercial Street, which is a block past Clay on Grant, is the Chinese Historical Society. The Pacific Heritage Museum is at 608 Commercial. Four blocks later, at Bush Street, you leave Chinatown via "Dragon's Gate." Turn left on Bush Street, skirting the Financial District, until you reach Market. Turn left on Market and head for the Ferry Building.

For the **SoMa stroll**, turn left from the Ferry Building along Embarcadero Promenade. Up-close views of the Bay Bridge serve as a backdrop. On your right, between Spear and Steuart streets, is Rincon Center, where you'll find a zesty food court and a series of WPA murals depicting California history. Continue toward South Beach Park and Marina, where brew pubs and cafes are springing up, lured by the opening of the

Coit Tower, Washington Square

Giants' Pac Bell Park. The classic brick ballpark is about a mile from the Ferry Building. A walk around the park—go left as you reach it—takes you to the bay, passing South Beach Marina, Seals Plaza, and McCovey Cove, where home runs to right field splash into the water. Take this stroll during a game so you can view for an inning or two for free through openings in the fence. Circling the park, you'll reach Willie Mays Plaza with its 24 palm trees planted to signify the center fielder's jersey number.

From Willie Mays Plaza, walk across King Street on Third. At 615 Third is the birthplace plaque of Jack London. Jog right on Brannan and then left on Jack London Alley, walking through South Park to Bryant Street. Go left on Bryant and then right on Third. Stay on Third for four long blocks, through a gritty area with work-live lofts and the occasional gallery. You'll reach the Museum of Modern Art, at Third and Minna Streets. The MOMA building is an art form, both inside and out; visit its changing exhibits and take a peek inside from the excellent gift store. Across the street from MOMA is Yerba Buena, with its gardens, fountains, galleries and eclectic view of San Francisco. Bordering Yerba Buena, on the Fourth Street side, is Metreon, featuring movie theaters, cool shops and eateries, where the with-it come to hang around.

History buffs will want to take a short walk down Mission Street, which is the north border of Yerba Buena, to the California Historical Society at 678 Mission. Across the street is the Ansel Adams Center for Photography. Then jog back to Fourth Street, passing the Marriott, where you can take an elevator ride to the top to enjoy the view out its arched glass windows. Continue to Market Street and turn right toward the Ferry. At Kearney and Market is Lotta's Fountain, the city's only water supply after the 1906 earthquake, where a yearly ceremony has been held ever since. On the way down Market, you can explore the remarkable interior design of two hotels: At New Montgomery Street is the historic Sheraton Palace, featuring a garden court dining room with an expansive glass ceiling. Farther down, at Drum and Market, is the Hyatt Regency, which features an indoor glass elevator rising through the world's largest atrium.

MB: For a **San Francisco to Sausalito Ferry loop**, a fairly flat ride of about 14 miles, turn right at the Ferry Building and follow the bike path along The Embarcadero—you'll see signs for Bike Route 5. After about 1.5 miles, at North Point Street, Bike Route 2 takes you west; or, to pedal through Fishermans Wharf, proceed another two blocks on The Embarcadero and go left on Jefferson Street. Either way, you'll go one mile and then run into Van Ness Avenue at Aquatic Park, where you hang a right and follow a bike path through Fort Mason to Crissy Field. From there, hug the route along the water and follow signs to the Golden Gate Bridge. Across the bridge, follow signs to Sausalito. From the center of Sausalito, take the Golden Gate Ferry, in the middle of town at Anchor Street.

See **Sausalito**, TH18, and **Larkspur Landing**, TH29, for bike trips in Marin after taking a ferry ride from the city.

2.   HAIGHT ASHBURY

Best for: A whiff of Flower Power lingers at San Francisco's famous intersection. Nearby are two parks with city views and an excellent children's museum.

Parking: From the north or south, take Highway 1, which is 19th Ave., to Fulton St. on the north border of Golden Gate Park. Turn east on Fulton. *Note:* Traveling south, you can't turn left off 19th Ave.; turn right on Cabrillo, the street before Fulton, and then make two lefts in order to cross 19th Ave. on Fulton. Head about a mile east on Fulton and turn right on Stanyan St. Go 4 blocks to Haight St. and park—you may have to park in the vicinity and walk to the corner of Haight and Stanyan to begin the stroll. *Bus:* SF Muni 33, 43

Agency: San Francisco Recreation and Park Department; *Special Interest: Kids

ST: **Haight Ashbury and Panhandle loop (1.25 mi.); Haight Ashbury, Buena Vista Park and Corona Heights loop (2.75 mi.)**

All strolls begin at historic Alvord Lake Bridge, a pond and small park that is the tunnel entrance to the east end of Golden Gate Park. This is the oldest roadway tunnel in California. Cross Stanyan and proceed up Haight Street. The block was once home to the Grateful Dead, Janis Joplin and Jefferson Airplane. The Haight still resonates sixties themes, with colorful clubs, ethnic cafes, head shops, used records, tattoo parlors, vintage clothing, and psychedelic junk stores—visited by tourists of every stripe and this century's version of street kids. For the full effect, begin this stroll after noon on weekends; this is not an early-bird type of street. Two blocks past Haight and Ashbury, at Central Avenue, the street scene fades. For the **Panhandle loop**, go left on Central for two blocks until you hit the Panhandle, a block-wide and .75-mile-long greenbelt tagged on to the east end of Golden Gate Park. Take the bike path to your left, about .5-mile back to Stanyan Street.

For the **Buena Vista and Corona Heights loop**, cross Central Street, and then Buena Vista Avenue West. Go up the broad set of concrete stairs, followed by a steep asphalt path. Buena Vista is a hilltop park with several meandering paths, large cypress and eucalyptus trees and, as its name suggests, views of almost all quadrants of the city. At the top of the first asphalt path is a playground with northward views. From the playground, wind your way up to the buena vista, a grassy knoll on top with tree-filtered views. Then head down the utility path on the south side of the knoll to get an enticing glimpse of Corona Heights, a primitive chert crag juxtaposed above the hubbub of upper Market Street. To get there, continue to the corner of Upper Terrace and Buena Vista Avenue. Go down Upper to a quaint, five-street intersection, where you hang a sharp left, downward, on Roosevelt. After one block veer left at Museum Way into the park—to your left will be a dog park with city views. Take the path around and up. From the top, you'll see Sutro Tower due west; Twin Peaks are to the south.

To the Randall Museum, head down the railroad tie stairs and keep to your right—the only building in the area is the museum. To get back to the Haight from the children's museum, head out the front door, turn right and go left down the stairs to a playground below. At States Street, jog right and then *immediately left* down a short flight of stairs to the top of Douglas Street. Take another short flight of stairs up to your right, which leads to Ord Court and Vulcan—go straight across and go up the Vulcan Stairs, about eight flights with landings in between, through the gardens of adjoining homes. At the top, go left on Levant and then right on Lower Terrace. Go right again when you come to busy Roosevelt Street, coming in short order to Loma Vista Terrace, where you veer left. After a short block on Loma Vista Terrace, you'll run into the top of Masonic—go down Masonic, take a left on Piedmont and then your first right on Ashbury. Go down Ashbury back to Haight Street, passing ornate and colorful Victorians for which San Francisco is known.

*Special Interest: *Kids:* The friendly Randall Museum, part of the San Francisco Recreation and Park Department, is a premier children's museum. To get there by car, head east on Fulton Street from 19th Avenue and then turn right, or south, on Masonic. At the top of Masonic, veer left on Roosevelt. Then veer right on Museum Way to free parking and admission at 199 Museum Way. Randall Museum features interactive science and art exhibits, as well as a live animal area, greenhouse and gardens, woodworking and ceramics studios, and a darkroom. Children will also enjoy Buena Vista Park playground, described in stroll above.

3.   GOLDEN GATE PARK EAST   ST, MB, J, R

Best for: Museums, gardens, arboretums, fountains—parks within a park—all in one of the world's most renowned urban playgrounds.

Parking: *From Highway 1,* which is 19th Ave., turn east on Lincoln Ave. From Lincoln, veer left after 4th St. on Kezar Dr. and park at John F. Kennedy Dr., near McLaren Lodge. *From Highway 101 south or the Bay Bridge,* follow freeway signs toward "Golden Gate Bridge." Take the Fell St. exit and proceed west on Fell into the park, entering at McLaren Lodge, park headquarters. *Notes:* Going south on 19th Ave., you can't turn left on Lincoln; pass Lincoln, turn right on Irving St. and double back to cross 19th on Lincoln. *To only visit the museums and gardens:* Turn east off 19th Ave. on Martin Luther King Dr. and park near Friend Gate. Parts of Kennedy are blocked off to traffic on Sundays. *Bus:* SF Muni 21, 44

Agency: San Francisco Recreation and Park Department; *Special Interest: Kids, boating, group picnics, tennis, lawn bowling, horseshoes. See *Resource Links* for the park's wide range of activities.

ST: **Golden Gate Park East loop (3.5 mi.)**

Once windswept sand dunes extending several miles inland, Golden Gate Park was first surveyed by William Hammond Hall in 1876. In 1887, and for the next 50 years, John McLaren became the park's superintendent, and most of what we see today is a tribute to his skill in landscape design and love of nature. This get-acquainted loop takes you everywhere in the 400-acre east end, which features most of the park's developed gardens, museums and other man-made attractions.

For the **Golden Gate Park east loop**, start at park headquarters, McLaren Lodge. This Moorish-Gothic structure, built in 1896, was once McLaren's home. From there, follow a multi-use path heading south to the Alvord Bridge. Drop down through the tunnel. You'll then pass through Mothers Meadow and reach Childrens Playground, which has been delighting kids since the '06 quake. Check out the merry-go-round at the west end of the playground—originally built in 1912 and usually open from September through May. Then head past the lawn bowling area on Bowling Green Drive.

Go left down a path into AIDS Memorial Grove. This gentle .25-mile path through the dell, surrounded by redwoods and tree ferns up to 20 feet high and a 100 years old, might leave you speaking in hush tones. In 1996, Congress conferred national status on the grove, as a gathering place for people touched by AIDS to heal, hope and remember. Take the path out the end of the grove, coming to Middle East Drive, behind the California Academy of Science. *Note:* For a shorter loop, go right, around to the front of the academy and into the Music Concourse, the large open area around which the museums are situated.

To your left behind the academy building is the Shakespeare Garden, the perfect setting for a wedding. Go left through the garden and then left again on Martin Luther King Drive. After a short distance, turn right into the Strybing Arboretum & Botanical Gardens. These 55 acres support some 7,000 species of plants from around the world that thrive in San Francisco's Mediterranean climate. The gardens and arboretum were established in 1940. Go straight, across the main lawn, passing a fountain and crossing a footbridge and the Wildfowl Pond to exit onto Martin Luther King Drive via the Friend Gate.

Go left from Friend Gate and then make your way up an embankment to Stow Lake. A multi-use path, encircles the lake and the large island which is its center. Cross Rustic Bridge, erected in 1893 and take a left toward the red-roofed Chinese Pavilion, a gift frm the City of Taipei. As you circle the island, head up the steep path paralleling Huntington Falls for a nice view. Returning down, you can walk across the Roman Bridge on the other side and continue around the lake's perimeter. On the north end is a boathouse which provides paddle boat and bicycle rentals. Park yourself on one of the many green benches for some quiet contemplation; the ducks will keep you company. *Note:* The Rose Garden is to your left, across John F. Kennedy Drive as you leave the east end of Stow Lake; it contains 53 beds of spectacular roses.

Golden Gate Park

Leaving the east end of Stow Lake, descend stairs, and continue to the five-acre Japanese Tea Garden. Estabished in 1901, its ornate gardens, designed to create a Japanese village atmosphere, feature a large bronze Buddha, cast in Japan in 1790, and a 9,000-pound Lantern of Peace. Throw a penny and make a wish atop the steeply curved drum bridge. The shady tea house terrace is a good place to recharge with cup of jasmine tea and a sesame cookie. No admission charged on the first Wednesday of every month.

To your left as you exit the Tea Garden is the M.H. de Young Museum which offers major traveling exhibits, as well as American work spanning centuries and fine art from around the globe. The de Young has expanded and improved continuously since its beginning in 1895. *Note:* Extensive remodeling will keep the museum closed until the spring of 2005.

The Temple of Music heads the large Music Concourse at the center of the park where he Golden Gate Park municipal band performs for free every Sunday at 1 pm from mid-April to October. Swing dancers, boogiers and family picnicers also share this century old space. Weekday mornings be on the lookout for Chinese sword and fan dancers gracefully practicing their traditional moves.

Across from the de Young is the park's most-visited attraction, the California Academy of Sciences, which includes the Morrison Planetarium, Steinhart Aquarium and the Natural History Museum. Families can visit here often without truly repeating the experience. In the space of an hour, the kids can feel a simulated earthquake, stand eyeball-to-eyeball with a shark and take a close-up look at a real moon rock. An admission is charged; the academy is open seven days a week.

To complete the park loop, head out the east end of the Music Concourse, veering to your right on a path through the McLaren Rhododendron Dell, and coming out to Kennedy Drive. Go right along the multi-use path along Kennedy. On your left you will come to what many consider a favorite attraction: the Conservatory of Flowers. Unfortunately, the 12,000-square-foot Victorian greenhouse—built in 1878 and the oldest glass and wood conservatory in the United States—was closed in 1995 due to wind damage and wear. Fortunately, an effort is underway to restore its indoor tropical rainforest of some 10,000 specimens. From the Conservatory, continue along Kennedy Drive to Kezar drive, completing your loop.

MB: Although bicycles are not permitted on some paths, Golden Gate Park is ideal for exploring on two wheels. Meander around. One specific ride, however, is the **Ocean Beach loop**, a ride of about 7 miles. Start at the east end of the park at Kennedy and Kezar and head west on the multi-use path along Kennedy, all the way to the Beach Chalet at the west boundary of the park. Take the path behind the Beach Chalet, heading south, to the Murphy Windmill—not toward the Dutch Windmill and tulip garden. At the Murphy Windmill, cross over Martin Luther King Drive and head east on a bike trail that runs parallel to King Drive on its south side. About halfway back, at Traverse Drive, turn left, or north, on a bike path that takes you back to Kennedy Drive.

To get to the **Presidio** and **Golden Gate Bridge**, exit the park on Arguello, which is toward the east end of the park off Kennedy Drive, behind the Conservatory of Flowers. Follow Bike Route 65 into the Presidio. Staying on route 65, you veer off Arguello onto Washington Street and follow it until meeting Lincoln Avenue, which is Bike Route 95 that takes you to the bridge.

J: The Bay to Breakers race, with some 50,000 zany runners, is routed through Golden Gate Park along John F. Kennedy Drive. Many runners like the Kennedy path for their daily exercise. The path around Stow Lake, about a mile long, also makes for a fine running track. The Golden Gate Park east loop, as described above, is also a good jogging route, since much of it is off-limits to bikes.

R: **Skates:** Try Kennedy Drive when the road is closed to cars on Sundays and holidays. Although it's generally downhill going west, the road is not steep anywhere. This is a prime-time path to do the Walkman glide, or learn how to do so. **Strollers**: On the east side of the park, Mothers Meadow and Children's Playground are favorite strolling areas, as are the grounds of Strybing Arboretum & Botanical Gardens. The path around Stow Lake and the Japanese Tea Garden are also excellent for strollers. **Wheelchairs**: In general, the east end of Golden Gate Park is wheelchair friendly and offers some excellent paths. Strybing Arboretum & Botanical Gardens and the Stow Lake path are two of the best. The Music Concourse is a place to wheel around in the center of things. For a workout, roll onto the Kennedy Drive path.

*Special Interests: *Kids:* Tots will enjoy the Childrens Playground, particularly during the summer when the carousel is in operation. Older children will get a Disneyland-type rush from the waterfall and paddleboats on Stow Lake, and the entire family can have fun at the California Academy of Science's Steinhart Aquarium. Golden Gate Park offers a wide range of sports and activities. See *Resource Links* for a complete listing.

4.   GOLDEN GATE PARK WEST   H, MB, J, R

Best for: A hike or bike on the wild side of the park, with forests, lakes and room to roam.

Parking: *From the Golden Gate Bridge*, take Hwy. 1, which is 19th Ave. Go south on 19th Ave. and turn right, or west, on Geary Blvd. Near the coast, veer right on Point Lobos Ave., continue, and then go south on the Great Highway. Park at the Beach Chalet Visitors Center. *From the south*, take Hwy. 280 to Hwy. 1, go west on Lincoln Ave. Then go north on the Great Highway to the Chalet. *From the Bay Bridge*, follow freeway signs to "Golden Gate Bridge," take Fell St. exit. Go right, or north, on Masonic Ave. and then left, or west, on Geary Blvd. Turn left, or south, on the Great Highway to Beach Chalet. *Bus:* SF Muni 18

Agency: San Francisco Recreation and Park Department; *Special Interest: Horse stables, fly casting, archery, model yacht sailing

H: Windmills loop (1 mi.); Windmills and Chain of Lakes loop (2 mi.)

For **both hikes**, begin at the Beach Chalet, the visitors center. Built in 1925, the Spanish Colonial-style building is known for its 1,500 square feet of frescoes depicting sights and activities of San Francisco, designed in the 1930s. The colorful murals were created by Lucien Labaudt as part of a WPA project. Upstairs is the Beach Chalet Brewery & Restaurant which offers commanding views of the Pacific.

Cross John F. Kennedy Drive, to the Dutch Windmill. Some 75 feet high, the windmill was built in 1903 to pump irrigation water to Stow Lake in the center of Golden Gate Park. The mill was restored in 1981, although electricity now provides the pumping power. The adjoining Queen Wilhelmina Tulip Garden's 10,000-plus tulips provide a riot of color in the spring.

Walk across Kennedy Drive from the tulip garden and drop down to the path at the short tunnel that runs under the street. After about .5-mile on the path you come to Murphy Windmill. Now decrepit, it was the largest windmill in the world when built to pump water in 1905. For the **windmill loop**, turn left up Martin Luther King Drive and then veer left on a short path section that takes you up to Bernice Rogers Way—a short road section between Kennedy and King drives. Take the path on the west side of the road, alongside Kennedy Drive, which takes you back to the Chalet.

For the **Chain of Lakes loop**, cross Martin Luther King Drive at Murphy Windmill. Take a short path that will connect with a multi-use path running along the south side of King Drive. After .25-mile on this path you cross Chain of Lakes Drive, where you turn left. Cross King Drive again, and pass South Lake, which will be on your right. Just past South Lake, get on the path on the east side of the road, with Middle Lake on your right. You then cross Kennedy Drive, just west of the Buffalo Paddock. Buffalo have roamed here since 1894, although the current herd was relocated from Wyoming in 1984. The path continues until reaching the north end of North Lake, where it goes west, or left, past the archery fields and back to the Chalet.

MB: The **Golden Gate Park loop** covers about 8 miles through verdant forests on both roads and bike paths. Head east on John F. Kennedy Drive, which begins just north of the Beach Chalet. Follow Bike Route 30. Just past Portals of the Past at Lloyd Lake—cross right over the street and pick up the bike path, Route 830. Take this path behind the de Young Museum and turn right on Middle East Drive, opposite the the Conservatory of Flowers. Veer right on Martin Luther King Drive. At Traverse Drive, turn right on Bike Route 75 for a short stretch, until you come to John F. Kennedy again. Pick up Bike Route 830 headed west. The path continues through the forests that takes you back out to the Great Highway, where you turn right back to the Chalet.

Notes: Bicycle rentals are available at the Beach Chalet. Bike Route 95 is at the west end of Golden Gate Park along the Great Highway. Northbound it takes you toward Lands End, the Presidio, and Golden Gate Bridge; southbound is toward Fort Funston, TH6.

J: If you enjoy cross-country running with minor elevation changes, the west end of Golden Gate Park will be a wonderland. Try the longer loop hike described in the hiking section. Or, use Chain of Lakes drives—West and East—for a mile-long oval that takes you on equestrian trails along the three lakes. For a more regimented run, try the track around the Polo Field at Golden Gate Park Stables, which is off John F. Kennedy Drive near Spreckels Lake. It's about .75-mile around the field.

R: **Skates:** On Saturdays and holidays, Middle Drive West is closed to cars between Metson Road and Traverse Drive, providing about a mile of smooth pavement for skaters. For access from the west end of Golden Gate Park, head east on Martin Luther King Drive and veer left on Middle Drive West until you reach the closure. **Strollers:** Most of the paths on the west end are stroller friendly, particularly the path behind the Beach Chalet heading north to the tulip garden and Dutch Windmill. Other popular spots for strollers are North Lake, at the 43rd Avenue and Fulton Park entrance; and Lloyd Lake, on Kennedy Drive just west of Cross Over Drive—which you access on the north side of the park at 25th Avenue. The small scenic lake features Portals of the Past, the portico of a Nob Hill mansion that was moved here after surviving the 1906 earthquake and fire. **Wheelchairs:** The east end of the park features more flat, paved paths for chair riders. But the path behind the Beach Chalet that runs through forest between the Dutch and Murphy windmills is worth a go.

*Special Interests: To find out about the wide range of esoteric field sports and activities available in Golden Gate Park, see *Resource Links*.

5. STERN GROVE   H, MB, J, R

Best for: A serene, small lake tucked away off two busy streets in the Sunset District, with easy paths through forest and glade.

Parking: From the Golden Gate Bridge take Hwy. 1, which is 19th Ave. Continue south through Golden Gate Park to Sloat Blvd., which is Hwy. 35. Turn right on Sloat and make an *immediate* right into Stern Grove. Follow road down about .5-mi. to parking area. *Bus:* SF Muni 23

Agency: San Francisco Recreation and Park Department; *Special Interest: Stern Grove is the site of a popular concert series.

H: Stern Grove-Pine Lake Park (2 mi.)

Check out the historic Stern Grove office set among redwoods just above the parking area, the locale of a 1906 shoot-out involving the city's mayor. Bullet holes still remain in the front door. Proceed to **Pine Lake Park**—on part of the Bay Area Ridge Trail—by taking the path that begins to the right of the sign for the Rhoda Goldman Concert Meadow. Go west just above the meadow through the terraces that provide rustic viewing spots during concerts.

In less than .5-mile you drop down into the parking area for the park, a popular dog exercise spot. Continue on a path through the large grass field. At the end of the field you reach marshy Laguna Puerca. Keep right on the trail that takes you on the short loop around the lake proceeding back to Stern Grove. For variations on your return, you can bear right at the parking area on a wide path, or, better yet, cut through the middle of the amphitheater. *Additional Access:* To directly access the dog area in Pine

Lake Park, go west on Sloat Boulevard .25-mile from 19th Avenue and veer right on Crestlake Drive. From Crestlake, turn right on Vale Avenue, which takes you down to parking.

MB: Stern Grove is too small to bike within, but two cross-city routes intersect here: Bike Route 75, which goes north along 20th Avenue to Golden Gate Park and south toward San Francisco State University; and Bike Route 60, which, westbound, follows Vincente to the Great Highway at the coast. Go north a short distance on Bike Route 75 and you will intersect Route 60.

J: The hike described above is a wooded, two-mile running loop, mostly on flat surfaces but with options to take steeper trails that wind through the wooded hollow that holds Stern Grove.

R: **Strollers and Wheelchairs:** On the south side, or to your left, of the Stern Grove Amphitheater is a wide, roughly paved path that leads to Pine Lake Park and Laguna Puerca, the marshy lake. Stern Grove's paths, enshrouded by redwoods, eucalyptus, and cypress trees, are a close-in respite from city life.

6.   FORT FUNSTON   H, ST, MB, J, R

Best for: Coastal bluffs above a wild beach, where hang gliders soar. And, the tranquil paths of huge Lake Merced, sitting right next to the city's fine zoo.

Parking: *For Fort Funston:* From Hwy. 1, which is 19th Ave., go west on Sloat Blvd., which is Hwy. 35. Just past Sunset Blvd., veer left on Skyline Blvd., which is the continuation of Hwy. 35. Continue on Hwy. 35 about a mile past the jct. with the Great Highway and turn right into the Fort Funston parking area. *For Lake Merced:* From Sloat Blvd., go left on Skyline Blvd., which is the continuation of Hwy. 35. After .25-mi. on Skyline, veer left on Lake Merced Blvd. and park immediately at curb on right. *For San Francisco Zoo:* Continue west on Sloat Blvd., past the intersection with Skyline Blvd. You'll see on-street diagonal parking on your left beginning near 45th Ave. *Bus:* SF Muni 18, 23, 88

Agency: Golden Gate National Recreation Area; San Francisco Recreation and Park Department; *Special Interest: Boating; Kids

H: **Fort Funston to: Sunset loop-Battery Davis (1 mi.), or Sand Ladder Trail to beach (.5-mi. or more); Lake Merced-North lakes loop (1.75 mi.).**

Fort Funston: For **all Fort Funston hikes,** take right fork as you enter, driving toward the main parking area. Park at the far left side of the lot. An observation deck is a short walk away. The deck is suspended about 200 feet above the water, affording a view of Ocean Beach and the rugged coastline to the south. You can also watch hang gliders from here, but stay clear of landing and take-off areas.

For the **Sunset loop**, take the marked trail that begins to the right of the observation deck. The trail ascends slightly, over dunes typical of San Francisco's original terrain, to Battery Davis. You'll see two large tunnels punched through the hill. Funston's bluffs have seen defense installations in World Wars I and II, as well as missile silos during the Cold War. Go through the tunnel farthest from the trailhead, and turn left on the sandy path that leads back. *Be aware*: The bluffs at Fort Funston are unstable and dangerous; some areas are off-limits.

For the **Sand Ladder Trail,** walk to the left of the observation deck. After crossing the flat sand, you make a steep walk down, aided by rough-hewn stairs, coming to where the miles of sand of Ocean Beach transition to rugged cliffs southward. Going south on the beach is limited due to cliffs, but during low surf and tides you can walk more than a mile to Thornton State Beach. Going north, you can walk the four-plus miles of Ocean Beach. *Be aware*: High tides and large surf can make beach walks in this area dangerous, particularly going south.

Lake Merced: The **North lakes loop** is a pleasant stroll around the lake under cypress trees and through the golf course. Begin at the Lake Merced parking described above. As you face the lake, go to your left on the multi-use path, which is part of the Bay Area Ridge Trail. After about .25-mile, depending on where you parked, walk to your right, down a ramp and stairs that lead to an isthmus between the two, smaller portions of Lake Merced. At lake level, walk across the bridge and then up the stairs to the Harding Park golf clubhouse. From the clubhouse, follow Harding Road, passing the boating and recreation area, back to the multi-use path.

ST: The **San Francisco Zoo** is revamping its already popular park, creating natural habitats and educational experiences. If it's been a while, or you've never visited the zoological park, you will be surprised at its new facilities. Admission is charged. *Note*: The wheelchair access to the zoo is on Herbst Road, off Skyline Boulevard, which is a left turn off Sloat Boulevard.

MB: The multi-use path runs for about 4.5 miles around **Lake Merced**, most of it part of a 30-mile City Loop as mapped by the San Francisco Bicycle Coalition. You can extend the Lake Merced loop, and get great coastal view, by jogging south on Skyline Boulevard at the west shore of Lake Merced. From Skyline, enter Fort Funston. A bike path leads over the top of Battery Davis and drops down to the north at the Great Highway. Turn right on the Great Highway, back to Skyline, where you cross and pick up the multi-use path that leads around the lakes. *Be Aware*: Skyline Boulevard and the Great Highway are high-speed traffic areas.

J: The Lake Merced multi-use path runs for about 4.5 miles, encircling all three lakes. It's a flat run, and the water makes for pleasant viewing, although you're close to streets along the east shore. This is a well-used running track.

R: **Skates and Scooters:** The multi-use path around Lake Merced, although some if it is rough, is a high-speed track for conditioned skaters and recreational scooters. **Strollers:** The Sunset loop at Fort Funston is good for strollers, especially for tots who like dogs. And, of course, the San Francisco Zoo is a kid-pleaser. **Wheelchairs:** The Sunset Trail is designed for wheelchairs. The north side of Lake Merced, as described in the North lakes loop, is also a pleasant roll. The Recreation Center for the Handicapped is on Herbst Road, off Skyline, just across from Lake Merced Boulevard.

Special Interests: Boating: Lake Merced has boat rentals and kayak access, as well as fishing. *Kids:* Kids will like the zoo. And the boating on Lake Merced is for the family.

7. OCEAN BEACH   H, MB, J, R

Best for: Miles of open beach, flanked by the city's historic esplanade.

Parking: *From the north on Hwy. 1*, which is 19th Ave., go right on Geary Blvd. Veer right on Point Lobos Ave., which curves down to the Great Highway. Go south and park along the coast at the north end of the mile-long parking lot. *Coming from the south*, go north on Hwy. 280 and follow signs to Hwy. 1. Go west on Noriega Ave. and then north on the Great Highway to north end parking, across from Balboa Ave. *From the Bay Bridge*, follow freeway signs toward "Golden Gate Bridge." Take the Fell St. exit and proceed west on Fell. Turn right, or north, on Masonic Ave. and then turn left, or west, on Geary Blvd. Continue to the Great Highway. *Bus:* SF Muni, 5, 31, 38, 18, N, 48

Agency: Golden Gate National Recreation Area

H: Ocean Beach (up to 8 mi.)

Ocean Beach is where Golden Gate Park meets the sea, a broad swath of sand running about 4 miles, from below the Cliff House to Fort Funston. Beginning at the north end and extending south for about a mile is **The Esplanade**, a sidewalk off which wide stairs lead down to the beach through regular openings in a 15-foot high seawall. South of The Esplanade, the path continues, intermittently paved, for the last several miles, with openings through dunes. At the far south end of Ocean Beach, where the bluffs of Fort Funston slope upwards from sea level, is an improved parking area—a good spot to begin walks along wilder sections of coast. You may wish to begin your Ocean Beach hike on the sand, go until you're half-tired, and then loop back up to The

Esplanade or path on the return leg. *Be Aware*: Ocean Beach is not safe for swimming. Shorebreak, riptide, cold water, and rogue waves contribute to the hazard.

MB: Try a 10-mile ride from the **Cliff House through Fort Funston**. Begin by going down the coast along the Great Highway, part of Bike Route 95. At the south end of Ocean Beach, where the Great Highway veers away from the coast, is a bike path leading over the Fort Funston dunes. You can take that path to the parking area at Fort Funston, where you ride out to Skyline Boulevard and double back on Bike Route 95.

J: The Esplanade, a coastal path, and the wide-open beach make for several options heading south on Ocean Beach. On temperate days, this is a great place for people-watching runners. Across the Great Highway, south of The Esplanade, is another paved running path, where you won't have to dodge people.

R: **Skates and Scooters**: The wide sidewalk of The Esplanade is ideal for in-line skaters, as is the parking lot which runs along the sidewalk. Except on the day of the Bay to Breakers race, when this area serves as the finish line, the lot is a wide open skate. **Strollers and Wheelchairs**: The Esplanade is an excellent surface for wheeling amid the sea air. The 4-foot beach wall that runs along it, however, limits the sea view from a sitting position, except at the stair openings. South of The Esplanade, the path is mostly unpaved, but packed hard enough to allow wheels; in some places you may encounter drifting sand.

8. LANDS END   H, ST, MB, J, R

Best for: With a world-class museum, relics of San Francisco's gilded years, and dramatic coastal bluffs and parks, this area scores at the top of everybody's fun list.

Parking: From Hwy. 1, which is 19th Avenue, turn west on Geary Blvd. Near the coast, veer right on Point Lobos Ave. and, just past El Camino del Mar, turn right on your Merrie Way. Park in large lot. *Note*: Additional parking described in sections below. *Bus:* SF Muni 18, 38

Agency: Golden Gate National Recreation Area; *Special Interest: Kids

H: **Sutro Heights Park (up to 1.5 mi.); Sutro Bath ruins (up to 1 mi.); Coastal Trail to Legion of Honor (1.75 mi.); Eagles Point viewing platform (.25-mi.)**

Lands End features rugged cliffs that form the most westerly portion of the south side of the Golden Gate. Numerous shipwrecks have been logged in these treacherous currents, rocks and high surf. When the freighter *Ohioan* ran aground in 1936, sparks from her steel hull were said to have illuminated the dark night. Lands End is part of GGNRA's Sutro District, named in honor of Adolph Sutro, an engineer and later mayor of San Francisco, whose mansion and lavish Sutro Baths supplied a fantastical architectural accent to the area's striking natural beauty. Sutro, an immigrant from Germany with little to his name, made his fortune in the 1860s by designing a tunnel through the base of a mountain which drained water from the silver and gold mines in the Comstock Lode in Virginia City, Nevada.

Sutro Heights Park is the site of Sutro's mansion, with views of Ocean Beach and Seal Rock. Cross Point Lobos Avenue to a parking lot and walk left to the end of the lot and up a short, fairly steep ramp to the park. At the top is a paved path that makes a large circle through a varied arboretum that includes cypress and Norfolk pines—the grounds of the estate of a man who had his pick of all of San Francisco. The gardens were planted at the time as a marvel for the public, as Adolph was prone to parlaying his fortune to amuse others as well as himself. On the west end of the loop is the park's hidden treasure, a path up to a viewing area. Sutro died in 1898 and his mansion was demolished in 1939.

To **Sutro Bath ruins**, take the steps down from the Merrie Way parking lot. You can also take a wide trail down from the sidewalk a few hundred feet up from the Cliff House. The substantial remains of the bath's foundation today form a pool for shore-birds. But when Sutro's incredible site opened in 1896, the foundations supported seven large saltwater pools, enclosed by a two-acre glass roof and surrounded by curio shops with Egyptian artifacts, galleries with restaurants, and a tiered grandstand that seated 5,000 people. Some 500 private dressing rooms served up to 20,000 swimmers each day. In the mid-1900s, the weather-bashed baths were converted to a skating rink, and in 1966 the remaining structure was destroyed by fire. You can roam around the concrete labyrinth—to the right of which you'll also find a 200-foot long tunnel leading to crashing waves. And don't miss the higher paths up to the right that lead to walled-in coastal perches. *Be aware*: High surf is a hazard all along the shoreline.

Queen Wilhelmina's tulips, Laughing Sal at the Musee Mecanique, The Esplanade

The **Coastal Trail to the Legion of Honor** features a tree-filtered view of Lands End and the Golden Gate Bridge. Head out from the trailhead at the north end of the Merrie Way parking lot on a spur trail that soon joins the Coastal Trail. Go left on the Coastal Trail, and, when the Golden Gate Bridge comes into view, take a staircase with cable railing that goes up to the right. The stairs lead to the Fort Miley parking area, which is also accessible via El Camino del Mar. Proceed on a road out the northwest part of the parking area, to your right as you face the water. This old road, a former railroad bed for the Sutro line that serviced the Cliff House and baths, is the Camino del Mar Trail. The forested trail with ocean views leads to a series of steps—jog right— and then to a paved part of El Camino del Mar. As you walk up, the Legion of Honor is to your right and the golf course on the left. Explore the museum's beautiful grounds, if you like, and then pick up the Coastal Trail, which is off the the large circular drive, where Legion of Honor Drive ends at El Camino del Mar. The Coastal Trail loops back to the Merrie Way parking lot.

For **Eagles Point**—a spectacular viewing area of the Golden Gate Bridge—you need to drive: From the Merrie Way parking lot, turn left and then make an immediate left toward Fort Miley. Then turn right on Clement, continue for a number of blocks, and turn left on Legion of Honor Drive. Drive past the Legion of Honor and go right on El Camino del Mar. Look for GGNRA's Land End sign, just west of 32nd Avenue, and park along the golf course. The short trail, down railroad-tie stairs, leads to the John C. Scully bench.

ST: Cliff House; Musee Mecanique; GGNRA Visitors Center; Legion of Honor

To the **Cliff House Restaurant**, a San Francisco tradition since 1863, walk to the right down the broad sidewalk from the Merrie Way parking lot. The elegant structure has had many incarnations. The original modest place was sold to Sutro in 1881, who built a rail line to it, before it burned down in 1894. Sutro's grand re-build, fashioned after a French chateau, survived the 1906 earthquake, but burned a year later. The third, and existing, Cliff House was built by Sutro's daughter, Emma, in 1909. The National Park Service acquired the restaurant in 1977. Sunset views and fine food make it one of the most popular restaurants in the country.

Below the Cliff House—accessible via stairs or a ramp that begins off the sidewalk about 200 feet down the hill—is the **Musee Mecanique**, a wondrous, low-tech arcade of antique games from yesteryear. Your kids will have so much fun they won't realize they're getting an education on pre-electrical automated amusements. Across from the Musee is a **GGNRA Visitors Center** featuring an excellent gift shop and bookstore. Offshore from these attractions is a view of misnamed Seal Rocks. Once a more popular hangout for local sea lions, these guano-covered crags now feature an array of shorebirds.

The **Legion of Honor** is one of San Francisco's world-class art museums. Drive east on Point Lobos Avenue until it becomes Geary Boulevard, and then turn left on 34th Avenue. At Clement Street, 34th becomes Legion of Honor Drive, which you take a short distance up to the ample and scenic parking area. Dedicated in an extravaganza on Armistice Day 1924, the museum is a slightly down-scale replica of the neoclassical Legion of Honor in Paris. Check out the view from the east end of the parking area. You can sit outside the museum doors with Rodin's *The Thinker*. Inside are traveling exhibits, as well as ancient, medieval and European art from the 16th century forward to modern times. Also inside is the huge Ernest M. Skinner organ, built in 1924 and featuring 4,526 pipes.

MB: For a 10-mile round trip ride to **Fort Funston**, head down Point Lobos Avenue to the Great Highway and pick up Bike Route 95 on the right, which runs all the way to Fort Funston's dunes. For a **Lands End loop**, a 3-mile ride that takes in some of the Coastal Trail and the Legion of Honor, turn left from the Merrie Way parking lot and go left on El Camino del Mar. After a short distance, when Clement Street is on your right, go left on the Coastal Trail. Continue until the trail comes out to El Camino del Mar, leading to the Legion of Honor. Head over the hill past the Legion of Honor and down to Clement. Turn right and follow Bike Routes 10 and 95 back to your starting point. *Be Aware*: Point Lobos Road around the Cliff House is an area where drivers tend to be looking at the view.

J: The Coastal Trail to the Legion of Honor, described above, is also called the Railroad Bed Loop, in honor of Sutro's old tourist line. It is a mostly flat cross-country run with great views. From Merrie Way, jog up El Camino del Mar—with an option of taking a side trip up to Fort Miley to your right—and then pick up the old service road from the parking lot at the end. That trail takes you to the Legion of Honor, from where you take the Coastal Trail back.

R: **Strollers and Wheelchairs**: Check out Sutro Heights Park for a wheel through pleasant greenery with spectacular views. For easy access to the park, head up Point Lobos one block to 48th Street and you'll see the two lion statues, faithfully guarding the entrance to a mansion that no longer exists. A level path leads around the park. Sutro Bath ruins is also accessible by wheel, via the route from the sidewalk up the street from the Cliff House. The surface is not smooth and the path is fairly steep.

*Special Interests: *Kids*: The Musee Mecanique, as described in stroll section, is a hoot for the kids, especially if they've never seen Laughing Sal. The tunnel at Sutro Bath ruins will give kids the fun kind of creeps.

Baker bluffs

9. BAKER BEACH

Best for: A movie director's favorite beach, set below Seacliff mansions and adorned with dunes, rolling surf and romantic views from the Pacific side back to the Golden Gate Bridge.

Parking: From the Golden Gate Bridge, go through the far-right toll booth and make an immediate right, on Merchant Rd. Follow Merchant a short distance to Lincoln Blvd., turn right, continue about .75-mi. Veer right on Bowley St., following signs to Baker Beach. *Bus:* SF Muni 29

Agency: Golden Gate National Recreation Area

H: **Baker Beach-Battery Chamberlain (.75-mi.); China Beach via Seacliff (1.25 mi.)**

To walk **Baker Beach and Battery Chamberlain**, veer to the right on Chamberlain Road as you drive in toward Baker Beach on Bowley Street—note the grassy picnic area under pines to your right as you drop down. Park at the far right side of the parking lot. You'll see Battery Chamberlain, a 95,000-pound cannon emplaced here by the Army in 1904. Park rangers provide tours of the huge gun and small museum. Drop out to the beach and stroll right, taking in views of the famous bridge and Marin Headlands across the gate. You'll see access to the Coastal Trail, heading off to your right as you get to the beach near Battery Chamberlain. *Be Aware*: Rip currents and drop-offs make Baker a dangerous swimming beach.

To **China Beach via Seacliff**, veer left on Gibson Road as you drive in on Bowley Street from Lincoln Avenue. From the parking area, start to your left along a sandy path that skirts the beach dunes. You pass coastal flora and then go up railroad tie stairs to the wrought iron gate that marks an entrance to Baker Beach from tiny North 25th Avenue in Seacliff. From here, jog left out to Seacliff Avenue and turn right, walking almost .5-mile through the grand and picturesque estates, some of the most desirable dwellings in the world, including one owned by comedian Robin Williams. You'll come to the end of Seacliff and a parking area that marks the short path down to the beach. China Beach, set in a rocky cove, was a Gold Rush-era Chinese fishermen encampment. Tucked away, this beach gets less tourist traffic than most. *Direct Access:* Continue driving south on Lincoln past Bowley Street. Turn right on 26th Avenue and go one block to Seacliff Avenue, veering left at Scenic Way. Park at the dead end.

MB: A scenic, 6-mile **Baker Beach loop** takes in both beaches, the Legion of Honor, and part of the Presidio. Park at north end of Bowley Street near Lincoln Avenue, as per parking directions above. This ride requires some navigation. Head down Bowley, doing in-and-outs to Baker Beach on both Chamberlain and Gibson roads. Continue along Bowley to where it circles out to Lincoln. Veer right off Lincoln at El Camino del Mar—you'll be veering off Bike Route 95 onto 395—and then turn right on 26th Avenue to Seacliff in order to visit China Beach. Come back out to El Camino del Mar and continue up past the golf course, turning left on Legion of Honor Drive. Pass the museum and ride down the hill to Clement Street. Turn left on Clement, now on Bike Route 10, and then left on 30th for a short distance to Lake Street. Take Bike Route 10 east on Lake, along a bike lane, and hang a left on 15th Avenue, joining Bike Route 65. Follow Bike Route 65, coming to Washington Boulevard. Ride Washington, taking in a dramatic Pacific view, until you come to Lincoln Avenue. Turn left and continue the last .75-mile to the Baker Beach entrance at Bowley Street.

10. THE PRESIDIO   H, ST, MB, J, R

Best for: Overlooking the Pacific and San Francisco Bay, the entire Presidio is a National Historic Landmark of nearly 1,500 acres. You'll find buildings of at least nine different architectural styles that reveal a diverse history dating from the late 1700s—all set amid trees ranging from garden palms to forests of cypress, eucalyptus and pine.

Parking: At William Mott Visitors Center. *From the Golden Gate Bridge,* pass through the far-right toll booth and turn right immediately past the bridge office building, on Merchant Rd. Then turn right immediately again, following the road under the bridge roadway to the parking lot on the east side. Keep right to stop sign at Lincoln Ave. Turn left on Lincoln, follow for about 1 mi. and veer right on Sheridan; cross Taylor Road and turn left on Montgomery—you'll now be in a large parking lot and see the visitors center to your left. *From Highway 1* *south*, which is 19th Ave., continue to north side of Golden Gate Park and turn right on California St. Go about .75-mi. on California, just past 2nd Ave. and turn left on Arguello Blvd. Follow through the Arguello Gate to the Presidio, and then all the way down to Sheridan; jog left on Sheridan and then right on Montgomery St. to visitors center.. *Bus:* SF Muni 29

Agency: Golden Gate National Recreation Area

H: Ecology Trail from Main Post to Inspiration Point (1.5 mi.); Bay Area Ridge Trail to: San Francisco National Cemetery (1.25 mi.), or Fort Winfield Scott Parade Ground (3 mi.); Mountain Lake Park to Rob Hill via Juan Bautista de Anza Trail (3 mi.)

Prior to becoming part of the National Park Service's GGNRA in 1994, the Presidio had been a military garrison for 220 years—under the flags of three different nations. First, in 1776, Spanish troops constructed an adobe quadrangle that became the northernmost outpost of their empire, then called Alta (upper) California. In 1821, the Mexican flag flew here, when the newly independent republic annexed Alta California as part of its territory. In 1846, American forces landed during the war with Mexico, and, as a result of treaty in 1848, the Stars and Stripes were raised. The garrison was the staging area for U.S. troops bound for the Philippines in 1898, during the Spanish American War, and many of the brick barracks were built during that period. Today, since many of the buildings are no longer needed for military personnel, a whopping 6-million square feet of spread-out office space is being leased through private-public partnership to nonprofit groups and other park-friendly organizations, under the stewardship of the Presidio Trust. The Trust is charged with making sure the park is financially self-sufficient by 2013.

San Francisco
National Cemetery

Ft. Point during construction of the Golden Gate Bridge.
Photo collection of Golden Gate National Recreation Area, National Park Service

For the **Ecology Trail from Main Post to Inspiration Point**, walk directly away from the visitors center across the former Parade Ground, veering right across Pershing Square to Moraga Street. Go to Funston Street—you'll see the old Officers Quarters, built in 1862, in a line along Funston. From the corner of Moraga and Funston, join the Ecology Trail, which heads up, climbing over 200 feet, through eucalyptus and cypress forest to the recently renovated Inspiration Point. Near the top of the trail, stairs lead up to the point from the trail. From the point are views of the bay toward Crissy Field and Alcatraz. *Note:* Inspiration Point is accessible by car; see description for Bay Area Ridge Trail hike below.

For **both Bay Area Ridge Trail hikes**, begin at the Presidio Golf Course parking, just inside the Arguello Gate. Drive winding Arguello up from Moraga Avenue near the visitors center. The Ridge Trail was begun some 30 years ago as the brainchild of conservationist William Mott. When completed, the BART will connect parks and open space on a 400-mile swing around the greater Bay Area. Begin the hikes by heading north, entering a tunnel of towering cypress and eucalyptus trees. In about .5-mile you come out to Washington Boulevard—just before you do, note a spur road to your left that gives you an option of scaling Presidio Hill. Then go left on Washington, following BART signs.

For the **San Francisco National Cemetery**, veer to the right on Nauman Road just past a crosswalk that takes the BART path to the other side. Pass a few 1940s-circa officers' family homes and go right on a trail marked by upright pipes. This short spur trail leads to a view from the uppermost portion of the cemetery grounds. This glimpse is bound to cause a patriotic beat of the heart even among cynics, especially on holidays when flags are flying over the sea of headstones dating from the late 1800s. *Note:* The return leg of the Fort Scott loop also goes through the cemetery.

To continue to the **Fort Winfield Scott Parade Grounds**, stay on Washington, following BART signs to Compton. Head up Compton, turning right on the dirt trail. You walk up through dense eucalyptus forest, passing a picnic area and popping back out to pavement at Harrison Street. Walk down Harrison and turn right on Hitchcock Street—part of the San Juan de Bautista Trail. Then look for a left-jog of the trail, which leads via Greenough Avenue to the parade grounds. The grounds are surrounded by Fort Scott barracks, which date from 1910. If you're lucky, you'll see the equestrian United States Park Police training on their thoroughbreds in the field. Leave the parade ground at the south end, going uphill on Upton Avenue before going left on Kobbe Avenue. At the bottom, cross busy Park Boulevard to a short trail that leads up to the San Francisco National Cemetery. You'll need to step over a two-foot high wall. Keep to your right, going steeply uphill through the cemetery. At its southern corner, go out a spur trail and then go left at the first street—this takes you out to Washington Street, where you retrace your steps to the Arguello Gate.

For **Mountain Lake Park to Rob Hill via Juan Bautista de Anza Trail**, leave the Presidio driving south on Arguello, and then turn right on Lake Street. Continue 12 blocks and park near the corner of Lake and Funston. Walk up Funston to Mountain Lake Park, and take the serene trail that goes around the lake to your right. You'll loop north away from the lake, cross under Highway 1, and then head south again along Battery Caufield Road, which becomes a segment of the Anza Trail. In 1775, Juan Bautista de Anza, frontier captain of New Spain, led some 200 immigrants and a herd of livestock northward hundreds of miles to the far reaches of Alta California, terminating at what is now the Presidio. In 1990, Congress made the Anza a National Historic Trail. Continue almost a mile along Battery Caufield Road until you reach more off-street trail. Rob Hill—highest spot in the Presidio—is up through the forest to your left, a short distance north of Compton Street. To return, take a trail to your right just after Battery McKinnon-Stotsenberg; you'll be on a section of the BART trail that leads out to Washington Boulevard. Go left on Washington and, after about one-eighth mile, turn right on a trail across from Park Boulevard. The Park Presidio Tunnel will be below the earth you trod, as you walk south for almost .5-mile, coming to the trail from Mountain Lake. Go left on this trail.

ST: William P. Mott Jr. Visitors Center; San Francisco National Cemetery

The **William P. Mott, Jr. Visitors Center** is a must-stop to get acquainted with the park's history and present-day goings on. Free maps are offered, helpful in navigating the park's spider web of roads and trails. They also have an excellent book and gift store and beautiful exhibits. The center also offers guided tours—including walks of the National Cemetery, Main Post, and Crissy Field.

To drive to the **San Francisco National Cemetery**, go south on Montgomery in front of the visitors center and turn right on Sheridan. After a short distance, just before Lincoln Avenue, veer left on Sheridan, up through the main gate of the cemetery. Park at the buildings on the right as you enter, and walk rather than drive around the grounds. The 28-acre cemetery, set on a hill under towering cypress trees in view of the Golden Gate, is particularly striking on Memorial Day and Veterans Day.

MB: The Presidio is ideal for exploring on a bike, but be ready for exercise with elevation changes of some 200 feet. And bring a road map to avoid getting lost in a network of lesser streets and alleys. For a specific route, try the **Fort Scott loop**, as described in the hiking section above.

For a 6-mile **Presidio loop**, begin at the Mott Visitors Center. Head toward the bay on Montgomery Street and turn right on Lincoln Avenue. At Halleck Street you join Bike Route 55. Stay on route 55 as Lincoln blends with Presidio Boulevard—be mindful of traffic in this area. After about .5-mile on Presidio Boulevard, turn right on West Pacific Avenue, following a wide-curb bike lane and passing the Arguello Gate. Just past the gate, continue on a bike path, which takes you to Mountain Lake Park. The path loops around the lake to the north, goes under Highway 1, and then turns south before hitting 15th Avenue near the hospital. From here, follow Bike Route 69 north along Battery Caufield until you come to Washington Boulevard. Go left on Bike Route 65—passing a spectacular vista point looking out to sea—until you come to Lincoln Avenue. You can follow Lincoln around, under the bridge approach, and back to the visitors center; or, to avoid traffic, turn right on Storey Avenue and make your way across the Presidio to hit Lincoln much closer to the center.

J: The Fort Winfield Scott Parade Grounds make a flat, scenic jogging track, circling the grounds on the interior of the buildings. You can access Fort Scott from Lincoln Avenue at Ralston Street. The Bay Area Ridge Trail to Fort Scott loop, as described in the hiking section, is probably better as a run that a walk, since half of the route is on surface streets.

R: **Wheelchairs and Strollers:** The Main Post Walk is nearly a mile if you include the roll from the visitors center to the beginning of the walk at Pershing Square. Pick up a detailed pamphlet at the center for the 12-stop tour of the historic buildings around the Main Post. For a more nature-oriented roll, start at the parking area near the Arguello Gate, as noted in the BART loop hikes—with this variation: Head out as described above, but double back before the trail reaches Washington Boulevard, taking a spur trail that goes back toward the golf clubhouse. Less than .25-mile from the parking area, you'll see the trail to the left. Also, be sure to take in Inspiration Point, which is just north on Arguello Boulevard from this trailhead parking.

11.   ALCATRAZ   ST, R

Best for: For a more than a hundred years "The Rock" was a fortress and prison, but since 1972 its tide pools, historic buildings and bird colonies have attracted millions of visitors—now with round-trip tickets.

Parking: Trips to Alcatraz are with Blue & Gold Fleet Ferry service from Pier 41 in San Francisco, which is on The Embarcadero at Powell Street near Fishermans Wharf. Reserve ahead on summer weekends and holidays.

The Blue & Gold Ferries serve Fishermans Wharf from Sausalito, Tiburon, Vallejo and Richmond. Trolley and bus service to the wharf is available in front of Ferry Building at Market Street. Cable cars run from downtown San Francisco on Powell Street to Fishermans Wharf.

Agency: Golden Gate National Recreation Area

ST: **Alcatraz Island (up to 1.5-mi.)**

Alcatraz is a small island, but you're bound to get plenty of exercise wandering around the old Army barracks, cellhouse and numerous other buildings. In 1850, just two years after California became a state, the U.S. military installed cannons on Alcatraz, making it the first permanent military outpost on the Pacific Coast. No shots were ever fired and by about 1900 other defenses at the Golden Gate had made Alcatraz obsolete. The Rock's history as a prison began in 1895 when 19 Hopi people were imprisoned here. Although Spanish-American War captives, military miscreants, and overflow city jail prisoners during the 1906 earthquake also did time on the little island, Alcatraz was not made a Federal penitentiary until 1933. It was a Federal pen until 1962, boasting no escapes among 14 attempts—although Frank Morris and the Anglin brothers went over the wall in June of 1962 and were never heard from again. From 1969 to 1971, about 100 Native Americans occupied the island and proclaimed it as Native Land.

Alcatraz is not without its greenery. Dirt was hauled from Angel Island when the gun fortifications were installed in the 1800s, and this soil later became the basis for the gardens of military and prison personnel. The cellhouse sitting atop the center of the island is a popular attraction. Also a favorite is the Agave Trail along the seawall on the island's west shore, leading to stairs up to your own private "lock-up." One of the island's best features is its tremendous view of the San Francisco skyline and the Golden Gate Bridge. *Note:* Off-limits areas include the north shore of the island, and, from August through January, the Agave Trail. Closures are to protect nesting birds and keep people away from dangerous cliffs.

R: **Strollers and Wheelchairs:** Areas are steep, but Alcatraz is accessible for rolling visitors. An on-island shuttle is available to wheelchair riders who need a lift up the steepest .25-mile path.

Alcatraz

12.   FORT MASON ST, MB, J, R

Best for: Captivating natural beauty, historic sites, and an array of tourist amusements combine for an only-in-San Francisco walk to remember.

Parking: From the Golden Gate Bridge, stay on Hwy. 101 and keep left. You'll blend with Marina Blvd. Go about 1 mi. and park on left at Fort Mason at Buchanan St. and Marina Blvd. Some parking is by permit only on weekends and holidays. *Bus:* SF Muni 29, 47, 19, F

Transportation: Blue & Gold Ferry service direct to Fishermans Wharf. Trolley and bus service from downtown Ferry Building.

Agency: Golden Gate National Recreation Area; City of San Francisco; *Special Interest: Kids, Swimming

ST: Fort Mason to Pier 39 (3 mi.); Fort Mason to Crissy Field (2.25 mi.)

On a walk from **Fort Mason to Pier 39**, you'll encounter centuries-old military sites, Aquatic Park, Ghiradelli Square, Hyde Street Pier, Fishermans Wharf and a host of other sites that inspire the development of scads of Kodak prints. Begin by taking a paved path up through Fort Mason's Great Meadow from the corner of Laguna and Bay streets. Head toward the obelisk statue near the top—by Benny Bufano—and take the stairs. Check out the community gardens on your right then veer left behind the Fort Barry Youth Hostel. Walk through Black Point Battery, set in a cypress grove with great bay views. Up the stairs to your right will be the site of Battery San Jose, built by the Spaniards in 1797, the oldest of the Golden Gate's many gun emplacements.

Take the railed stairs from Black Point Battery, leading down to the northern terminus of Van Ness Avenue at Aquatic Park. The park is a man-made cove for fishermen, swimmers, and rowing clubs. If you wish, take a side-trip out the Municipal Pier where you can almost touch the passing sailboats or see what the locals are catching. Then continue around the inner crescent of Aquatic Park, with its beach and tiered steps, below the Maritime Museum and National Historic Park. The Maritime Museum, offering free admission, displays excellent exhibits of San Francisco's seagoing history and is good place to spend a rainy day. The large complex of red brick buildings behind the museum on Beach Street is Ghiradelli Square, enticing visitors with its chocolate factory, trendy shops and restaurants. Stop in for their famous hot fudge sundae.

Leave Aquatic Park at the corner of Hyde and Jefferson streets. Immediately left is the Hyde Street Pier, a National Historic Park that moors more than a half-dozen vessels, most open to visitors. The ships date from the late 1800s to World War II—square-rigged Cape Horn sail boats, steam schooners, paddle tugs and side wheel ferries. Among them is the *Balclutha*, launched from Scotland in 1886. Traditional seafaring skills are on display. *Note:* An admission is charged.

Continue down Jefferson Street—you'll now whiff the crab, sourdough, and cotton candy—while wandering past curio shops, sidewalk seafood restaurants, and the moored fishing boats of Fishermans Wharf. Look for dock openings on your left to wander out among the working boats, the muscle behind the glitz and gaucherie of the wharf. Then walk left at Taylor Street, past the ferry terminals at Pier 43. To the right of the Red and White Ferry, head out toward the Public Shore sign to the pier, which features a display commemorating a system of bells that kept ships from rocky shoals all around the Golden Gate. Then continue, passing Pier 41 with service to Alcatraz, to Pier 39.

Pier 39 is a two-level circus of colorful shops and restaurants set in rough-hewn buildings on a broad plank walkway that juts about 1,000 feet into the San Francisco Bay. At the end of the busy boardwalk is a viewing area, looking out toward Alcatraz and Angel Island. Go left at the viewing area to see Pier 39's most-boisterous crowd: a hoard of up to 600 barking, frolicking and sunning sea lions gathered at K-dock. The migrating mammals began hanging out after the earthquake of 1989, enjoying a ready supply of herring in the shoreline waters. They have increased in number and migrated less since then, perhaps enticed and amused by an adoring human audience. You can then proceed along the outside of Pier 39.

Retrace your route back through Aquatic Park, but then stay to your right and head up the wide, paved path along the water to Fort Mason. At the top of the ramp, head down a long staircase to a half-dozen long, large buildings with red roofs set on piers. Poke around the bookstore, Mexican Museum, or lunch at the renowned Greens Restaurant. Fort Mason was the Army's main Pacific supply center during World War II.

To walk the other way, from **Fort Mason to Crissy Field**, head to your left as you face the bay, walking the path or sidewalk nearest the water. For the first mile, the Marina Yacht Harbor will be on your right and the Marina Green, a playfield for locals, will be on your left. At the far end of the Marina Green, you'll pass the yacht clubs, after which is the eastern end of the Golden Gate Promenade. This path follows the bay to the bridge; see Crissy Field, TH13.

MB: The entire San Francisco Bay shoreline, from **Fort Mason to the Ferry Building**, and, going the opposite direction, to **Fort Point and the Golden Gate Bridge**, is bike friendly. For a touristy, sight-seeing ride, pedal up the multi-use path beside the Great Meadow, which takes you to Aquatic Park. From there, hug the shore-side streets, Jefferson, and then The Embarcadero, for a rolling look at the sights mentioned in the stroll above. Be mindful of traffic, although cars move slowly through the wharf area. Continue along The Embarcadero, past piers going away from the buzz of Fishermans Wharf. Stay on a dedicated bike lane of Route 5 to the Ferry Building in the heart of downtown. You can have a picnic under skyscrapers at Justin Herman Plaza. The round trip from Fort Mason to downtown is almost 7 miles.

From **Fort Mason to Fort Point** at the Golden Gate Bridge is a level ride of about 6 miles, round-trip. You can hug the water all the way, along the Marina Green and then Crissy Field. This is a breezy, big open view, "look ma, no-hands" ride.

J: The multi-use path over Fort Mason's Great Meadow to Aquatic Park is a popular jogger's route. From Aquatic Park, continue through the wharf, a path used by many runners in spite of sharing the route with autos.

R: **Skates, Strollers, Wheelchairs**: The paved path from Fort Mason to Aquatic park—and then out the Municipal Pier—is well-suited for all rollers looking for city scenery with their exercise. Factor in, however, the steepness of the path over Great Meadow. To wheel out the pier and around Aquatic Park, avoiding Fort Mason, continue past Fort Mason on Bay Street and then make a left on Van Ness.

*Special Interests: *Kids:* Young ones through the teen years can spend days at Pier 39 and Fishermans Wharf. *Swimming:* Swimmers who like cold water do laps just offshore at Aquatic Park.

13.   CRISSY FIELD   H, ST, MB, J, R

Best for: Urban walking that draws people from around the globe: Dramatic seascapes, marine wildlife and historic sites—all beneath the luminous beauty of the Golden Gate Bridge.

Parking: *From the Golden Gate Bridge,* pass through the far-right toll booth and make an *immediate* right turn. Then turn right again at your first opportunity, circling below the bridge roadway to the parking lot on the east side. Bear right to Lincoln Ave. Turn left, curving along Lincoln for about a mile and then turn left on Halleck St. Go under the bridge approach to Mason St. and turn right. Follow to signed parking. *From the Bay Bridge or Hwy. 101 south,* follow signs for Hwy. 101 north, Golden Gate Bridge and take Van Ness St. exit. Follow Van Ness several miles and turn left on Bay St. Turn right off Bay at Laguna St., which takes you to Marina Blvd. Follow Marina Blvd. past Marina Green and veer right on Mason St. Look for Crissy Field parking. *Bus:* SF Muni 29

Agency: Golden Gate National Recreation Area; San Francisco Recreation and Park Department; *Special Interest: Kids, Kites, Kayaks

H: **Golden Gate Promenade to Fort Point (3 mi.); Yacht clubs and Fort Mason (4 mi.)**

Crissy Field, recently bequeathed by the Army to the National Park Service, has been transformed from a WWI-vintage airfield with a potholed parking lot to a lagoon, with a path through vegetation along the sandy shore of San Francisco Bay. On most days, and for sure on sunny weekends, the Golden Gate Promenade is filled will sight-seeing exercise lovers—and their strollers, bikes, skates and pets.

Begin the **Golden Gate Promenade to Fort Point** by going left along the path. You can also walk the beach, a popular dog exercise area. You'll cross a bridge over a developed lagoon, bordered by native plants, and then reach the visitors center for the Gulf of the Farallones National Marine Sanctuary on your right. Those interested in the marine life will want to drop in for a visit. The Farallones Sanctuary protects a large portion of ocean, extending offshore beyond the Farallon Islands—which are 29 miles west of the Golden Gate—and northward beyond Point Reyes Seashore to Bodega Bay. Designated in 1981, this sanctuary was the first among 13 in the country today.

Pass the Farallones Center on the water side. In another .25-mile you come to Fort Point Wharf, built in 1908, used by fishermen and walkers who want to get out on the water. Just past the wharf, the Promenade blends with Long Avenue, the car route to Fort Point. Construction of the brick fort took nine years, beginning in 1853. The only west coast example among 30 similar fortifications on the Atlantic coast, Fort Point was designed to house 500 soldiers. Once a massive sentinel at the south head of the gate, the fort now is dwarfed by the Golden Gate Bridge, directly overhead.

The walk the other way from Crissy Field, toward **Fort Mason**, is a look at city life along the Marina, and features a scenic yacht club jetty. Go right along the beach as

Golden Gate Promenade

you face the water, curling around to the St. Francis Yacht Club. Walk past the club, with the sailboats moored on your right, and continue out the breakwater, toward the statue of a lighthouse. You'll be immersed in a spectacular view of Angel Island, Alcatraz, and the city. Pass the small Golden Gate Yacht Club and continue to the end of the jetty. There you can quizzically observe the "ocean organ," a system of pipes and rock work that emits sounds caused by tidal action below. Double back on the breakwater, all the way to the St. Francis, turn left, and continue along the Marina Green, where city dwellers play various field games on weekends. At the end of the green is another yacht harbor, Gashouse Cove, and just beyond that is Fort Mason. The Great Meadow above Fort Mason is a great picnic area and the site of the annual San Francisco Blues Festival. Above the meadow are the youth hostel and community garden.

ST: Palace of Fine Arts and Exploratorium (1 mi.); Chestnut Street (2.25 mi.)

The **Palace of Fine Arts** is a landmark most will recognize—a tall Romanesque rotunda designed in 1915 by Bernard Maybeck for the Panama-Pacific International Exposition. To get there, walk diagonally from Crissy Field across a field of young cypress to the corner of Marina Boulevard and Baker Street; you'll see the palace dome across the street. The Palace of Fine Arts, whose huge columns are decorated with Greek statuary, is surrounded by a lagoon replete with swans and ducks—a favorite photo backdrop among brides and grooms. On the grounds of the palace is the **Exploratorium**, an educational playpen for kids of all ages. It features all sorts of whizzing, beeping interactive gizmos and displays designed first for fun, but all with learning as a by-product. The Exploratorium is a long-standing favorite among parents, kids, and educators.

If you're up for a beverage or meal, and want a glimpse at neighborhood life in the Marina, head for **Chestnut Street**. Walk away from the Palace of Fine Arts on the lagoon side, on Beach Street. Go two blocks, turn right on Divisidero Street, go four blocks, and then walk left on Chestnut. The entire Marina District, which sustained significant damage during the '89 quake, is built on marshland that was filled during the 1915 Panama Pacific Exhibitions. The vibrant part of Chestnut, with florists, bars, boutiques and cafés, runs a half-dozen blocks, from Divisidero to Fillmore.

MB: A ride from **Fort Point to the Ferry Building**, about 12 miles round-trip, gives you a cross section of San Francisco—the bridge, beaches, historic sites, Fishermans Wharf and the skyscrapers of downtown. Park at the end of Crissy Field closest to the Golden Gate Bridge, and do an out-and-back to Fort Point. Then continue away from the bridge—there's a path close to the water and also a paved bike route along Mason Street. Continue along the Marina Green to Fort Mason. Go up the Great Meadow at Fort Mason, over to Aquatic Park and on to Fishermans Wharf on Jefferson Street. You come to The Embarcadero, where you turn right and follow Bike Route 5, a bike lane that runs along the piers to the Ferry Building.

J: The Golden Gate Promenade, as well as the paths going the other way to Fort Mason, are excellent, flat runs. People come from all over the Bay Area, and down from flats throughout the city, to jog the shoreline and take in sea air and scenery.

R: **Skates and Scooters:** The Golden Gate Promenade is used by skaters, but the surface is rough in places, and you may encounter sand. For the skate toward Fort Point, try the multi-use path that runs in that direction along Mason Street; it later dovetails with the road to Fort Point. **Wheelchairs and Strollers:** The Golden Gate Promenade is a wheeler's dream. The Palace of Fine Arts is also a tranquil spot to wheel around.

Special Interest: Kids: The Exploratorium ranks at the top among fun places—an ideal solution to bring cheer to a rainy day. *Kayaks:* Put in at Crissy Field; or, for a calmer locale, try the dock at the corner of Marina Boulevard and Baker Street at the St. Francis Yacht Club. *Be Aware*: Tides, surf, and boat traffic all may pose hazards for paddlers offshore of Crissy Field. *Kites:* Marina Green, with shore breezes typical, is a popular spot for kite enthusiasts.

14.   GOLDEN GATE BRIDGE SOUTH   H, MB, J, R

Best for: An up-close-and-personal view of the world's beloved bridge—from its pedestrian walkway or the historic gun emplacements that rim the southern bluffs of the Golden Gate.

Parking: *From north of the Golden Gate Bridge* on Hwy. 101, go through the far-right toll booth. Then make an *immediate* right on Merchant St. and another immediate right, traveling under the roadway to the east side of the bridge. Veer right to a stop sign at Lincoln Blvd. Turn left on Lincoln and then turn left after a short distance into GGNRA parking for Battery East. *From the south of the Golden Gate and the Bay Bridge*, head toward the Golden Gate Bridge on Hwy. 101 and take the vista point exit on the San Francisco side, immediately before the toll plaza booths. Follow directions above to Battery East parking lot. *Note:* You could use the metered parking at vista point, which is closer to the bridge. Pay attention to the abnormal hours of meter operation. *Bus:* SF Muni 28, 29

Agency: Golden Gate National Recreation Area; Golden Gate Bridge District.

H: **Golden Gate Bridge** (2.5 mi.); **Fort Point** (1 mi.); **Fort Scott overlook** (1.75)

For all hikes, go down the stairs to a trail as you face the bridge—not the bike route that takes off to the left. On your right is Battery East, the oldest U.S. gun emplacement, built in 1876. A hop to the top reveals its splendid vantage point. To **Fort Point**,

Upper Presidio, San Francisco commuter

which is also described in TH13, drop down the trail, just to the right of Battery East. You'll go down stairs, through a eucalyptus and cypress grove with lush undergrowth. After descending about 200 feet, the trail reaches Long Avenue, which leads a short distance along a seawall. Often wet with crashing waves, this wall is where Kim Novak flung herself into the sea and was saved by Jimmy Stewart in Hitchcock's *Vertigo*. The massive brick fortress is not far to your left.

For the **Golden Gate Bridge** and **Fort Scott overlook**, continue on the trail past the battery, going through a brick tunnel, and coming to the vista point parking area. Among the sights here are a segment of the bridge's huge cable and a statue of Joseph Strauss—The Man Who Built The Bridge. Then head up to the roadway to begin the bridge walk. You'll notice the clean Art Deco detail built into the bridge, and might be surprised by how much it curves upward in the middle. The towers are 500 feet above the roadbed, and it's 220 feet to the sea. *Be Aware*: It's usually breezy on the span.

To **Fort Scott overlook**, head down the stairs at the bridge observation area, leading to a path that takes you under the bridge. You'll be on the Coastal Trail, and also portions of the Bay Area Ridge Trail and De Anza Trail. Keep right along the bluffs, coming to stair sections here and there. Along a .25-mile section you pass the Coastal Defense Batteries in this order: Battery Cranston, built in 1897; Battery Marcus Miller, 1891; Battery Boutelle, 1900, where the bike route joins the hiking trail; and finally to Battery Godfrey, emplaced in 1895. Just south of the parking area at Battery Godfrey is the Fort Scott overlook. This spot is across the street from the Presidio's Fort Winfield Scott. *Be Aware:* Crumbling cliffs are hazardous.

MB: To head over to **Marin north across the Golden Gate Bridge**, take the bike route leading out the left side of the Battery East parking lot as you face the bridge, which takes you to the toll plaza. *Note:* As signs will indicate, the bike route on weekdays is shared with pedestrians on the east side of the bridge; on weekends, you cross under the bridge and ride the walkway on the west side. See Golden Gate Bridge North, TH15, for Marin-side bike routes.

Battery East is also a good parking spot for rides down to Crissy Field toward downtown, as well as rides toward the Pacific side of the Golden Gate toward Fort Funston. You can also go south through the Presidio to Golden Gate Park. To **Crissy Field**—and the shoreline ride to the Ferry Building described in TH13—ride down Lincoln and take Long Avenue, which is the first street to your left, a sharp turn. To head down the **Pacific Coast,** turn right on Lincoln Avenue, which takes you to Bike Route 95. A more scenic route is to head toward the bridge from Battery East on the bike path, go under the bridge, and come around to Merchant Street, which takes you to Lincoln Avenue. If headed farther south, you may also want to veer off Lincoln at El Camino del Mar for a more scenic route, on Bike Route 395, which goes past the Legion of Honor and back out to Bike Route 95.

The ride through the **Presidio to Golden Gate Park** is 3 miles, with a couple hundred feet of up-and-down. Pedal to your right on Lincoln Avenue from Battery East. You circle under the bridge, and then veer left on Bike Route 65 at Ralston Avenue. Follow route 65 as it curves, climbs, and blends with several different streets, eventually popping out of the Presidio at 15th Avenue and Lake Street. Take Bike Route 69 south along 15th Avenue. Go left at Cabrillo Street and right on Funston into the park.

J: Runners may access the bridge from here, as described in hiking section above, although on nice-weather days you may find yourself jogging around a number of people. The Coastal Trail, to Fort Scott overlook as per hiking section, is also a good cross-country jog, with stairs and minor elevation gains. The views are fantastic and you're essentially in natural surroundings. For a more citified jog, head down to Fort Point on Long Avenue, which is to your left as you run away from Battery East on Lincoln Avenue. This takes you to Crissy Field.

R: **Wheelchairs and Strollers**: The Golden Gate Bridge is wheel-accessible, and the openings in the railing allow views from chair level. You may wish to park at the toll plaza, although the bike path from Battery East is a pleasant roll.

Marin Peninsulas

Hawk Hill

The written history of Marin may have begun 175 years earlier if it hadn't been for fog. Around 1600, an English sailing ship and at least two Spanish vessels made landfall on the far shores of Marin. But the doors of the Golden Gate had been veiled by the white vapor, and it wasn't until 1775 that the Spanish vessel *San Carlos*, under the command of Lt. Juan Manuel de Ayala, sailed through and made landfall off the Tiburon Peninsula at Angel Island.

The next 75 years, slow as they were in terms of written history, were turbulent times in the lore of the Coast Miwok who had inhabited the bays and valleys of the Marin peninsulas for centuries. Their culture was substantially lost as the Spaniards— later the Mexicans when the country was annexed—established forts, missions, and a

Battery Spencer

system of huge rancheros. Then in 1849, the Mexicans themselves were displaced as the Mother Lode shocked their world as much as they had the Miwok's.

   Tiburon and Sausalito, Marin's two cosmopolitan towns greet tourist ferries that shuttle from San Francisco. Today, galleries, restaurants, quaint seaside streets and yacht harbors draw the crowds. In the 1850s, the sites were attractive for their deep-water harbors along a coast of mudflats and cliffs, and in the lee of the prevailing weather. Richardson Bay, between the peninsulas, was safe anchorage for full-rigged ships awaiting their loads of wheat from Port Costa, farther up San Pablo Bay. A few decades later, the towns came into their commercial being as the ports at the end of the line for railroads that connected them to redwood mills and quarries. The materials were hoisted on ferries and shuttled across the bay to build San Francisco. Those days in southern Marin were filled with industrious labor, and the free-for-all Barbary Coast spirit was alive at night.

   When the Golden Gate Bridge opened in 1937, the peninsula towns began a slow transition from can-do villages to high-end residential communities with the scenic resources to draw tourists from around the globe. In the post-WWII boom, residential demand increased exponentially, and the scenic resources that attracted the multitudes—beaches, trails, vistas, wetlands, coastal bluffs—were in jeopardy. In recent decades steps have been taken to keep southern Marin's scenic gifts intact, and real estate prices have gone through the roof.

In 1962, Angel Island was made a California State Park. In 1972, Congress established the Golden Gate National Recreation Area, the world's largest urban park, three-quarters of which—54,000 acres—is in Marin County. The Marin Headlands portion of the GGNRA covers most of the Marin Peninsula. In 1982, Ring Mountain Preserve was established by the Nature Conservancy, a park that has since been taken over and expanded by the Marin County Open Space District. In between these peninsula ridges are large city parks run by Mill Valley and Tiburon with paths along the shores of Richardson Bay.

Visitors to San Francisco may not truly appreciate its splendor until they catch the views from the Headlands, Angel Island, and the Tiburon Peninsula. In the Marin Headlands are the high cliffs west of the Golden Gate Bridge, offering vistas of one of the world's great waterways, as well as routes down to the rugged coast, at Kirby Cove and Fort Baker. The Headlands roll north from the gate—high, rounded ridges covered by dwarf coastal shrubs, grasses and seasonal flowers. Two major valleys extend inland from the Pacific, at Rodeo and Tennessee beaches. Rodeo Beach is the center for this portion of the National Recreation Area, with a visitors center, several nonprofit organizations and numerous trailheads. Northward from Rodeo is the ridge that separates it from Tennessee Valley, which has its own beach and system of view trails. And

Lyford House, Horseshoe Bay,
Blackie and friends,
Battery Wallace picnic

Bayfront Park, Battery Cavallo, Tiburon waterfront

still northward from Tennessee is the ridge that falls to Muir Beach—which lies below the forests and chaparral on the southern slopes of Mount Tamalpais.

Between the Headlands on Marin Peninsula and the Tiburon Peninsula is large Richardson Bay, into which small Strawberry Peninsula protrudes. Bayfront Park and Bothin Marsh, a city park and county open space, offer trails along the west bay shore. On the other side of the Strawberry Peninsula—the crest of which is a greenbelt thanks to the large Golden Gate Theological Seminary—is Blackies Pasture, with Richardson Bay paths that extend into Tiburon.

Although residences encircle much of the Tiburon Peninsula, and cover its swank Belvedere and Corinthian islands, most of the high ground is parkland, including Tiburon Ridge, Ring Mountain, and Old St. Hilarys open space preserves, as well as the Tiburon Uplands Nature Preserve. The ridge top of the Tiburon Peninsula is like the Headlands in that it is open with dwarf vegetation and boasts a big view of the Bay Area. But Tiburon's geology and flora are quite different, and many of its wildflowers are unique. From Ring Mountain and Old St. Hilarys high points, you can visually fit all the pieces of southern Marin and San Francisco into a geographic whole.

Outdoor excursions in the Marin Peninsula, whether up high or at water's edge, are vibrant with the entire cityscape of the San Francisco Bay. But tempering the charms of the city are the pleasures of being someplace that is essentially natural. You can choose from a breadth of experiences: short walks to ceremoniously enjoy a sun setting over the Golden Gate, long hikes to find solitude in wild lands, or strolls to find a double latte while shuffling through interesting harbor towns.

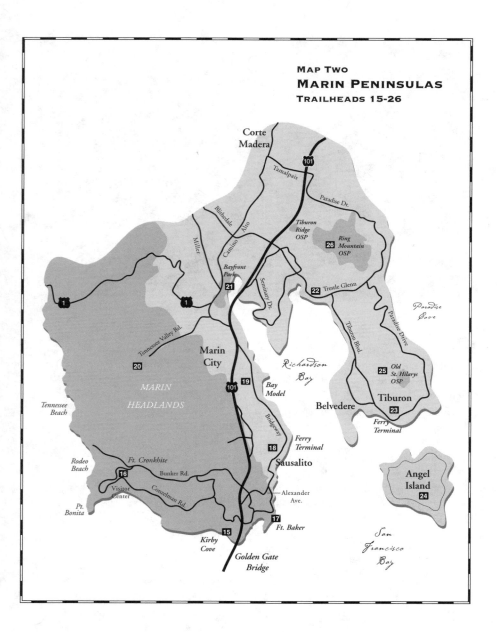

MAP TWO
MARIN PENINSULAS
TRAILHEADS 15-26

Corte
Madera

101

Tamalpais

Paradise Dr.

Blithedale

Camino Alto

Miller

Tiburon
Ridge
OSP

Ring
Mountain
OSP
26

Bayfront
Park

21

Seminary Dr.

22   Trestle Glenn

Paradise
Cove

Tiburon Blvd.

Paradise Drive

Tennessee Valley Rd.

Marin
City

20

MARIN
HEADLANDS

101

19

Richardson
Bay

Bay
Model

25   Old
St. Hilarys
OSP

Tiburon

23

Tennessee
Beach

Belvedere

Ferry
Terminal

Rodeo
Beach

Ft. Cronkhite

Bunker Rd.

16

Visitor
Center

Conzelman Rd.

Pt.
Bonita

Bridgeway

Ferry
Terminal

18

Sausalito

Alexander
Ave.

Angel
Island

24

17   Ft. Baker

15

Kirby
Cove

Golden Gate
Bridge

San
Francisco
Bay

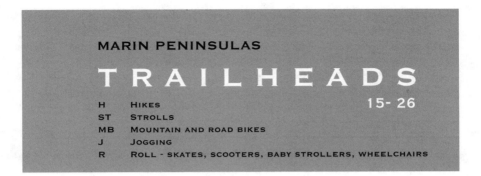

MARIN PENINSULAS

T R A I L H E A D S

15- 26

H   HIKES
ST   STROLLS
MB   MOUNTAIN AND ROAD BIKES
J   JOGGING
R   ROLL - SKATES, SCOOTERS, BABY STROLLERS, WHEELCHAIRS

All hike and stroll distances are ROUND TRIP except as noted for shuttles.
Please contact Agency to obtain current rules and regulations. See Resource Links for all telephone numbers.
See also special Doggie Trails section.

15. GOLDEN GATE BRIDGE NORTH   H, MB, J, R

Best for: Take a walk across the graceful steel span from the north side, or look down upon the bridge towers from vantage points atop the Marin Peninsula.

Parking: *From Hwy. 101 north*, take the Sausalito exit after coming through the Waldo Tunnel—your last exit before the bridge. Veer right on the uphill grade toward the Marin Headlands, and then turn left into a large, unpaved parking area. *From Hwy. 101 south*, take the Alexander Ave. exit, just past the Vista Point exit, on the Marin side of the Golden Gate Bridge. Turn left, going under the freeway and turn back toward the bridge; keep right toward the Marin Headlands, and then turn left into the parking lot. *Note:* Additional parking described in hiking section.

Agency: Golden Gate National Recreation Area; Golden Gate Transit; *Special Interests: Group Camping

H: Golden Gate Bridge (up to 2.5 mi.); Battery Spencer (.5-mi.); Kirby Cove (2 mi.); Hawk Hill (.75-mi.)

To walk the **Golden Gate Bridge**, go down the stairs to your right as you face the roadway. You'll go under the roadway superstructure to Vista Point. Go down the stairs that lead to the 10-foot-wide walkway. You'll reach the north tower, with its curved railing section and deco light stanchions, after about .25-mile. Pedestrians may walk the bridge until 9 p.m. After nightfall is a film-noir time to venture out, with city lights in the distance and the artfully lit bridge towers above dark waters.

To **Battery Spencer**, drive uphill on Conzelman Road for about .25-mile and park on your left. Wander out through the relic cannon emplacement, at a height about halfway up the bridge towers. Huge freighters churn in and out the Golden Gate. Battery Spencer is a small walk with a big scenic payoff. To **Kirby Cove**, walk down the gated road adjacent to Battery Spencer parking area. The road winds down through conifers to a fairly large beach, usually strewn with driftwood logs. Pine needles carpet a forested flat above the beach—a group campsite is located here. The beach features a Pacific-side view of the bridge. This is a ruggedly beautiful beach and the only one readily accessible on the steep southern shore of the Marin Headlands. *Be Aware*: Surf conditions make for unsafe swimming.

To **Hawk Hill**, continue driving up Conzelman Road from Battery Spencer. Some 20,000 eagles, hawks, falcons, and other raptors soar over the hill each year. After 2 miles, past a turnoff to McCullough Road, park on your left. This is where Conzelman becomes a one-way road down to Marin Headlands. You will see two tunnel openings on your right. The short trail to the top is near the beginning of the one-way road. As the raptor flies, Hawk Hill is little more than a mile from the north bridge tower, and about 150 feet above it. Migrating raptors don't like to fly over water, and both east and west of the Golden Gate are vast sheets of the wet stuff. On the short walk back, you have the option of taking trails through either of the large but short tunnels bored as part of the WWII-vintage Battery 129. *Note*: Conzelman continues to the Fort Cronkhite, an alternate route from that described in TH16.

MB: This trailhead parking is a good starting point for trips across the **Golden Gate Bridge** into San Francisco. Use the west walkway on weekends. On weekdays cross under the bridge to use the east walkway. See TH14 for cycling options on the south side of the bridge—to Crissy Field, Presidio, or the Pacific coast.

Conditioned road bikers may opt for a **Headlands loop**, beginning at the north side bridge parking. The route follows paved roads with ups-and-downs totaling about 1,000 feet over about 7 miles. Start up Conzelman from the bridge parking, climbing steeply at times for the first 2 miles, to the Hawk Hill parking. The road becomes one-way, lessening traffic concerns, as you drop some 800 feet through open country. From the bottom of the valley, pick up Bunker Road going east, which climbs gradually to the long Barry-Bunker Tunnel; it has an adequate bike lane. Come out of the tunnel and turn right on Alexander Avenue, climbing back to the parking area.

J: The Golden Gate Bridge is a classic run. Over and back, including the approaches is about three miles. On nice weekends, runners will be dodging people.

R: **Wheelchairs and Strollers:** The bridge is wheel-accessible from both sides, but you must access the east-side walkway from Vista Point. Going north across the bridge, take the Vista Point exit. From the south drive over the bridge and double back: Stay in the far-right lane, make your first right after going through the toll plaza, then make a right again, driving under the bridge offices to the other side, where you can get back on the roadway going north. You'll need to pay the bridge toll to do this.

*Special Interest: *Group camping:* Kirby Cove is one of the better campgrounds in the Bay Area—forested, on a rugged beach and with Golden Gate views; call GGNRA for reservations.

16.   MARIN HEADLANDS   H, ST, MB, J, R

Best for: The ingredients for a full day: Open highlands with grand Pacific views, a big beach, a placid lagoon, and nonprofit centers featuring art, history and conservation.

Parking: *From 101 north*, take the last exit, toward Sausalito after coming down the grade from the tunnel. Turn right at first stop sign on Alexander Ave. and follow road around under freeway. Turn left on Bunker Rd., go through light-metered tunnel and continue about 3 mi., veering right as you approach the coast. Park at Rodeo Beach, next to Fort Cronkhite. *From 101 South*, take the Alexander exit toward Sausalito just after crossing the Golden Gate Bridge and follow directions above. *Note:* Additional parking in hike, stroll and bike descriptions. *Bus:* SF Muni route 76

Agency: Golden Gate National Recreation Area; *Special Interest: Backpacking, Kids, Surfing

H: **Rodeo Beach (up to 1 mi.); Rodeo Lagoon loop (1 mi.); Battery Townsley loop (1.25 mi.); Wolf Ridge loop (5 mi.); Point Bonita Lighthouse (1 mi.)**

Rodeo Beach is a .5-mile long, wide swath of sand, set between the bluffs of Tennessee Point on the north and Bird Island, just offshore, to the south. A valley spreads inland, beginning with a large lagoon. *Be Aware:* Unsafe to swim due to riptides.

View from Conzelman Road

A trail encircles **Rodeo Lagoon**. Some of the lagoon's many shorebirds are endangered species. From the Rodeo Beach parking, head toward the lagoon and go left, away from the beach. You'll cross the bridge and then head toward the beach on the south side of the lagoon, below the visitors center; you can also access this trail from the center. Half of the trail is near the road and the other half contours above water. *Additional Access:* Another option for this hike is to begin at Battery Alexander, which is just up the hill from the visitors center on Field Road. A trail with great views leads down to the least-peopled part of the lagoon. From Battery Alexander you will also find the South Rodeo Beach Trail, a short walk to the cove just south of the main beach.

The **Battery Townsley loop** takes you for a bird's-eye view of the Headlands and a good look at the Farallones offshore. Begin at the parking at the far west end of Bunker Road, near Fort Cronkhite. Starting as pavement, the Coastal Trail climbs about 200 feet to the old defense bunker. Either retrace your steps down, or come down Old Bunker Road, which drops down behind Fort Cronkhite.

The **Wolf Ridge loop** is a fairly difficult walk, gaining some 1,000 feet, but offers a big-view payoff. Start on the Coastal Trail at Fort Cronkhite. You climb past Battery Townsley and up to where the Coastal Trail joins the Wolf Ridge Trail. Looking north, you'll see Tennessee Valley. You have an option of taking the short scamper up to Hill 88, the highest point around. Then continue to your right on the Wolf Ridge Trail for another .75-mile, where you hit the Miwok Trail and turn right. Head down 2 more miles to Bunker Hill Road.

Point Bonita Lighthouse is one of the most spectacular short walks this side of the moon. Veer left onto Field Road, as you approach Rodeo Lagoon, heading toward the visitors center. Continue about a mile, passing an excellent picnic area at Battery Wallace, to signed Point Bonita parking. The trail winds down a rocky spine and then through a rough-bored tunnel. You emerge at the western extremity of the Golden Gate and then walk a suspension footbridge that may give acrophobics sweaty palms. The lighthouse has aided ships since 1855. *Be Aware*: The trail is normally open 12:30 p.m. to 3:30 p.m., weekends and Mondays; call to verify times. To view Point Bonita from a distance, drive to the scenic turnout at road's end, near Battery Mendell.

ST: Headlands Visitors Center; Headlands Center for the Arts; Marine
        Mammal Center; Headlands Institute.

To visit **Marin Headlands Visitors Center**—in the former Fort Barry Chapel, built in 1941—veer left off Bunker Road on the east end of Rodeo Lagoon. The center has a tasteful gift store, a wealth of books and other information, as well as displays that befit its historic setting. The **Headlands Center for the Arts** is located in the quaint assemblage of buildings, next to the hostel, up the hill on Bodsworth from the visitors center. The Center for the Arts is a nonprofit artists-in-residence program for a wide range of artists. The best time to visit is during one of the several open houses.

The **Marine Mammal Center** treats hundreds of sick and injured sea lions, elephant seals, dolphins and other warm-blooded marine critters. Its clinic is located on Old Bunker Road; veer right just before you reach Fort Cronkhite. The center is also active in research and education, and is well known for coming to the aid of beached whales. Open to the public daily, they also have a volunteer program. The **Headlands Institute**, which offers highly respected environmental studies programs for children, is located on Bunker Road headed toward Fort Cronkhite. Look for signs. The institute welcomes visitors, especially parents who wish to tour the campus.

MB: The ride to **Hill 88** is a steep pump up about 900 feet along a section of the Coastal Trail that is open to bikes. You start the open upslope at the end of Bunker Road at Fort Cronkhite. The summit is just under 2 miles from the trailhead. You have a great view of Mt. Tam and the long view toward the Pacific. You need to roll back down, as the trails from here are closed to bikes.

The **Tennessee Valley loop** is a challenging ride of about 8 miles, gaining and losing more than 500 feet twice. Start out at the Rodeo Valley trailhead that is on Bunker Road about .5-mile east of the bridge at the lagoon. After a short distance, veer left on the Miwok Trail, and begin a mile-long ride, the steepest of the entire ride. The Miwok Trail joins Old Springs Trail, which drops down to the north, all the way to the Miwok Stables in Tennessee Valley. Before the stables parking, take Marincello Road to your right and loop back to the south, climbing at a manageable grade to join the Bobcat Trail. Go right on the Bobcat Trail, dropping through wide-open Gerbode Valley.

J: Rodeo Lagoon trail makes for a good running loop, although sand on the west end makes for tough slogging. For an inland run, try going east on the Miwok Trail, beginning at the trailhead off Bunker Road at the east end of the lagoon—across from the bridge. After about .5-mile, go right on the Rodeo Valley Trail, which is fairly flat for another .75-mile before heading to the upper reaches of the Headlands. You can cut right off Rodeo Valley Trail, coming out to the road to make a loop.

R: **Wheelchairs and Strollers:** Point Bonita trail is ready for rollers, but be aware of the steep grade going down on the first part of the path. The Marin Headlands Visitors Center has a view of the lagoon and attractive grounds to wheel around. Battery Alexander and Battery Mendell, up the road from the center, will also be a plus for the day.

*Special Interest: *Camping:* Backpacking is available at several camps seasonally, including Haypress, Hawk, and Bicentennial; call for details. *Kids:* Special environmentally oriented programs at the Headlands Institute. *Surfing:* Experienced boardheads flock to Rodeo Beach when the surf is right. Conditions are considered hazardous.

Horseshoe Bay pier, Fort Baker

17. FORT BAKER

H, ST, MB, R

Best for: An active cove with a fishing pier, Coast Guard Station, and children's museum, all in the shadow of the Golden Gate Bridge.

Parking: *From Hwy. 101 north*, take the last Sausalito exit after coming down the grade from Waldo Tunnel. Turn right at stop sign toward Sausalito and loop under freeway. Now headed downhill on Alexander Ave., turn left toward GGNRA. Turn right before entering light-metered tunnel, on Bunker Rd. Follow Bunker Rd. to bottom, and park near pier. *From Hwy. 101 south*, take the Sausalito-Alexander Ave. exit just north of the bridge. Turn left toward GGNRA and East Fort Baker and follow directions above. *Bus:* City of Sausalito Shuttle Bus from Sausalito.

Agency: Golden Gate National Recreation Area; *Special Interest: Kids, Kayaks

H: **Horseshoe Bay (up to 1 mi.)**

Horseshoe Bay, around which Fort Baker's 46 historic buildings are situated, is more a place to walk around rather than a hike. Begin with a stroll out the fishing and crabbing pier, the end of which offers a point-blank look at the Golden Gate Bridge rising above the lighthouse at Lime Point. In the 1850s, the Army detonated 25 tons of gunpowder inland from Lime Point—its largest blasting operation then to date—with plans to construct a brickwork fort similar to Fort Point across the strait. Although it was never constructed, the Army's efforts weren't totally wasted, since some of the earth removal was helpful in constructing the big bridge some 80 years later.

Head around the interior of Horseshoe Bay, part of the Bay Trail, past the Coast Guard Station to the Presidio Yacht Club, where you can walk onto a jetty. Beyond and above the yacht club is Cavallo Point, site of Battery Yates and, farther inland, Battery Cavallo.

These low-slung emplacements afford big views across the bay to the city. *Additional Access:* Driving up Baker Road, you'll find a wide path that goes up a eucalyptus-covered hill above Murray Circle, which may be of interest to a spouse left with the dog while the other spouse is with the kids at the museum.

ST: Bay Area Discovery Museum

The **Bay Area Discovery Museum**, designed for children 10 and younger, is located within and around a half-dozen wood-frame former military barracks, set on 7.5 acres. They have been converted to an interactive learning center and inventive playground. Art, science and multimedia play centers give kids a hands-on good time. Children's birthday parties can be arranged as well, and the museum stages special entertainment, like dancers and storytellers, on event days. The lovely grounds are often abuzz with active toddlers amid a traffic jam of strollers. *Note:* An admission fee is charged; yearly passes available for up to four persons.

MB: Fort Baker is the scenic, relatively traffic-free way to get from above **Sausalito to the Golden Gate Bridge**. After climbing out of Sausalito on Alexander Avenue, veer left on Baker Road and glide down to Horseshoe Bay. Stay to your right and head up Conzelman Road—closed for much of 2001 during a seismic retrofit of the bridge—pumping up from the base of the towers to the bridge's roadway.

R: **Wheelchairs and Strollers:** Aside from the stroller action around the Discovery Center, seated wheelers might find a trip onto the fishing pier and on the path toward Lime Point, at the base of the bridge, worth the roll. You can also wheel around Horseshoe Bay, through quiet parking lots.

Special Interest: Kids: Toddlers delight at the Bay Area Discovery Museum, and will also enjoy the crabbers on the fishing pier. *Kayaks:* The deep-water paddling here is dramatic, along the battery bluffs looking up at the Golden Gate Bridge. But be very careful of strong current, tidal action, and boat traffic.

18.   SAUSALITO
H, ST, MB, R

Best for: A blend of Mediterranean burg and the old Barbary Coast with views of San Francisco and Angel Island. Sausalito lures sightseers from all over. Above the town is access to the high trails of the Marin Headlands.

Parking: *From Hwy. 101 north*, take the Sausalito-Marin City exit. Turn left at stop sign, go under freeway and turn right on Bridgeway. Follow Bridgeway about 1.5 mi. and park near Napa Street, across from Dunphy Park. *From Hwy. 101 south*, take the Alexander Ave. exit north of the bridge, follow Alexander into Sausalito, merging with Bridgeway. Continue through Sausalito to Napa St. *Note:* Additional parking in hiking descriptions. *Bus:* GGT routes 10, 20, 50; Sausalito Shuttle for cross-town rides.

Agency: Golden Gate National Recreation Area; Sausalito Parks & Recreation Department; *Special Interest: Kids, Backpacking; Kayaks

H: **Rodeo Avenue Trail to: Wolfback Ridge (2 mi.), or Hawk Camp (6 mi.); Morning Sun Trail from Spencer to: Alta Trail (.75-mi.), or SCA Trail overlook (1.75 mi.)**

For the **Rodeo Avenue Trail**, take the Rodeo Avenue exit, just north of Sausalito. Look for trailhead parking on your right. An unpaved road switchbacks about 400 feet up a small ravine, with a good view back toward Richardson Bay. Near the top, the Alta Trail—see TH19—comes in from the right. You curve left, joining the **Wolfback Ridge Trail**, which in turn comes to Bobcat Trail. You'll get views down the Gerbode Valley to Rodeo Beach. To continue to **Hawk Camp**, turn right, or north, on Bobcat Trail. After about .5-mile, take the Hawk Trail to your left. Hawk Camp, situated below Vortac Peak, is a permit-only backpacking camp. *Additional Access:* The Bobcat Trail, if you go south, drops into Rodeo Beach at the Marin Headlands, descending almost 800 feet over 2-plus miles; a fork off the Bobcat Trail, the Rodeo Valley Trail, takes a 3-mile route down. These make good car-shuttle hikes.

The **Morning Sun Trail** is a locals' favorite with Sausalito and San Francisco views. From Highway 101, take the Spencer Avenue-Monte Mar exit, the next exit south of Rodeo. A variety of coastal flora and fauna complements the views on the 300-foot climb to Wolfback Ridge. From the Ridge, you can drop about 800 feet over 3-plus miles to Fort Cronkhite, via the Rodeo Valley Trail—a very good car-shuttle hike. The **SCA Trail overlook** offers an astounding look down at the bridge, the bay, and the city, as well as the Marin Headlands. Keep going past the Rodeo Valley Trail and veer left on the SCA Trail. *Notes:* You can also access the SCA Trail and upper Headlands at Wolfback Ridge Road, off Highway 101. Take the narrow overpass spanning the highway. However, a large sign at the trailhead says parking is prohibited.

ST: Sausalito (3 mi.)

Sausalito began in 1838 as *Rancho Del Saucelito*—Ranch of the Little Willow Grove— part of a Mexican land grant received by Englishman William Richardson. After Richardson died, the Saucelito Land and Ferry Company purchased 20,000 acres and laid out lots for development. Sausalito received a major growth spurt when, in 1871, a railroad connection to the town's docks linked Northern California's timber with San Francisco's building boom. After the Golden Gate Bridge opened in 1937, ferry and suburban train service to the city ceased and the town languished prior to its beginnings as a quaint tourist attraction. Ferry service was re-established in 1970.

Begin with a **Sausalito stroll** through Dunphy Park, with its gazebo and small sandy beach. From Dunphy Park, stay left along the water, heading along the plank walkway of the Sausalito Yacht Harbor. Emerging from the yacht harbor, to your left you'll see Sausalito Point—a short walk out Spinnaker Drive. Ahead is the Ferry Terminal and Gabrielson Park, a perfect place to occupy a bench where the town meets the bay. Then turn to your right on El Portal, out to Bridgeway, where you'll see Del Mar Plaza with a grand fountain, bordered by redwood and palm trees—the center of Sausalito. Turn left on Bridgeway. On your right is Princess Street, heading uphill. Many visitors will just want to walk around; about 20 galleries, and as many historic buildings, are located on Princess Street and in the 500 and 600 blocks of Bridgeway.

Urban hikers can continue south on Bridgeway. Just past Princess Street on the water side, is Yee Tock Chee Park, named in honor of a beloved local grocer, which marks the spot where the *Princess*, a small paddlewheeler, docked in 1868 on Sausalito's first ferry run. Continue along .25-mile shoreline path and veer left at the far end of town on a boardwalk that takes you in front of a restaurant that is the former Valhalla—a restaurant once owned by Sally Stanford, a fabled San Francisco madam who became mayor of Sausalito in the late 1960s. Go up to Second Street. Turn left and then left again, toward the water, on Valley Street. After a short block, take a long flight of stairs down to Swedes Beach, a cove tucked away beneath beach cottages and condos.

To return, either backtrack on the other side of Bridgeway, taking in shops and galleries; or, for a look at a neighborhood perched above the town, cross Second Street and go right up Third Street. At the top is pleasant South View Park. You're now in Sausalito's "banana belt," known for its sunshine. Walk right on Atwood Avenue, which joins with Bulkley Avenue, heading back toward town above Bridgeway. Sitting spots offer places to enjoy the charming neighborhood, nestled amidst flowering gardens and trees. Where Princess Street joins Bulkley Avenue, look for Alta Mira Hotel and Restaurant, a Sausalito tradition. Pass the Alta Mira on Bulkley. To return to the town,

Gate Six, Del Mar Plaza

turn right down a flight of stairs on Excelsior Lane; or pass Excelsior and take another flight of stairs on El Monte Lane. Both take you back near Del Mar Plaza.

MB: Not many cyclists will begin in Sausalito, but many pedal through, perhaps stopping for libation, taking the bike path from Richardson Bayfront, TH21, to Fort Baker, TH17. Buffed bikers also may begin a loop at the **Rodeo Avenue**. You pedal up about 400 feet initially, on a nicely graded road surface. From the top, turn right, or north, on Old Marincello Road, whizzing down into Tennessee Valley. Then take Tennessee Valley Road out—cross under Shoreline Highway—and head out along the wetlands to the Mill Valley-Sausalito bike path. Turn toward Marin City, crossing over Bridgeway and under Highway 101. Then take Donahue Street up—you'll do most on the climb back on pavement—to the Alta Trail. The Alta Trail joins with the Rodeo Avenue Trail, which you take back down to parking. This ride involves about 1,200 feet of climbing over 8 miles.

R: **Wheelchairs and Strollers:** Although you may wish to avoid the sidewalk and street traffic during Sunday brunch time, the center of Sausalito, around Del Mar Plaza, combines a seaside with a town experience. The yacht harbor is also worth a roll.

Special Interest: Kids: South View Park has a view playground, which can be combined with a walk down to Swedes Beach. *Backpacking:* For primitive camping at Hawk Camp, contact GGNRA, Marin Headlands. *Kayaks:* Put it at Schoonmaker Beach, just north of Dunphy Park on Liberty Ship Way. This is among the most popular paddling places people park for trips to Angel Island and Richardson Bay. Outfitters are available for lessons and rentals.

19. MARINSHIP   H, ST, MB, J, R

Best for: Learn about San Francisco Bay and Marin history along Sausalito's working waterfront; or take a hike to the upper Marin Headlands from a less used trailhead.

Parking: From Hwy. 101 take the Marin City-Sausalito exit. Head toward Sausalito on Bridgeway. *For longer stroll:* Park near the houseboats on Gate 6 Road, which begins just south of the freeway on ramp. *For shorter stroll:* Go toward Sausalito on Bridgeway and then turn left on Harbor Drive. From Harbor, make first right on Marinship Way and follow signs to Bay Model. Park at Bay Model. *Note:* Additional parking in hiking descriptions. *Bus:* GGT routes 10, 20, 50

Agency: Marin County Open Space District; Sausalito Park & Recreation Department; *Special Interest: Kayaks, Kids.

H: Alta Trail (2.5 mi. or more); Cypress Ridge Open Space Preserve (up to .75-mi.)

The **Alta Trail** begins high above Richardson Bay. You'll have vistas of the Strawberry and Tiburon peninsulas. From the Marin City exit on Highway 101, turn toward Marin City, and follow Donahue up through condos to road's end. After about .25-mile on an unmarked road, you get to an open space sign noting the Alta Trail. The trail undulates through eucalyptus and cypress. About a mile up, you reach the end of MCOSD and then beginning of GGNRA. Pets are prohibited beyond this point. Continuing south on the Alta Trail another .5-mile, you come to the Rodeo Avenue; see TH18. You can go for another .75-mile south on the Alta Trail coming to several trails that drop into the Marin Headlands at Fort Cronkhite.

Cypress Ridge is a small, eucalyptus and cypress forest, offering a sublime view of Mount Tam above Richardson Bay. The preserve is secluded visually, ideal for a rustic picnic, but ears will note the presence of Highway 101. From Bridgeway in Sausalito, turn west, away from the bay, on Nevada Street and curve up and around to Rodeo Avenue. If you're going north on Highway 101 from the bridge you can get to this preserve by taking the Rodeo Avenue exit.

ST: *Longer Stroll:* Sausalito Houseboats to Schoonmaker Beach (3.25 mi.); *Shorter Stroll:* Bay Model to Schoonmaker (1.5 mi.)

Both strolls take you through north Sausalito, former site of Marinship, which played a vital role in winning World War II in the Pacific. From 1942 through 1945—from three months after Pearl Harbor to the Japanese surrender—shifts of 20,000 men and women worked around the clock to build 93 ships in record time. These Liberty cargo ships and oil tankers supplied U.S. forces in the Pacific. Eight Marinship vessels were among the American Fleet gathered in Tokyo Bay to accept Japanese surrender on August 14, 1945. The monument commemorating this effort is at the Bay Model.

For the **Longer Stroll**, head out Gate 6 Road, taking options to meander out on the docks of the houseboat community. The only conflict ever waged on Marin soil, or mudflats, took place here: the "Houseboat Wars" of the early 1970s. The County of Marin needed help from law enforcement over a period of many months during zoning squabbles with houseboat dwellers. The houseboats remain, now zoning compliant, but still a delightfully ragtag assemblage of structures on pilings sticking into Richardson Bay. Come back out Gate 6 Road, go south, and turn left on Gate 5 Road. Immediately tucked away on your left are more houseboats. Continue, on foot or by car, along Gate 5 Road, passing chandlers and warehouse work spaces. In less than .5-mile you get to Harbor Road. Turn right and then left on Marinship Way. Follow signs another .25-mile to the Bay Model. *Note:* Martin Luther King Park, a dog exercise area, is across Bridgeway from Gate 5 Road.

The **Shorter Stroll** begins at the San Francisco Bay Model—a three-dimensional replica, 1,000 times smaller, of the greater San Francisco Bay. Covering some 1.5 acres, the model is carved out of 286 five-ton slabs of concrete. The waters in the model simulate tides, currents, and river action. Dozens of well-designed exhibits surround the Army Corps of Engineers indoor complex. Kids will be gaga, even if they don't understand everything, and all visitors will receive a tour of the region in miniature. The Marinship exhibit and a bookstore are located in the building.

In front of the Bay Model is Marinship Park. Its long concrete pier is where Marinship vessels were outfitted. Now the pier is home to one or more large, vintage square-rigged ships that sail the coast to Seattle and the Pacific to Hawaii. Continue south, hugging the shoreside, and veer to your left along Liberty Ship Way toward the palm trees of Schoonmaker Point. The beach at Schoonmaker has kayak rentals for paddlers of Richardson Bay and Angel Island. Walk around Schoonmaker Point on a path, which brings you back out to Bridgeway at Dunphy Park. To head back, take the multi-use path that runs below the bulkhead of Bridgeway. Cross Bridgeway to Caledonia Street to visit the non-touristy neighborhood businesses of Sausalito.

MB: Park at Gate 6 Road off Bridgeway. You can ride from here via a paved bike path through Bothin Marsh to **Richardson Bayfront,** TH21, where numerous central Marin cycling options are available. This parking is also good to head toward a town ride of **Sausalito** and on to **Fort Baker** and Golden Gate Bridge North. For a traffic-less route to Sausalito, turn left on Gate 5 Road and then right on Harbor. From Harbor, turn left on Marinship Way and follow to its end. A bike path runs below Bridgeway to Dunphy Park. From Dunphy Park you can hug the water through long parking lots, quiet streets, and a wharf path to the center of Sausalito.

From **Alta Trail,** as described in the hiking section, you can begin a fairly difficult 7-mile loop down to Tennessee Valley via the Old Marincello Road. This route is described in TH18, as it can also be accessed from the Rodeo Avenue trailhead. The Alta Trail access may be preferable, because you start out high, at the top of Donahue Street, rather than beginning down at freeway level on Rodeo Avenue.

J: Head down the multi-use path, going north from Gate 6 Road. A round-trip run through Richardson Bayfront, TH21, to Blithedale Avenue is about 5 miles. After jogging along the Bothin Marsh on the paved path, you can loop through the dog park on an unpaved path closer to the water, and then come back out to multi-use path.

R: **Skates and Scooters:** From parking at Bridgeway and Gate 6 Road, get on the 2.5 miles of flat, paved path that runs through Bothin Marsh along Richardson Bay. This is Rollerblade City. **Strollers and Wheelchairs:** The initial .25-mile of the multi-use path is an open straightaway for exercise only, but after that, as you reach Richardson Bay, scenic values are enhanced. The Bay Model, as well as the long concrete dock in front of it, are also good choices for rollers.

*Special Interest: *Kids:* The San Francisco Bay Model is a great rainy day stop for childre. *Kayaks:* Put in at Marinship Park or Schoonmaker Beach.

20. TENNESSEE VALLEY

H, MB, J, R

Best for: Quick access from central Marin to a dramatic beach, and hikes up to the high, open ridges on either side of this narrow coastal valley.

Parking: From Hwy. 101, take Hwy 1-Shoreline Hwy. exit toward Stinson Beach. After about .5-mi. on Hwy. 1, turn west on Tennessee Valley Rd. and continue about 1.5 mi. Park at road's end. *Note:* Additional parking noted in hiking description.

Agency: Golden Gate National Recreation Area; *Special Interest: Backpacking

H: **Tennessee Beach (4 mi.); Tennessee Beach overlook (4.5 mi.); Pirates Cove (6.25 mi.); Coyote Ridge loop (4 mi.); Hill 88 (4.75 mi.); Oakwood Valley loop (2.5 mi.)**

With a good-sized beach, a small lagoon, and wildly sculpted cliffs, Tennessee Valley is a favorite among hikers and joggers. **For all hikes**, with the exception of Oakwood Valley, head down the road from the parking lot, which ends at **Tennessee Beach**. You have an option to take a trail down the center of the valley about a mile into the walk, if this trail is not closed due to flooding. A lagoon just inland from the beach is usually the home for waterfowl and shorebirds. *Be Aware*: High surf and undertow make swimming and even walking near water's edge a potential danger.

Tennessee Valley beach

To **Tennessee Beach overlook**, take a steep trail up from the north side of the cove, near a bench at the beach. The quick climb of almost 200 feet brings you to a concrete-reinforced bunker. Big ships from the Golden Gate can usually be seen steaming toward Asia. *Be Aware:* Stay away from unstable cliffs. To **Pirates Cove**, a craggy nook in the coastal cliffs between Tennessee and Muir Beach, take the road to Tennessee Beach and turn right, or north, on the Coastal Trail after a mile. After .75-mile, and almost 500 feet of upping, make sure to stay left as the trail contours the coast. After about .5-mile, as the trail dips to its lowest point between two ridges, look for the steep trail down to the cove—gravelly and strewn with driftwood.

To get the spectacular views north to Muir Beach from **Coyote Ridge**, look for a trail junction on your right, about .5-mile from the parking area. Head right on the Fox Trail and ascend almost 800 feet over 1.25 miles to the top. Near the top, you'll see a left junction with the Coyote Ridge Trail, which is your return route. Backtrack after drinking in the view. After about 1.5 miles of almost steady dropping, you reach the road to Tennessee Beach.

Hill 88, named by the military during WWII, sits inland from Tennessee Point, the south entrance to the beach. To make the walk, veer left on the trail in Tennessee Valley that is about a mile from the parking area. After a short distance, turn left, or south, on the Coastal Trail. The trail takes a circuitous and steep route for more than a mile, and then hits Wolf Ridge Trail. From the ridge, jog right and then take a short spur to the top of Hill 88. On clear days you'll be looking down to Rodeo Beach. The **Oakwood Valley loop**, along a woodland stream, is a hiking choice if weather is inclement at Tennessee Valley. Look for the trailhead on your left about .75-mile in on Tennessee Valley Road from the Shoreline Highway. Trails run parallel on either side of the creek; start in on the first trail you reach. After 1.25 miles, look for a junction to your right, where you cross over and turn back.

MB: **Tennessee Valley Beach** is a good destination from other trailheads. Try taking a path off the Mill Valley-Sausalito bike route and then ride out Tennessee Valley Road and down the beach road. Start from Richardson Bayfront, TH21.

For a monster off-road ride from Tennessee Valley, try the **Coastal Trail-Miwok Trail loop**. This ride gains and loses more than 1,000 feet over a 5-mile course. From the Tennessee Valley parking area, roll down the main road 1.25 miles and veer right on the Coastal Trail. You climb steadily about 800 feet—and steeply during the first part—for the next 1.5 miles. The turn right, or east, on the Coyote Ridge Trail, climbing gradually to a summit at just over 1,000 feet during the next .75-mile. At the summit, the road hairpins back to your right, joining the meandering Miwok Trail on a very steep descent back to Tennessee Valley.

Two other mountain bike routes begin behind the Miwok Stables, near the parking lot, and head south out of Tennessee Valley. The **Old Springs Trail** goes due south—

up and down about 500 feet—over a 2.5-mile course ending near Rodeo Lagoon at Fort Cronkhite. The **Old Marincello Trail** starts out eastward, but then hooks south and up, climbing about 600 feet, before gaining the ridge. The Old Marincello Trail joins the Bobcat Trail, which you can take down for 2 miles. Making a loop—Marincello to Bobcat and then back on the Old Springs trail—is a fairly strenuous 7-mile ride.

J: The downhill run to Tennessee Beach is well used by runners, a 4-mile round-trip with some 200 feet elevation loss on the way. For something different, try the Oakwood Valley loop, as described in hiking section. Part path and part trail, the loop offers some up-close detail of ferns, oaks and a variety of coastal plants.

R: **Strollers and Wheelchairs:** The trail to Tennessee Beach is fairly steep, a workout, particularly for wheelchairs. At the beach, sand makes the last part difficult. But all in all, Tennessee Valley scores high marks for rollers.

*Special Interest: *Backpacking:* Permit-only primitive camping is available at Haypress Camp, off the Tennessee Valley Trail. Call GGNRA for information.

21.   RICHARDSON BAYFRONT   H, MB, J, R

Best for: An exercise break along a wide bay and its wetlands; or a choice of bike rides toward all points on the compass in central and southern Marin.

Parking: *From the north on Hwy. 101*, take the Mill Valley-E. Blithedale exit. Turn right, or west, on East Blithedale, go about 1 mi., and turn left at traffic signal on Camino Alto Ave. From Camino Alto, turn left on Sycamore Ave. and continue .25-mi. Park at Bayfront Park. *From the south on Hwy. 101*, take the Hwy. 1-Shoreline Hwy. exit toward Stinson Beach. Proceed to traffic signal and turn right on Almonte Blvd., which becomes Miller Ave. From Miller Ave., turn right on Camino Alto Ave. and then right on Sycamore Ave. Continue to parking at Bayfront Park. *Bus:* GGT route 10

Agency: Mill Valley Parks & Recreation; Marin County Open Space District; *Special Interest: Kayaks, Kids

H: Bayfront loop (.75-mi.); Bothin Marsh (2 mi.); Richardson Bay overlook (1.5 mi.)

The **Bayfront loop** is a walk along the west shore of Richardson Bay and Mill Valley's popular pooch park. Head toward the bay, staying to the left of the large lawn field that is surround by a low chain-link fence. Then turn right along the shore. At the far end of the dog park, the path curves to your right, and then comes to the multi-use path that leads back to the parking area.

To walk to **Bothin Marsh**, a Marin County Open Space Preserve, you can take the first part of the loop trail described above, or simply head out southbound on the multi-use path. Leaving Bayfront Park, you enter wide-open spaces of the marshland—though Miller Avenue is not far away at times. You eventually come to the bay's waters, under the Richardson Bay Bridge.

For the **Richardson Bay overlook**, where fewer visitors venture, go across the arched plank bridge, heading east over the creek that feeds the extreme north end of Richardson Bay. On the other side, at the south end of a rough-hewn field, make sure to head right on a path marked as Public Shore. This path leads up a short distance through eucalyptus trees to a rock-walled overlook, with a tree-filtered look across the shallow bay.

MB: Richardson Bayfront offers many choices for cyclists wishing to explore southern Marin. For a **Tiburon loop**—a ride of about 6 miles around Strawberry Peninsula—head over the footbridge eastbound from Bayfront Park. Cross the park, to Hamilton Drive and turn right to Redwood Highway, a frontage road. Go south and take the pedestrian overpass over Highway 101; go left, or north, on the other side for a short distance and then right on Ricardo Road. From Ricardo make a right on Seminary Drive, which loops around the Golden Gate Theological Seminary along the shores of the Strawberry Peninsula. You'll want to bear left near the tip of the peninsula, where Seminary Drive becomes Strawberry Drive, rather than going right around Great Circle Drive. After a mile, make a right on Harbor Cove Drive, going steeply downhill, behind a school. You'll come to Greenwood Beach Road and turn right. Greenwood takes you to the Tiburon Bike Path at Blackies Pasture, TH22. From Blackies, take the path all the way to Tiburon. To return, retrace your route through Blackies Pasture and Greenwood. Then go right to Tiburon Boulevard at Blackfield Drive. Ride west, crossing the car overpass at Highway 101. On the west side of Highway 101, Tiburon Boulevard is East Blithedale; continue a short distance to Camino Alto, where you turn left and take the multi-use path .25-mile to Bayfront Park.

To **Sausalito, Fort Baker and Tennessee Valley**, go south on the multi-use path from Bayfront Park. For Sausalito and Fort Baker, simply stay on the path, heading under the Richardson Bay Bridge and continuing to north Sausalito; See Marinship, TH19, to continue from there. Downtown Sausalito is about 4.5 miles from Bayfront; Fort Baker is just over 6 miles. To get to the beach at Tennessee Valley—about a 10-mile round trip—take an unpaved path to your right, after crossing a bridge a mile from Bayfront Park—before reaching the Richardson Bay Bridge. This path follows a canal for less than .5-mile and then goes under two-lane Shoreline Highway on a low-clearance path. On the other side is Tennessee Valley Road. Trail fragments border the road during the first part, but you'll wind up merging to the main road.

To hang out in downtown **Mill Valley**, without having to drive or park, pedal west on Sycamore, the street leading into Bayfront Park. Continue through neighborhood bungalows, about .5-mile to Park Street. You need to jog left on Park out to busy Miller

Avenue for a short distance, and then jog right on Wood Street. From Wood make an immediate left on Presidio Avenue, which blends into Laurel Wood Avenue, as you take back streets into town. The flat, round-trip ride to Mill Valley is almost 3 miles.

To head to **Corte Madera** and **Larkspur**—and from there to other central Marin destinations—go north on the bike path and cross E. Blithedale. Continue on Lomita, the street below the bike path, up to the elementary school. Turn right, still on Lomita, and take it up to Horse Hill at Highway 101. Turn left here, and take the connector bike path along Highway 101, coming to Casa Buena Drive in Corte Madera. Continue to Tamalpais Drive. At Tamalpais, you can go left to Larkspur, TH50; or turn right, over Highway 101, connecting with Shorebird Marsh, TH27.

J: The Bayfront Park loop is a good training track with an opportunity to greet dogs at the south end of the park. If you want to get out and go, take the multi-use path south through Bothin Marsh—a 2-mile round trip to the Richardson Bay Bridge.

R: **Skates and Scooters:** The county's multi-use path—sometimes called the Mill Valley-Sausalito Bike Path or Bicentennial Bike Path—is a flat, long run along good surface that is shared by walkers, dog-walkers, and high-speed road cyclists. Even on busy weekends there seems to be enough room for everyone. You can roll south about 2 miles, impeded only by the occasional plank bridges, all the way to Gate 6 Road at the north end of Sausalito. Going north on the path, you reach East Blithedale Avenue after about .25-mile. **Wheelchairs and Strollers:** The multi-use path toward Bothin Marsh is an exercise run. For a quieter roll, but with some unpaved and uneven surfaces, try the Bayfront loop described in the hiking section; or roll over the bridge to the less used east side of the park.

*Special Interest: *Kayaks:* Put in at the dock at Bayfront Park, or under the Richardson Bay Bridge, using the Highway 1-Stinson Beach exit from Highway 101. *Kids:* A children's play park is over the footbridge from Bayfront Park.

22.   BLACKIES PASTURE   H, ST, MB, J, R

Best for: A scenic shoreline path for all muscle-powered modes, with many benches along the way to sit and take it easy in front of inspiring city views.

Parking: From Hwy. 101 take Tiburon Blvd. Go east on Tiburon Blvd. for about 1.5 mi. and turn right into Blackies Pasture parking lot, across from Trestle Glen Blvd. *Bus:* GGT route 10.

Agency: Town of Tiburon; *Special Interest: Kids.

H: **Richardson Bay Park loop (1.25 mi.); Tiburon (5 mi.)**

South-of-the-Knoll Park

Blackie was a swaybacked horse who for 25 years, until his last days in 1966, stood guard in the pasture right where his statue stands today. For the **Richardson Bay Park loop**—which is the official name for the park that includes several smaller ones—start down the paved multi-use path. Bear right at the big grass field, McKegney Green. You'll skirt the shore, passing Little Lady Lorie Gazebo at water's edge. Continue to the point that has several benches to enjoy a view of the San Francisco skyline and the sailboats frolicking in the bay waters. From the point—this is the South-of-the-Knoll Park—follow the path up to the multi-use path and turn left to the parking area.

To walk to **Tiburon**, you can begin on the shore route described above; or, just keep left on the multi-use path leading from Blackies Pasture. Beyond South-of-the-Knoll Park, the path runs along the bay shore for about .75-mile, but it's also right next to busy Tiburon Boulevard. If the tide is out, you can drop down and walk a rocky beach. Then, after crossing San Rafael Avenue, the path continues away from the boulevard, for a tree-shaded .75-mile until you merge with Tiburon Boulevard. Duck in along shops during the last .5-mile to the center of town, where you enjoy the view of Angel Island and San Francisco. *Additional Access:* To make a semi-loop, walk to your right when the multi-use path reaches San Rafael Avenue; a pleasant path follows Public Shore. San Rafael Avenue curves left and reaches Beach Boulevard, where you go left by yacht harbors to the center of town.

ST: Audubon Bay Center & Sanctuary (up to .75-mi.)

The ornate Victorian Lyford House, subject of more than one movie set, is the jewel in the setting of the striking **Audubon Bay Center & Sanctuary**. You can walk there, about .5-mile away, by taking Greenwood Beach Road, the road that is blocked to cars from the west end of the Blackies Pasture lot. Or, to drive, go west on Tiburon Boulevard from Blackies about 1.5 miles and turn left on Greenwood. On the grounds of the center, a National Audubon Society education and conservation facility, is a .5-mile nature loop that takes in the knoll and shoreline. The Lyford House, which features artwork by John James Audubon, is usually open Sundays for tours. *Note:* An admission is charged to tour the grounds.

MB: For a **Tiburon Town loop**, a flat ride of about 6 miles, pedal down the multi-use path, as described above, only turn right on San Rafael Avenue. Continue to Beach Street and then left to Tiburon. For a recommended variation, to take a look at the posh Belvedere Island, veer right along the water line on West Shore Road, where San Rafael Avenue hooks left. West Shore comes to an end after about a mile, where you ride a steep, short switchback to your left. You'll reach the top at Belvedere Avenue. Go right, passing large, stately homes with bridge and city views. Continue around the south tip of the island, to Beach Road. Follow Beach around and down to Tiburon. To return, ride west along Tiburon Boulevard until you pick up the bike path, on your left across from Mar West Street.

For a **Tiburon Peninsula loop**, a popular 8-mile run for ten-speeders, head down the multi-use path all the way, dovetailing finally with Tiburon Boulevard. When you reach the water in the center of town, hang a left on Paradise Drive. For the first .5-mile, the road is flat along the shore. Then you climb and curve, losing and gaining minor elevation, for the next 2 or 3 miles, with views down through conifer and laurel forests toward Paradise Cove. At the only stop sign on this route, about 3 miles from Tiburon, go left on Trestle Glenn Boulevard. This takes you to Blackies Pasture. *Be Aware:* Watch for traffic on Paradise Drive; portions are without shoulder.

For a more-adventurous **Tiburon Peninsula grand loop**—taking in the entire land mass on a run of 13 miles—do the Tiburon Peninsula loop, only do not turn left on Trestle Glen. Continue on Paradise Drive. You'll curve above the water for another 1.5 miles, passing Paradise Cay, and then drop to sea level. Ride the straightaway for another mile, and then turn left, or south, on Koch Road, which is straight ahead through the traffic signal at Paradise. Take this frontage road, all the way to the top, where it ends at a cul-de-sac next to condos. Then comes the adventurous part. You need to go through an unsigned Marin County Open Space gate, jog left, and push your bike up .25-mile of steep trail. At the top, continue straight, south, down a steep unpaved road that takes you to Central Drive. Roll down to Tiburon Boulevard. Cross, go left about a mile, and turn right on Greenwood Beach Road, which takes you to Blackies.

J: Use the Richardson Park loop as a jogging track, or make the run into Tiburon. Both routes are described in hiking section above.

R: **Skates and Scooters:** The multi-use path all the way to the outskirts of Tiburon, a 2-mile run, is mostly flat, except for the gentle rise up to the left of McKegney Green, just south of Blackies Pasture. **Strollers and Wheelchairs:** Try the Richardson Bay Park loop, described above. Instead of making a loop, chair riders might prefer to backtrack to avoid the steeper section of the multi-use path.

Special Interest: Kids: At South-of-the-Knoll Park, which is just beyond the McKegney Green, are two beautifully situated and well-designed children's play areas, one for tots and one for older kids. Exploration trails lead up the knoll behind the park.

23. TIBURON

Best for: Tourists from around the world are drawn to these quaint streets and dockside nooks, alongside a glamorous view of San Francisco and the bay.

Parking: From Hwy. 101 take Tiburon-E. Blithedale exit and go east on Tiburon Blvd. Drive about 2 mi. and park in lots or on street near Mar West Street. *Note:* Additional parking described in stroll section. *Bus:* GGT route 10 *Ferry:* Blue & Gold Fleet from Ferry Building in San Francisco and Fishermans Wharf.

Agency: Town of Tiburon; Marin County Department of Parks

ST: Shoreline Park and Main Street (.75-mi.); Main Street to Belvedere Island (2.25 mi.); Paradise Beach Park (up to .5-mi.)

Punta de Tiburon—Shark Point—was among the first sites named by the Spanish in the late 1700s, but the town itself was Marin's last to be incorporated. Now an exclusive residential community and tourist attraction, Tiburon's roots are as a raucous railroad hub and seaport. In 1884 Colonel Peter Donahue brought in trains of the Northern Pacific Railroad from San Rafael, which connected with big ferryboats to booming San Francisco. Main Street was developed as a business hub for the rail service, featuring bawdy hotels and bootleg bars that thrived during prohibition.

For the **Shoreline Park** stroll, head to the water at the corner of Main Street and Tiburon Boulevard. You'll pass the Blue & Gold Fleet dock and then walk left on a paved waterside path that has several benches. You'll come to the Tiburon Railroad & Ferry Depot Museum, standing alone, which is opened spring through early autumn by the Belvedere-Tiburon Landmarks Society. At the end of Shoreline Park is Elephant Rock, slightly offshore down a steel walkway. From the rock's viewing perch is a water-level look across Raccoon Strait to Angel Island.

Double back on the path and take a walk down **Main Street**, with its shops, galleries, and restaurants, a dozen of which are catalogued by the Landmarks Society. One alley close to Tiburon Boulevard leads to the Angel Island Ferry dock. As you stroll, be sure to poke in a restaurant or two to take advantage of back decks on the water. As Main Street makes a right turn at the end of the block, you can turn left down an alley for a look at seagoing life at the Corinthian Yacht Club, which dates from 1886.

To continue to **Belvedere Island**, continue on Main Street as it curves right along Ark Row, a series of tree-shaded boutiques and galleries housed in restored arks, each about 100 years old. At the end of Ark Row take a side trip by walking left on Bellevue Avenue onto Corinthian Island. At the tip you'll find a viewing area over the yacht harbor and Tiburon, with eye-popping looks at San Francisco, Alcatraz, and both bridges. You could walk around Corinthian Island from here, on East View Terrace, and drop back to Main Street at the base of Ark Row. Or, to continue on a longer stroll, double back on Bellevue, go straight to Beach Road, and turn left.

On the water, at 52 Beach Road, is China Cabin, a historical site—the restored Social Saloon of the *SS China*, which beached in 1886 in Belvedere Cove. China Cabin is normally open from April through October. Continue on Beach Road to where it makes a left turn. Look to your right for Pagoda Lane, and head up the 200 stairs that lead to Bayview Avenue on Belvedere Island. Walk left on Bayview until you come again to Beach Road. Head left back to Tiburon. You'll pass the San Francisco Yacht Club, an opportunity to stroll dockside among some finely outfitted ocean cruisers.

Paradise Beach Park is on the north side of the Tiburon Peninsula, about 4 miles from Tiburon on Paradise Drive. Paradise Drive continues to Tamalpais Drive and Highway 101 in Corte Madera, making for a scenic route back from Tiburon. The Marin County-run park features 19 acres of lawn and picnic area, leading down to a sandy beach. A long pier extends over the bay. *Note:* Admission charged for day use.

MB: Blue & Gold Fleet passengers from San Francisco can bring bikes across to ride around in Marin. See TH22, **Blackies Pasture**. Also see Richardson Bayfront, TH21, for connections to other Marin destinations.

R: **Wheelchairs and Strollers:** The path along Shoreline Park to Elephant Rock, and its wheel-accessible circular dock, is sublime. Tiburon lends itself to wheeling.

24.   ANGEL ISLAND   H, MB, J, R

Best for: Several beaches, an 800-foot-high peak to view the entire Bay Area, and 738 forested acres—an island home to wildlife, and the site for dozens of historical buildings that date from the Civil War.

Angel Island

Parking: From Hwy. 101 take Tiburon-E. Blithedale exit and proceed east on Tiburon Blvd. Start looking for parking after you cross Mar West St. on Tiburon Blvd. *Ferry to Angel Island:* The Tiburon-Angel Island Ferry is on Main Street, near where Tiburon Blvd. becomes Paradise Drive. Other ferry service is available from Fishermans Wharf. *Note:* Schedules may vary seasonally and during inclement weather; call for current information. *Ferries to Tiburon:* Blue & Gold Fleet ferry direct from Fishermans Wharf and Ferry Building in San Francisco. *Bus:* GGT route 10

Agency: Angel Island State Park; *Special Interest: Kids, Kayaks, Backpacking, Group Picnics

H: **Perimeter Road loop (5 mi. or more); Interior Fire Road loop (4 mi.); Mount Caroline Livermore loop (4 mi.)**

Angel Island sits off the tip of the Tiburon Peninsula, across Raccoon Strait. On the island's trails, you'll see a variety of grasses and flowers as well as many species of trees—eucalyptus, cypress, oak, bay, madrone, Douglas fir, cypress and Monterey pine among them. Western culture set foot on Angel Island in1775, from the decks of the Spanish vessel *San Carlos*—the first known to have entered the Golden Gate—under the command of Lt. Juan Manuel de Ayala. U.S. Army garrisons and batteries were constructed during the Civil War period and expanded during the Spanish-American war, circa 1899. An immigration station was established on the north shore in 1910, which was used primarily for detainment of Chinese immigrants, deemed less desirable after the railroad construction and mining booms of the late 1800s. In 1940, the North Garrison Immigration Station was abandoned. In 1962, all of Angel Island was made a California State Park, ending a 15-year effort that was hampered during the 1950s Cold War, when a Nike Missile facility was built on the island's southeast shore.

All hikes begin at Ayala Cove, where ferries dock. For the **Perimeter Road loop**, the best introduction to Angel Island, take a road to the right, just up the path from the ferry dock. All around the island are spur trails leading out from the perimeter route to points of interest—which all totaled would add another 2.5 miles to the hike. About .75-mile from Ayala Cove is a loop trail to Point Stuart, a scenic view of the Golden Gate and a worthy final destination for less energetic hikers. About .5-mile past the Point Stuart Trail is a short trail down to Alcatraz Gardens, and about a mile past that is another spur trail toward Point Blunt, near the Nike Missile site.

Most perimeter hikers will want to detour halfway around to explore the East Garrison at Fort McDowell and stroll Quarry Beach, the island's best beach. You may also want to save time for a walk to the former Immigration Station at North Garrison, about .75-mile north of Fort McDowell, which is also reachable via a coastal trail taking off from the road to Quarry Point. The North Garrison, features exhibits detailing Chinese immigration history on the island at China Cove.

Angel Island ferry, Tiburon Uplands nature loop

An **Interior Fire Road** contours the island, maintaining an elevation of about 400 feet, about halfway between sea level and the top of Mount Livermore. This loop is for visitors less interested in history and wishing more natural surroundings. A half-dozen trails and roads connect the Fire Road with the Perimeter Road, and several trails lead from it to the top of Mount Livermore. For this loop, head up the Sunset Trail, beginning at Perimeter Road where the main path comes up from Ayala Cove. The trail switchbacks up 200 feet to the Interior Fire Road. Start to your right, beginning your counterclockwise route.

For the **Mount Caroline Livermore loop,** take the Northridge Trail, which begins to your left as you disembark the ferry, before reaching the snack bar. The peak is named for the Marin conservationist who led the long effort to make Angel Island a park. You'll cross Perimeter Road as the trail curves to the north, and then goes directly up the ridge. Near the top you'll find a pleasant picnic area to enjoy a multifaceted panorama. The last part of the trail is a spur from where the Northridge and Sunset trails join. On the trip back, return to this junction and go right on the Sunset Trail. *Be Aware:* Make sure to time your hikes to be back for the last ferry.

MB: Angel Island is perhaps best seen from a bicycle seat, with some 12 miles of biking roads. Not all trails are open to bikes, but you will be able to take most of the spur options from the 5-mile **Perimeter Road loop**. You also have the option of a hike 'n' bike: riding, locking the wheels, and walking.

On an **Angel Island Double loop**, of about 10 miles with 600 feet of elevation, you ride both the Perimeter Road and Interior Fire Road. Start out to your right on Perimeter Road. The road undulates as you go, but basically maintains a contour at about 200 feet above the sea. After about 4 miles—on the north side of the island just before North Garrison—take the road turning back south, and up. You gain about 200 feet over .5-mile before reaching the Interior Fire Road. Go left, or clockwise. Continuing on the Fire Road, you'll pass five hiking trail and road junctions, before making a complete circle and rolling down to the Perimeter Road at North Garrison. Turn left and complete the double loop back to Ayala Cove.

J: Both the Perimeter Road and Interior Fire Road make excellent running paths. Angel Island is an excellent jogging area, for both runners in training and those just recreating.

R: **Strollers and Wheelchairs:** All the buildings at Angel Island are wheelchair accessible. Perimeter Road, though it gains and loses a hundred or so feet of elevation, is not steeply graded. The paths and picnic areas around Ayala Cove are destination enough, and rolling travelers don't need to circumnavigate the island to enjoy its scenery. *Be Aware:* At low tide, the ramp leading onto the ferry may be steep. **Skates and Scooters:** Skates, scooters and skateboards are not allowed on Angel Island.

Special Interest: Kids: Starting with the ferry over, Angel Island has much to offer for outdoor families. *Kayaks:* Professional outfitters offer tours of the island's shore, for all levels of paddlers, including novices. Make sure to get tide and current information from a professional before venturing across Raccoon Strait to Angel Island. Boat traffic is also a significant concern. Angel Island is a top-rated kayaking destination but not one to approach without planning and experience. *Camping and Group Picnics:* Angel Island has 10 environmental backpack camping sites and several group picnic sites. All are available by permits that must be reserved in advance.

25. OLD ST. HILARYS PRESERVE   H, ST

Best for: A grassy ridge with arm's length looks at an astounding number of different wildflowers, and a panorama of Tiburon.

Parking: From Hwy. 101 take Tiburon-E. Blithedale exit and proceed east on Tiburon Blvd. Follow Tiburon Blvd. for almost 3 miles and turn left on Lyford Dr., just past Needs Way. Follow Lyford up nearly to the top, jog left on Sugar Loaf Dr. and turn right on Heathcliff Dr. Park at MCOSD gate at end of Heathcliff. *Note:* Additional parking in hiking and stroll descriptions.

Agency: Marin County Open Space District; Marin County Department of Parks

H: **Top of Old St. Hilarys Preserve (up to 1 mi.); Tiburon Uplands Nature Preserve to: nature loop (.75-mi.), or Old St. Hilarys Preserve (1.5 mi.)**

From the Heathcliff Drive access, you are nearly at the **Top of Old St. Hilarys**, at the preserve's northern boundary. Walk from the MCOSD gate along an undulating, grassy ridge top for about .5-mile. You'll look down the tip of the Tiburon Peninsula toward Angel Island. The preserve hosts many species of wildflowers, two-thirds of them native to the Tiburon Peninsula, including the Tiburon Paintbrush and the rare Black Jewel, which blooms in early summer.

To Old St. Hilarys from the **Tiburon Uplands Nature Preserve**—the best hike in this trailhead—you need to access from the northeast side of the peninsula off Paradise Drive: Either drive through Tiburon and continue around the tip on Paradise Drive, or come in on the north, by using the Tamalpais Drive exit in Corte Madera and going east on Paradise Drive. The trailhead is near the south entrance to Tiburon Romberg Center at 3150 Paradise Drive. Park on the large shoulder opposite the Romberg main gate and walk down the road less than .25-mile to a short flight of railroad-tie stairs.

The **Tiburon Uplands nature loop**—starting out left, or clockwise—takes you through a Sherwood Forest of ferns under a canopy of bay trees, gaining some 200 feet. After about .5-mile you come to a bench with a San Pablo Bay view. To the left of the bench is the trail to **Old St. Hilarys**, unmarked. You climb, through oak and grassland, another 250 feet and pop out near the top, not far from the Heathcliff Drive access. Backtrack down to the view bench and continue on the Nature Loop trail, on this drier-side exposure of the Tiburon Uplands Preserve.

ST: Old St. Hilarys Church (up to .5-mi.)

Old St. Hilarys Church, of Carpenter Gothic design, was built as a Roman Catholic church in 1888. It is a modest structure that sits by itself on an open, 4-acre hillside—a rare combination in Tiburon. To get there, head up Mar West Street, which is between Beach and Lyford off Tiburon Boulevard. Then turn left up short Esperanza Street to its end. A short trail leads from the church grounds up to the Vistazo West fire road. The Belvedere-Tiburon Landmarks Society opens the building, normally spring through early fall on Wednesday and Sunday afternoons.

26.   RING MOUNTAIN   H, MB, R

Best for: Many trailhead options on this wide-open ridge, easily accessible from central Marin and affording vistas of the entire North Bay and Mount Tamalpais watershed.

Parking: Ring Mountain has access on both its north and south slopes, close by foot but far apart by car. *For north-access trailheads:* Take the Tamalpais Dr.-Paradise Dr. exit from Hwy. 101 in Corte Madera. Go east on Tamalpais Dr., turn right on San Clemente Dr., and continue to Paradise Dr. *For south-access trailheads:* Take E.-Blithedale-Tiburon Blvd. exit from Hwy. 101 and go east on Tiburon Blvd. *Note:* Further instructions in hiking section.

Agency: Marin County Open Space District

H: **Tiburon Ridge: long walks (4.5 mi.); mid-distance walks (1.75 mi. to 2.25 mi.); Phyllis Ellman Trail (1.75 mi.); Ring Mountain Summit: from Taylor Road (1 mi.), from Shepherd Way (2.25 mi.)**

Ring Mountain Open Space Preserve and Tiburon Ridge Open Space to its west form the base of the Tiburon Peninsula, featuring a system of trails about 2 miles long and up to a mile wide. Ring Mountain, the 602-foot top of a rock-strewn grassy ridge, was established as a preserve by the Nature Conservancy in 1982 and transferred to the county in 1995. You'll see blue and green schist, as well as igneous, greenish serpentine—an inhospitable environment for most plant life. But connoisseurs will find rare and endangered plant species. Walkers with keen eyes may also spot 2,000-year-old petroglyphs among the rock outcroppings.

Tiburon Ridge long walks: Both hikes traverse the Tiburon Ridge Open Space and Ring Mountain. *From the north side:* Turn right where Paradise meets San Clemente. Then go left, or south, on Koch Road, a frontage road, for about .5-mile to its end, and park at a cul-de-sac. Go through the unsigned MCOSD gate and jog left to a trail that leads steeply up a short distance to Taylor Ridge Fire Road. *From the south side:* Turn left just east of Highway 101 on Tiburon Boulevard, on N. Knoll Road. Follow N. Knoll Road up and turn right on Central; go to the end at gate amid a condo complex. Head steeply up the unpaved road for a long .25-mile to Taylor Ridge Fire Road.

For both north and south access points, head east on Taylor Ridge Fire Road. You'll walk through the grass and oak woodlands of small Tiburon Ridge Open Space. After curving through some modest elevation gains, nearly a mile from the trailheads, you come to the MCOSD gate for Ring Mountain. From here, you begin a 200-feet gradual climb to Taylor Ridge. The high ridge, with its sitting rocks and circular view, is a worthy destination. Ring Mountain is the rounded peak to the south, with a near a water tank. From Taylor Ridge, you drop down about 150 feet through a saddle and continue for .75-mile, now on the Ring Mountain Fire Road.

The **Tiburon Ridge mid-distance**: On both hikes you reach the ridge fire road just east of the Taylor Ridge summit. *From the north side:* Take Paradise Drive east and turn right on Westward Drive, which is just past Verona Place. Take Westward to its end, at a MCOSD gate. Take the winding trail up, beginning under pine and laurel trees and continuing by lichen-splotched rocks. You reach the fire road after a curving .5-mile, gaining about 200 feet in the process. *From the south side:* Heading east on Tiburon Boulevard, turn left on Reed Ranch Road, which is between Celia Way and Trestle Glen Boulevard. Take Reed Ranch all the way to the top and park at MCOSD gate. A short trail, the Reed Ranch Fire Road, climbs gradually through grassland and meets the ridge fire road after about .75-mile. *For both mid-distance hikes*, continue east on the fire road, climbing steadily but gradually to Ring Mountain.

The **Phyllis Ellman Trail** begins at bay level, bordering an ephemeral brook and meandering up through small laurels and native bushes, finally reaching the ridge fire road about 400 feet up. Access is from the north side of the peninsula, at a MCOSD gate that is on Paradise Drive, just east of Westward Drive. This is the site of a prehistoric rockslide. Bird lovers will enjoy this quieter look at the Ring Mountain Preserve.

To the **Ring Mountain Summit from Taylor Road,** a short walk, begin on the north access, traveling east on Paradise Drive. After passing Robin Drive, turn right on Taylor Road and follow it to the top. A MCOSD gate sits beside trophy homes. Take the paved road that heads up to your right from the gate. You'll pass a junction with the Ring Mountain Fire Road coming in on the right, and curve around left to the peak, which is to the left of a large water tank. Amazing views provide a lesson in the geography of the San Francisco Bay.

To the **Ring Mountain Summit from Shepherd Way**—one of the best, but least-used trailheads in the preserve—take either Tiburon Boulevard or Paradise Drive toward Tiburon. Turn on Trestle Glen Boulevard and at the top, turn up Shepherd Way to its end. The trailhead is an unmarked path leading out of the far end of the church parking lot. After about 200 feet, you come to a low pipe gate and a sign noting the Tiburon Ridge Trail. The trail becomes more of a road, passing a noble stand of eucalyptus, and gaining some 400 feet in total. Turn right when you hit the paved road at the top, and then veer left of the water tank. On the return walk you'll head toward views of San Francisco and the towers of the Golden Gate Bridge.

MB: The taxing **Ring Mountain loop ride** covers the length of the ridge. Begin at the south side access off Central Drive, as described in Tiburon Ridge long walks above. Ride up from Central and turn right on the Taylor Ridge Fire Road. You'll do a steep climb through sparse oak hills, hit a straight stretch, and reach a gate marking beginning of Ring Mountain Preserve. You then make a major pump up Taylor Ridge. After descending the ridge, you cross the saddle and climb again toward the summit, but not all the way. You'll pass the road that comes in from Taylor on your left. Veer right, dropping over the last .75-mile. The road comes out at Shepherd Way, which you ride down to Trestle Glen Boulevard. Turn right, descending to Tiburon Boulevard. Cross over to Blackies Pasture and go right through the parking area to Greenwood Beach Road, which is closed to cars on this end. Follow Greenwood to Tiburon Boulevard, near Central.

R: **Wheelchairs and Strollers:** The paved road from Taylor Road, though not signed as handicapped access, provides a relatively easy path to the summit of Ring Mountain. The road is fairly steep, and becomes roughly paved past the water tank near the top; chair riders should have help as a back-up. Ring Mountain is one of the most panoramic destinations in the Bay Area readily reached by wheelchair. Active Moms & Dads will be able to negotiate strollers on most preserve roads.

Bay Wetlands

Gallinas Creek

By 1815, the Spaniards had been settling the Golden Gate region for 30 years, building a military stronghold at the Presidio and dividing Marin County up into a number of large rancheros, which were granted to those who had served the empire. The Coast Miwok who had lived these lands for thousands of years were subjugated as ranchero workers or conscripted by the missions. Seeking a site to build Mission San Rafael Archangel, a Spanish exploring party sailed up San Rafael Creek. They did battle with a village of Coast Miwok, and captured their leader, El Marinero—or Chief Marin as we later named him.

Chief Marin was shipped off to be converted to Christianity at Mission Delores in San Francisco, and also enlisted to aid the Spanish in their ferry operations on the bay. In 1824, Mexico achieved independence from Spain. And Chief Marin, along with the last band of free Miwok, achieved independence as well. They fled in canoes, taking refuge on the two, tiny Marin Islands less than a mile offshore the marshlands of San Rafael Bay. Although facing superior numbers and armaments, the Miwok were able to defend the rugged island until food supplies ran out. The warriors were killed and captured. The very last Coast Miwok warrior, known to us as Quintin, made a run for the Golden Gate, but the tides were against him and Spanish vessels captured his canoe at today's Point San Quentin—now the site of the famous prison.

During the remainder of the century, the marshlands of the east shore of Marin—that extend north from Tiburon Peninsula to the Petaluma River, which is the border with Sonoma County—were left relatively untouched, in spite of the Gold Rush fervor that shook the rest of the bay region. The wetlands had been a horn of plenty for the Miwok, but the new settlers applied different values. Although wondrously level, unlike the ridges of Mount Tamalpais, these mudflats were of no use: No timber, little deep water for fishing, no firm ground for railways, no pastures for grazing, no damn good. By the time California became a state, the wetlands were considered less-valu-

Mission San Rafael, Marin Islands

China Camp shrimper George Quan,
Pt. San Quentin, Marin Civic Center

able extensions of the Mexican land grants that were sold to enterprising Americans who were in the right place at the right time.

Until rail lines were laid down along the dry western fringes of the wetlands, the creeks that ran through them were used for the transport of the timber, aggregates, and rock that was shipped to booming San Francisco. Creeks were excavated to improve the waterways for barges. Corte Madera, San Rafael, Las Galinas, Rush and Novato creeks, as well as the Petaluma River, were used to float materials, along with dairy products and produce. When the rail lines to Tiburon and Sausalito were laid in the late 1800s, the waterways became less significanct. Dairy and grazing, on reclaimed marsh, continued on these eastern reaches of the rancheros.

But one part of the bay shore that saw its activity increase during the late 1800s was the north shore of San Pedro Mountain, the 1,000-foot high ridge that is the noted exception to marshlands on the bay coast. Chinese immigrants in the 1870s established a fishing village, mainly harvesting shrimp that hungry San Francisco couldn't get enough of. Unlike other out-of-work railroad workers in California who found themselves doing labor on rancheros, the fishermen here established a community that has lasted into the 21st century—now within the grounds of China Camp State Park, established in 1977.

Some 1,500 acres of San Pedro Mountain is included in the state park. The rest of the mountain's considerable mass is in San Pedro Mountain Open Space Preserve and San Rafael's undeveloped Barbier Park. With an intertwined system of trails that are enjoyed by hikers, dog walkers, cyclists, and equestrians, San Pedro Mountain is a recreational getaway that is not far from Marin's urban area.

Recreational areas in the rest of the wetlands—all east of the freeway corridor—are a patchwork of different agencies, including the following: Marin County Open Space District; California Department of Fish and Game; San Rafael and Corte Madera park departments; and the Marin County Department of Parks. The Open Space Preserves, in addition to the lands on San Pedro Mountain, include Deer Island, Rush Creek, Santa Margarita Island, and Santa Venetia Marsh. Hikers can walk among the waterfowl on raised trails along the creeks and bay shores, or on oak islands—woodland-and-grass hillocks that rise from the marshes. In the pre-canal and levee days, floodwaters and tidal surge surrounded these oak islands. Two state public areas, at Black Point and Corte Madera Marsh, offer trails onto the marsh habitat, as do the paths at McInnis County Park and Shoreline Park. Hikers can explore the creek canals at McInnis also, as well as at Bel Marin Keys, Shorebird Marsh, and Larkspur Landing.

Conversion of the marshlands to public lands began in the mid-1970s, as the public and scientists began to appreciate the fundamental importance of the wetlands—where land and water mix, and where oceans meet the rivers—to the overall ecology of the region. Where fresh water flows from rivers and meets salt water, turbulent eddies result, known as the salt-water wedge. Organic plant nutrients roil in the eddies, important to hundreds of marine species and attracting millions of tiny shrimp, which in turn feed bass and other fish. Plans are underway near Old Hamilton Field and Bel Marin Keys to restore a 2,500-acre tract of bay wetlands to its pristine condition.

Deer Island

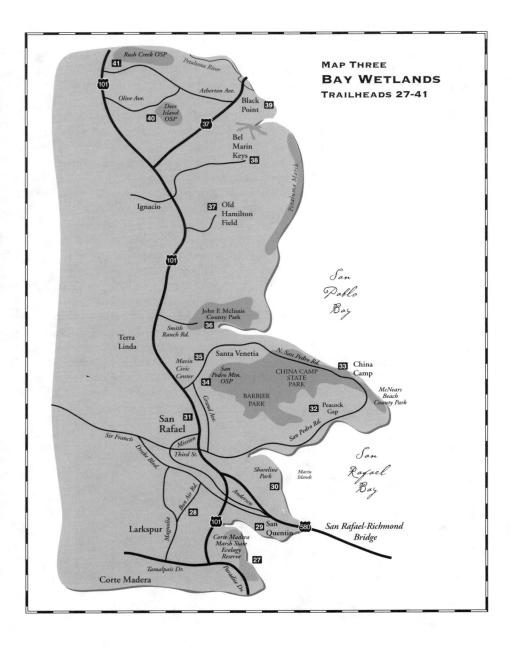

MAP THREE
BAY WETLANDS
TRAILHEADS 27-41

Rush Creek OSP

41

101

Petaluma River

Atherton Ave.

Olive Ave.

Deer
Island
OSP

40

37

Black
Point

39

Bel
Marin
Keys

38

Ignacio

37

Old
Hamilton
Field

Petaluma Marsh

101

*San
Pablo
Bay*

John F. McInnis
County Park

36

Smith
Ranch Rd.

Terra
Linda

35

Santa Venetia

N. San Pedro Rd.

China
Camp

33

Marin
Civic
Center

San
Pedro Mtn.
OSP

CHINA CAMP
STATE
PARK

34

BARBIER
PARK

McNears
Beach
County Park

32

Peacock
Gap

San
Rafael

31

Grand Ave.

San Pedro Rd.

Sir Francis

Mission

*San
Rafael
Bay*

Drake Blvd.

Third St.

Shoreline
Park

Marin
Islands

30

Bon Air Rd.

Andersen

28

Magnolia

Larkspur

101

29

San
Quentin

580

**San Rafael-Richmond
Bridge**

Corte Madera
Marsh State
Ecology
Reserve

27

Tamalpais Dr.

Paradise Dr.

Corte Madera

BAY WETLANDS

TRAILHEADS

H	HIKES
ST	STROLLS
MB	MOUNTAIN AND ROAD BIKES
J	JOGGING
R	ROLL - SKATES, SCOOTERS, BABY STROLLERS, WHEELCHAIRS

27-41

All hike and stroll distances are ROUND TRIP except as noted for shuttles.
Please contact Agency to obtain current rules and regulations. See Resource Links for all telephone numbers.
See also special Doggie Trails section.

27. SHOREBIRD MARSH   H, MB, J

Best for: A large marsh preserve—hiding in plain sight along the urban corridor of central Marin—with paths along the San Francisco Bay and views of Mount Tam.

Parking: Take the Tamalpais Dr.-Paradise Dr. exit from Hwy. 101 in Corte Madera and go east on Tamalpais Dr., toward the bay. Park near corner of Tamalpais and Paradise; or, at The Village shopping center. Turn left at signal on Redwood Highway and make first left into the The Village. *Bus:* GGT local route 21

Agency: California Department of Fish and Game; Corte Madera Parks and Recreation Department

H: **Corte Madera Marsh loop (2.75 mi.); Muzzi Marsh (up to 2 mi.); Shorebird Marsh Park (0 mi.)**

Shorebird Marsh is comprised of several wetlands, the largest of which is Corte Madera Marsh, a state ecological preserve. The Corte Madera Creek enters the bay at the north side of the marsh, site of the Larkspur Ferry Terminal—so walks on the marsh usually include views of ferries offshore heading to and from the city. On the south end of the wetland is San Clemente Creek. The inland area of the marsh supports stands of pampas grass, and along portions of the paths are acacia trees, blooming yellow in late winter. A variety of birds roost on the high wires hung between huge power towers. Eastward, across open water is "The Q"—San Quentin State Prison.

For the **Corte Madera Marsh loop**—beginning from the parking lot at The Village shopping center—take the crosswalk at the corner of Tamalpais and San Clemente.

Pass the first unpaved road that borders a canal and then walk left on a second, which you come to shortly thereafter. The route heads toward the bay and then back left, or north, encircling the entire wetland. On the northeast sector of the loop, a spur trail leads out to the mouth of Corte Madera Creek, close to passing ferries. *Additional Access:* To access the marsh from its north end, use the above parking instructions, only continue north on Redwood Highway, passing The Village. Proceed straight through a traffic signal, passing a shopping center, and turn right on aptly named Industrial Way. Continue down Industrial and go right to a parking area. A scenic spur road leads into the marsh.

To walk **Muzzi Marsh**, a smaller preserve bordering San Clemente Creek, take the paved bike path to your right after crossing the crosswalk at the southeast corner at The Village parking lot. After a short segment that parallels busy San Clemente Drive, you turn left. The unsigned path to Muzzi Marsh heads eastward off the bike path. You can walk straight out to the mouth of the creek, or use another levee path to make a loop out of it.

Shorebird Marsh Park has no hiking trails, but its lagoon is a popular spot for migratory birds and waterfowl—and for stationary brown-baggers taking a lunch break. The small park is located just north of The Village on the Redwood Highway frontage road. Shorebird Marsh lies just east of the lagoon, creating a mile-wide backdrop. The park is next to the freeway, so noise is a factor.

MB: Pedaling is a good way to acquaint yourself with **Shorebird Marsh**. Cutting through the marsh, when headed to or from Tiburon on Paradise Drive, is also a scenic byway. If coming from Tiburon, veer right off the bike path at San Clemente and take the unpaved road along the slough. The road comes out at Industrial Way, by the Sir Francis Drake pedestrian overpass.

This trailhead is a convenient central departure point for many destinations around Marin. To go north to **Larkspur Landing, TH29,** take the bike path going north across from The Village. Continue past Shoreline Park, skirting busy Redwood Highway. After passing the pedestrian overpass, look for an opening in the fence to your left, and take the elevated sidewalk north over a freeway off-ramp. At the other end of the ramp, which is Sir Francis Drake Boulevard, is the Corte Madera Creek bike path. From this path you can either head west toward Kentfield or east on the scenic route to San Rafael; see, TH28-29.

To **Larkspur**, head north on the bike path, past Shorebird Park, and turn left on the Wornum underpass. Continue across Vista Boulevard after crossing under Highway 101. Follow a bike path through a greenbelt that heads right at Mt. Tam. Turn right when you reach a canal, toward nearby Lucky Drive. At Lucky, go left behind Redwood High School on a path that leads to the old railroad easement behind Larkspur. *Note:* A bridge over the canal at Wornum is due to be constructed.

To **Mill Valley** from Shorebird Marsh, head west on Tamalpais Drive, crossing Highway 101 on the elevated sidewalk. On the other, cut left across busy Tamalpais and keep left, following Casa Buena Drive south, over Horse Hill, to Richardson's Bayfront; see TH21. To **Tiburon** from the marsh, take the bike route south, along San Clemente, and then go left on Paradise Drive. You then climb on curving Paradise Drive and come to Trestle Glen Boulevard. Turn right on Trestle Glen and drop down to Blackies Pasture on Tiburon Boulevard. A bike path leads from Blackies into Tiburon; see TH22.

J: The Corte Madera Marsh is designed for jogging. Flat and with good footing, you can divert your eyes to the view across the water, thanking your lucky stars you're not wasting away in the Big House. Waterfowl, shorebirds and a mix of woodland birds share the open space.

28.   CORTE MADERA CREEK   H, MB, J, R

Best for: A multi-use path through the heart of Marin that makes a loop alongside both banks of wide canal, with a view of Mount Tamalpais.

Parking: From Highway 101, take Sir Francis Drake Blvd. west. Continue for about a mile and turn left, toward the hospital, on Bon Air Rd. Park parallel on road, beginning at Creekside Park, .25-mile from Drake Blvd. *Bus:* GGT routes 1 and 21.

Agency: Marin County Department of Parks; *Special Interest: Kids

H: Corte Madera Creek (1.5 mi.); Creek loop (2 mi.); Creekside Park (up to .5-mi.)

The **Corte Madera Creek** walk begins about 2 miles upstream from the Larkspur Ferry Terminal on the navigable creek, in Mount Tam's rain shadow. After about .75-mile on the paved path, you'll come to where the creek enters a concrete canal, and another creek forks in from the left. Select one of the view benches here, or one of the many that line the path on your return walk.

For the **Creek loop**, continue a short distance along the concrete canal, often a swimming pool for ducks and fish. Cross over a footbridge and turn left. *Note*: The path to the right continues for .25-mile to College Avenue at the College of Marin. Heading back down the creek, the unpaved loop path comes to the confluence of two creeks. Veer right on a trail that skirts fenced Peiper Field. You continue around to your right to a roughly paved parking area. Across this parking area, to your left, you'll see a footbridge. Cross the parking lot and the footbridge. You're now on the unpaved road that heads back on the opposite bank of Corte Madera Creek.

The path to **Creekside Park** is at the north end of the parking for Corte Madera Creek. After a short walk, you come to the large lawn, picnic area, and tree-shaded playground. To the left, steps lead to a Coastal Conservancy interpretive kiosk and views of the creek and Mount Tam—one of the better lowland looks at the noted peak. *Note:* The path continues from Creekside Park for another .25-mile, to Drake Boulevard, near Marin Catholic High School and Wolfe Grade.

MB: This trailhead lies midway along the Corte Madera Creek bike path that transects Marin from Larkspur Landing to Ross. It's convenient to get from here to anywhere in central and southern Marin. To **Larkspur Landing, TH29**, cross Bon Air Avenue and pedal South Eliseo .75-mile over a rise. You drop down to the creek bike path that goes to the ferry terminal. From there you can take the bay route to San Rafael and China Camp; see TH29. To downtown **San Rafael, TH31**, take the bike path from Creekside Park, as per the hiking description above. At the end of the path, cross Sir Francis Drake and take Wolfe Grade, which goes over a hill and becomes D Street in San Rafael.

To **Ross and Phoenix Lake, TH47**—where you can continue to Mt. Tam or Fairfax—head north on the bike lane to Kentfield. Cross College Avenue, and pedal through College of Marin parking lots, keeping right, and follow a narrow bike lane along the creek that comes out behind the post office in Ross; see TH47. *Be Aware:* Watch for pedestrians on the creek route from the college. For a faster route to Ross from College of Marin, veer left out of the parking lot and turn right on Kent-Poplar Avenue.

To go south to **Larkspur, TH50**, from this trailhead, cross over the creek using the bike lane on the Bon Air bridge. When you get to Magnolia Avenue, take a bike lane that runs on the east side of Magnolia. This takes you to Larkspur and along the old railroad easement that runs behind town to Corte Madera. See TH50 for directions to connect with Mill Valley and Richardson Bayfront.

J: The Creek loop, in spite of the pesky double-back spot, makes for a good running track, and at the college you can loop around the athletic track to make this jog a distance of your liking.

R: **Skates and Scooters:** Use the path described in the hiking section. You can extend that route another .5-mile, round trip, by continuing over the footbridge to Kentfield. **Wheelchairs and Strollers:** This trailhead, across from Marin General Hospital, is excellent for convalescing patients and their family members. Also try the wheel around Creekside Park; ditto for Moms & Dads with strollers.

Special Interest: Kids: Creekside Park has a fun play area shaded by big oaks next to a large lawn. The Tam viewing kiosk and creek trails add a nature-educational component to the day.

Creekside Park, Larkspur Landing

29. LARKSPUR LANDING

Best for: Connect via bike to anywhere in Marin, or put the bike on a ferry and pedal the waterfront in San Francisco. Or visit Point San Quentin without being ordered there by the court.

Parking: *From Hwy. 101*, take the Sir Francis Drake Blvd.-San Anselmo exit and go east toward the Hwy. 580, Richmond-San Rafael Bridge. Parallel park opposite the Larkspur Ferry Terminal on E. Sir Francis Drake. Spaces may be hard to come by on weekdays. Only ferry passengers may use the ferry parking area. *Note:* Additional parking described in sections below. Ferry: Golden Gate Ferry from San Francisco Ferry Building. *Bus:* GGT route 30 or a dozen free commuter buses.

Agency: Golden Gate Transit; Larkspur Parks & Recreation; Marin County Department of Parks; *Special Interest: Windsurfing, Kayaks

H: Remillard Park (1.25 mi.); Point San Quentin (up to .5-mi.); Corte Madera Creek (2.25 mi.)

For **Remillard Park**, begin your left along the multi-use path as you face the bay at the pedestrian overpass. This bayside stroll, past the quixotic conquistador sculpture, follows the bay to the San Quentin Prison west gate. It dips away from the noisy boulevard in places, and is a walk you might take while waiting for the ferry, to watch windsurfers or passing ferryboats. The park is the site of an 1890s brickyard; the brick kiln tower still stands across the street.

For **Point San Quentin**, with its driftwood cove, you need to drive east on E. Sir Francis Drake, toward the Richmond-San Rafael Bridge. Take the last Marin County exit and then turn right on Main Street. Not far down the street are steps leading down through eucalyptus trees to a small beach. On the beach you can go right to a low promontory. The cove is just down the street from the east gate of the prison. There you will find a gift shop that has inmate-made items and a small post office, established in 1859, from which you can postmark cute "wish-you-were-here" cards and letters. San Quentin has been a place of imprisonment since an Army brig barge was anchored here in 1852. The point is named for a Coast Miwok warrior, *Quintin*, the last to be captured by Mexican soldiers, here in 1824.

The **Corte Madera Creek** walk follows a multi-use path. Begin walking toward the freeway from the pedestrian overpass on the ferry terminal side of the boulevard. During the first part of the walk, traffic noise is an issue, as this is where Richmond Bridge drivers join Highway 101. But as you go under the freeway, relative quiet begins. Walk left on a dock section that runs under the road infrastructure and along a restored marsh area bordered by decorative light stanchions. You leave the concrete ceiling behind, during the last part of the multi-use path, which ends at South Eliseo behind the Bon Air Shopping Center. The path curves along the creek, pointing toward Mount Tam from the green margins of an upscale townhouse neighborhood.

MB: Larkspur Landing is an excellent place to start pedals to central Marin, San Rafael Bay, San Rafael, Tiburon, or San Francisco. One of the best biking adventures is to ride the ferry on a **one-way ticket to San Francisco.** From there you ride The Embarcadero to Crissy Field, TH13, and then across the bridge. From Golden Gate Bridge North, you ride through Sausalito to Richardson Bayfront, TH21. Connect from Richardson Bayfront to Shorebird Marsh, TH27, and from there back to Larkspur Landing. This is an all-day ride but you don't have to be in great shape.

To **downtown San Rafael** head toward San Quentin on the bike path and past the prison gate on a bike lane. At the top of the hill you need to cross over E. Sir Francis Drake and head down the bike path along Andersen. This a busy street with a good bike lane that takes you into San Rafael at A Street; see TH31.

To **San Rafael Bay** at **Shoreline Park**, follow the ride to San Rafael as described above, only keep right and pass Andersen. Ride down the freeway, on a more than adequate shoulder, and take the last Marin County exit to San Quentin. Go left at the stop sign and then left again on the other side of an underpass. Follow Francisco Boulevard for about a mile and turn right on Pelican Way. At the end you'll find the Shoreline Park bike path. Go left, or north, on the path almost 2 miles to Pickleweed Park; see TH30.

To get to **Ross and Phoenix Lake,** or **San Anselmo and Fairfax**, follow the Corte Madera Creek hike described above. At the end of the path, take South Eliseo to the Corte Madera Creek trailhead. Continue on to Ross; see TH47, Phoenix Lake.

To **Shorebird Marsh**—where you can pump toward Tiburon, Mill Valley, or Larkspur—start out as directed on the Corte Madera Creek hike. Pass the left turn on the dock walkway and continue a short distance to an opening that leads to an elevated sidewalk section that runs along the Sir Francis Drake freeway off-ramp. *Be Aware:* This sidewalk, though highly convenient, borders heavy traffic. Ride south on the frontage road past the shopping center, where you pick up a shore-skirting bike path and continue to Shorebird Marsh; see TH27.

J: Corte Madera Creek path, allowing for a drab first .25-mile, is a good running path—not used by as many joggers as other multi-use paths. You can extend the jog by continuing over the hill on South Eliseo on a .75-mile road run that connects with TH28, by Marin General Hospital.

R: **Skates and Scooters:** The Corte Madera Creek path is a good run, but watch out for cars at the ferry terminal entrance. A short plank section just before Highway 101 will also slow you down. **Wheelchairs and Strollers:** Traffic noise and roads to the ferry terminal make this a less desirable starting point for rollers. Instead, drive west on Sir Francis Drake, turn left at the first signal on Barry Way, and go left again on Drake's Landing Road. From the end of this road is a paved path, that takes you to the multi-use path along Corte Madera Creek. To the right, the path extends a long .5-mile, and to the left you can explore the restored marsh area.

Special Interest: Kayaks: A paddling club puts in near the railroad trestle at Highway 101. A better option for kayakers—and one of the best creek paddles—is to go west on Sir Francis Drake to the Bon Air Landing. Follow the instructions in the wheelchair access above. *Windsurfing:* When the wind is up, sail boarders flock to Remillard Park faster than K-Mart shoppers to a blue-light special.

Corte Madera Marsh trail

30. SHORELINE PARK   H, MB, J, R

Best for: Marin's longest and least traveled shoreline multi-use path, along San Rafael Bay, perfect for an after-work or morning stroll.

Parking: *From Hwy. 101 north of San Rafael,* take the Francisco Blvd.-Richmond Bridge exit, and veer right off overpass. Continue to traffic light at Bellam Blvd. and turn left. *From Hwy. 101 south of San Rafael,* take Francisco Blvd. exit and turn left on Bellam. *For both directions:* From Bellam Blvd., continue across Francisco and turn left at traffic signal on Kerner Blvd. Follow Kerner to end at Canal St. and turn right. Park near Pickleweed Park. *Bus:* GGT route 20 or 35

Agency: San Rafael Community Services Department

H: **Lagoon point (1 mi.); San Rafael Bay shoreline (3.75 mi.)**

Hidden east of an industrial park and the Highway 101 corridor, Shoreline Park's scenery may come as a surprise. For **both Shoreline Park walks**, start east, away from Pickleweed Park along the bay. A mile offshore in the bay are the two Marin Islands, a National Wildlife Refuge. An exercise station and benches mark **lagoon point,** at the end of a straight section. You have a view of the Richmond-San Rafael Bridge, whose double steel suspensions echo those of the Bay Bridge in the far background.

To walk the entire **San Rafael Bay shoreline**, continue on the path along the south side of the lagoon for a short distance, and then turn left, or south, on the long, stretch of path that follows the shoreline. The multi-use path ends on the north side of Pt. San Quentin. *Additional Access:* The south side of Shoreline Park path may be accessed from Pelican Way. Using the above parking directions, turn right on Francisco from Bellam. Go left on Pelican and park in signed area.

MB: Shoreline Park's multi-use path is a scenic secret route for cyclists to get from Larkspur or Corte Madera to San Rafael or Peacock Gap—and continuing along the shore to China Camp State Park. To **Larkspur Landing, TH29**, take the multi-use path, hugging the shore. Turn right before the path ends, on a paved path that leads in from Pelican Way. Go out Pelican, turn left on Francisco, and ride until you see an opening in the chain link fence. Take that opening, heading up a wide bike lane on the Sir Francis Drake exit off Highway 580. Continue over a rise. At the bottom of the hill beyond the prison, cross Sir Francis Drake to a bike path at Remillard Park, and continue to the ferry terminal; see TH29.

To downtown **San Rafael or Peacock Gap**, head away from Pickleweed Park on Canal Street all the way to Harbor Street. Go left, out to Francisco Boulevard, where you turn right. Hook around to your right, now on Grand Avenue, crossing over San Rafael Creek. **To continue on to Peacock Gap and China Camp**, turn right on Third Street, which becomes Pt. San Pedro Road. Continue all the way around the point past China Camp State Park to the Marin County Civic Center. *Note:* To go directly to the Civic Center, stay on Grand Ave, after riding Francisco Boulevard from Canal Street. Grand Street comes to a freeway on-ramp, which cyclists may safely and legally ride to the next exit, which is San Pedro Road.

To downtown San Rafael from Shoreline Park, follow the directions above, only don't turn right on Third Street. Continue on Grand Avenue and turn left on Mission Street, which is just past Fifth Street.

J: The San Rafael Bay shoreline hike, described above, is one of the best bayside runs. You also get good views inland across the lagoon toward Mt. Tam. To make a 2-mile loop of the run, taking another multi-use path back, continue straight after rounding the point at the south end of the lagoon. A paved multi-use path, along a lagoon, connects with Baypoint Drive. Follow Baypoint, past some of the homes, and then turn right on a paved path when you reach Playa del Ray. This path comes out at parking for Shoreline Park on Canal Street.

R: **Skates and Scooters:** Take the multi-use path to lagoon point, as described above. You can continue for another long .25-mile east on a paved path, or make a loop back to Pickleweed Park as per the jogging description. **Wheelchairs and Strollers:** With the inland view across the lagoon toward Tam, and offshore looks at Marin Islands in San Rafael Bay, this is one of the best shoreline roller paths. Wheelchair riders will want to park at the playground, Schoen Park, on Canal Street just east of Pickleweed Park.

31. SAN RAFAEL   H, ST, MB

Best for: Nearly two centuries of California living come together—from the missions of the early 1800s to avant-garde films of today—along the Victorian neighborhoods and parks around downtown San Rafael.

Parking: From Hwy. 101, take the central San Rafael exit. *Coming from the south*, you will be on Grand Ave; continue to Fourth St. and turn left. *Coming from the north*, you will be on Heatherton; turn right of Fourth St. For both exits, continue west on Fourth St. for a few blocks and park on street near Lootens Pl. *Note:* Additional parking in hike descriptions. *Bus:* Many routes to GGT center at Third and Heatherton

Agency: City of San Rafael; *Special Interest: Kids

H: San Rafael Hill (1 mi.)

San Rafael Hill offers a great view of the city and its setting. Turn right on Court Street, just past Lootens Place on Fourth Street, and continue 2 blocks to Mission Avenue. Turn left on Mission and then make an immediate right on Wilkins Street, just before Boyd Park. Turn at next left, on Laurel and then veer right on Dollar Scenic Drive. Take Dollar to the top, just before Tampa Drive; you'll see parking on your right and a fire road going up to your left. Start up the road, an unsigned entrance to the upper part of Boyd Park. You'll make lazy switchbacks on the main road, climbing 350 feet to the top, which is marked by a small telecommunications installation. On the way, notice along the road a series of masonry benches, a remnant of bygone days of the Dollar Estate. You'll have view all the way—a 3-D map of San Rafael directly below and distant looks at the San Francisco skyline and Sutro Tower.

ST: San Rafael stroll (1.5 mi. to 2.75 mi.)

Immigrants of the Western world first took up full-time residence in Marin in 1817, when the Spaniards built Mission San Rafael the Archangel. Saint Raphael is the angel of bodily healing. The mission was established as a sanitarium for ill Coast Miwok and other Indians who could not recover, from illnesses brought by the Europeans, in the damp clime of San Francisco's Mission Delores. The town, now Marin's county seat, was laid out in 1850. Begin the **San Rafael stroll** by walking north on Lootens place to Fifth Street, jogging right one block to Nye Street, and continuing one block north again to Mission Street. *Note:* During weekday business hours, you may wish to pick up a San Rafael walking tour map from the San Rafael Chamber of Commerce at 817 Mission.

On Mission Avenue over the next six blocks are some ten buildings rated exceptional or excellent by the California Office of Historical Preservation: At 823-825 Mission is a Queen Anne Victorian built in 1881; at 828 Mission is a Stick-Eastlake house, built in 1884 and once the home of the city's first mayor; at 907 Mission is another Stick-Eastlake, built in 1880 on Fourth Street and moved to this site in 1903; at 1130 Mission is the Coleman House, built between 1849 and 1852, the oldest building in San Rafael; At Mission and B Street—the entrance to Boyd Park—is the Boyd Gate House, a High Victorian Gothic built in 1879, home to the Marin History Museum.

For a woodsy side-trip, head into Boyd Park, featuring a children's play set near the museum and a short trail leading around large redwoods. A little farther west of Boyd Park is the piece de resistance among Mission Avenue mansions: the Falkirk Cultural Center at 1408. Set on 11 acres of landscaped gardens, the 5,000-plus square-foot estate was built in 1888. In 1974, city taxpayers, led by Marin Heritage, bought the mansion, once home to steamship tycoon Robert Dollar. Today, Falkirk Cultural Center presents visual and performing arts, lectures, and art and poetry classes.

From Falkirk, backtrack and take C Street to your right one block to Fifth Street and turn left on Fifth. At 1104 Fifth is the site of Mission San Rafael Archangel. The existing church, built in 1949, is a close replica of the original Spanish Colonial structure. The mission was secularized and taken over by the civil government in 1833. It was raided for equipment, and even plants and trees, by General Mariano Vallejo, and torn down in 1861. The new church is open for mass.

From the church, head down A Street to Fourth Street, and turn right. Fourth Street is alive with a number of coffee shops, bookstores and restaurants, where you can stroll to pick out a sidewalk lunch or dinner spot. At 1108 Fourth is the Rafael Film Center, a major independent film venue for Northern California. Built originally for silent movies in 1920, and restored for talkies after a fire in 1937, the Rafael became a victim of the multiplex trend and closed down. Then filmmaker George Lucas, a Marin resident, and others helped restore the building and opened the center in 1998.

You may wish to drive the next section of the stroll, which ends at WildCare center. On foot, backtrack on Fourth Street, head right, or south, down B Street. Along B Street are four historic buildings rated from excellent to exceptional: The addresses are 848, 840, 810, and 724—all originally built the early 1880s. Cross busy Second Street, and into the palm-tree lined entrance to Albert Park. Walk past the large field and then left to WildCare center at 76 Albert Park Lane.

Founded by Elizabeth Terwilliger, the grandame of Marin environmental conservation, WildCare gives treatment to thousands of orphaned and sick birds and wild critters. They also provide classes and nature hikes for thousands of children and adults throughout the Bay Area. Once inside the center's gates, you are in an oasis among herons, pelicans, hawks, egrets—raccoons, squirrels, who knows—on the grounds of the wildlife hospital.

MB: San Rafael has marginal bike routes. To head west toward **San Anselmo**, take Mission Avenue, just north of Fifth Street. Turn left on H Street and right on Fourth Street. Cross the busy intersection and turn right on West End Avenue. West End merges with Greenfield Avenue, which you can take to San Anselmo; see TH46.

Falkirk Cultural Center, WildCare

To **Greenbrae and Kentfield**, take D Street south from San Rafael. D Street becomes Wolfe Grade, which goes over a hill and drops down to Sir Francis Drake. To get to the Corte Madera Creek bike path, go right on Sir Francis Drake and then left on College Avenue. Look for the bike path near the post office in Kentfield.

To head north to **Terra Linda or China Camp**, go south on Mission Avenue, or Fourth Street, and turn left on Lincoln Avenue. Follow busy Lincoln all the way, past a freeway on-ramp. To China Camp, you climb partway up Puerto Suello Hill and keep right, taking a short bike lane section that connects with North San Pedro Road. Turn right on North San Pedro toward the Marin Civic Center, TH32. To Terra Linda, turn left on San Pedro, at the bottom of the bike path, and then turn right on Los Ranchitos Road. Los Ranchitos leads to Freitas Parkway, and continues north as Las Galinas Avenue to Marinwood, TH95.

*Special Interest: *Kids:* Children will enjoy a trip to WildCare, or a field trip to one of Marin's wildlife areas. Toddlers will love Boyd Park's play area under the redwoods.

32.   PEACOCK GAP   H, MB, J

Best for: Take a jetty walk onto San Rafael Bay; or hike up 1,000 feet to look down on it from some of San Pedro Ridge's secluded trailheads.

Parking: From Highway 101, coming from either north or south of San Rafael, take the central San Rafael exit. Head east on Second St., a one-way street. Second blends with Third St., which in turn becomes Pt. San Pedro Rd. *Note*: This trailhead has several access points, which are listed below in succession, heading from west to east on Pt. San Pedro Rd.

Agency: San Rafael Community Services Department; China Camp State Park; Marin County Department of Parks; *Special Interest: Kayaks, Kids

H: **Loch Lomond Jetty (1.25 mi.); Main Dr. to San Pedro Mountain (3.75 mi.); Knight Drive to: San Pedro Mountain (3 mi.), or Bay View Trail loop (2 mi.); McNears Beach (up to 1 mi.); Biscayne Drive-Shoreline Trail loop (4.75 mi.)**

The Peacock Gap trailhead covers the uplands and shore of San Rafael Bay, beginning from the south at San Rafael Creek and extending north to Point San Pedro. The **Loch Lomond Jetty** takes you onto the harbor to a spot less than a half-mile from Marin Islands. Continue east on Pt. San Pedro Road and turn right on Loch Lomond Drive. Go all the way to the left in the marina parking lot, where you'll see the path leading out to the jetty. Marin Islands were a last refuge for Coast Miwok—led by a warrior later called Chief Marin—who tried to fight off Mexican soldiers in 1824.

To hike **San Pedro Mountain from Main Drive**, turn left on Main Drive off Pt. San Pedro Road, which is after Bayview. This is a less traveled, scenic hike. Take Main up to its end, under eucalyptus trees with a gated fire road going up to your left. This access is through Harry A. Barbier Park, San Rafael's undeveloped open space adjacent to the south side of China Camp State Park. You climb more than 800 feet, if you make the San Pedro Summit.

Bear right a short distance from the trailhead; the left road is a spur coming in from the end of Bayview Drive. The road ascends fairly steeply, soon coming to open oak-and-grass hillsides with big bay views. Stay on the main road, Bay Hills Fire Road, ignoring side trails and roads. After about .75-mile, and a 400-foot gain, you'll level out on open hills studded with oaks—a good turnaround spot for those not wishing to make the top. The road then enters dry forest and climbs steeply on the last surge to the ridge. On top, you come to a roughly paved ridge road. To San Pedro Mountain, go right on the road, passing the big fenced antenna. After an undulating .25-mile, the road goes over the top of the mountain, which is a large, flat clearing fringed by madrone and oak trees.

For **both Knight Drive hikes**, which access the upper east side of China Camp State Park, turn left on Knight Drive, just past Main Drive off Pt. San Pedro Road. Take Knight to its end at the top and park at a gate. A steep connector trail brings you from the gate to China Camp trail signs. Go left on the main fire road, toward the Back Ranch Fire Road junction, .75-mile distant. For the **Bay View Trail loop** hike, turn right when you get to the fire road. You descend about 200 feet over a short distance, and then intersect the Bay View Trail. Turn right on Bay View and begin an eastward contour, mainly through madrone and oak forest back to the Knight Drive trailhead. To continue to **San Pedro Mountain from Knight Drive**, walk past the Back Ranch Road junction, ascending about 200 feet on a half-mile segment. You reach the San Pedro Ridge Fire Road. Turn left, or south, on the paved ridge road, grunting up 100 feet steeply and briefly to the rounded top of San Pedro Mountain.

To **McNears Beach County Park**, 55 acres of beachfront on the San Pablo Bay, turn right on Cantera Way. The turnoff is up the hill from Point San Pedro, occupied primarily by historic McNears Brickyard. Tons of red brick were barged from here to build San Francisco. Nearby, G.F. Steigerwalt's concrete block company provided much of the material that was used to help re-build Pearl Harbor. McNears Beach, the county's most popular park, features a seasonal swimming pool, sand beach, picnic areas—and a fishing pier that juts 500 feet into San Pablo Bay. *Note:* Admission fees are required for all use.

The **Biscayne Drive-Shoreline Trail loop** begins at the east boundary to China Camp State Park. Pass Cantera Way. At the top of the rise, park on the left at the intersection of Biscayne Drive and Pt. San Pedro Road. Or, just as your make a left on Biscayne, park at a gate. Both parking areas have trails that lead to the same point. You soon cross the state park boundary on the Shoreline Trail. After a pleasant woodland contour, the Shoreline Trail reaches the ranger station at Bullhead Flat. Cross the road and take the trail up on the other side. Continue west, to your right, on the Shoreline Trail past the Peacock Gap Trail junction. After another 1.5-miles—walking with tree-filtered views from 100 feet above San Pablo Bay—you come to the Miwok Trail. Turn on the Miwok Trail and begin chugging up about 400 feet over .75-mile, where you join the Oak Fire Trail. Head east, or to your left, on this rugged, higher contour. After another .75-mile you reach the spur trail from McNears Drive, and then switchback down to the Peacock Gap Trail. Go left on this trail to the ranger station, where you rejoin the Shoreline Trail. *Be Aware:* Poison oak does well throughout the area.

MB: Road cyclists can take San Pedro Road around the point to the **Marin Civic Center** and circle back to the south side of San Pedro via Grand Avenue. See TH35. For a hefty pump up **San Pedro Mountain**, use the Main Drive access in the hiking description above. From just north of the top of the mountain, turn right from the ridge trail, coming to Knight Drive. Then descend on asphalt to Pt. San Pedro Road. Return to Main Drive to complete a loop of 6 miles, with some 1,000 feet in elevation gain. From the paved ridge trail at the top of the Main Drive access, you can turn left and, .25-mile later, go right down **Gold Hill Grade** to the Dominican University Campus. From there, take Grand to Third Street, and go left toward Peacock Gap.

J: Only the fittest runners will enjoy taking to the high trails listed above. For a more moderate cross-country run, try the Shoreline Trail from the Biscayne Drive access. For a bayside run, along a multi-use path next to Pt. San Pedro, park just after Main Drive.

Special Interest: Kayaks: Access San Rafael Bay and Marin Islands from Loch Lomond. Or access San Pablo Bay from McNears Beach County Park. *Kids:* Peacock Gap Neighborhood Park, at the end of Biscayne Drive, has a large rolling lawn and a big playset. You can also take the little people for a walk. The park is close to the Peacock Gap Trail, off Biscayne at Partridge Drive. The short walk up to a viewpoint will be an adventure for active kids.

33.   CHINA CAMP   H, MB

Best for: A full day trip: Picnic or stroll along several miles of bay coastline trails and bluffs, visit a historic fishing village, or venture inland on woodland trails spread out over 1,500 acres.

Parking: *From south of San Rafael* on Hwy. 101, take the central San Rafael exit and then turn right Second St., which blends with Third St. Continue east as Third becomes Pt. San Pedro Rd. East boundary of the park is about 5 miles from Highway 101. *From north of San Rafael on Hwy. 101*, take the Marin Civic

Center-N. San Pedro Rd. exit. Drive east on N. San Pedro for about 3 miles, to west boundary of China Camp. *Notes:* China Camp State Park covers about 3 miles of shoreline with numerous access points. Hiking descriptions below are referenced from the east boundary. Parking fees may be required at some areas.

Agency: China Camp State Park; *Special Interest: Kayaks; Camping

H: **China Camp Village-Rat Cove (up to .75-mi.); Bullhead Flat loop (3.75 mi.); Chicken Coop Hill (.25-mi.); Turtle Back loop (1 mi.); Back Ranch Meadows loop (4.5 mi.).**

In the early 1800s, this area and surrounding hills became part of a large Mexican ranchero. In the late 1850s, when ranchero grantee Timoteo Murphy died, the area was subdivided, and in 1868 the present-day park was purchased by George McNear—whose descendents today run the brickyard on San Pedro Point. In the 1870s, some 10,000 Chinese grass shrimp fishermen lived along the coves and beaches of San Pablo Bay. A few buildings, a dock, and foundations remain—as does shrimp fisherman Frank Quan, the village's only resident and descendent of the early shrimpers. The state purchased the China Camp acreage in 1977.

To explore **China Camp Village**—and take the short walk to adjacent **Rat Rock Cove**—turn right about .5-mile from the park's east boundary. The trail to the cove is one-tenth of a mile west of the top of the road down to the village. You'll see tiny Rat Rock,

China Camp Village

one of the shrimping spots, a short distance offshore. The village site is down the road. The camp's plank pier and vintage buildings will give you a sense of history. To make the history come alive, stop at the China Camp snack shop and talk to Georgette Quan, Frank's cousin, or drop by the building complex on the water to talk to one of the park's informed docents. A grassy picnic area sits on a knoll above the village.

The **Bullhead Flat loop**, which gives you a look at coastal as well as woodland flora, is about a mile from the park's east boundary. Park at the beach parking or on the road, and walk in a short distance to the ranger station. Take the trailhead up to your right along split-rail fencing, and keep right, on the Shoreline Trail. After almost 2 miles on this contour, 100 feet or less above sea level, turn left on the Miwok Trail. After some 400 feet of climbing over the next .5-mile, you'll come to the Bay View Trail. Turn left, returning to Bullhead Flat, a mile away over a rough contour. *Note:* Bay View Trail and Oak Ridge Fire Road run close together along this last part of the hike, intersecting in two places. Both routes wind up back where you want to be.

The short walk to the top of **Chicken Coop Hill**, a knoll with a good bay view, begins about 2 miles from the east boundary—across from the road into Miwok Meadow. Start to your left as you face the hill. A trail curves around to the bay side and then to the oak-studded top. The **Turtle Back loop** is the best wetlands walk in China Camp. Begin 2.5 miles from the east boundary, or just .5-mile in from the west. A nature trail encircles the oak island, with interpretive signs along the way. Off the tip of Turtle Back, is smaller Jakes Island.

For the **Back Ranch Meadows loop**, the most strenuous hike for this trailhead, begin at the campground entrance that is about .25-mile from the west boundary of the park. Go to the left of the ranger station and you'll see Back Ranch Fire Road, a reddish scar going straight up the hillside. Start up this road, beginning nearly 600 feet of upping, the last part on switchbacks. Near the top, you join the Bay View Trail— China Camp's high trail contour. Go to your right. After .5-mile you'll come to a

Jakes Island, aprés-trail bikewash

junction leading to Bayhills, which you pass, keeping right. You'll dip in and out on a contour toward the bay through leafy forest. About .75-mile past the Bayhills junction—and where a power-line road goes to your left—you begin a quick descent via switchbacks, coming out near the campground entrance.

MB: San Pedro Ridge is a popular mountain biking area that can be accessed from all points on the compass; you'll also want to check out TH34, San Pedro Mountain Preserve, and TH32, Peacock Gap. For a relatively leisurely ride through China Camp State Park, try a **Shoreline Trail loop** of about 6 miles. Start at either the entrance to Back Ranch Meadows Campground on the west end of the park, or at Bullhead Flat Ranger Station. From either, get on the Shoreline Trail, which dips in and out of woodlands, making a contour about 100 feet above shoreline. You can return via San Pedro Road to your starting point.

For a more ambitious **Bay View Trail loop**, start at the Back Ranch Campground Road. Take the Shoreline Trail to the right of the gate at the road. In less than .25-mile, take the Bay View Trail to your right. After about .25-mile, the Bay View Trail begins a series of switchbacks, gaining almost 200 feet in short order. At the beginning of the switchbacks, you have an option of taking Powerline Road to your right; this road takes the climb on a big, sweeping turn and joins the Bay View Trail. Either way, after the elevation gain, you continue a fairly steep ascent of some 300 feet over the next .75-mile—where you pass a Bay View Trail spur that leads to Bayhills Road and the Nike platforms. The Bay View Trail follows a ragged contour, passing the Back Ranch Fire Trail. About a mile past this junction, turn left, going downhill on a segment of the Ridge Fire Trail that joins the Miwok Fire Trail. Keep left at the Miwok junction and drop down another 300 feet, reaching the Shoreline Trail. Go left on the Shoreline Trail, for your return to Back Ranch.

*Special Interest: *Kayaks:* Bullhead Flat parking area is the best place to put in kayaks to paddle San Pablo Bay. You can also launch at Camp Village. *Camping:* Back Ranch Meadows, near the park's west boundary, has 30 walk-in campsites. Reservations may be made up to 7 months in advance; some sites are available daily on a first-come basis.

34.   SAN PEDRO MOUNTAIN PRESERVE   H, MB

Best for: A short drive to long hikes up San Pedro Ridge—through oak, laurel, and the ridge's only redwoods—to big views from San Pablo Bay to Tamalpais.

Parking: *North side access:* From Hwy. 101, take the Marin Civic Center-N. San Pedro Rd. exit and proceed east on N. San Pedro Rd. *South side access:* Coming from south of San Rafael on Hwy. 101, take the central San Rafael exit; turn right on Second St. and then make first left, on Grand Ave. Coming from north of San Rafael on Hwy. 101, take the central San Rafael exit, turn left at first opportunity, and then turn left again, on Grand Ave. *Note:* North and south access points are referenced in hiking description below. *Bus:* GGT route 23

Agency: Marin County Open Space District; San Rafael Community Services.

H: **North side access: Bayhills Drive to Nike viewing platform loop (2.75 mi.); Woodoaks Trail (2 mi.); San Pedro Ridge via Scettrini Fire Road (4.5 mi.); South side access: San Pedro Ridge via Aquinas Fire Road (3.5 mi.); Gold Hill Grade to San Pedro Mountain (4 mi.)**

San Pedro Mountain Open Space Preserve is about 350 acres comprising the western-most portion of a San Pedro Ridge landmass that also includes China Camp State Park and San Rafael's undeveloped Harry A. Barbier Park. Combined, these three parklands are almost 2,500 acres. The county began purchase of the preserve in 1971, staving off ever-present pressure for residential development.

North side access: The **Bayhills Drive to Nike platform loop** begins up a paved road that is closed to all but local residents, and leads to a splendid viewing platform. Just past Vendola Drive on your left, turn right on Sunny Oaks Drive. Follow the winding narrow street and turn left on Bayhills Drive. You'll find limited on-street parking at the MCOSD gate, at the end of Bayhills. After about .75-mile walking up the steep road, you'll see the Bay View Trail—this is where you rejoin Bayhills after completing a loop. At the top—you gain some 700 feet on the mile-long paved section—you'll see a sign on your right, marking the San Pedro Preserve. To the left is a sign noting Harry A. Barbier Park, more than 500 acres that was purchased by the city in 1969 from "Ol' Blue Eyes," Frank Sinatra. Heading into Barbier Park, you come at once to the Nike Missile concrete platforms, which offer the best views from the San Pablo Ridge—better than the peak itself. To continue the loop, take the road leading away from the Nike platform. In less than .5-mile, you'll see a China Camp trail junction. Go left, down the Back Ranch Fire Road—but keep a lookout for Bay View Trail, which will be about one-eighth mile down on your left. Take this trail back Bayhills—making sure to bear left on a spur trail about .5-mile after joining the Bay View Trail.

The **Woodoaks Trail** is the only hike that is mostly on trail rather than a fire road. Just past the Jewish Community Center on N. San Pedro Road, turn right on Woodoaks Drive and go to the end. Park at MCOSD gate. The trail takes you up through tawny madrones and maroon manzanita, with a few redwoods thrown into the mix. When you top out at a saddle on the San Pedro Fire Road, the Nike platforms are about .75-mile to your left. These are not a style of shoe. Both **San Pablo Ridge hikes** traverse the preserve from west to east. The **Scettrini Fire Road**, on the north, involves 300-plus more feet in elevation gain. From N. San Pedro Road, make the first right, on San Pablo Avenue, then the first left, on Meadow Oaks Drive. Turn right on Village Circle and drive to the back of a quiet condo complex. Park at the gate. The road climbs more than 500 feet, largely through eucalyptus.

South side access: The **Aquinas Fire Road** climbs 300 feet to the ridge. From Grand Avenue, turn right on Mountain View Avenue. Then, in a series of quick maneuvers, turn left on Sienna, right on Dominican Drive, and right again on Aquinas Drive. Park at the top of Aquinas. Both ridge hikes bring you to the San Pedro Fire Road about 1.25 miles from the eastern boundary of the open space.

For the **Gold Hill Grade to San Pedro Mountain** hike, you enter from Barbier Park and not the county open space. From Grand Avenue, at Dominican University, turn right on Locust and then veer left on Gold Hill Grade Road. Park at the end, at un-signed gate with a road leading up under a eucalyptus-and-laurel overstory. The Gold Hill hike, perhaps the best in this trailhead, features a mixed woodland forest, including a few redwoods. You'll reach a paved utility road that services the telecommunications towers on the ridge. Turn left. After a short distance you pass the road coming in from the Main Drive access in Peacock Gap, and after another .5-mile you reach the unremarkable top of San Pedro Mountain, elevation 1,058 feet.

MB: All roads on San Pedro Ridge are well used by cyclists and all require an initial climb. For an intermediate ride, try an **Aquinas-Gold Hill loop**, which involves about 600 feet of upping over a 3.5-mile course. Start at the Aquinas trailhead, which is very steep at the beginning. Then head along the ridge fire road, entering Barbier Park and passing the Nike platforms on the paved road. About .25-mile beyond the platforms, pass a trail on your left that leads to China Camp, after which you make a short, steep ascent to San Pedro Mountain. Continue south off the mountain and avoid any left-turning options. Just before the paved road ends, at a telecommunications installation, hang a right and descend Gold Hill Grade. At the bottom, ride back out to Grand Avenue and finish the last portion of the loop on pavement.

For a longer ride, but with the same elevation gain, try an **Aquinas-Main Drive Access loop**. This 7.5-mile loop takes you over the top of San Pedro Mountain, exactly as described above—only you make a left on a fire road before reaching Gold Hill Grade. This road—coming up from Main Drive-Bayview in Peacock Gap—is about .25-mile south of San Pedro Mountain, located at the mini-power tower with satellite dishes hanging on it. After dropping 800 feet, very steeply at times, over a mile-long run, you hit pavement. Head down surface streets to Pt. San Pedro Road, on which you turn right and ride all the way back to Grand Avenue.

35.   MARIN CIVIC CENTER   H, ST, MB, J, R

> **Best for:** Stroll Frank Lloyd Wright's futuristic, architectural work of art; or take a short hike with the shorebirds at your choice of three marsh and lagoon parks.

Parking: From Hwy. 101, take the Marin Civic Center-N. San Pedro Rd. exit. Turn left at first light, which is Civic Center Dr., and then turn right on Armory Dr., just past post office. Follow signs to Civic Center Lagoon Park. *Bus:* GGT routes 1, 23

Agency: Marin County Open Space District; Marin Department of Parks; *Special Interest: Kids

H: Civic Center Lagoon Park (up to 1 mi.); Santa Margarita Island loop (.25-mi.); Santa Venetia Marsh loop (1.25 mi.)

Paths go around both the lagoon and rolling lawn at **Civic Center Lagoon Park**— totaling about a mile if you walk both. Noontime strollers usually roam the park's 20 acres, descending from civic center offices. Picnic tables and trees at one end of the lagoon create quiet spots among frolicking waterfowl and gulls, while a bridge at the east end gives you an open-water look back toward the civic center.

Santa Margarita Island is an oak-studded, 9-acre preserve surrounded by the waters of Gallinas Creek. Drive from the Marin Civic Center on N. San Pedro Road about .75-mile, turn left on Meadow Drive, and continue to the end. The oversized bridge to the tiny island was constructed by a would-be developer, prior to the county's purchase of the island in 1978. **Santa Venetia Marsh** is another open space preserve. From the civic center, drive almost 2 miles farther east on N. San Pedro Road and turn left on Vendola Way. Park at the end of Vendola. The marsh loop is along a levee that protects the Santa Venetia homes, which are below sea level, from flooding. On the far end of the loop walk is a good spot for viewing shorebirds and waterfowl. Across Gallinas Creek is McInnis Park, TH36.

ST: Marin Civic Center

To the **Marin Civic Center**, turn left off Civic Center Drive, on the road that takes you up to and under the building. Renowned architect Frank Lloyd Wright was 90 years old in 1957 when he designed the sleek building, although he didn't live to see its completion in 1969. A central, 80-foot-diameter dome is flanked by two wings—one 584 feet in length and the other 880 feet. Inside are open atriums, four-stories high. Wright designed the low-slung civic center to "bridge these hills with graceful arches." Wright artfully realized his organic intent, although some say the center's signature bright blue roofs don't quite match the sky. The Marin County Civic Center is a National Historic Landmark. Some of the recent sci-fi flick *Gattaca* was filmed here. A cafeteria, open to all, features an outdoor picnic area. Docent-led tours are given weekly.

MB: The Marin Civic Center is a crossroads of sorts for trans-Marin cycling. To go **north toward Terra Linda and Lucas Valley**, ride under the freeway on N. San Pedro Road and turn right on Los Ranchitos, which later becomes Las Gallinas Avenue. To head **south toward San Rafael**, go under the freeway on N. San Pedro and turn left on Merrydale. A bike path connects the top of Merrydale with Lincoln Avenue in San Rafael. From Lincoln, if you want to ride the bay shore via Shoreline Park to Larkspur Landing, turn left on Linden, following a sign that points to Dominican University. Linden goes under the freeway in a short tunnel to Grand Avenue. You then turn right on Grand. See Shoreline Park, TH30. To downtown San Rafael, turn right off Lincoln on Mission Avenue. See also San Rafael, TH31.

J: Civic Center Lagoon Park and Santa Venetia Marsh both serve as flat running tracks about a mile around, for runners who wish to train in a circle but don't want the monotony of a track.

R: **Strollers and Wheelchairs:** Feed the ducks and geese on a spin around the Civic Center Lagoon. The Civic Center building is also wheel accessible. Take the elevator to the top floor, close to the continuous skylight that beams rays down on the four-story atrium. The parking lot below the north side of the building is the site of a twice weekly farmers' market featuring fresh local produce and flowers.

*Special Interest: *Kids:* A children's area is beautifully situated in trees and water, with ducks flapping about, near the entrance to Civic Center Lagoon Park. Children might also be enchanted by the mini-walk around Santa Margarita Island.

36.   MC INNIS PARK   H, MB, J, R

Best for: A large marsh where the confluence of two creeks and wildlife ponds combine for one of Marin's best places to explore wetland ecology.

Parking: From just north of San Rafael on Hwy. 101, take the Lucas Valley Rd.-Smith Ranch Rd. exit and drive 1 mi. east on Smith Ranch Rd. to park entrance. Park at Lot 2, to your right after passing entrance sign. *Note:* Other parking areas described below.

Agency: Marin County Department of Parks; *Special Interest: Kayaks

H: **McInnis Marsh to: Gallinas Creek confluence (1.5 mi.), or McInnis loop(3.5 mi.); Las Gallinas Wildlife Ponds loop (up to 2.5 mi.)**

McInnis is a 441-acre park that includes a developed area with four playing fields, a golf course, picnic areas, and four tennis courts, all surrounded by the wetlands of San Pablo Bay. The park is adjacent to additional public marshlands, which combined make more than 800 acres of open space. For **both McInnis Marsh hikes**, head out on the road with the golf course's trees on your left and the creek canal on your right.

McInnis Park

After about .75-mile, you reach a creek-side bench that overlooks the **confluence of Gallinas Creek** and its south forks. Mount Tam rises in the background.

For the **McInnis loop,** continue past the bench bearing right. In less than .25-mile, you come to a fork. Go right along the creek banks toward Santa Venetia Marsh. The trail then heads toward the bay for a while, but loops back well before you get to the shore. About .5-mile later, look to your left for a return trail back toward the bench and confluence. It's difficult to get lost, since these routes are on levees.

The **Wildlife Pond loop** is a wide path around three reclamation ponds. You need to drive left, rather than into the park. Go past the county honor farm, following signs to Public Shore, reaching the Las Gallinas Valley Sanitary District. Being near a treatment plant is not a great selling point for the hike, but the birds love this 385-acre open. The Audubon Society has cataloged almost 200 species of birds around the ponds. You can make varying length loops by taking connector paths between the ponds, or make the grand circle around all three. *Additional Access:* A path extends eastward away from the far end of the loop route. This public trail hooks north toward Hamilton Field, about 1.5 miles away.

MB: You'd cover more than 8 miles of marshland levee exploring McInnis Park and the Las Gallinas ponds by bicycle—a good way to get to know the area. A seldom-pedaled path is the one from the Las Gallinas ponds to Hamilton Field.

J: All the hikes described above are well suited for running—flat, long distance tracks with fairly even footing. You can vary your route in many other ways than those described above, lessening monotony. Runners may enjoy McInnis Park the most among recreational users.

R: **Strollers:** Surfaces are not always smooth. Avoid this park after heavy rains, but the paths are popular among jogging Moms & Dads with babes on wheels.

Special Interest: Kayaks: A boat dock and ramp near trailhead parking in McInnis Park provide excellent access to Gallinas Creek, and out to San Pablo Bay. Beyond the mouth of the creek is the China Camp State Park coastline.

37.   OLD HAMILTON FIELD   MB

Best for: Bike tours lead into the past beside the rolling lawns of tile-roofed bungalows on this Spanish-style, retired military base; or ride along a levee to preview what is planned to be the largest wetland park in the Bay Area.

Parking: From Hwy. 101, take the Hamilton Field-Nave Blvd, exit. Go north on Nave Blvd. and then turn right on Main Gate Rd. Veer left on Palm Dr. and then veer right on S. Palm Dr. Follow S. Palm to stop sign and turn right on Hangar Ave. Follow Hangar to its end, at a small park across from Stern Dr.

Agency: City of Novato

MB: Perimeter Levee loop (3.25 mi.); Old Hamilton Tour (1.5 mi.)

Begun as an Army Air Corps base in 1935, Hamilton Field today is transitioning to a dense, high-end residential development, surrounded by more than 2,600 acres of wetlands. Plans are underway to restore the marsh. For the **Perimeter Levee loop**, proceed just past the park and keep to your left. The levee road, bordered by a low wall, runs behind the outermost block of new homes and continues northward for more than a mile, passing the huge hangars that are being converted to an industrial park. At the far end of the levee road is where MCOSD plans a preserve. All to the east and north as you ride, are lands proposed for wetlands restoration. *Note:* From the southeast corner of levee road is a route that goes south to McInnis Park.

For the **Old Hamilton Tour**, backtrack on Hangar Avenue and turn left on San Pablo and then, at the circle, go left on Sunset Drive. You'll pass the old Officers Club and Historic Spanish Housing. Continue up Sunset, reaching another circle, where you can ride up Buena Vista, a cul-de-sac, for an even better view. As you ride back down, veer right at Las Lomas around in a circle that takes you out to Oakwood Drive. Follow woodsy Oakwood down to the circle and take N. Oakwood out the opposite side. On your right, you'll see signs noting the old amphitheater and church, where you can cut through and drop back down to Hangar Avenue. *Note:* Old Hamilton's roads connect at odd angles; you may be better off following your nose around, rather than paying attention to street signs. Plan on getting semi-lost.

38. BEL MARIN KEYS   H, MB, J, R

Best for: Walk, pedal or run along a large lagoon and through a huge wetland to the shores of the San Pablo Bay.

Parking: From Hwy. 101 take the Ignacio Blvd.-Bel Marin Keys exit and turn right on Bel Marin Keys Blvd. Follow the boulevard for almost 2 miles, passing Pacheco Pond, and park on the right in an unimproved lot near the water just before entering the Bel Marin Keys residential area.

Agency: County of Marin; California Department of Fish & Game

H: Bel Marin Keys lagoon (2.5 mi.); San Pablo Bay (5.25 mi.)

Bel Marin Keys is a residential community surrounded by a system of lagoons that are fed, via locks, by Novato Creek. **For both hikes,** head through the opening in a chain link fence, taking the broad, unpaved path that runs along the water's edge. To your

Bel Marin Keys marsh

right, or south, are agricultural lands, oft-slated for development, that now appear to be included in a proposed wetlands restoration. You'll curl around the south shore of the wide lagoon, headed for a large stand of eucalyptus trees—at a ramshackle homestead that is the end of the **Bel Marin Keys lagoon hike**.

To **San Pablo Bay**, turn right, following the road when you reach the first stand of eucalyptus. The road continues due east along a canal. In the distance, you'll see a small structure, which is an old pump house at the shore of San Pablo Bay. But you won't be able to see water until you get there and walk up to the levee. The last few steps take you to a vast sheet of water eastward and thousands of acres of marshlands spreading out to the west. Just south of the mouth of both Petaluma River and Novato Creek is where fish congregate, so you may see hunting shorebirds or a curious sea lion.

MB: Park at scenic **Pacheco Pond** and ride to **San Pablo Bay**, as described in hike above. Curious cyclists will also find other roads, heading south toward Hamilton Field. Bel Marin Keys is a low-key family bike outing. *Be Aware:* Some roads are private; heed signs.

To head **northbound toward Novato**, turn left on Frosty Lane, just as Bel Marin Keys Boulevard bends to the right, or east. A dedicated bike path runs .75-mile north along a railroad easement, under Hwy. 37 to Hanna Ranch Road, which is just south of the Vintage Shopping Center on Rowland Avenue in Novato. Ride up, next to the freeway, to the end of Hanna Ranch Road, and drop down to Rowland via some unsigned and unsightly dirt roads. From here you can go north on Rowland, turn right on Rowland Way, and connect with Novato.

J: If you're looking for a flat, 5-mile run along water that has a pleasing destination, the San Pablo Bay hike route will be to your liking.

R: **Wheelchairs:** Although you want to avoid this path after heavy rains, you'll most often find good rolling on this wide, flat route. The broad swathe of water, frequented by white egrets and other birds, and an elevated look across the wetlands make this a good choice. **Strollers:** Whether walking or pushing on the run, both hikes described above are good for tots on wheels. You'll find rougher going past the lagoon, heading out toward the bay.

39.   BLACK POINT   H, J

Best for: A levee walk in a wildlife preserve in the northeastern corner of Marin, where an oak island sits at the mouth of the Petaluma River.

Parking: From Hwy. 101, take Hwy. 37 toward Vallejo. Turn right, opposite at Atherton Ave., and go toward Black Point on Harbor Dr. Then turn right on

Grandview Ave. and follow for 1 mi. through narrow residential streets—making a sharp right at "five corners" after .5-mi. Park at the gate, on street, at the end of Grandview. *Note:* Additional parking area described in hiking section.

Agency: California Fish & Game; Marin Department of Parks; *Special Interest: Kayaks

H: Day Island levee (1.75 mi.); Day Island Lagoon and Petaluma River view (1.25 mi.)

From 1865 to 1891, when the Navy logged oaks from the high ground at the point to build its shipyards at Mare Island just to the north, Black Point was the main post office for Novato and northern Marin. Now the eastern tip of Black Point is a State Wildlife Area. Plenty of oaks have returned, which attract woodland birds, while shorebirds flock to two lagoons. For the **Day Island levee** hike, take a grassy road to your right after coming through the gate from the parking area. This road makes a short inland loop around a marshy area. You'll come to a levee where a gated road goes to your right. Walk left, toward the oak knoll of Day Island, which is about .5-mile away. Across marshland to the south is Novato Creek and Bel Marin Keys. Nearing Day Island, the trail passes one of the wildlife area's lagoons and then climbs a short distance, up through oak forests and coming to an unpaved Day Island Road.

For **Day Island Lagoon and Petaluma River view**, drive to the main entrance of the wildlife area. Just after making the right turn on Grandview, turn left on Iolanthus Avenue and then, after a long .25-mile, turn right again on funky Norton Avenue. Park on street outside the gate at Norton-Day Island Road. The wide, unpaved road soon breaks into the open as you pass the lagoon on your left and make a short climb up into the oak knoll that is Day Island. Bear left when you have a choice and follow the road to its end. *Note:* Private residences in this area; heed signs.

J: This is one of the more remote places in Marin. The wide roads of Day Island are probably better suited for runners than hikers. Use the Grandview gate and try the loop hike, with a side trip to the end of the road to look toward the river.

Special Interest: Kayaks: Black Point Boat Launch is a one-acre Marin County park at the mouth of the Petaluma River, and beneath the superstructure of Highway 37. To get there, stay on Harbor Drive, which loops around under the highway. Paddlers can head up the Petaluma River, along the banks of the Petaluma Marsh Wildlife Area, or out toward the San Pablo Bay, where the shore immediately north of the river mouth is a National Wildlife Area. Fishing boats, sail boats, tides and currents all must be considered when venturing into these waters. *Note:* Parking fee required.

40. DEER ISLAND   H, J

Best for: A wealth of flora and fauna on this 135-acre oak knoll that rises from the wetlands—a quick getaway for an afternoon run or sunrise hike.

Parking: From Hwy. 101 in Novato, take the DeLong Ave. exit. Go west on De Long, toward Novato, turn right at light on Redwood Blvd. Follow Redwood .5-mile and turn right on Olive Ave. Follow Olive for 1.5 mi. and turn right on Deer Island Ln. Park at end at MCOSD gate.

Agency: Marin County Open Space District; *Special Interests: Kids

H: Deer Island perimeter loop (2 mi.); Deer Island crest loop (1.75 mi.)

Deer Island truly was surrounded by water—the flood plane of Novato Creek and the high tides of San Pablo Bay—until the late 1800s. Novato's marshlands were dried out by a series of dikes and canals, and made into pasturelands. Some of the old structures around the perimeter of the island date from the dairy days. A host of ground critters—squirrels, raccoons, skunks, coyote—are common in the preserve, joining the island's namesake. For the **Deer Island perimeter loop**, start to your right from the MCOSD gate, which is near some unappealing warehouse buildings. Pass the De Borba Trail on the left and, after about .25-mile, pass a spur trail on your right that goes out to a knoll. The perimeter trail continues at the toe of the oak-studded hills, with marsh and pasturelands spreading to the south. Curl inland to laurel and oak woodlands, and pass the De Borba Trail coming down from the top about .75-mile from the trailhead.

For the **Deer Island crest loop**, start to your right from the MCOSD gate, but take De Borba Trail that goes up and to your left after a short distance. After about .5-mile you reach a junction with the Arnold Baptiste Trail—a short spur to your right that runs along the crest of the island. The De Borba Trail switchbacks down to join the perimeter trail. A pond, near the eucalyptus grove at the base of the trail, is an active area for wildlife viewing, if you sit and be quiet for a while. *Be Aware:* Poison oak does well on Deer Island. Also, avoid unofficial trails in this small preserve, as erosion is harming flora.

J: The Deer Island loop is popular among cross-country runners. Some people like a double loop: Do the perimeter run, around to the start, and then take the De Borba Trail up and over. This double loop, without doing the Baptiste Trail at the crest, is about 3.75 miles, with some 175 feet of elevation gain.

*Special Interests: *Kids:* The Deer Island loop is short enough not to wear young kids out, but long enough to give them a sense of accomplishment.

Rush Creek

41. RUSH CREEK   H, MB, J

Best for: With a wildlife marsh spreading to the north beneath a 300-foot-high oak ridge, hikers and joggers will see—and hear—a wide assortment of birds, along with woodland critters that descend from the hills to visit the creek.

Parking: From Hwy. 101 in north Novato, take the San Marin Dr.-Atherton Ave. exit. From Atherton Ave., make an immediate left on Binford Rd., a frontage road. Park at MCOSD gate about .25-mi. from Atherton. *Note:* Additional parking described in hiking section. *Bus:* GGT route 80

Agency: Marin County Open Space District

H: **Rush Creek loop (3.75 mi.); Pinheiro Ridge Fire Road loop (2.75 mi.)**

Until the late 1800s, the trail along Rush Creek marked the boundary between two large Mexican land grants: Rancho Olompali to the north and Rancho Novato to the south. Rush Creek, which flows just north of today's trail through marshlands, was used to barge supplies about 5 miles downstream to the Petaluma River, and then onto the San Pablo Bay. The Marin County Open Space District established the preserve in

1986. The preserve, in effect, is made larger by some 200 adjacent acres to the north, which are part of the Rush Creek Marsh Wildlife Area.

For the **Rush Creek loop**, start down Pinheiro Fire Road, named after an early settler. The reeds and marsh grasses of meandering Rush Creek will be on your left, and the oak and laurel ridge rises to your right. Numerous species of birds flit about in this transition habitat. After about 1.25-mile you reach a fork. Take the levee trail to the left onto the marsh, beginning a loop around the lagoon. Across the levee, go right on the Rush Creek Fire Road, heading now on the opposite side of the lagoon, for about .5-mile, where you rejoin the Pinheiro Road.

The **Pinheiro Ridge loop** provides a look at the oak hills of the preserve as well as the marsh loop portion of Rush Creek. You need to use a different trailhead: Continue east on Atherton Avenue from Highway 101 for about a mile, and turn left on Saddle Wood Drive, which is just before Bugeia Lane. From Saddle Wood, look for the MCOSD gate on your left near Trailview Court. You'll see the Pinheiro Ridge Fire Road heading up the ridge toward a large water tank. You hike up about 200 feet into oak grasslands and then drop down to the lagoon that is described above.

MB: Rush Creek Open Space Preserve is open to bicyclists, although too small to be considered a biking area.

J: The Rush Creek loop is an easy-access jogging trail that will be a favorite among north Marin cross-country runners. Runners seeking more of a challenge can run the Pinheiro Ridge Fire Road around the ridge, using the Atherton Avenue trail to the right at the Binford gate, although this route brings you into closer contact with homes and traffic.

*Civic Center lagoon,
poison oak*

Mt. Tamalpais

Muir Woods

If gold can be said to have built San Francisco, then the rainwater that fell upon Tamalpais formed Marin. Meaning "Bay Mountain" in the language of the Coast Miwok, Tamalpais is steeply fissured. From its peak, steep ridges radiate in all directions, covered by a thicket of greenery that is nourished by subtropical amounts of rain—60- to 90-inches yearly is not uncommon. California's first publicly owned water district, the Marin Municipal Water District, was formed here in 1912, insuring equal water for all and effectively preserving the entire watershed of Tamalpais from any activity that would spoil the supply.

Tamalpais has always drawn people who love to hike, and the mountain stands as testament to how this attraction can be held as most valuable in the sensibilities of a community. While San Francisco drew seekers of gold, The Sleeping Maiden, as the mountain's silhouette has been dubbed, allured lovers of nature. This appreciation of nature translated directly into land use, as Tamalpais was the site of the state's first official park, a flourishing tourist trade, and one of the nation's first national monuments.

Muir Woods National Monument, a large grove of virgin redwoods, was due to be logged in 1905. But William and Elizabeth Kent stepped in, bought the place, and gave it to the public. Similar redwood groves in Larkspur and Mill Valley, which were more conveniently located, had already been made into boards. Today, a million or more people visit the monument yearly, paying a small entrance fee that over the years adds up to far more income than would have been gained by cutting the trees down.

Ridgecrest Boulevard

*Baltimore Canyon,
lupine, summer in Fairfax*

In 1928, the public's love of Tam's natural qualities was again evident, when Mount Tamalpais State Park was created, the first in California. The park includes the mountain's three peaks, the mixed conifer forests that envelop Muir Woods, and the high oak-and-grass ridges that slope westward to the Pacific. On the coast, Stinson Beach was a popular camping spot, at a time when camping was a new phenomenon in America. It was later made a state park and then included in the Golden Gate National Recreation Area.

The beginnings of Mount Tamalpais State Park were the hiking clubs and tourist railways around the turn of the twentieth century. Marin was a vacation retreat, an island getaway of sorts, for people who ferried over from San Francisco. In the 1890s nature lovers waited in line for tickets on the train from Mill Valley to the Tavern at the top of Tamalpais. And in the early 1900s, tourists in newfangled automobiles paid good money to travel Ridgecrest Boulevard along the shoulder of the mountain, named "California's Most Scenic Road." During the same period, European-Americans, drawing upon their outdoor traditions, built trails and established clubs, like the Tamalpais Conservation Club, California Alpine Club, and Tourist Club—whose members not only enjoyed the mountain but also were instrumental in preserving it.

This movement—harmonizing the values of nature with those of commerce near a cosmopolitan city—continued well into the twentieth century, when the Bolinas Ridge west of Tamalpais, as well as large areas of West Marin and San Francisco, were made part of the Golden Gate National Recreation Area. Millions of visitors each year spend tourist dollars on both the manmade attractions of San Francisco and the wonders of Tamalpais that nature has provided for free.

The trailheads in this section circle the mountain, starting in the north at Fairfax, with access to the lake-reservoirs—Lagunitas, Alpine and Bon Tempe—in a relatively remote slope of the watershed. From Fairfax also is access to forested open space preserves in Cascade Canyon and Deer Park. The towns that rim the peak, heading around to the east—San Anselmo, Ross, Larkspur, Corte Madera and Mill Valley—all have a history that involves outdoor recreation in early Marin. Today, all have access to Marin County Open Space Preserves, with ridges, creeks, and forests that fan from the mountain. Each town has a different personality.

The Sleeping Maiden's sunny face—one familiar to those viewing it from San Francisco—includes Muir Woods National Monument, Mount Tamalpais State Park, and the high trails of the Marin Municipal Water District, including both Coast Miwok routes and the paths blazed by the early hikers. The west slope of Tamalpais is where the Bolinas Ridge falls to the Pacific, and includes Stinson Beach and Audubon Canyon Ranch.

Old Mill Park,
Corte Madera Ridge, Stinson Beach

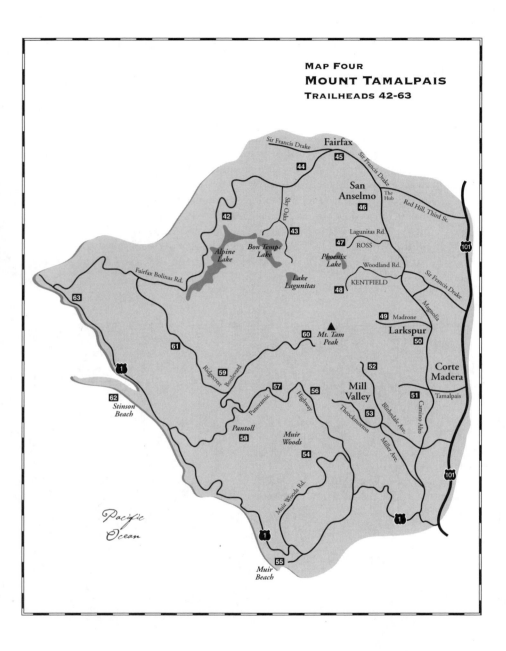

MAP FOUR
MOUNT TAMALPAIS
TRAILHEADS 42-63

Sir Francis Drake

Fairfax
45
44

Sir Francis Drake

San
Anselmo
46

The Hub

Red Hill, Third St.

Sky Oaks

42
43

Lagunitas Rd.

47   ROSS

Alpine
Lake

Bon Tempe
Lake

Phoenix
Lake

Woodland Rd.

Sir Francis Drake

Fairfax Bolinas Rd.

Lake
Lagunitas

KENTFIELD

48

101

63

Magnolia

49   Madrone

60   Mt. Tam
Peak

Larkspur

50

61

52

Corte
Madera

Ridgecrest   Boulevard

59

57   56

Mill
Valley

51   Tampalpais

1

62
Stinson
Beach

Panoramic

Highway

Throckmorton

53

Blithedale Ave.

Camino Alto

Miller Ave.

Pantoll
58

Muir
Woods

54

101

1

Pacific
Ocean

Muir
Woods
Rd.

1

55
Muir
Beach

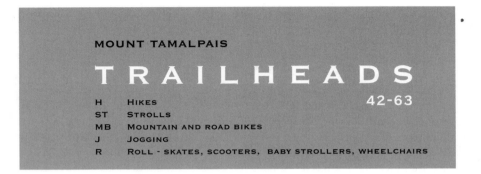

MOUNT TAMALPAIS

T R A I L H E A D S
42-63

H	HIKES
ST	STROLLS
MB	MOUNTAIN AND ROAD BIKES
J	JOGGING
R	ROLL - SKATES, SCOOTERS, BABY STROLLERS, WHEELCHAIRS

All hike and stroll distances are ROUND TRIP except as noted for shuttles.
Please contact Agency to obtain current rules and regulations. See Resource Links for all telephone numbers.
See also special Doggie Trails section.

42.   ALPINE LAKE   H, MB

Best for: Remote Marin vistas from 1,500-foot-high ridge tops with peculiar geology and trees; or a white-water creek, deep in a conifer forest reminiscent of the Pacific Northwest.

Parking: From Hwy. 101, take San Anselmo-Sir Francis Drake Blvd. exit and proceed on Sir Francis Drake about 6 mi., past San Anselmo. *Note:* From north Marin, take the central San Rafael exit and go east on Third St. to San Anselmo, where you join Sir Francis Drake Blvd. At Fairfax, veer left on Broadway, to center of town, and turn left on Bolinas Rd. Continue winding up 3 miles on Bolinas Rd. It becomes Fairfax-Bolinas Rd. Pass Meadow Club Golf Course and the MMWD gate. *For Pine Mountain hikes:* Park on left at trailhead 1.25 mi. after entering the MMWD gate. *For Alpine Lake hikes:* Park at Alpine Dam about 5.25 mi. after entering the watershed lands. *Note:* MMWD gates close in the evening and reopen in the morning.

Agency: Marin Municipal Water District

H: Pine Mountain trailhead to: Azalea Hill (.75-mi.), or Pine Mountain summit (5 mi.), or Sargent cypress grove (3.75 mi.), or Oat Hill Ridge (up to 9 mi.); Alpine Dam hikes to: Kent Lake view (4 mi.), or Cataract Creek and Laurel Dell (3.25 mi.)

From Pine Mountain parking: For **Azalea Hill**, a short walk with a huge view, head up the road that is on the same side of the street as the parking area. The road curls to the east side of the hill, rising about 150 feet on the short hike to the 1,217-foot top. The trail continues down to Bon Tempe Meadow at Sky Oaks Ranger Station.

For **Pine Mountain, Sargent cypress grove** and **Oat Hill Ridge**, head out rocky Pine Mountain Road, across the street from the parking area. On open chaparral, you ascend straight and fairly steeply over the first mile, climbing more than 200 feet, where you reach a road junction.

To **Oat Hill Ridge**, turn left at this junction. Oat Hill is the ridge running back toward Alpine Lake that you can see on your left during the first part of the hike. During the next 1.5 mile, heading south, you drop down to a saddle and then up again, through a gap between two 1,400-foot, tree-covered peaks: Liberty on your left and Cliff on your right. About 1.75-miles from Pine Mountain Road, the Old Vee Road drops to the right toward Kent Lake. The trail continues in deep fir forest, another mile south along the ridge. You emerge in an open oak forest. Veer left at a fork near the end that leads to short uphill walk to Oat Hill, a grassy mound with views down more than 600 feet to Alpine Lake. You'll often see raptors soaring below.

For **Pine Mountain**—one of Marin's best peak walks—continue straight, past the Oat Hill Road junction. After about .5-mile across the rough ridgeline, take a left on Pine Mountain Road. From the junction with the San Geronimo Road to Pine Mountain, you climb almost 300 feet in .75-mile. At 1,762-feet, Pine Mountain is Marin's second-tallest summit on public land. Look for a very short spur trail leading right from the main trail. On the top of Pine Mountain, you will find only a humble pine sticking out of the chaparral. But take note of the low rock walls at the summit, built by Chinese laborers in the late 1800s and used to separate the rancheros.

To see the **Sargent cypress grove**—pygmy cypress trees unique to California—continue straight at the junction with Pine Mountain Road. The grove is a hedge on either side of the San Geronimo Ridge Road for .5-mile, beginning at the Pine Mountain Road junction and ending beyond the junction with Repack, or Cascade Road, which drops to the right into Cascade Canyon. These diminutive cypress smell like juniper, and you might be reminded of upper elevations of Arizona. The greenish rock you see is serpentine, an igneous—or volcanic—mineral comprised of magnesium silicate.

From Alpine Dam parking: To **Kent Lake view**, park when you first get to the dam, on the north side. Start down drably named Kent Pump Road, entering a dense mixed conifer forest. Botanists will be busy observing flora in this near-rainforest. Lagunitas Creek, which drains Lake Alpine will be down a steep embankment to your left all during the hike. At 2 miles, still about 500 feet above the lake, you'll come to the junction with the Old Vee Road, that climbs steeply to your right up to Oat Hill Ridge—you may want to turn around here. The Kent Pump Road continues for another 2.5 miles, contouring around another tentacle of the lakeshore formed by Little Carson Creek. From the Old Vee Road back to Alpine Dam, you gain almost 200 feet.

The **Cataract Creek Trail to Laurel Dell**, the most popular route at Lake Alpine, begins on the left .25-mile past, or south, of the dam. Only a few parking spots are

*Pine Mountain,
Sargent cypress*

available on Fairfax-Bolinas Road, and turning around is difficult, so you may wish to park at the dam on weekends. Water gushes over bedrock along this fern-and-conifer creek walk—leading to the picnic glade at Laurel Dell. You'll cross the creek within the first .25-mile, after which the trail climbs the hillside to the right of the creek, now a series of cascades and pools. After about .5-mile, you pass the Helen Markt Trail, which goes left back toward Alpine Lake. Almost 1.5 miles up the creek canyon, after more gushing whitewater and significant falls, the trail levels out. You then come to the junction with the High Marsh Trail, which heads on a high contour back toward Alpine and Bon Tempe lakes. Near the junction, some 700 feet above the surface of Lake Alpine, is the picnic area of Laurel Dell. Poppies, popcorn flowers, and a host of other wildflowers may join you for lunch during the springtime months. *Note:* Laurel Dell can also be reached from Ridgecrest Boulevard, TH61; Cataract Trail can be accessed from Rock Springs, TH59. *Be Aware:* Be extra careful to stay on trail, as heavy use has caused damage in places.

MB: Well-conditioned mountain bikers will like **Pine Mountain Road.** One difficult and exciting loop of wild country—of about 12 miles, with numerous up-and-downs—is to continue north of Pine Mountain Road on San Geronimo Road. Over the next 4 miles, dubbed 17 Knolls, you do some serious pedaling along the ridge, which varies between 1,200 and 1,500 feet. After passing three roads that lead to your right—the last of which drops down to Buckeye Circle in San Geronimo—turn west, or left, from what has been a northerly course. About .75-mile beyond that juncture, just west of the climb to Green Hill, you meet up with Pine Mountain Road, which drops down to your left. Pine Mountain Road begins a big loop through the Carson creeks drainage above Kent Lake. The road then turns east, up and over tall Pine Mountain, and back to the junction with San Geronimo Ridge Road.

43. SKY OAKS LAKES

Best for: Three lakes pocketed into evergreen forests of the north Tamalpais watershed, fed by numerous streams and visited by a variety of wildlife.

Parking: From Hwy. 101 take San Anselmo-Sir Francis Drake Blvd. exit and proceed west on Sir Francis Drake about 6 mi., past San Anselmo. *Note*: From north Marin, take the central San Rafael exit and go west on Third St. to San Anselmo, where you join Sir Francis Drake Blvd. At Fairfax, veer left on Broadway, to center of town, and turn left on Bolinas Rd. Continue about 2 mi., to near 799 Bolinas Rd., and turn left uphill on Sky Oaks Rd., toward MMWD's Bon Tempe Lake and Lake Lagunitas. Go almost 1 mi. to Sky Oaks Ranger Station. Note: Entrance fee charged. *For Bon Tempe Lake hikes*: Turn right about .25-mi. beyond entrance station and go another .5-mi. on Bon Tempe Rd. Park on left at bottom. *For Lake Lagunitas hikes:* Go straight from entrance station, following Sky Oaks Rd. about 1.5 mi. to large parking lot at Lake Lagunitas.

Agency: Marin Municipal Water District; *Special Interest: Fishing.

H: Bon Tempe Lake hikes to: Alpine Lake-Hidden Lake loop (5.5 mi.), or South Shore-Rocky Ridge loop (4 mi.); Lake Lagunitas hikes to: Lake Lagunitas shore loop (1.75 mi.), Pilot Knob loop (2 mi.)

Bon Tempe Lake hikes: **For all hikes**, head up a short connector road from the parking area, toward the Shadyside Trail and walk across the wide dam that forms the west shore of Bon Tempe Lake. Bon Tempe is a more recent reservoir, built in 1948—75 years after flagship Lake Lagunitas, which is out of view to the southeast, and 30 years after Alpine Lake, whose easternmost shore is visible below the dam to your right.

The **Alpine Lake-Hidden Lake loop** takes you along 2 miles of lakeshore before beginning an inland swing to the ridge above both lakes. Bear right after you cross the dam, on the Kent Trail. You begin close to lake level, but then the trail ascends through redwood and Douglas fir forest. About 2 miles from the dam, where the Helen Markt Trail continues along the lake, hang a left on the Kent Trail. You'll climb some 400 feet over the next mile, amidst redwoods, laurel and oaks—and come to the Stocking Trail, where you want to go left. Walk through a hollow containing Hidden Lake, which is now a bog, and reach Rocky Ridge Road. Go left on this road, coming to the hike's high-point and view area after a short distance. Then begin the tromp back down to lake level. *Note:* About halfway down on Rocky Ridge Road is Casey Cutoff, a shorter and steeper way to get to the bottom.

For the **South shore-Rocky Ridge loop**, go left after crossing the dam, on the Shadyside Trail. You'll dip in and out along the dimpled shore, staying fairly close to the water in a thick conifer and broadleaf forest; the variety of trees on this walk is remarkable.

After about a mile, you reach the Lower Berry Trail, where you go right. You'll climb fast, about 250 feet in less than .25-mile, before joining the Rock Spring-Lagunitas Road. Stay on the road, going up another 350 feet over the next .75-mile, until you reach Bay Tree Junction, where you join Rocky Ridge Road. Here you go right, or north, and begin a steady descent to Bon Tempe Dam. *Additional Access:* Rock Spring-Lagunitas Road continues south, climbing and reaching Mountain Theater, TH59, after about 2.5 miles.

Lake Lagunitas hikes: The **Lake Lagunitas shoreline loop** is a lovely lakeshore walk among redwoods, ferns, and a variety of trees. Cross the bridge to the far right in the parking area. Then bear left on the road, ascending gradually through mossy forest. You'll come to the dam, which has a decked viewing area that can be crossed to make a short loop back to the parking area. Continue, with the lake to your left, walking under the boughs of large Douglas fir and crossing a series of footbridges. After the third bridge, you reach Lakeview Road—a drier area with madrones and oaks. After .25-mile on the road, bear left at a picnic area and take a trail that leads back to the dam. From the dam, walk down through the redwoods to trailhead parking.

On the **Pilot Knob loop** you'll get splendid views of Lake Lag and vistas all the way to the East Bay. Take the Lakeview Road that heads east, away from the picnic area, just as you enter the trailhead parking area. *Note:* You could also walk up the road to the left of the stream from the parking lot to the dam, and bear left on a trail to join Lakeview Road. In either case, after about .5-mile, make sure to stay left on Lakeview, rather than go right on the road that goes around the lake. In another .5-mile, go left on Pilot Knob Trail. The trail rises gradually through oak, madrone, and some firs for about .25-mile—to where a spur trail leads left. The spur trail goes to 1,200-foot Pilot Knob, taking you up some 250 feet in short order. Backtrack down the spur trail, and go left again, passing lovely madrones, and rejoin Lakeview Road.

MB: The Sky Oaks lakes are on the circuit for loop rides that connect with Phoenix Lake, TH47. For one short and interesting option—of a little more than 3 miles—begin on **Concrete Pipe Road**, which goes south from Bolinas Road from the intersection with Sky Oaks Road. You'll see a gate, with limited on-street parking. After about 1.5 miles of contour, you reach Five Corners, above Phoenix Lake. Turn right, up Shaver Grade, climbing about 250 feet in .5-mile. You come to Sky Oaks, where you turn right and ride out to Bolinas Road. You might do this loop in combo with taking the continuation of Concrete Pipe Road on the other side of Bolinas Road—which is sometimes called Pine Mountain Tunnel Road. You ride a wiggling contour for about 1.5 miles, to Happersberger Point, which overlooks Cascade Canyon.

Another Sky Oaks' option is to bomb down **Southern Marin Line Road,** that takes off to the east—from just north of the Lake Lagunitas parking area. You drop down almost 200 feet and come to Eldridge Grade after about 1.25 miles. Go left on Eldridge, dipping down and then up a little, covering .75-miles and reaching Five Corners.

From Five Corners you can go short and steep to the left on Shaver Grade to Sky Oaks Road; or veer left and contour on Concrete Pipe Road, out to Bolinas Road. From Bolinas Road you go left up Sky Oaks Road about 1.5 miles back to the Southern Marin Line Road. The long version, via Concrete Pipe, is about 6 miles.

Hardcore mountain bikers like the **Rocky Ridge Road** that takes off to the south from the Bon Tempe Dam, heading toward Rock Spring up on Mt. Tam; see TH59.

J: Both Lake Lagunitas and Pilot Knob are excellent cross-country jogging routes. The easier and prettier is the lake run.

R: **Wheelchairs:** The MMWD has constructed a wheelchair lake access at Pine Point, which is on the east shore of Bon Tempe Lake—take the road toward Lake Lagunitas. Bon Tempe Meadows, accessed via a parking area to the right just after the Sky Oaks Ranger Station, is a level path suitable for off-pavement chair rides. **Strollers:** The Lake Lagunitas loop is cross-country terrain, but woodsy Moms & Dads will enjoy pushing a stroller on this trail.

*Special Interest: *Fishing:* Permitted in Lake Lagunitas and Bon Tempe Lake; call MMWD for permit information.

44.   CASCADE CANYON   H, MB, J

Best for: A tucked-away nature preserve close to Fairfax, featuring a cascading creek and trails to the steep ridges that rise above it.

Parking: From Hwy. 101 take San Anselmo-Sir Francis Drake Blvd. exit and proceed west on Sir Francis Drake about 6 mi., past San Anselmo. *Note:* From north Marin, take the central San Rafael exit and go west on Third St. to San Anselmo, where you join Sir Francis Drake Blvd. At Fairfax, veer left on Broadway, to center of town, and turn left on Bolinas Rd. After a short .5-mi. on Bolinas Rd., veer right on Cascade Dr. to end. Limited on-street parking.

Agency: Marin County Open Space District

H: Elliott Nature Preserve (.5-mi.); Cascade Falls (1.75 mi.); Cascade Canyon Road to Sargent cypress forest (5.5 mi.)

The **Elliott Nature Preserve** is an inviting glade just beyond the entrance to Cascade Canyon Preserve, washed by Cascade Creek and fringed by Douglas fir, oak, and madrone. A trail, broken at times by the creek's high water flows, leads through the center; a road goes to the same place but stays out of the creek bed. **For both hikes**, continue straight, avoiding left-side trail options that lead on rutted routes to Carey Camp Trail and Happersberger Point. You'll reach a bridge, a little more than .5-mile from the trailhead. **For Cascade Falls**, cross the bridge and veer right up the creek. You'll ascend gradually for about .25-mile before reaching the falls—a 15-foot-high cataract spilling over shaded bedrock into a pool. *Additional Access:* The road going up to your right before crossing the bridge loops back up toward Blue Ridge Road.

On the **Cascade Canyon Road to Sargent cypress forest** hike, you climb 1,200 feet to the open San Geronimo Ridge Road, near Pine Mountain. Go left on road after crossing the bridge. At the outset, avoid a spur trail to the left that heads up San Anselmo Creek. Continue up Cascade Canyon Road, the reddish scar you can see from the Elliott Nature Preserve. It is also called Repack Road because its bumpy surface causes cyclists to repack their wheel bearings after coming down. After 2 miles of a direct assault on the ridge, mostly through chaparral, you come upon San Geronimo Fire Road. Going left here would connect you with Pine Mountain Road, TH42. To the left and right of the junction, you are in the Sargent cypress forest; the dwarf conifers are unique to California, some of which are more than 100 years old.

*Additional Access: A*ccess to upper Cascade Canyon is off Toyon Drive: Turn right off Cascade Drive at stop sign on Laurel Drive. Follow steep, winding Laurel, turn right on Oak and follow to Toyon Drive. Turn left on Toyon and park at MCOSD gate near 90 Toyon, with limited on-street spaces. The Toyon Trail goes up steeply and connects with the Blue Ridge Fire Road, which continues toward White Hill. In the first .5-mile, keep left and avoid other options that lead toward private Camp Tamarancho.

MB: Thrill seekers who want to find out why they call it **Repack Road** can try a 5-mile **Cascade Canyon loop**, a little more than half of which is via surface streets. Park on Cascade Drive, where it veers off Bolinas Road, and start riding up Bolinas. About 3 miles later—after climbing 700 feet over 1.25 miles and entering MMWD lands—turn right at trailhead for Pine Mountain Road. Take this rocky road, pumping up 400 feet and passing the Oat Hill Road on your left. Go straight on San Geronimo Road as Pine Mountain makes a left. About .25-mile later, look for Repack Road, a.k.a. Cascade Canyon Road, going down to your right. Hang on down to the bottom, cross the bridge at Cascade Creek and ride out to the MCOSD trailhead at Cascade Drive. It's about 1.5 miles to rejoin Bolinas Road.

Yahoo cyclists can also charge up **Blue Ridge Road**, via Middle Fire Road, which takes off to your right just before the bridge on Cascade Creek, as described in hiking section. Blue Ridge Road takes you over **White Hill** and then connects with San Geronimo Ridge Road a mile north of Repack Road. You turn left on San Geronimo Road, climb 1,000 feet, and reach Repack—your return route. The route up to White Hill from Cascade Canyon via Blue Ridge is a steep rollercoaster.

J: If you feel like some serious communing with nature on a cross-country run, strap on your mud-shoes during or after a rainstorm and head up to Cascade Falls.

45. FAIRFAX

Best for: Find an organic snack or offbeat gift in bohemian Fairfax, followed by a hike or bike ride at nearby Deer Park, a redwood-studded gateway to the Mt. Tam watershed.

Parking: From Hwy. 101 take San Anselmo-Sir Francis Drake Blvd. exit and proceed west on Sir Francis Drake about 6 mi., past San Anselmo. *Note*: From north Marin, take the central San Rafael exit and go west on Third St. to San Anselmo, where you join Sir Francis Drake Blvd. At Fairfax, park in long lot between Sir Francis Drake and Broadway. *For Deer Park:* From Broadway, turn left at stop sign on Bolinas Rd. and go about .5-mi. to veer left on Porteous Ave. Follow Porteous through neighborhoods and park at lot in trees just before Deer Park School. *Bus:* GGT route 23

Agency: Marin County Department of Parks; Town of Fairfax.

H: Bald Hill (3 mi.); Deer Park Ridge Trail loop (1.5 mi.); Yolanda Trail loop to Phoenix Lake (6 mi.)

Deer Park is a wooded 54-acre county park, enveloped by the Mount Tam watershed. To **Bald Hill**—for an overview of San Anselmo and the Ross Valley—go to your right, through the gate and around the school. Then go left across the field. Take Deer Park Trail, snaking up about 600 feet through mixed broadleaf forest for about .75-mile, coming to Worn Springs Road. Go right, curving along a ridge for another .75-mile. You'll gain a few hundred feet and break out to a grassy dome. Avoid a left-forking fire road, just to the north of the top. Bald Hill sits at 1,141 feet, an elevation that allows you to see detail of the towns below, and yet feel high above them. And you get an intimate look at Tamalpais, just three miles away as the hawk flies.

For the **Deer Park Ridge loop**, a woodsy twirl through the creek's varied flora, go to your right from the picnic-parking area before entering the school grounds. Take the

Fairfax

trail from the back of the picnic area up the creek through redwoods. The trail rises through oak, madrone, redwoods, fir, and an occasional pine, up some 400 feet on a .5-mile course. You then descend somewhat to Boy Scout Junction—where an absurd number of trails join. You want take a left option, down Deer Park Road. Another trail, Six Points Trail, drops down to nearly the same place, and you won't go wrong if you end up taking it. Once at the creek, amid the mint-colored moss dangling from oak trees and a jumble of vines, go left on Deer Park Road.

The **Yolanda Trail loop to Phoenix Lake** takes you on a woodsy walk to vistas from Bald Hill. From the parking, cut around to the right through the school grounds and go straight across the field to Deer Park Road. After about .5-mile along creek, go left on Six Points Trail, and stay on it for .5-mile, up a few hundred feet to the Yolanda Trail. Take the Yolanda Trail to your right, following a rough contour, for 1.25 miles. Cut left on a short connector trail just before, and above, the shores of Phoenix Lake. The connector trail takes you to Worn Springs Road, where you go left, on the return leg. You make lazy switchbacks northward, ascending 900 feet, right over the top of Bald Hill. About .75-mile after dropping down the north side of Bald Hill, look for the Yolanda Trail on your left. Take the mile-long contour that goes back to Six Points, your trail back down.

ST: Fairfax (.5-mi.)

In 1839 Fairfax was part of a 6,500-acre Mexican land grant. This genteel estate was acquired in 1855 by Lord Charles Snowden Fairfax, a British royal who was lured west by the Gold Rush, leaving a little estate his family owned back east—called Virginia. Fairfax, a politico and congenial host, gave the town its resort reputation, which was maintained after his death in 1869. His estate became Pastori's Hotel & Restaurant, and later the Marin Town & Country Club, which stands today, although in a decrepit state. The town was a movie mill during the early 1900s, when Bronco Billy Anderson cranked out westerns filmed in the area. In 1917, when the Alpine Dam was constructed, Italian workers arrived, giving it the "Little Italy" designation, and spawning bars and restaurants, some of which remain. Fairfax embraced the Hippies in the early 1970s, and, today, its shops and restaurants exude an organic, laid-back atmosphere.

For the **Fairfax stroll**, cross Broadway to the vintage Tamalpais Theater and turn right. From Broadway, turn left, heading up Bolinas Road for several blocks, ducking in and out of quirky shops. Then go across the street to the Fairfax Pavilion—you'll see it sitting up behind a green space and redwood trees. The Pavilion stands in Fairfax Park, what remains of the original 65-acre plot around which the town was built. From Fairfax Park, head back down Bolinas Road, and then hang a left on Broadway, which is interesting for another block or so.

MB: To get to **San Anselmo and Ross**—and connect with the Corte Madera Creek bike path, TH28—take Broadway east out of town. When you get to the stop sign at Center Boulevard, veer right on to Landsdale. Landsdale blends into San Anselmo Avenue, which takes you all the way to San Anselmo, on a mellow residential route. At San Anselmo, you can cut right on Laurel and wind your way through residential streets on the west side of the town, or just take San Anselmo Avenue. Turn right on Bolinas Avenue and then left on Shady Lane. Shady Lane brings you into Ross. From Ross you can go right to Phoenix Lake or left behind the post office to the Corte Madera Creek bike path.

Two country-city loops are popular from Fairfax: For a **Phoenix Lake loop** of about 8 miles, ride up to Deer Park—see hiking—and take Deer Park Fire Road. After about 1.25 miles, climbing a few hundred feet, you'll come to Five Corners, where you want to take Shaver Grade down to Phoenix Lake. From the lake, ride down to the parking area and out to Lagunitas Road. Then turn left on Shady Lane, taking the route back to Fairfax described in the paragraph above.

For a shorter loop, about half on dirt, try a 5.5-mile **Sky Oaks loop**. Head to Deer Park, as described in hiking section, and pedal up the 1.25 miles to Five Corners. At Five Corners, go right on the Concrete Pipe Trail, which contours for about 1.5 miles before popping out on Bolinas Road. You then roll down Bolinas Road back to Fairfax. As a variation on this loop, you can also take Shaver Grade up from Five Corners—up about 300 feet over .5-mile—and come out on Sky Oaks Road past the ranger station. You then pedal less than a mile back out to Bolinas Road and ride back to Fairfax.

46. SAN ANSELMO   H, ST

Best for: The top of "Old Baldy," combined with a luncheon date and a stroll of the town's antique shops and theological seminary.

Parking: From Hwy. 101, take San Anselmo-Sir Francis Drake exit and go about 4 mi., through Kentfield. Turn left at Bolinas Ave. Then make immediate right on San Anselmo Ave., drive through town and park near Tamalpais Ave. *Note*: Additional parking in hiking descriptions. *Bus:* GGT route 20

Agency: City of San Anselmo; Marin County Open Space District.

H: **Bald Hill from: Redwood Road (1 mi.), or Oak Avenue (1.25 mi.)**

Bald Hill Open Space, a 32-acre preserve, was acquired by the district over a three-year period, beginning in 1994, thus preventing trophy homes from overtaking San Anselmo's landmark hill. Bald Hill can also be accessed from Phoenix Lake, TH47, and Deer Park, TH45. Below are shorter hikes from above San Anselmo.

Redwood Road provides a direct route through ferns and redwoods on a short, very steep trail. Head toward Fairfax on San Anselmo Avenue. Veer left on Center Boulevard and turn left at Redwood Road. Head up the narrow, winding road for nearly a mile. Just past 390 Redwood, on a bend, look for a MCOSD gate on your right. Begin walking up a steep hillside on a little used trail under a canopy of bay, oak, and redwoods. You'll need hands in a spot or two. You emerge at Worn Springs Road and proceed left. You'll enter MMWD lands, climbing and breaking into the open. Baldy is a 1,141-foot grassy mound—either tawny or Irish green, depending on the season. Forest green Mount Tam lies westward across a ravine. Once you've been up Bald Hill, you'll notice it from all over Marin.

The **Oak Avenue** access is near Redwood, but via an easy, connecting road rather than the steep trail. Continue on funky Redwood Road, as described above. After rounding a couple of sharp inside bends, turn right on funkier Gerlach Road, a short connector. Then make a right on Oak Avenue. You might want to drive to the top to check out the parking, which is prohibited by private drives in places, and then double-back down and park lawfully as close as you can to the top. You could add about .5-mile, round-trip, to the hike walking on pavement to the trail. Then walk up Oak past homes to the unpaved MCOSD road that will bring you up to Worn Springs Road, not far south of where the Redwood Road trail comes in. Turn left on Worn Springs, and saunter the .5-mile to the top of Bald Hill.

ST: San Anselmo (1.5 mi.)

Today, San Anselmo is the Hub, crossroads between San Rafael, Fairfax and the Ross Valley. To the Miwok, until early 1800s, the region was a hub for hunting and an encampment along San Anselmo Creek. In the mid-1800s, these same lands were the boundary zone between two Mexican land grants. After that, the town was literally called Junction, in the late 1800s, when trans-Marin railroad lines connected here. The railroad served rustic resorts along San Anselmo Creek. The town's early impetus for growth was the building of the San Francisco Theological Seminary in 1892.

From the parking at San Anselmo and Tamalpais avenues, start the **San Anselmo stroll** by walking toward town. Jog left at bridge, crossing the creek, and turn right to walk through Center Creek Park—the former camping spot for both Miwok and tourists from San Francisco. Turn right down Art Alley, crossing back over the creek, and walk left again down San Anselmo Avenue. After leaving the concentration of shops, cross over the avenue, and turn right on Mariposa Avenue. Then go left on Richmond Road, beneath the San Francisco Theological Seminary's castlelike campus. Take a long flight of stairs up to your right. You come out at Montgomery Hall. Veer left to Geneva Hall and its big sunny entrance facing Mt. Tamalpais. The ivy-covered towers of Scott and Montgomery halls are original landmarks from 1892. Double back from Geneva Hall, coming down from Seminary Hill on Kensington Road.

From Kensington, jog left on Ross Avenue, right on Sunnyside and right on Woodside—you'll be going around Wade Thomas School. On the other side of the school, go left on Crescent Road. Proceed to 237 Crescent, to Robson-Harrington mansion, built in 1910 and now a city park and community center. Head through the historic gardens and down through brick terraces with tile inlays. From the garden's street level picnic area, take Magnolia Avenue back to San Anselmo Avenue. Continue your stroll through the town, perhaps for a bargain among its antique stores.

47. PHOENIX LAKE
H, ST, MB, J, R

Best for: Avoid busy weekends and feel far away at this close-in woodsy lake, tucked into the steep folds of Tamalpais—a gateway for watershed hikes and bicycle rides.

Parking: From Hwy. 101, take Sir Francis Drake-San Anselmo exit and drive about 3 mi. to Lagunitas Rd. Turn left, continue 1 mi. through Ross to Phoenix Lake parking at end of Lagunitas Rd. *Note:* Different parking in stroll section.

Agency: Marin Municipal Water District; Town of Ross; *Special Interest: Fishing

H: Phoenix Lake shoreline loop (2 mi.); Tuckers Camp loop (4 mi.); Lake Lagunitas via Fish Gulch Trail (4 mi.)

Built in 1905, Phoenix Lake is Marin's second-oldest reservoir, some 35 years younger than Lake Lagunitas, which is just up the mountain. With an arboretum-like forest extending above it steep banks, Phoenix Lake has high aesthetic values, often appreciated by a variety of birds as well as fishermen. **For all hikes**, take the .25-mile road up from Natalie Greene Park, which lies at the entrance to MMWD lands; you can also take a beautiful trail that goes up the shaded creek. Both paths reach Phoenix Lake at the dam. For the **Phoenix Lake shoreline loop**, go left at the lake. You follow a road along the east shore for about .5-mile and then cut back to your right on the Williams Trail. This trail contours above the water—amid redwoods, bay, madrone, and ferns—for about 1.25 miles along the scalloped south shore of the lake. You then come to Phoenix Lake Fire Road, where you turn right and complete your circle of the shore.

The **Tuckers Camp loop** is a more obscure jaunt. Go left once you reach the Phoenix Lake dam. This route was used in the old days by a woodsman who worked the forests of the canyon south of the lake. At the tip of the lake, continue south on the road, which soon becomes a trail. For the next mile you climb about 500 feet, crossing minor stream drainages as you curl right around the narrow canyon. Not far beyond Tucker's campsite, you come to Eldridge Grade, where you turn right, making a swerving descent over 1.25 miles to lake level at Phoenix Lake Road.

Cascade Canyon, bay laurel

To hike to **Lake Lagunitas via Fish Gulch Trail**—a lake that can also be reached by car from Fairfax—walk to your right on Phoenix Lake Road after reaching the dam. You'll come to where Shaver Grade goes up to your right, Eldridge Grade to your left, and Fish Grade continues more-or-less straight. Go up Fish Grade, but bear right on Fish Gulch Trail that veers off it. Once you top out—now more than 500 feet above Phoenix Lake—pretty Lake Lagunitas is about .5-mile to your left. On the return trip, either retrace your route, or, for a loop, take Lakeview Road eastward from Lake Lagunitas. Lakeview drops to Eldridge Grade, where you can turn left and head down to Phoenix Lake. The Eldridge option will add another 1.5 miles to the hike.

ST: Marin Art and Garden Center (about .5-mi.)

The **Marin Art and Garden Center** entrance is across from the intersection of Sir Francis Drake and Lagunitas Road in Ross. The historic 21.5-acre center was the estate of Ross pioneers George and Annie Worn. The center's well-known octagonal house was built in 1864, and the barn on the hill—used for performances by the Ross Valley Players—also dates from the late 1800s. The gardens feature inviting benches surrounded by a leafy wonderland of blossoming shrubbery and a rainbow of flowers. On the grounds you'll also find a library and museum, restaurant, and a gift shop.

MB: Phoenix Lake is a popular biking trailhead, so much so that you should consider parking in Ross or Kentfield and biking to the lake, especially on weekends. The Corte Madera Creek bike path leads to Ross. One good loop from the lake is to **Fairfax via Five Corners.** This 8-mile run delivers a good slice of the Mount Tam watershed along with some pleasant Marin road biking. Head up to Phoenix Lake and bear right on Phoenix Lake Road. About .5-mile from the lake, go right on Shaver Grade, humping up several hundred feet in 1.25 miles to Five Corners. Go straight across at Five Corners, taking Deer Park Road another 1.25 miles down to Deer Park. Follow Porteous Avenue to Bolinas Road, and turn right to the town. In Fairfax, hang a right on Broadway. When you reach Center Boulevard, take Landsdale-San Anselmo Avenue to San Anselmo. Go through San Anselmo, turn right on Bolinas Avenue, and immediately left on Shady Lane, which takes you back to Lagunitas Road heading to Phoenix Lake.

Lake Lagunitas loop, into the higher country above Phoenix Lake, is a 5-mile run with more than 600 feet of climbing. From Phoenix Lake parking, head up to the dam, keep right and after .5-mile take Shaver Grade up to Five Corners. At Five Corners, take Shaver, climbing to the left, until you hit Sky Oaks Road—about 250 feet up over .5-mile. Go left on the paved to Southern Marin Line Road; to see the lake, continue down Sky Oaks Road and then double back. After about .25-mile down Southern Marin Line Road, veer left onto Fish Grade, which takes you very steeply down to Eldridge Grade. From Eldridge, take Phoenix Lake Road back to the lakeshore.

Additional Access: You can make a couple of variations on the above loop toward Lake Lagunitas. One is to head away from Five Corners on Concrete Pipe Road—veer left between Shaver Grade and Deer Park roads. This road contours out to Bolinas Road, where you turn left and ride Sky Oaks Road up to the Shaver Grade junction described above; this adds about 1.5 miles to the ride, but is easier pedaling. Another option is to continue down Southern Marin Line Road rather than going left on Fish Grade. This is a less steep, paved descent. Then go left on Eldridge Grade and curve back down to Phoenix Lake; this option adds about 1 mile to the ride.

J: The Phoenix Lake shoreline loop is ideal for adventure running. You'll need to pay attention to foot placement and will encounter minor undulations along an overall flat course. Aesthetic values are high, with ever-changing glimpses of the forest and lake inlets.

R: Strollers and Wheelchairs: The initial push up to Phoenix Lake from Natalie Greene Park is steep, but manageable. The road to the right along the north shore gains some elevation also, but in general this is a very good place for kids on wheels and chair-riding outdoor enthusiasts. For more manicured surroundings, with a trip to a gift shop in the offing, try the tranquil grounds of the Marin Art and Garden Center. A number of paths wind through the flora in the shade of towering trees.

*Special Interest: Fishing: Anglers shore cast at Phoenix Lake; contact MMWD for permit information.

48.   BALTIMORE CANYON   H, MB, J, R

Best for: A long contour road along the top of a lush, forested canyon; or trails to vistas from the green shoulders of Tamalpais.

Parking: From Hwy. 101, take Sir Francis Drake-San Anselmo exit and go 2 mi. to Kentfield. Turn left on College Ave. and after less than .5-mile, turn right on Woodland Ave. *For Northridge hikes:* From Woodland turn right on Goodhill Rd., follow up for a long mile, turn left on Crown Rd. and follow to end—Crown becomes Phoenix Rd. Park on street at MCOSD gate. *For Baltimore*

Canyon contour hikes: From Woodland turn left on Evergreen Dr., follow for about a mile, and turn left on Crown Rd. Park at end at MCOSD gate.

Agency: Marin County Open Space and Marin Municipal Water districts

H: **Northridge to Knob Hill (2.75 mi.); Baltimore Canyon to: Southern Marin Line contour (up to 5.75 mi.), or Hoo-Koo-E-Koo-Blithedale Ridge loop (3.5 mi.)**

Acquired over an 11-year span, the 196-acre Baltimore Canyon Open Space Preserve includes Northridge, the forked spur of Mount Tam that separates Mill Valley from Larkspur and Corte Madera. Baltimore Canyon shared boundaries with several other MCOSD preserves, as well as the huge tract of MMWD public lands.

Northridge hike: The **Knob Hill** hike begins from an appealing trailhead under redwoods, already at 600-feet in elevation. You have a choice of routes, which join about .5-mile into the hike. On your left, through the MCOSD gate is the Windy Ridge Trail, more shaded and featuring a redwood forest. On your right—the recommended route—is the Indian Fire Road, through the MMWD gate. With steep Williams Canyon, down to your right, the Indian road rises steeply, in a series of ramps and benches. You come to the Blithedale Ridge Road after about 1.25 hard miles. For Knob Hill, with San Francisco views as well as looks into Mill Valley, go left on the Blithedale Ridge Road. The hill will be to the right of the trail within about .25-mile after the junction, just after passing the Hoo-Koo-E-Koo Road, which is also on the right. *Additional Access:* You'll see Eldridge Grade across the canyon, making a rising lateral toward Tam, as you walk up Indian Fire Road. To get to the grade, keep right at the Blithedale Road junction. If you go left on Eldridge, you make switchbacks another 800 feet up, reaching Tamalpais. To the right takes you down 1,200 feet to Phoenix Lake.

Baltimore Canyon hikes: **For both hikes**, from the lower Crown Road parking, head through a MCOSD gate. For the **Southern Marin Line contour**—an unflattering name for this delightful curving path through redwood, maple, and madrone forest— just keep on truckin'. The 2.75-mile course of the road sweeps around the top of Baltimore Canyon and ends at Sunrise Lane in Corte Madera. You'll get tree-filtered looks toward the bay at San Quentin. You also pass trail and road options to both left and right. The options to the left that drop into the canyon, including Dawn Falls, are described in King Mountain, TH49. The right-heading options lead up to Blithedale Ridge—the hike described below. In all but the driest time of the year, water ripples and spews down rocky fern gardens at several places, as the road dips in and out along the steep shoulders of the ridge.

For the **Hoo-Koo-E-Koo-Blithedale Ridge loop**, which takes you up and back down about 175 feet, you need to go right on the Hoo-Koo-E-Koo Trail shortly after starting out. In thick forest, the trail—named after a band of Miwok—notches up a bit and then contours. In about a mile, you reach the Blithedale Ridge Road, with classic looks at Tamalpais over chaparral that will be blooming in the spring. Turn left on the road, go for a little less than .5-mile, and take a left again, in a shaded saddle, on the H Line Road. This fire road makes a switchback down and joins the Southern Marin Line Road near a small pumping station. Turn left and take the meandering road back—about 1.25 miles to the trailhead.

MB: Only thunder-thighs mountain bikers can hang in the pedals heading up **Indian Fire Road**. You can ride to connect with Eldridge Grade and then go right down to Phoenix Lake. From Phoenix Lake, you need to go right at Ross toward the College of Marin, and then take Woodland back up to trailhead parking. The **Southern Marin Line Road** is an excellent family ride of almost 6 miles.

J: The Southern Marin Line Road contour of Baltimore Canyon is a four-season favorite. You'll be in the shade on the sunniest of days—which is good or bad, depending on whether it's August or a morning in January.

R: **Wheelchairs and Strollers:** Try the Southern Marin Line Road. You don't have to roll the whole route to feel like you've been somewhere. This is one of the better forested wheelchair routes in Marin. You'll encounter minor hazards, such as branches and rocks, and find muddy going after rains. Jogging Moms & Dads with babes on wheels will find the run to their liking.

49.   KING MOUNTAIN   H, J

Best for: A trail around the peak of Larkspur's mini-Tamalpais; or a cool hike among ferns and redwoods to the east slope's popular falls, and the sunny ridge above it.

Parking: From Hwy. 101, take the Paradise Dr.-Tamalpais Dr. exit in Corte Madera. Go 1 mile on Tamalpais Dr., turn right on Corte Madera Ave., which becomes Magnolia Ave. At stand of redwoods in Larkspur, turn left on Madrone Ave. *For King Mountain:* Go up Madrone, turn right on Redwood Ave. and left on Oak Rd. From Oak, turn left on Wilson Way and follow to top. Park on street at end below water tank. *For Dawn Falls:* Continue on Madrone to end, stay left; it becomes Water Way. Park on street near MCOSD sign. *Note:* Additional King Mountain access described in hiking section. *Bus:* GGT route 20.

Agency: Marin County Open Space District

H: King Mountain loop (1.75 mi.); King Mountain from Citron Road (3.25 mi.); Baltimore Canyon Trail to: Dawn Falls (2.25 mi.), or Baltimore Canyon loop (2.75 mi.), or Blithedale Ridge loop (3.5 mi.) Note: All Baltimore Canyon hikes include the falls.

The **King Mountain loop** takes you on a small-scale version of Tam's varied ecosystems, ranging from oak forests to redwoods and ferns. The mountain is named for Patrick King, a rancher who in the late 1800s owned the land on which Larkspur stands. At MCOSD signs, start around to your right, at first through laurel and oaks, with views toward the Bay Bridge and San Francisco. About halfway around, you cross the Citron Fire Road. You then enter moister environs, cross a drainage with redwoods and ferns, and then begin switchbacking up steps. After topping out the steps, keep left, passing a fire road that comes in from Ridgecrest Road in Kentfield. When almost back to the trailhead, on your right you'll see the Ladybug Trail, which connects with the Baltimore Canyon hikes.

For a longer hike, try the **Citron Fire Road**, beginning near the theater in Larkspur. Turn off Magnolia Avenue on Ward Street, toward the post office, and then turn right on Hawthorne. Make a left off Hawthorne on tiny Ajax Street, and go left again on Cedar Avenue to MCOSD gate. The fire road meanders up through scrub and oak trees, before meeting the King Mountain loop trail.

The **Dawn Falls Trail** is popular, following Larkspur Creek up Baltimore Canyon beneath an overstory of redwoods, madrones, laurels, and occasional maple trees. From the parking, drop down to creek level and cross the bridge. Turn right, upstream—the trail also goes left for about .5-mile to Larkspur. In a clearing about .5-mile in, are old dam remnants. You'll climb much of the route's 200 feet over the russet tones of fallen leaves, switchbacking the last distance before reaching Dawn Falls. Two forks of the creek meet at the falls, gathering on a basalt ledge and falling about 25 feet to a pool.

For **both loop hikes**, continue up the trail above the falls, coming to the Southern Marin Line Road. For the **Baltimore Canyon loop**, go left on the pleasant contour road, continuing on a level path beneath the dimpled slopes of the ridge. Looking out from the tree tunnel, you'll catch glimpses toward the bay. After a mile—and after passing H-Line Fire Road on your right at a small pump station—look for a post marking the Barbara Spring Trail going down to your left. This trail, also called the Edwin O. Hagstrom Trail, makes a steep descent and joins the Dawn Falls Trail near the trailhead.

For the **Blithedale Ridge loop**, which breaks out to big views of Tam and the bay, continue straight across the Southern Marin Line from above Dawn Falls. The falls trail continues for a short, steep segment and joins the Hoo-Koo-E-Koo Trail. Go left, on one of Tam's better trails, and you'll reach Blithedale Ridge Road after about a mile. Go left for about .5-mile, to where the H-Line Road drops off to the left in a shaded saddle. Descend to the Southern Marin Line Road, take a right, and then start looking for the Barbara Springs-Hagstrom Trail on the left. It's marked only by a post. This steep route comes out near the trailhead parking.

J: The King Mountain loop is a ready-made, scenic running track for adventure runners. You probably want to go counterclockwise, as described in the hiking section, to run up rather than down the steps on the loop's northwest quadrant. The Dawn Falls Trail is also an excellent cross-country run—including the loop portion that takes in a stretch along Southern Marin Line Road and drops down the Barbara Springs Trail. During rains, the trail is especially dramatic.

50. LARKSPUR   H, ST, MB, J, R

Best for: A lunchtime stroll among the high-end shops and restaurants of this former redwood logging town; or a walk in the park that reveals the town's surprising origins as a port.

Parking: From Hwy. 101, take Paradise Dr.-Tamalpais Dr. exit in Corte Madera. Take Tamalpais Dr. to Corte Madera Ave. and turn right. Corte Madera Ave. becomes Magnolia Ave. Park in public lot at Ward Street and Magnolia. *For Piper Park:* Continue past Ward Street and turn right on Doherty Drive. Turn left off Doherty at police station, continue to parking lot. *Bus*: GGT route 20

Agency: City of Larkspur; *Special Interests: Kids, Kayaks

H: Piper Park loop (1.5 mi.)

The **Piper Park loop** takes you around the tree-lined grass field that leads to a point on wide Corte Madera Creek. Start on the path, with the athletic fields to your right and Larkspur Canine Commons dog park on your left. Continue out to the point, where you'll find benches to observe shorebirds and rowers on the creek. Piper Park has a number of picnic tables, ball fields, tennis courts and volleyball pits—a family picnic park. It is also home to the Larkspur Community Gardens, a veggie and flower co-op, located near the dog area at the west side of the park.

Piper Park

ST: Larkspur (up to 1 mi.)

The redwood trees along Magnolia Avenue in Larkspur and in Baltimore Canyon are the adolescents that survived the logging of old growth giants, beginning in the early 1800s. Shipments were largely to San Francisco from an official U.S. port that was designated in 1846, using Corte Madera Creek to convey the timber to the bay. The town was laid out in 1887 by C.W. Wright—whose wife is credited with naming the town after a lupine wildflower she misidentified.

Begin the **Larkspur stroll** at Ward Street. You're across Magnolia from the former Hotel Larkspur and Blue Rock Inn, constructed in 1895 with stone from a quarry in Baltimore Canyon. At 476 Cane is where the Rosebowl Dance was held every Saturday night for 50 years, ending in 1963. Continuing up Magnolia, you'll pass boutiques, cafés and restaurants—and the venerable Silver Peso Saloon which harks back to the town's bawdy origins. At the top of the rise on Magnolia is St. Patrick's Church. Beyond that landmark, at Madrone Avenue, is Dolliver Park, with play sets under tall redwoods alongside the banks of Larkspur Creek. Across the street is the Lark Creek Inn restaurant, set in an old Victorian, next to a number of gift shops set in old cottages. Head back down Magnolia to the beginning—or jog left on King Street and explore the old hillside residential area, with some streets connected by stairways.

MB: Larkspur is a pleasant crossroads for cyclists traveling central and southern Marin. To get to **Phoenix Lake** and **San Anselmo**, go down Cane Street and turn left on the bike path. At Bon Air Road, jog right, cross the road, and go over the bridge. At Corte Madera Creek, TH28, you turn left on the bike path that leads through Kentfield and on to Ross.

To get to **Shorebird Marsh**, TH27, where you can connect with **Larkspur Landing** or **Tiburon**, take the bike path behind at William Avenue, which heads east. When you reach a canal—if the bridge is not up yet—cut left to Lucky Drive. Follow Lucky toward the freeway. To Larkspur Landing, go left up the bike path on the Sir Francis Drake on-ramp, and turn right on the bike path on the other side of the creek. To Tiburon, via Paradise Drive, take the pedestrian overpass to the east side of Highway 101, and turn right on the frontage road. After the shopping area, you'll hit a bike lane that goes for miles.

To **Mill Valley**, take a right on the bike lane behind Larkspur, heading south, which comes out to Tamalpais Drive in Corte Madera. Road cyclists go over busy Camino Alto Avenue. For a safer route, and not much out of the way, roll down Tamalpais Drive toward Highway 101. Veer right on Meadowsweet, and stay near the freeway. Buena Drive is a frontage road that takes you up to the bike lane at Horse Hill. From there it's an easy pedal to Bayfront Park, TH27—with easy access to Mill Valley and Sausalito.

J: Larkspur's bike paths, along tree-lined railroad easements and canals with Tam views, are excellent running tracks. For a loop of about 2.5 miles, go down Baltimore Avenue and run left on the railroad easement path. Then veer right before Williams Avenue on the path that runs east through a field along a canal. When the path hits another canal, before reaching Tamal Vista Boulevard, go right through a chain link fence. Following a path along the canal, you'll cross Lakeside and come out at the large field at Corte Madera Town Park. From the park, take Redwood Avenue to your right to Corte Madera town. Then go right down the railroad path, before reaching Corte Madera Avenue. The railroad path takes you into Larkspur.

For a shorter run, of about 1.75 miles, head east on the Williams Avenue path, as described above, only turn left toward Redwood High School when you reach the canal. You jog out to Lucky Drive and then turn left on Community Fields Path. This path runs along the school fields and connects back with the path you ran out on.

R: **Wheelchairs and Strollers:** The Piper Park loop is easy to get to and a pleasant roll, with a water view at the end and a good look at Mount Tam on the homestretch.

Special Interest: Kids: Try Dolliver Park, at the corner of Madrone and Magnolia, with its creek-side setting under redwoods. *Kayaks:* Higgins Landing is a small crafts dock operated the City of Corte Madera. You'll find limited on-street parking, near Redwood High School, at the corner of Doherty and Lucky drives. This is access to a wide channel that branches off Corte Madera Creek.

51.   CORTE MADERA RIDGE   H, MB

Best for: Many access points on this central Marin ridge that ramps up from near the bay to the shoulders of Mount Tamalpais.

Parking: From Hwy. 101, take the Tamalpais Dr.-Paradise Dr. exit in Corte Madera. Take Tamalpais Dr. to Corte Madera Ave., and proceed straight across intersection to Redwood Ave. Follow narrow winding road and then turn left on Summit Dr. Follow even narrower, very steep Summit to the top. *Be Aware:* Few parking spaces are available at MCOSD gate; driving up this road is not for the faint of heart in large cars. *Note:* Several open spaces share boundaries in this trailhead. Additional access points are described in hiking descriptions.

Agency: Marin County Open Space District

H: **Corte Madera Ridge to Blithedale Ridge (1.75 mi.); Bob Middagh Trail-Alto Bowl (1 mi.); Horse Hill (2 mi.); Escalon Road-Lower Ridge (1.5 mi.)**

Northridge is a 1,200-foot-high buttress of Tamalpais, separating Mill Valley from Larkspur and Corte Madera. The ridge forks on its jagged descent, with the Corte Madera Ridge going more northerly. The **Corte Madera Ridge to Blithedale Ridge** hike begins at a 900-foot elevation in the Camino Alto Open Space. From the Summit Drive trailhead, you'll have vistas of the San Francisco Bay, as well as closer looks down to the green creases of Mill Valley. But the best views may be the near-yet-far looks at Tam as you make your way westward. About .5-mile into the walk, just after a redwood grove, the road descends to a saddle. You pass Huckleberry Trail, coming up on your right from the Southern Marin Line, near Sunrise Lane in Corte Madera. Then on the left is the Glen Fire Road coming up from the Warner Creek, as described in TH52. Not long after this junction, and an uphill burst, you reach the Blithedale Ridge Fire Road. You'll find some terrific view spots among oak trees, now at about 950 feet in elevation. Going right on the Blithedale Ridge Road takes you on a roller coaster, but always up, toward Knob Hill, described in TH48.

The **Bob Middagh Trail** links the upper ridge of the Camino Alto with the lower of the Alto Bowl Preserve. Go south toward Mill Valley on Corte Madera Avenue, which becomes Camino Alto—the "over the hill" route linking Corte Madera with Mill Valley. Park at the top of the hill, near Chapman Street. On your right you'll see a MCOSD gate for the Camino Alto Fire Road, and just down to the left of that is the MCOSD sign for the Middagh Trail. Not far on the Middagh Trail you'll pass under large oaks and be rewarded with San Francisco views—similar to those once enjoyed by rock 'n' roll promoter Bill Graham, who owned the Masada estate just up the hill. The trail continues along the grassy ridge, crossing over the Alto Tunnel, the now-defunct railroad route built in 1884, back in the old days when Marin had mass transportation. Farther on the trail, you pass a spur trail leading up from Upperhill Road, on the Mill Valley side. Then the Middagh Trail ends at the Alto Bowl Fire Road. This short road links Sausalito Street on the Corte Madera side with Midhill Road from the Mill Valley side. You could go right on the Alto Road, and then turn left to continue walking on the Horse Hill Road.

Horse Hill is a 400-foot climb to a grassy hill with a great view, but hampered by freeway noise. Turn left on E. Blithedale Avenue at the bottom of Camino Alto; you can also take the E. Blithedale exit from Highway 101 and drive toward Mill Valley. Either way, just east of Camino Alto, turn on Lomita. The trailhead is at a MCOSD gate, near 43 Lomita. You'll see Horse Hill Fire Road snaking its way up to the ridge. Head to your left along the ridge, the most pleasant part of the walk, under the shade of stately oak trees. The trail descends to join the Alto Bowl Fire Road—the terminus of the Middagh Trail. You'll probably want to turn around at the high-point rather than make this descent and climb back up.

The **Escalon Road-Lower Ridge** hike is a fairly flat and easily accessible hike in Camino Alto Preserve. Turn on Overhill Road, which is about .5-mile up from E. Blithedale Road on Camino Alto. Follow Overhill up and stay right to end of cul-de-sac, as

Escalon Drive goes off to left. You start out in a nice corridor of oaks and proceed straight. After less than .25-mile Escalon Road crosses Camino Alto Road; bear left. You'll get good looks at Mt. Tam peeking over Blithedale Ridge. About .75-mile into the hike, you'll reach a junction of many roads. You can continue up the ridge by bearing left, but not hard left, staying on the Middle Summit. *Additional Access:* For the longest Camino Alto hike, take the Del Casa Fire Road. To get there, take E. Blithedale past Camino Alto and turn right on Elm Avenue. Then go right on Sidney Street, left on Alvarado Avenue, right on Manor Drive—and finally left on Marlin Avenue. You'll see an unsigned gate near 115 Marlin.

MB: Camino Alto bike rides are all about steep. The best access is **Escalon Road off Overhill**, described in hike above. You can make some wonderful but strenuous loops by continuing up the Corte Madera Ridge—taking Middle Summit Road after you reach the many-points junction at the top of Escalon Fire Road. After climbing about 500 feet over a grueling .5-mile, you reach the top of Summit Drive. From there you take Corte Madera Ridge Road, dropping a little. You can then make your first major left, which takes you down **Glen Fire Road**, and then down Vista Avenue to E. Blithedale. Ride out to Camino Alto and up to Overhill. This is about a 6-mile trek.

You can also continue a little farther on Corte Madera Ridge Road and turn left to come down **Blithedale Ridge Road**. By keeping left near the bottom of the, you come out on Elinor Avenue. Elinor drops to Carmelita Avenue, the road leading into the Mill Valley Golf Course off E. Blithedale.

52.   BLITHEDALE SUMMIT   H, MB, J, R

Best for: Trails that have been hiked for a century, from redwood valleys to chaparral ridges of Tamalpais—and other view trails on public lands that are brand new.

Parking: From Hwy. 101, take E. Blithedale-Tiburon Blvd. exit and go toward Mill Valley on E. Blithedale. Pass traffic light at Camino Alto; further directions in hiking descriptions below. *Bus:* GGT route 21

Agency: Marin County Open Space and Marin Municipal Water Districts.

H: **Warner Canyon to Corte Madera Ridge from: Glen Drive (1.75 mi.), or Elinor Avenue (3 mi.); Blithedale Ridge to Corte Madera Ridge from Greenwood Way (2 mi.); W. Blithedale Park to: Blithedale Ridge loop (1.5 mi.), or Old Railroad Grade to Summit Avenue (3.5 mi.) Note: The W. Blithedale Park hikes, though listed last for ease of driving descriptions, are the most popular.**

The 561 acres of Blithedale Summit Open Space Preserve have been acquired over an 18-year span. At the trailheads, thick forests of redwood, oak, fir, and maple provide a canopy. The trails climb to the low-lying vegetation, the chaparral, on the higher points of Blithedale Ridge. The open space is next to water district lands, which have been public since the early days of Marin.

Warner Canyon, featuring a gushing creek, is the deep crease between Corte Madera and Blithedale ridges. For **Glen Drive** access, turn right on Carmelita Avenue from E. Blithedale, and right on Buena Vista. Continue to the top, keeping left—Buena Vista becomes Glen Drive; look for MCOSD gate. This is the sunny route up the canyon, on a brush-cut road fringed by oaks. You'll meet the Elinor Fire Road about halfway up the nearly 500-foot climb to a saddle in the Corte Madera Ridge.

For the **Elinor Drive** access—longer, shaded and prettier—you want to turn left on Buena Vista, after coming up Carmelita Avenue. Then turn right on Oakdale Avenue and immediately right on Elinor Avenue. Follow winding, hairy Elinor up. Park, in limited spaces, near where pavement ends. Walk down to your right and you'll come to a gate amid redwoods. About .25-mile from the first gate, where the road begins switchbacks, you pass the Tartan Road connection to your right—described in the access note below. After that, on your right, is the signed Warner Canyon Trail, which heads about .5-mile up the canyon to end a lovely cataract—an option for trailblazers. Continue on Elinor Fire Road, on sweeping switchbacks beneath tall laurels and red-woods, with ferns carpeting the hillsides. After a mile from the trailhead, you meet the Glen Fire Road and begin the last .5-mile to Corte Madera Ridge. *Additional Access:* Adventure seekers can make a loop hike: Drive up Glen Drive and turn left on Tartan Road. A path from here goes across to Elinor Fire Road, which you take up to its junction with Glen Fire Road.

The hike from **Blithedale Ridge to Corte Madera Ridge from Greenwood Way** is an open view hike with easy parking, after a fairly complicated drive. Continue into Mill Valley on E. Blithedale. Veer right on W. Blithedale Avenue, and turn right on Eldridge Avenue. Then turn right on Woodbine, twisting up, and turn left on Upland Avenue and follow to Greenwood Way. Go straight up Greenwood and park near fire road at water tank. The Blithedale Ridge Road rises over a succession of ramps and benches. Topping out, you reach the oak-studded clearing that is the junction with Corte Madera Fire Road. Over Mill Valley's treetops you can see San Francisco.

For **W. Blithedale Park** hikes—the premier access for this trailhead—take E. Blithedale into Mill Valley and veer right at the stop sign on W. Blithedale. Follow to signed, creek-side parking at gate. Both hikes begin up Old Railroad Grade, the rail bed for the 1896 single-track tourist line that made a crooked course over 22 trestles to the top of Mount Tamalpais.

For the **Blithedale Ridge loop**, start up through the tree tunnel, alongside and above the creek. After an initial elevation gain of 200 feet over .5-mile, take Horseshoe Fire Road off an outside turn. Horseshoe Road climbs 200 feet over just .25-mile to join Blithedale Ridge Road. After reaching the top, turn right on the road, and, after .25-mile, turn right again—on the H-Line or Tank Turns Road. This road drops several hundred feet, over a little more than .5-mile, to join the Old Railroad Grade near trailhead. *Additional Access:* After a short distance on Horseshoe Road, Corte Madera Creek Trail goes off to the left for about .5-mile to join the Hoo-Koo-E-Koo Trail. Turn right on the Hoo-Koo-E-Koo to join the Blithedale Ridge Road. The creek trail option lengthens this loop hike by about a mile and 300 feet of elevation.

The **Old Railroad Grade to Summit Avenue** hike follows the lower part of the old train route. On the way, you get good panoramic views of Mill Valley and the bay. Continue around the bend from Horseshoe Fire Road. The road dips in and out of sunny, exposed contours below the East Peak of Tam before coming to Summit Avenue above Mill Valley, which is described in TH53. The upper portion of the walk is in low chaparral which allows for good vistas.

MB: Blithedale Park is a good biking trailhead. One popular **loop of Blithedale Ridge** is to take the H-line or Tank Turns Road, up to the right just after setting out on Old Railroad Grade. After paying a price of about 300 feet on this .75-mile connector, you hit Blithedale Ridge Road. From there you roll right, 1.5-miles down the spine, veering right before the end to come down the Greenwood Way access. You drop down Greenwood, via Upland, Woodbine, and Eldridge, to Blithedale Avenue—which you ride back to the park. This loop is about 4 miles. You can also do an **Old Railroad Grade loop**, the first part of which is described in the hiking section. Ride down Summit Avenue after reaching it from the Old Railroad Grade. In Mill Valley, take Throckmorton through town for a short distance, and then ride left on W. Blithedale to the trailhead parking. This 6-mile loop is on surface roads for some 4 miles.

Cyclists also make a loop out of **Elinor and Blithedale Ridge roads**. The tricky part is connecting between the two. You want to start at the Greenwood access, go up the ridge, and hang a right on Corte Madera Ridge Road. Then come down the Glen Fire Road at the saddle—veering right partway down on Elinor. After coming out the gate at the bottom of Elinor, look for the short connector going up to your right behind the fire hydrant and gas meter. This short trail brings you back to Blithedale Ridge Road.

J: Cross-country runners will like Old Railroad Grade. It's a workout, but not so steep that the downhill part will tear up the knees.

R: **Strollers and Wheelchairs**: Old Railroad Grade from Blithedale Park is a nice wide path—assuredly uphill but not too steep—under pleasant tree cover and beside the creek. The segment to Horseshoe Fire Road—about 1.25 miles round-trip, gives you a good slice of the canyon.

53.   MILL VALLEY

Best for: Marin's reigning capital of hip & cool—always good for an enter-taining evening stroll—is also steeped in hiking tradition, with clubs and races that go back a century or more.

Parking: From Hwy. 101 take E. Blithedale-Tiburon Blvd. exit and drive about 2 miles to park near the corner of Blithedale and Throckmorton Ave.; or, from south of Mill Valley on Hwy. 101, take Hwy. 1-Stinson Beach exit and turn right on Almonte Blvd. Almonte becomes Miller Ave.; continue to Mill Valley, turn right on Throckmorton and park at Blithedale. *Note:* You might end up parking a block or three away from this intersection. *Bus:* GGT routes 10, 21

Agency: Mill Valley, Parks & Recreation; Marin Municipal Water District; *Special Interest: Kids

H: **Old Railroad Grade loop from Summit Ave. (2.25 mi.); Cascade Falls (.75-mi.); Dipsea Trail Steps (.5-mi.)**

The **Old Railroad Grade loop** begins at a 1,000-foot-high trailhead, from which you may also hike to Tam's East Peak. You'll need to drive. Go down Throckmorton to Old Mill Park. Jog right on Old Mill Street, left on Lovell Avenue and then right on Sum-mit Avenue. Follow winding, narrow Summit, to a junction with Fern Canyon; here, a gravel road to the right leads to Old Railroad Grade coming up from Blithedale Park, TH52. Continue driving left, now on Fern Canyon, another .25-mile to where the road ends. Park on street at one of 10 or 12 spots. Head through the MMWD gate, on this inviting redwood fringed portion of upper Old Railroad Grade. In about .75-mile, keep right when passing the Gravity Car Grade road coming up from Mountain

Mill Valley

Home, TH56. Continue for another .25-mile and go right on Hoo-Koo-E-Koo Road. On your left at this junction, you'll see the Vic Haun Trail; this trail makes a direct approach to the top of Tam, over about 1.25 miles and 1,400-feet of elevation. Meanwhile, back on Hoo-Koo-E-Koo, after .5-mile you'll come to the Temelpa Trail, which you take down to your right; the Temelpa Trail also goes left, steeply and directly toward Tam, meeting the Vic Haun Trail. Taking the Temelpa Trail down, you hit pavement and need to go right about .25-mile to trailhead parking.

For **Cascade Falls**, which fueled Mill Valley's historic mills, drive up Throckmorton past Old Mill Park. Throckmorton ends and you veer right on Cascade Avenue. You'll see the Cascade Falls trailhead sign on your right. The short, mossy trail leads up the creek to the falls, through a dark redwood forest. This is an easy hike to combine with a stroll of Mill Valley.

The **Dipsea Trail Steps**, some 675 of them, are at the beginning portion of the venerable 6.8-mile race from Mill Valley to Stinson Beach. Start at Old Mill Park on Throckmorton. Walk through the park on Cascade Drive, across Molino Avenue, and up a continuation of dead-end Cascade Way. You'll see the first 330-plus flight of stairs that lead to little Millside Lane. Jog right on Millside to Marion Avenue, at the beginning of which you'll see the second 200-plus staircase, this one leading up to Hazel Avenue. You go left on Hazel and then right up the remaining 140 steps that take you to busy Edgewood Avenue. The Dipsea Trail is really only a complete trail on race day, since it hits pavement at a number of places. Dipsea greats include Sal Vasquez, Jack Kirk, and Vic Sagues.

ST: Mill Valley (1 mi.)

Mill Valley's lands first were possessed by John Reed, courtesy of a Mexican land grant in 1834—acquired using the time-honored tradition of marrying the commandant's daughter. Mill Valley was the first Marin grant. It was made by the Presidio's Jose Antonio Sanchez in deference not only to daughter Hilaria's hand in marriage, but also in exchange for many board-feet of redwood that were to help build the garrison, courtesy of Reed's sawmills that gave the town its name. Logging was king here for the remainder of the century and into the next. But leisure, too, has always been a Mill Valley pursuit. Tourist railroads, resorts and taverns date from the late 1800s and early 1900s. Mill Valley's Dipsea Race was begun in 1905, second in seniority only to the Boston Marathon. In more recent times the Mill Valley Film Festival has become the flagship among many events that bring tourists to a town where the person who steams your cappuccino may well have penned the next hot screenplay.

Begin the **Mill Valley stroll** at the corner of Throckmorton and Blithedale. Right there is the Mill Valley Outdoor Art Club, designed in 1905 by Bernard Maybeck. Across the street is the Mt. Carmel Catholic Church, whose copper spire and 18-foot gold-leaf cross is the tallest in the country. Walk down Throckmorton—the stroll takes you up one side of Throckmorton, to Old Mill Park and the library, and back down the other. On your left is El Paseo, with its winding brick passage and just beyond that is the Mill Valley Theater, the main venue during the film festival.

Opposite the redwoods in the center of town is Lytton Plaza. The plaza is the center of things: the starting point for the Dipsea Race, the former railroad and bus depot, and currently ground-zero for hanging out. Cross the street and keep heading up Throckmorton. You'll leave the shops and eateries and come upon Old Mill Park, a few blocks up. The park is home to the remnants of Reed's historic sawmill, and of one of the old railroad cars. Backtrack down Throckmorton, catching the stuff you missed while walking up the other side of the street.

MB: For a mellow, neighborhood ride to **Richardson Bayfront,** TH2—with easy bike path links to Sausalito or north to Corte-Madera Larkspur—take Miller Avenue from Mill Valley and turn left on Sunnyside. From Sunnyside, go right on Laurelwood and continue as that street blends with Presidio Avenue. Presidio takes you to Millwood, where you jog left out to E. Blithedale for a short distance, and then veer right on to Sycamore Avenue. Sycamore takes you to Bayfront, crossing busy Camino Alto very near the park. To ride **Old Railroad Grade** up toward Mt. Tam, see TH52, Blithedale Summit.

*Special Interest: *Kids:* Cascade Falls will be an adventure for children, as will playing under the redwoods in Old Mill Park. Moms & Dads should also check out Boyle Park, which is off E. Blithedale coming into town; its large, open grounds feature lots of play stuff.

54. MUIR WOODS   H, MB, R

> **Best for:**   Feel small among behemoth redwoods; or hike above the treetops for a big view of the Pacific Ocean.
>
> **Parking:**   From Hwy. 101 north of Sausalito, take Hwy. 1-Shoreline Hwy. exit toward Stinson Beach. Follow up and turn right on Panoramic Hwy. After about 1 mi., turn left on Muir Woods Rd. Continue for about 2 mi. to monument parking. *Note:* Entrance fee charged. *Bus:* Commercial tours from San Francisco
>
> **Agency:**   Muir Woods National Monument; Mt. Tamalpais State Park.

H: **Muir Woods loop (up to 2 mi.); Hillside Trail loop (2.25 mi.); Ben Johnson Trail to: Cardiac Hill (4.75 mi.), or Deer Park Fire Road loop (4.75 mi.)**

In 1905, Marin Congressman William Kent and his wife Elizabeth Thacher Kent bought a 295-acre old-growth redwood grove that had been spared the sawyer's blade thanks to its relatively remote location—pocketed into a valley 2,000 feet below the south slope of Tamalpais. In 1908, President Theodore Roosevelt declared the woods a National Monument, honoring Kent's insistence to name the grove after John Muir. Roosevelt wanted the woods named in honor of Kent. Muir was pleased, calling the park "the best tree-lover's monument that could possibly be found in all the forests of the world." Muir Woods is now some 560 acres, enveloped by the sprawling lands of Mt. Tamalpais State Park and Marin Municipal Water District.

For all hikes, head straight through the entrance station and visitors center on a paved path alongside Redwood Creek. You'll pass four bridges on the way to the end of the flat path, which is lined by ferns and split-rail fences. After Bridge 3 and Cathedral Grove, a boardwalk leads to the Fern Creek Trail. To your right about 100 yards up the trail is the William Kent Memorial, where you can pay your respects at a plaque beside a huge redwood. Not far past the Fern Creek Trail, and after passing a trail that leads to your right up the canyon toward Camp Alice Eastwood and Bootjack, is Bridge 4.

For the **Muir Woods loop**, turn around at Bridge 4, double back, and then cross over to your right at Bridge 3. A trail on the other side of Redwood Creek goes back to the visitors center. For the **Hillside Trail loop**, which takes you back via a contour about 200 feet above Redwood Creek, cross Bridge 4 and head up the Ben Johnson Trail. You'll see the Hillside Trail on your left not far up from the bridge. This loop gives you a woodsy alternative when larger numbers of pedestrians are on the lower paths.

For the **Ben Johnson Trail to Cardiac Hill**, and for the **Deer Park Fire Road loop**, continue up the redwood-shaded stairs from the Hillside Trail Junction. These hikes are excellent, up through grand forest and ending with a spectacular view. From Bridge 4 you climb about 1,000 feet over the next 1.5 miles. After about 1 mile, you need to jog left, up a short connector trail that makes the last 200 feet up and joins the Deer Park Fire Road; the straight-ahead option from this connector trail, the Stapelveldt Trail, continues to Pantoll Ranger Station, TH58. To **Cardiac Hill**—so named for its physiological effects on Dipsea Trail runners—turn right on Deer Park Road. About .5-mile later you'll pop out the Douglas fir forest to an open hillside—joining the Coastal Trail—with airborne views of the Pacific and Stinson Beach.

For the **Deer Park Fire Road loop,** double back and then continue down the ridge instead of taking the connector trail to the Ben Johnson Trail. On your way down, the Dipsea Trail makes several intersections with the Deer Park Road, as both routes share the same ridge. After about 1.25 miles from the connector trail junction, the Dipsea goes left, and you want to go with it, dropping about 400 feet to Redwood Creek. The creek can be hard to cross in high water. At the bottom you are about .25-mile from the monument parking lot.

MB: Although the monument is closed to cyclists, you can ride the Bay Area Ridge Trail, up **Deer Park Fire Road**—either on an up-and-back to Cardiac Hill or on a

Muir Beach Overlook

Coastal Trail loop via Muir Beach. For the up-and-back, covering 4.5 miles and climbing about 1, 200 feet, begin at the Deer Park Fire Road gate, which is on your right, less than a mile downhill from the entrance to Muir Woods National Monument. Your toughest climb is during the first .5-mile. For the Coastal Trail loop—a ride of some 7.5-miles, the last 3 on scenic car roads—hang a left on the Coastal Trail when you come to the junction after humping 2.25 miles up Deer Park Road. You roll down the ridge, dropping almost 1,000 feet in 2 miles, and hit Highway 1 about a mile north of Muir Beach. Pedal left on Highway 1, dropping into Muir Beach, and then go left on Muir Beach Road. The Deer Park Road gate is less than 2 miles away, along an easy grade beside Redwood Creek.

R: **Strollers and Wheelchairs:** The Muir Woods loop trail is suitable for wheels, and sure to please or even inspire. Try to pick a weekday or come early to avoid crowds.

55.   MUIR BEACH   H, MB, J

Best for: A large sandy cove, rugged overlooks, and a verdant valley combine for a remarkable coastal experience.

Parking: From Hwy. 101 north of Sausalito, take Hwy. 1-Shoreline Hwy. exit toward Stinson Beach. Keep left on Shoreline at Panoramic Hwy., and continue another 2 mi. to Muir Beach. Turn left on Sunset Way to beach parking. Park at far-left side of parking lot. *Note:* Additional parking in hike descriptions.

Agency: Golden Gate National Recreation Area

H: Muir Beach stroll (up to 1 mi.); Coyote Ridge loop (3.5 mi.); Pirates Cove (2.75 mi.); Green Gulch Farm (1.75 mi.); Muir Beach Overlook (.25-mi.)

From the parking area, head across the bridge and onto the sands of **Muir Beach**. You'll cross Redwood Creek, adding its freshwater to the Pacific; from the bridge a wildlife path leads upstream away from the beach for about .25-mile. The broad sand crescent of Muir Beach is framed by bookend cliffs. The fresh water intrusion makes a good splash area for the kids. You can also augment your beach walk with treks on bluff trails near the south end of the beach.

The **Coyote Ridge loop** takes you 900 feet up to an open ridge of the Marin Headlands. Cross the footbridge and take the Coastal Trail on your left. You could also go to the right across the footbridge and find another trail on the left that heads to the ridge and joins the Coastal Trail. Either way, you jump up 400 feet after about .5-mile. You'll come to a fine view bluff at the top—sometimes called the Matt Sagues Overlook, because he was huffing so fast up the grade he overlooked it. Keep to your left past this overlook, climbing an open sweep of the Coyote Ridge Trail. Stay left, heading inland, as a spur of the Coyote Ridge Trail heads right, toward Tennessee Valley. A short distance past this junction go left on the Middle Green Gulch Trail, which makes a curving descent to the green fields just west of Green Gulch Farm. Make a left at the bottom, following Redwood Creek .75-mile back to the beach trailhead.

For **Pirates Cove**, a two-thumbs-up coastal experience, head out up the Coastal Trail, as described above. The Coastal Trail veers right toward Pirates Cove from the overlook. About .5-mile along this scalloping trail—that roughly contours 200 feet above a rocky shore—you'll see a spur trail dropping down the cove. The trail junction is at the low point between Muir Beach and Tennessee Valley; you could look down upon Tennessee Valley by continuing up to the next ridge south. The short, steep trail leads to the little rocky cove where pirates or anyone else would have trouble mooring.

The **Green Gulch Farm loop** takes in a huge organic garden and Zen center that is a West Marin institution. Go left at the footbridge and keep left on the Green Gulch Trail. Make sure to keep left and not go up Middle Green Gulch. The expansive gardens are a tranquil stroll for everyone, and a must-see for those interested in horticulture—acres of herbs, veggies, and flowers flourish among arbors under huge shade trees. Part of the San Francisco Zen Center, Green Gulch provides produce for the Greens Restaurant at Fort Mason, TH12, and also offers instructional programs, both spiritual and horticultural. From the lower end of the gardens, you'll see Lower Green Gulch Trail, which follows the creek back to Muir Beach. *Note:* You can drive to Green Gulch and just walk among the gardens. Go south on Highway 1 from Muir Beach and turn right, following signs to visitor parking.

The **Muir Beach Overlook** is a five-star short walk out a promontory above a wild seascape. Drive one mile north on Highway 1 from its junction with Muir Woods Road, which is just north of the road leading into Muir Beach. Turn left at a GGNRA sign and drive in a short distance to a parking lot. A series of steps lead out to a railed viewing area of the rugged coast between Stinson and Muir beaches—though you get a plain view of neither. *Additional Access:* Leading north from the parking lot is the Owl Trail, which descends along a coastal knoll to Slide Ranch, about 1 mile distant, from which dramatic trails lead down to a rocky shore.

MB: **The Coyote Ridge loop** is a keeper for fit cyclists—but you must ride in the opposite direction from that described in the hiking section, since Middle Green Gulch Trail is only open to bikes going uphill. Turn left at the trailhead across the bridge. Middle Green Gulch Trail begins its 800-foot climb to the ridge after you ride about .75-mile inland.

The **Coyote Ridge Trail** can also be accessed at a primo trailhead that is a long drive from Muir Beach. You start out at an elevation of nearly 600 feet, from the end of **Marin Drive in Tam Valley**. Take Highway 1 west from its intersection with Almonte Boulevard. Turn left on Maple Street and then turn right on Marin Drive, following its curving course to the top. From a gate, take a right-bearing trail that connects with the Miwok Trail, where you bear right again and connect with the northern end of Coyote Ridge. The Coyote Ridge Trail forks high above the coast on its southern end—with the right fork going to Muir Beach and the left to Tennessee Valley.

Another trailhead for a dramatic ridge ride—**Diaz Ridge Fire Road**—is also a drive from Muir Beach. Take Highway 1 and veer right on Panoramic Highway, at Muir Beach Road. Just after this junction, look for the fire road gate on your left. This 5-mile loop involves a 2-mile leg along Diaz Ridge and a return leg of about 3 miles up Highway 1. You climb gradually over the first 1.25 miles before beginning a steep descent to Highway 1. Turn left and start uphill, passing Green Gulch, on your way back to the trailhead parking. *Note:* Just before Panoramic Highway, the Miwok Trail on the left is a shortcut to rejoin the Diaz Ridge Fire Trail.

J: Runners might like the Redwood Creek Trail that follows water flow for about 2 miles. Coming down from Muir Woods, about .5-mile from the entrance, look for a sign on the left for the Miwok Trail. Start down the Miwok Trail. After .5-mile, veer right on the Redwood Creek Trail. You'll find two other junctions off this trail on the way down: the Kent Falls Trail, .5-mile from the fire road; and Santos Meadow horse camp, which is a mile downstream. The trail varies only about 100 feet over the entire distance, although you do climb a contour over the last .5-mile to the Highway 1 junction.

56. MOUNTAIN HOME INN
H, MB, J, R

Best for: Historic trails—those of the hiking clubs and tourist railroad of the early 1900s—lead up to the sunny shoulders of Tamalpais or down to forested creases above Muir Woods.

Parking: From Hwy. 101 north of Sausalito, take Hwy. 1-Shoreline Hwy. exit toward Stinson Beach. Follow up and turn right on Panoramic Hwy. Continue 2 mi. past junction with Muir Beach Rd. and park in lot on left, across from Mountain Home Inn. *Bus:* GGT weekend route 63

Agency: Marin Municipal Water District; Mount Tamalpais State Park; *Special interest: Group Camping, Lodging

H: Gravity Car Grade loop (2.25 mi.); West Point Inn via Old Railroad Grade loop (4.25 mi.)

The Mountain Home Inn has been offering libation to hikers since 1912, from a dining area hanging off a ridge of Tam that overlooks Mill Valley. **For both** the Gravity Car Grade and Old Railroad Grade hikes, walk up the highway a short distance to a right-hand turnoff. For the **Gravity Car Grade loop** veer right on an unpaved road and, after a short distance, continue through a MMWD gate. You begin a pleasant contour on Gravity Car Grade, in the shade of Douglas fir, madrone, and young redwoods, with a San Francisco view beyond Richardson Bay. After .75-mile you pass remnants of the Mesa Station railroad platform, and a right-hand junction of the Old Railroad Grade that heads down to Mill Valley. Stay left, now on the Old Railroad Grade, as it switchbacks upward over the next .25-mile. You'll pass the Hoo-Koo-E-Koo Road beginning its long contour toward Blithedale Ridge, and the Vic Haun Trail beginning its ascent of Tam. Continue west on Old Railroad Grade, climbing another 250 feet over about .5-mile. You reach the Hogback Road, down which you walk to the Mountain Home trailhead .5-mile away.

The **West Point Inn via Old Railroad Grade loop** takes you to the historic hiker's retreat built in 1904. Veer left, up toward the fire station, as you leave Panoramic Highway just up from the Mountain Home Inn. Head up the Hogback Road, the reddish scar of a trail that can be seen from the highway, rising more than 500 feet to Old Railroad Grade. Turn left on the grade, and continue for 1.5 miles, dipping into Fern Canyon before reaching West Point. The inn is perched at nearly 1,800 feet, on the most westerly bend of the former railroad route. From below the inn, take a short connector, the Nora Trail, which descends a quick 400 feet and joins the Matt Davis Trail. Go left on the Matt Davis, which contours around for .75-mile, well below the Old Railroad Grade, and rejoins the Hogback Road.

MB: Cyclists can take an 8-mile **West Point loop**, through chaparral, conifers and oak forests. The last 3 miles of the loop are on Panoramic Highway. Start up Old Gravity Car Grade, as per hiking directions, and continue left on Old Railroad Grade to West Point Inn; this first 3-mile leg of the ride takes you up 900 feet. From West Point Inn, go west on Old Stage Road, which takes you on a twisting descent of about 300 feet over 2 miles, coming out at Pantoll Ranger Station on Panoramic Highway. If you start early in the day, you'll have less traffic when heading east on the mild climb back to Mountain Home Inn.

J: Cross country runners will like the 5-mile round-trip route from the Alice Eastwood Road to Pantoll Ranger Station, using a series of trails that connect on a contour below the southern edge of Panoramic Highway. Start down the Eastwood Road and veer right at the bend on Troop 80 Trail. Stay on that all the way to Van Wyck Meadow, making sure not to stray left down the TCC Trail just before the meadow. You pass a connector trail to Bootjack in the meadow, and continue west another .5-mile on the Alpine Trail to Pantoll. Hardcore runners have the option of dropping down into Muir Woods—via Stapelveldt and Ben Johnson trails—and coming back up the Alice Eastwood Road. This loop means adding 1.5-miles and 600 feet of climbing to the run. Otherwise, reverse course and return to Eastwood Road.

R: **Wheelchairs and Strollers:** The Gravity Car Grade road, though on an unpaved surface, does little climbing over the first .75-mile to the Mesa Station platform—and passes through pleasant forest with a great view. The Alice Eastwood Road, located about .25-mile down the highway from the inn, is a paved, 1.25-mile drop to the campground, and its grade is not steep. But you will have to roll more than 300 feet up on the homestretch.

*Special Interest: *Group camping:* Available under the jurisdiction of Mount Tamalpais State Park, at Camp Alice Eastwood. Located near Fern Creek just outside of Muir Woods National Monument, the camp is named in honor of a California Academy of Sciences botanist who pioneered conservation and recreation on the mountain in the early 1900s. *Lodging:* Both private rooms and cabins are available at the rustic West Point Inn, which is still without electricity, faithful to its 1904 roots.

57.   BOOTJACK   H

Best for: A variety of ambitious Tamalpais hikes—redwoods, mixed conifer, and oak—both up and down the mountain from this mid-elevation trailhead.

Parking: From Hwy. 101 north of Sausalito, take Hwy. 1-Shoreline Hwy. exit toward Stinson Beach. Follow up and turn right on Panoramic Hwy. Park at Bootjack Picnic Area, about 2.5 mi. after Mt. Tamalpais State Park boundary. *Note:* Parking lot fee required. *Bus:* GGT weekend route 63

Agency: Mt. Tamalpais State Park; Marin Municipal Water District

H: Redwood Creek-Camp Alice Eastwood loop (5 mi.); Mountain Home-Matt Davis Trail loop (4.75 mi.); Muir Woods via Ben Johnson Trail loop (5 mi.)

The **Redwood Creek-Camp Alice Eastwood loop** takes you down a mossy, fern-embanked creek, over footbridges beneath redwoods, and then back up amid the sunny, drier forests of oak and manzanita. From the parking, head up toward the stone restrooms and go right to join the Bootjack Trail. You immediately cross the highway and follow the splashing waters of Redwood Creek along a merry 1,000-foot drop, over about 1.5 miles, to Camp Alice Eastwood. At the camp, turn left and look for the Sierra Trail. The Sierra Trail joins the Troop 80 Trail. Go left, weaving through redwoods, to Van Wyck Meadow, where you rejoin the Bootjack Trail.

For the **Mountain Home-Matt Davis Trail loop**—a long oval that goes both above and below the highway through a breadth of flora—go right on the Matt Davis Trail, from near the stone restrooms. Matt Davis was a champion trail builder for the Tamalpais Conservation Club in the early- to mid-1900s. You begin on a contour, through mixed conifer forests and with big ocean views. After 2.25 miles, it joins the Hogback. Head down for a steep .25-mile, cross Panoramic Highway, and, from the parking area across from the Mountain Home Inn, drop down to your right to join the Alice Eastwood Road. At the big bend in this road, veer onto Troop 80 Trail, which is a veritable Mt. Tam arboretum. Follow Troop 80 for 1.5 miles to Van Wyck Meadow go right on Bootjack Trail. *Additional Access:* A shorter variation on this loop goes up the mountain slope and also avoids crossing the highway. Go left from the Matt Davis Trail on the Nora Trail, about 1.5 miles from Bootjack. The Nora Trail climbs through an unusual combination of redwoods with chaparral, to West Point Inn. From there, take the Old Stage Road back to Bootjack. This loop is about 3.5 miles.

The **Muir Woods via Ben Johnson Trail loop** is a 1,200-foot descent through lush redwood and fir forest, followed by a climb beside a cascading creek. Begin by taking the Bootjack Trail down from the picnic area. On the other side of the highway, pass the Alpine Trail on your right. Continue in Van Wyck Meadow, where you turn right on the TCC Trail—a level meander through redwoods built in the old days by the Tamalpais Conservation Club. After 1.5 miles, you connect with the Stapelveldt Trail. Go left on a long descent that joins the Ben Johnson Trail. In Muir Woods, jog left across the bridge, and go left almost immediately, on the Bootjack Trail. Crossing bridges and weaving up Redwood Creek, the Bootjack climbs for about 1.75 miles.

58.   PANTOLL RANGER STATION   H, MB, J

Best for: Pop out of the lush forests on the western slopes of Tamalpais onto open, grassy knolls with glorious views from high above the Pacific Ocean.

Parking: From Hwy. 101 north of Sausalito, take Hwy. 1-Shoreline Hwy. exit toward Stinson Beach. Follow up and turn right on Panoramic Hwy. Continue 3 mi. past Mt. Tam State Park boundary, and .25-mi. past Bootjack, to Pantoll Ranger Station Parking on left. *Note:* Parking lot fee; some non-fee places available across street, at jct. with Pantoll Rd. *Bus*: GGT weekend route 63

Agency: Mount Tamalpais State Park; *Special Interest: Camping, Lodging

H: **Dipsea Trail-Steep Ravine loop (3.75 mi.); Coastal Trail-O'Rourkes Bench loop (2.75 mi.); Easy Grade-Mountain Theater loop (2.25 mi.)**

Pantoll is the headquarters for Mount Tamalpais, which was established in 1928 as California's first state park. The park now includes some 12-square miles, taking in the peaks of Tam and lands extending to the Pacific. The **Dipsea Trail-Steep Ravine loop** exacts a 1,100-elevation gain, but delivers with splashy Pacific views and creek-side wonder. Head down the road from the far right side of the Pantoll parking lot. After a few hundred feet, go left on the Old Mine Trail, through Douglas fir and oak forest. After passing the Coastal Fire Road and the Lone Tree Fire Road, go to your right on the Dipsea Trail. After only .25-mile on the Dipsea, you have an option of taking a spur trail up to your right to Lone Tree Spring, and its garden of redwoods and ferns.

Continue west on the Dipsea, which weaves in and out along the Lone Tree Fire Road, for .5-mile to a right-bearing junction toward Stinson Beach; this trail segment was used by Miwok long before Mt. Tam's recreational trails were constructed. The Dipsea Trail falls some 600 feet over the next .75-mile to the bridge at Webb Creek. Turn right at the bridge and head up Steep Ravine Trail. You may hardly notice the climb, distracted by its charms: ferns, pools and riffles, bridges and mossy rocks. About .75-mile up from the Dipsea junction you reach a 10-foot ladder that provides passage through

Pantoll, oak and bay laurel

monster rocks. Above the creek ladder, having ascended now 600 feet, the trail veers away into mostly Douglas fir forest over the remaining .75-mile back to Pantoll. *Additional Access:* Check the schedule for bus 63, and consider taking the Dipsea Trail all the way to Stinson and using public transportation back to Pantoll.

For the **Coastal Trail-O'Rourkes Bench loop**, a view hike heading up the mountain from Pantoll, cross the highway to the gate that is near the beginning of Pantoll Road. Heading to your left, start out on the Matt Davis Trail—which at this point is also part of both the Coastal Trail and Bay Area Ridge Trail. You begin on an open hillside, enter fir and laurel forest, and pop into the open again. Take a trail heading up to your right. Over a short distance, this trail ascends more than 300 feet to O'Rourkes Bench, a grassy open platform fringed by pockets of laurels and oaks. Veer right from the bench— heading toward Tam but avoiding a right-hand contour that leads directly to Pantoll Road. You meet Pantoll Road at Rock Springs. Cross the road, veer right, and pick up Old Mine Road. This route descends into a panorama on its 1.25-mile course back.

The trail for the **Easy Grade-Mountain Theater loop**, featuring lots of wildflowers in the early spring, is also across the highway from Pantoll Ranger Station. Go right on the Matt Davis Trail, which intertwines in the beginning with the Old Stage Road. After .25-mile head left up the Easy Grade Trail. You'll hit other junctions during the first part of the 500-foot "easy" trail up through oak woodlands. Near the top, you cross the Bootjack Trail and come in near the lower part of the amphitheater. Once you've spent some time in the terraced bowl, go left on the loop road leading out and go left again on the Old Mine Trail. On the way down you'll pass a granite-stubbed knoll with spectacular view.

Audubon Canyon Ranch, Mountain Theater

MB: Two long loop rides involve going down one ridge on a fire road, connecting via auto roads, and riding back up another fire road. For an 8-mile **Lone Tree Road-Coastal Trail loop**—with spectacular Stinson Beach views—head south on the Old Mine Road from the Pantoll parking area. After .75-mile go right on Lone Tree Road. You descend close to 1,000 feet over the next 1.75-miles, coming to Highway 1 just south of Stinson Beach. Go left on Highway 1, undulating as much as 200 feet for the next 3 miles, past Slide Ranch, and turn left on the Coastal Trail—before you get to Muir Beach Overlook. Make the steep, 2.5-mile pump back to Pantoll.

A similar ride, this one of 8.5 miles, is the **Deer Park Road-Coastal Trail loop**. Head down the Old Mine Road, as described above, and turn left on Deer Park Road. You drop about 1,200 feet to Muir Woods Road. Turn right and pedal a pastoral valley about 2 miles to Highway 1. Turn right toward Stinson on Highway 1, making up 300 feet of elevation on pavement. You reach the Coastal Trail, on your right about .5-mile past the Muir Beach Overlook.

J: The Easy Grade loop is not that easy, but it will score high marks among adventure runners. Also try the Matt Davis-Coastal Trail, as described in the O'Rourkes Bench hike, only don't go up the spur trail to the bench, but continue along the Coastal Trail. This trail is surreal when the fog is rolling up the mountainside.

*Special Interest: *Camping.* Pantoll Ranger Station has 16 campsites, each a short walk in from the parking area, available on a first-come, first-served basis. *Lodging.* Steep Ravine Environmental Camp, consists of 6 tent sites and 10 rustic cabins, all located on a rocky terrace above the ocean about 1 mile south of Stinson Beach. Rooms are available by reservation; call Tamalpais State Park up to 7 months in advance.

59. MOUNTAIN THEATER   H, MB, R

Best for: Stroll back in time through a stone amphitheater; or explore the less-traveled meadows, forests, and streams of north Tam.

Parking: From Hwy. 101 north of Sausalito, take Hwy. 1 toward Stinson Beach. Follow Hwy. 1 and turn right on Panoramic Hwy. Continue 3 mi. past Mt. Tam State Park boundary, to Pantoll Ranger Station. Turn right on Pantoll Rd. *For Rock Springs parking:* Park on left at MMWD lot after 1.25 mi., at intersection of Pantoll Rd. and Ridgecrest Blvd. *For Mountain Theater parking:* Go right of E. Ridgecrest Blvd. to signed parking after .25-mi. *Note:* Gates at Pantoll Rd. close in evening. Additional parking in hiking description.

Agency: Mount Tamalpais State Park; Marin Municipal Water District; *Special Interest: Kids

H: Mountain Theater (up to .75-mi.); Rock Spring-Lagunitas Road to: Potrero Meadows (2 mi.), or Lake Lagunitas (6.75 mi.); Rock Spring parking to: Cataract Trail-Simmons loop (3.25 mi.), or Potrero Meadows-Laurel Dell loop (4.25 mi.)

The Sidney B. Cushing Mountain Theater—sometimes "Theatre"—is named in memory of the president of the historic Mt. Tam-Muir Woods Railway. The outdoor venue is the backdrop for the Mountain Play, produced yearly since 1913. The Civilian Conservation Corps redesigned the natural, tree-fringed grassy bowl in the early 1930s, resulting in the Greek-inspired stone terraces and walls that are here today.

From Mountain Theater parking: To walk around the **Mountain Theater**, take the paved road and head to your right toward the Madrone Grove. You'll wind up near the bottom tiers of the amphitheater's many rows of stone-block seats. Wander up through the seating terraces, or around the amphitheater, to the top. Then take the paved loop road that leads back out to the parking area. *Additional Access:* The Rock Springs Trail, which takes off from the left side of the stage as you look down from amphitheater seating, is a less used, 1.5-mile route to West Point Inn.

For the **Rock Spring-Lagunitas Road** hikes, drive up E. Ridgecrest Boulevard from the theater parking, just around the bend, and park in the large lot to your right. The trailhead is across the road. For both **Potrero Meadows** and **Lake Lagunitas**, you begin on a slight uphill, climbing almost 200 feet in less than .5-mile, before beginning a steady fall on this ridge-and-meadow route that ends at MMWD's oldest lake. Potrero Meadows, a popular horseman's picnic area, lies to your left at the junction with Laurel Dell Fire Road. Continuing north on the road, you pass Rifle Camp, which dates from 1917. You gradually enter conifers, especially during the last .75-mile that descends 800 feet to lake level. You may wish to pick a view spot and turn around rather than go all the way to the lake.

From Rock Springs parking: The **Cataract-Simmons trails loop**, which follows two streambeds, is the prime-time hike for this trailhead. From Rock Springs, a pleasant open area with Douglas fir and mossy oaks, head to your left on the Cataract Trail. Follow the trail, on a rocky ledge at times, alongside Cataract Creek, amid a tumble of oak, madrone, fir, and many shrubs. After a mile you pass the Mickey O'Brien Trail—to which you will double-back. Continue another .25-mile to the picnic area of Laurel Dell. From there, head down the trail a short distance to view the falls of Cataract Creek, gushing water beginning a mile-long tumble that ends at Alpine Lake, TH42. Then backtrack and go left on the O'Brien Trail.

Barths Creek will be on your left as you ascend to join the Simmons Trail. Near this junction is Barths Retreat, now a picnic area, that was the getaway for an avid hiker, Professor Emil Barth, who first roamed these woods in 1886 when they were wild. On the mile-long return leg, Simmons trail ascends a rocky chaparral slope, crosses a hill-

Laurel Dell

top of oak and Douglas fir, and descends into a redwood ravine. You cross a bridge over a stream before reaching the Rock Springs trailhead.

The **Potrero Meadows-Laurel Dell loop** is a forest and meadow jaunt with a return leg on Cataract Creek. Go down the road to the left of the parking area, and then veer right on the Benstein Trail. As you leave the creek, you enter drier terrain, with mint-green moss adorning rocks and oak, and Douglas fir towering above. After about a mile, jog left on the Rock Springs-Lagunitas Road for a while, and then take a left-turn on the Benstein Trail. Continue over the greenish serpentine rocks, beside Sargent cypress. You'll cross Laurel Dell Road and enter Potrero Meadows. From the meadows, backtrack to Laurel Dell Road. After 1.75 miles, mostly through chaparral, you'll drop into the dell. Take the Cataract Trail a short distance downstream to view the trail's namesake. Backtrack on the lush riparian trail, 1.25 miles to the Rock Springs parking.

MB: This trailhead offers good back-country riding. For a fairly short ride through some wild country, try the **Rock Spring-Laurel Dell Roads loop**, which covers al-most 4 miles, all but 1.5 miles of which is off highway. Take the Rock Springs-Lagunitas Road, which begins on your left, .25-miles past the Mountain Theater. After a mile—climbing a little and dropping a little—go left on Laurel Dell Road. Laurel Dell undu-lates several hundred feet through varied country on its 2-mile route to W. Ridgecrest Boulevard. Turn left, enjoying splendid ocean views, and ride back to the trailhead.

Big time pedal pushers can take a longer ride—a **loop of Bon Tempe Lake and Lake Lagunitas.** This loop—of 10 tough miles—drops you down and back up 1,500 feet, with a lot of humps along the way. Take the Rock Springs-Lagunitas Road to Lake Lagunitas. Take the paved road away from the lake. Turn left toward Bon Tempe Lake, cross the dam at the lake, and begin a 1,200-foot climb up on Rocky Ridge Road. This road meets the Rock Springs-Lagunitas Road at Bay Tree Junction, which is 2.5 miles from trailhead parking.

R: **Strollers and Wheelchair**: The Mountain Theater road is paved, and the unpaved road through Madrone Grove is also okay for wheels. This is a serene setting. Try the Old Mine Road as well, which breaks out to big views above Rock Springs—enhanced in the near-view by wildflowers in the spring.

*Special Interest: *Kids:* Imaginative youngsters will enjoy running around the Moun-tain Theater, especially when it's empty and they can stage their own productions.

60. MOUNT TAM PEAK   H, MB, J, R

Best for: The ultimate Marin and San Francisco views on short walks to the top—or around—the summit of Mount Tamalpais; or the mother of all down-hill mountain bike rides.

Parking: From Hwy. 101 north of Sausalito, take Hwy. 1 toward Stinson Beach. Follow Hwy. 1 and turn right on Panoramic Hwy. Continue 3 mi. past Mt. Tam State Park boundary, to Pantoll Ranger Station. Turn right on Pantoll Rd. After 1.25 mi., go right of E. Ridgecrest Blvd. and follow for about 3 mi. to road's end parking. *Note:* Gates at Pantoll Rd. close in evening and reopen in morning. Additional parking described in hiking section.

Agency: Mt. Tamalpais State Park; Marin Municipal Water District; *Special Interest: Kids

H: **Tam East Peak Summit (.75-mi.); Tam Summit circle-Dunshee Trail (.75-mi.); North Side loop (4.25 mi.); South Side loop (2.75 mi.)**

At 2,571-feet, East Peak is the highest among the three peaks that form the curving summit ridge of Tamalpais. West Peak, with the white sphere military installation is 11 feet shorter, and in the saddle between the two is Middle Peak, standing at 2,490 feet. The three unimaginatively named peaks combine to create the curvature known, from the time of the Miwok onward, as the more poetic "Sleeping Maiden." The parking lot at road's end was the terminus for the tourist railroad that chugged up from Mill Valley, and also the site of the Tavern where travelers enjoyed their stay.

For the **Tam East Peak Summit**—with views of everywhere—take the road from the end of the parking lot and start up the plank trail. You circle around to the east face of the mountain, and walk up rocks for the last bit of this 200-plus-foot climb. On top is Edwin Burrough Gardner Lookout, constructed in 1936 and named for the first district fire warden. The lookout features a stone foundation that anchors the steel-frame and timber structure to the peak, withstanding winds of 100 mph and greater. You can wander southward from the peak on a little loop trail among the big rocks. On foggy days, the view from Tam can be ethereal, as the green peak often sticks above a puffy blanket.

For the **Tam Summit circle via the Verna Dunshee Trail**—which you don't want to overlook in your haste to see the peak—go right at the signed trailhead just down from the parking lot. The circular route, roughly paved with benches along the way, contours 200 feet below the summit. You view the Bay Area panorama in quadrants as you walk. As you complete the circle, coming down some railroad tie stairs, you pass what's left of an old railway station.

The **North Side loop** takes in Inspiration Point and Middle Peak. Start at Eldridge Grade, which is just down from the paved parking area—going up, it's on your left. Starting at 2,200 feet, Eldridge Grade drops about 300 feet over 1.5 miles and makes a big hairpin to Inspiration point—via a short trail to Collier Spring near the point. You descend through a variety of chaparral flora. After drinking in the views, leave the Inspiration Point heading west on the North Side Trail. After curving 1.5 miles, you come to Collier Spring, a lush butterfly habitat among redwood trees. Go left on the Collier Spring Trail, gaining 400-plus feet in .5-mile and coming to the road. Go left on the road for a short distance, and drop off to your left, on the Lakeview Trail. This trail goes around the north face of Middle Peak, reaching a fire road—on which you can take a quick jaunt to the top—and continues to meet the road again, a few hundred feet away from the Eldridge Grade.

The **South Side loop** is a short but strenuous hike, featuring a 1,000-foot down-and-up on some of Tam's historic trails. Head out to your right from below the parking lot on the Verna Dunshee Trail. After .25-mile, go right on the Temelpa Trail, a straight-down deal through chaparral. In less than .5-mile, be sure to veer right on the Vic Haun Trail, which drops some more, dumping you out on the Old Railroad Grade. Go right, making up 400 feet of elevation over the next mile and coming to Fern Creek Trail. Go right up the steep draw on the Fern Creek Trail, passing a water tank about halfway up, and coming to the parking lot at East Peak.

MB: East Peak is, literally, the seminal trailhead for mountain biking. In the early 1970s, at a time when ten-speeds were all the rage, teenagers like Gary Fischer, Brian Butler and many others pieced together "clunkers" from parts of old fat-tire bikes and pointed the wheels down the mountain. The craze caught on.

Many yahoo routes lead down the mountain to many different places in Marin. The trick is getting someone to give you a ride up. The best ride may be **Eldridge Grade**—beginning to your left off Ridgecrest below the parking lot. Eldridge makes a circuitous run to the north, over 6 miles to Phoenix Lake, TH47. Another option is to come down Eldridge for 2.5 miles, go right on **Indian Fire Road**, and then right again after .5-mile on **Blithedale Ridge Road**. You can ride Blithedale all the way to Greenwood in Mill Valley, as described in TH52; or veer left off Blithedale Ridge on **Corte Madera Ridge** and hit the pavement at Overhill in Corte Madera, as described in TH51. The Blithedale Ridge run is over 5 miles, and the Corte Madera Ridge option is more than 6 miles.

View from the top of Mt. Tam

Old Railroad Grade is another classic descent, with a saner line of fall than sections of the above routes. You wind up at Blithedale Park, TH52, in the heart of Mill Valley. The grade begins to your right before you begin the last uphill to the East Peak parking lot—it's before you get to Eldridge Grade. Following the bed of the historic tourist railway, you drop 2,000 feet over almost 7 miles, including a short paved stretch after about 4 miles, on Fern Canyon Road—be sure to go left on Old Railroad Grade and not continue down Summit Avenue. En route, you'll pass West Point Inn, after the first 1.5 miles, below the mountain's south face. You then head east, passing a turnoff on Gravity Car Grade that leads to Mountain Home Inn, TH56. From there the grade curves below East Peak, dropping down to the redwoods of Blithedale Park.

J: The Verna Dunshee Trail is the ultimate natural track run—although you may have to do a couple three circles to feel like you've had a workout.

R: **Strollers and Wheelchairs**: The Verna Dunshee Trail is paved and runs in a fairly flat contour with the best views in town. The pavement is rough in places, and narrow with drop-offs, so chair riders will want a companion. The bad news is that three-quarters of the way around are a dozen railroad tie steps, which will impede wheelchairs. The best plan may be to go halfway around on the trail and backtrack.

*Special Interests: Kids: The summit or Dunshee Trail are short enough for active kids, and both give them perspective on North Bay geography.

61. RIDGECREST BOULEVARD   H, MB, J

Best for: Once a toll road that was "California's Most Scenic Drive," and more recently the set for fantasy car commercials, this strip of asphalt offers several panoramic hiking choices along a wavy contour above the coast.

Parking: From Hwy. 101 north of Sausalito, take Hwy. 1 toward Stinson Beach. Follow Hwy. 1 and turn right on Panoramic Hwy. Continue 3 mi. past Mt. Tam State Park boundary, to Pantoll Ranger Station, and turn right on Pantoll Rd. After 1.25 mi., at Rock Springs, go left on W. Ridgecrest Blvd. *Note:* This trailhead covers a 4-mi. stretch of Ridgecrest, ending at Fairfax-Bolinas Rd.—you can also come in from Fairfax via that road. Hiking descriptions are given as distances from Pantoll Rd. junction.

Agency: Mount Tamalpais State Park; Marin Municipal Water District; Golden Gate National Recreation Area.

H: O'Rourkes Bench (.25-mi.); Ballou Point (up to .5-mi.); Laurel Dell (1.5 mi.); Willow Camp Road to Stinson Beach (4 mi.); Coastal Trail to Cooks Bench (1.5 mi.); Bolinas Ridge Road, north and south.

Ridgecrest Boulevard was during the advent of the automobile in the early 1900s one of California's first scenic drives, with people paying a dollar, big money then, to cruise the ridge up to Mount Tam. You may recognize the rolling curvature of the boulevard from footage of numerous sexy car commercials. Steep grassy slopes fall 2,000-feet to the ocean on the west, and the watershed's forested valleys are tucked to the east.

The turnout for **O'Rourkes Bench** is under oaks and fir trees, on your left .5-mile from the Pantoll Road junction. A trail leads down onto the bench, with options to loop around left or drop down the face to hit the Matt Davis-Coastal Trail. Bring wine and cheese. Not far past O'Rourkes, beginning at .75-mile from the Pantoll Road, is a trail on the right to **Ballou Point**, which skirts the road and rises gently to a rocky knoll. Engineer H. M. Ballou constructed the road for William Kent in 1926.

The **Laurel Dell**, **Willow Camp Road and Cooks Bench** trailheads are a study in contrasts from east to west. All begin 1.5 miles from Pantoll Road. To the right, down through thick Douglas fir forest into the deep folds of the Cataract Creek drainage is Laurel Dell. The dell is a picnic glade that is a very short distance upstream from the remarkable falls of the creek. On the west, Willow Camp Road drops 2,000 feet over 2 miles, through a grass carpet with tree splotches, coming out on Farallone Avenue above the country store at Stinson Beach. You probably won't want to go the distance, but you can reach tree-studded view knolls, about 400 feet and .75-mile down. To Cooks Bench, drop down the Willow Camp Road for .25-mile and go right, or north, on the Coastal Trail; this is a viewing spot of Bolinas Lagoon and Stinson Beach.

Additional Access: About 2.25 miles from Pantoll Road, on your left, is the McKennan Trail to Bolinas Lagoon, 1.75-miles, one-way and 1,700 feet down. A lateral trail of .75-mile connects with Willow Camp Road near the bottom, so you could make a monster loop, encircling Stinson Gulch, over 5.5 miles, using the Coastal Trail on top to connect the Willow Camp Trail back to McKennan.

Ridgecrest Boulevard ends after 4 miles, at the redwood shaded saddle that is the junction with **Fairfax-Bolinas Road**. To the north, Bolinas Ridge Trail goes for 11.5 miles; see TH82. Going to the south of the road junction, you can take the Coastal Trail on a contour for 2 miles until it comes out to Ridgecrest. You can also veer right after about .25-mile and venture into a forested thicket for a view of the Bolinas Lagoon.

MB: Most cyclists approach the **Bolinas Ridge Trail** from the north end, so it may be worth the drive to try this more secluded approach from the Fairfax-Bolinas Road at Ridgecrest. You can also make a **loop via Laurel Dell** down to Bon Tempe Lake and back up past Alpine Lake on the Fairfax-Bolinas Road. Also see Mountain Theater, TH59, and the Laurel Dell-Rock Springs loop.

Another option from Ridgecrest is a loop down **Willow Camp Road to Stinson Beach**. You drop steeply and dramatically for 2,000 feet over 2 miles, coming down through the quiet residences above Stinson to the highway in the middle of town. Of course, then you have to pedal back up every inch, via Highway 1 and then Panoramic Highway—not incredibly steep, but a workout for even the best-conditioned among cyclists. The road part of the ride is more than 10 miles.

J: The Coastal Trail makes a rolling contour below the ocean side of Ridgecrest Boulevard for 4 miles, extending from below O'Rourke's Bench to Fairfax Bolinas Road. The three best places to join the Coastal Trail are: At an open turnout just south of Fairfax-Bolinas Road; at McKennan Trail; and at Willow Camp Road. See hiking descriptions to spot locations. This trail is challenging, both with foot placement and negotiating elevation changes of 100- to 200-feet, but view-loving endurance runners will find it to their liking.

62. STINSON BEACH   H, J

Best for: Walk or jog miles along a usually sunny shore—with cliffs and crashing waves at one end and a sandy spit and huge lagoon on the other.

Parking: *From southern Marin:* Take Hwy. 1-Stinson Beach exit from north of Sausalito and follow about 13 mi. to signed beach parking. *From central Marin:* Take Sir Francis Drake Blvd.-San Anselmo exit and follow about 18 mi., through Fairfax to Hwy. 1 at Olema. Go south on Hwy. 1 for 10 mi. to Stinson Beach parking. *Bus:* GGT weekend route 63

Agency: Golden Gate National Recreation Area; *Special Interest: Surfing, Swimming, Group Picnics

H: **Seadrift Spit to Bolinas Lagoon (up to 5 mi.); Stinson Beach cliffs (1 mi.)**

Stinson Beach

The soft sands, gentle waves, and looming onshore views have been attracting beach-goers to Stinson since the late 1800s. The beach was then known as Eastkooks Beach after an eccentric seafaring captain, Alfred D. Eastkook, who built a home here in 1875 and warded off rowdy visitors with shotgun blasts. After the captain's unfortunate passing, at the turn of the century, the beach became know as Willow Camp, attracting hundreds of tent campers. Stinson Beach went public in 1939, as a state beach named for Nathan Stinson, whose 1906 subdivision formed the early community. The public lands were transferred to GGNRA in the 1974. The town itself is worth a walkabout, featuring galleries and several restaurants.

For the **Seadrift Spit to Bolinas Lagoon** hike, turn right as you face the water. You'll soon leave the GGNRA boundary. The beach northward is public access alongside Seadrift, a private community built on the .25-mile-wide spit between the Bolinas Lagoon and the Pacific. The end of the spit is a broad swath of sand fringed by sea grasses and scattered with driftwood. Across a narrow opening of the Bolinas Lagoon is the town of Bolinas; see TH64. Sea Lions may poke their heads up near the lagoon mouth—one reason why great white sharks have been spotted offshore, but not in numbers to evoke paranoia among swimmers.

To the **Stinson Beach cliffs**, walk left as you face the water. After about .5-mile you'll come to the end of the sand, as cliffs, rocks, and oncoming surf intrude. You can keep going, depending on the tides, but be mindful of shorebreak and high tide. While walking Stinson Beach, don't forget to look inland from the waves, where tall Bolinas Ridge frames the sky. *Additional Access:* Steep Ravine, an environmental camp that is part of Mt. Tam State Park, is about 1.5 miles south of Stinson on Highway 1. You can walk down the road, less than .5-mile, to venture onto Rocky Point, the rugged bench on which the cabins are situated. A trail to Redrock Beach, a wave-bashed cove in the cliffs south of Stinson Beach, begins about .25-mile south of the road into Steep Ravine; this trail is steep and subject to closures, so use good judgment.

J: From Stinson north along the spit to the lagoon—with nice flat sand during low tide—is one of the best beach runs anywhere. SoCal refugees may find themselves humming Beach Boys' tunes.

Special Interest: Swimming: Lifeguards are on duty from late May through mid-September. Stinson is one of the safer swimming beaches, but it does have riptides and can be dangerous when the surf is high. *Surfing:* Boardheads are more often found at Bolinas, but Stinson's rollers are some of NorCal's best—north of Santa Cruz—for boogie boarding or body surfing. *Group Picnics:* Facilities available, in shaded picnic areas close to beach; larger groups must call for information.

63. AUDUBON CANYON RANCH   H

Best for: Great blue herons and great egrets nest in dense woodlands, some atop redwoods, in the four steep canyons that rise from Bolinas Lagoon.

Parking: *From southern Marin:* Take Hwy. 1-Stinson Beach exit from north of Sausalito and follow about 13 mi., to 3.5-mi. north of Stinson Beach. *From central Marin:* Take Sir Francis Drake Blvd.-San Anselmo exit and follow about 18 mi., through Fairfax to Hwy. 1 at Olema. Go south on Hwy. 1 for about 8 mi., and look for signs on left as highway comes to Bolinas Lagoon on right. *Note:* Audubon Canyon Ranch, on private land, is open to the public four months during the year, from mid-March through mid-July, normally on weekends and afternoons, Tuesday through Friday.

Agency: Audubon Canyon Ranch

H: **Rawlings Trail to overlook (1 mi.); North loop (3 mi.); Griffin loop (2.75 mi.)**

Audubon Canyon Ranch's trademark, two-story ranch house dates from 1875, once home to Captain Peter L. Bourne. The nearby barn was added in 1932. The ACR is a nonprofit organization, not affiliated with the National Audubon Society, that offers guided walks and school programs. Take the **Rawlings Trail to the Overlook** to see the heron and egret rookery, with stick nests high up in redwood trees. Head up the trail to the left of the ranch house and headquarters. You walk a side-hill up a ravine about 250 feet in elevation. You can come back down the Kent Trail to make a loop hike of this bird-watcher's delight. *Note:* Bring binoculars.

For the strenuous **North loop**, head to the left at the entrance. You follow a steep shoulder, climbing 800 feet over .75-mile, with Pike County Gulch down to your left and Garden Club Canyon down right. Near the top, the trail enters Garden Club Canyon, crossing the stream, and then descends the shoulder on the opposite side, joining Kent Trail. For the **Griffin loop**, head to your right from the ranch house, following an unpaved road and crossing a stream. The road turns up the mountain—now the Bourne Trail—and you ascend 600 feet over the next .5-mile. The Bourne Trail continues up the shoulder—see *Additional Access*—but you want to contour around to your left into Picher Canyon. The trail heads into the canyon for .5-mile. You then cross the creek and come down on the middle ridge.

Additional Access: The upper part of the ranch can be accessed via the Bourne Trail, at the top of the Fairfax-Bolinas Road. Look for a trailhead on the south side of the road, about .25-mile west of Ridgecrest Boulevard. Begin near the site of Larsens Lodge. Named for the longtime caretaker, the lodge was formerly called Summit House, a stagecoach rest stop that burned down after it could not be sold in 1891. Some say hanky-panky was involved. The Bourne Trail follows a ridgeline down 850 feet.

Point Reyes

Alamere Falls

Visitors to San Francisco who want to see Southern California need go no farther than West Marin: Millions of years ago the entire landmass that is now the Point Reyes National Seashore was located more than 300 miles down the coast. It has moved north because this same day trip to West Marin is also a journey to a different continent.

The Point Reyes Peninsula—and the Farallon Islands that are 30 miles offshore— are part of the Pacific continental plate, while the mainland of Marin and San Francisco are part of the western edge of the North American Plate. These two plates, the largest of a dozen plates that comprise the 62-mile-thick crust of the earth, are grinding to-gether, with the Pacific Plate headed toward Alaska at a rate of about 2 inches per year, on average. The average was boosted on April 18, 1906, when a quiver in the San Andreas Fault launched the peninsula northward nearly 20 feet in a matter of seconds. The fault extends through Tomales Bay, runs offshore of the Golden Gate, and cuts into the California mainland at the southern end of the peninsula on which San Francisco is built. Two or three jolts like the Big One of '06 and, conceivably, both part of Marin and San Francisco could be islands.

As is often the case, this grand and peculiar land of Point Reyes was discovered by people who were looking for someplace else. In 1579, English adventurer and raconteur Francis Drake was sailing north in search of the Northwest Passage, searching in earnest since he and his 58-man crew were pursued by Spanish galleons, who, in turn, where motivated to recover a boatload of gold, silver, porcelain and spices that Drake had pirated from Spain some months earlier. Drake's ship, the *Golden Hind*—the last of five that had set sail from England on a mission to circle the globe on behalf of Queen Elizabeth—began to take on water in heavy seas off of Cape Mendocino. Drake sailed back to where he had seen the only safe harbor, at a large bay whose pale cliffs reminded his crew of Dover in their homeland—now called Drakes Bay. The ship was repaired during a six-week layover, during which time the Englishmen were entertained by their hosts, the Coast Miwok.

At the time of Drake's arrival, the Miwok had called Point Reyes home for several thousand years. Although two Spanish vessels would make landfall at Drakes Bay dur-ing the next 25 years, the Miwok would enjoy about two hundred more years of peace and quiet before their way of life, in a matter of decades, would be destroyed. At that time, the early 1800s, the Miwok lands were granted by the Mexican government's mission system to the three "Lords of Point Reyes": James Berry, Rafael Garcia, and Antonio Osio. By the mid-1800s, when the Americans took California from the Mexi-cans, Point Reyes was divided up and leased as dairy ranches.

Unlike other parts of California, where the story of a native culture's disappear-ance plays like a broken record, the lands of the Point Reyes Peninsula remain essentially unchanged from the Miwok days of antiquity. For the latter part of the nineteenth century, the lands of Point Reyes were preserved due to their value as dairy ranches, when ships from San Francisco would sail daily to reap a harvest of butter and other dairy goods. During the post-World War II boom that hit California, grand schemes were underway to construct multi-lane freeways through West Marin and build large suburban developments. But in the early 1960s—due to the miraculous efforts of many— almost the entire peninsula was designated a National Seashore.

Although many of the same plants and animals share both sides of the San Andreas Fault, keen observers will note differences between these two continental plates. On the mainland—the Bolinas Ridge—greenish outcrops of serpentine rock are apparent, having been thrust up from the ocean by tectonic movements. The peninsula consists largely of sedimentary rocks, overlaying a granitic basement. The mixed fir forests of the peninsula's ridges also contrast with the steep grassy slopes on the ridge, which are pocketed with redwoods and oaks.

As different as it may be from the North American plate, the seashore also varies as much along the 25 miles from its southern tip to its northern. On the south, the Bolinas Mesa is crumbling into the sea. Open bluffs face a large lagoon and the spreading waters of the Gulf of the Farallones Marine Sanctuary. Agate Beach offers tide pool exploration, and the southern trails of Palomarin lead to open seascapes.

Moving north from Bolinas—to the northern trails of Palomarin and those of Five Brooks and Bear Valley—the landscape becomes choked by a mixed Douglas fir forest, with tangled undergrowth of vines, ferns and shrubbery, all of it spreading over a narrow, 1,000-foot high ridge. With this portion of the seashore is the Philip Burton Wilderness Area, featuring backpacking campsites. Trails also run down the Olema Valley, the rift zone of the San Andreas Fault, where scrambled topography has caused Olema Creek to run northward to Tomales Bay, while nearby Pine Gulch Creek flows south to Bolinas Lagoon. Hikers also can take trails eastward across the fault line, up to the Bolinas Ridge, which is part of the GGNRA.

Beginning north of the Olema Valley is Tomales Bay, a narrow 12-mile inlet under whose waters runs the San Andreas Fault. The Bear Valley Visitors Center, with its system of trails, is located near where the valley meets the bay. Tomales Bay State Park, as well as portions of the PRNS, features calm-water beaches and pine-shaded hiking trails through lands where many Miwok archeological finds have been made. West of these bay beaches, Limantour Road heads over the Inverness Ridge toward the

Lifeboat Station, Drakes Bay

Palomarin, Kehoe Beach,
Bear Valley Headquarters, Miwok Village

ocean. Here visitors will find chaparral and California-laurel valleys, on trails offering supreme vistas.

The west end of the Point Reyes Peninsula, where it fans out to a 17-mile-wide hammerhead, is known for its huge, wave-battered beaches, including McClures, Kehoe, Great Beach, and Point Reyes Beach. On the southern head of the west side is the seashore's calling card: the Point Reyes Lighthouse, a historical attraction as well as a viewing area for migrating whales and birthing elephant seals. Chimney Rock, which shares the head with the lighthouse, is also a wildflower extravaganza and vista point, whose lands shelter Drakes Bay, beneath it, from prevailing winds.

On the northern tip of the peninsula is the geographically significant, as well as scenic, Tomales Bluff. The bluff is the northernmost point of the Pacific plate, situated where Tomales Bay opens to the Pacific. Sweeping up from the bluff, as well as from the beaches on the northern end of the peninsula, is Cow Heaven—sprawling green pastures that roll for miles. Many trails wander through these pasturelands, including those at Bull Point, Marshall Beach, and upper Muddy Hollow.

As if this ecological and topographical breadth were not enough, nature also has given the seashore large Abbotts Lagoon and huge Drakes Estero. Here stream runoff and the tide waters mix, creating a wonderland for shorebirds, raptors, waterfowl and just about every other kind of creature with a beak and feathers.

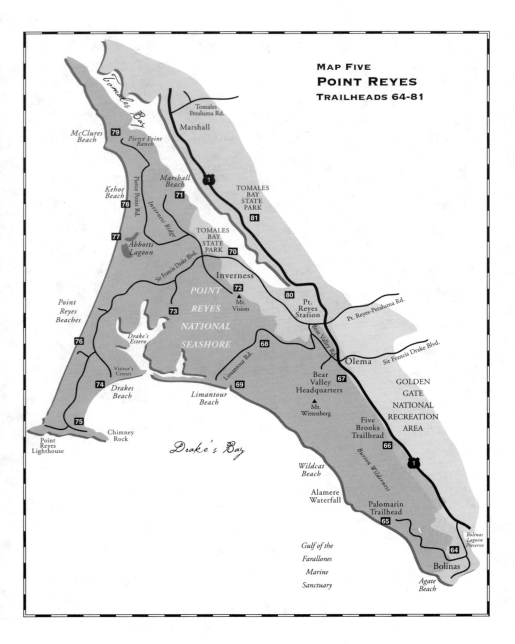

Tomales Bay

Tomales
Petaluma Rd.

Marshall

McClures
Beach 79 Pierce Point
Ranch

Marshall
Beach

71

1

TOMALES
BAY
STATE
PARK

81

Kehoe
Beach 78

Pierce Point Rd.

Inverness Ridge

77

Abbotts
Lagoon

TOMALES
BAY
STATE
PARK 70

Sir Francis Drake Blvd.

Inverness

POINT 72 Mt.
Vision

Point
Reyes
Beaches

73 **REYES**

NATIONAL

80 Pt.
Reyes
Station

Pt. Reyes-Petaluma Rd.

Drake's
Estero

SEASHORE 68

Bear Valley Rd.

Olema Sir Francis Drake Blvd.

76

Limantour Rd.

Visitor's
Center

74 Drakes
Beach 69

Limantour
Beach

Bear
Valley 67
Headquarters

GOLDEN
GATE
NATIONAL
RECREATION
AREA

Mt.
Wittenberg

75

Chimney
Rock

Point
Reyes
Lighthouse

Drake's Bay

Five
Brooks
Trailhead

66

Burton Wilderness

1

Wildcat
Beach

Alamere
Waterfall

Palomarin
Trailhead

65

Bolinas
Lagoon
Preserve

Gulf of the
Farallones
Marine
Sanctuary

64

Bolinas

Agate
Beach

POINT REYES

T R A I L H E A D S

64-81

H	HIKES
ST	STROLLS
MB	MOUNTAIN AND ROAD BIKES
J	JOGGING
R	ROLL - SKATES, SCOOTERS, BABY STROLLERS, WHEELCHAIRS

All hike and stroll distances are ROUND TRIP except as noted for shuttles.
Please contact Agency to obtain current rules and regulations. See Resource Links for all telephone numbers.
See also special Doggie Trails section.

64. BOLINAS

H, ST, MB

Best for: A large lagoon, tide pools, a surfer's beach, and a stroll of Marin's quirkiest town.

Parking: *From southern Marin:* Take Hwy. 1-Stinson Beach exit from north of Sausalito and follow about 13 mi. to 3.5-mi. north of Stinson Beach. Turn left on Olema-Bolinas Rd. Continue 2 mi. and park in town. *From central Marin:* Take Sir Francis Drake Blvd.-San Anselmo exit and follow about 18 miles, through Fairfax to Hwy. 1 at Olema. Go south on Hwy. 1 for about 7.5 mi., and turn right on Olema-Bolinas Rd. *Notes:* People have been tearing down the highway sign pointing to Bolinas for years, and officials have stopped trying to replace it. Additional parking directions in hiking descriptions

Agency: Marin County Department of Parks; *Special Interest: Surfing, Kayaks

H: Bolinas Lagoon (1.5 mi.); Agate Beach (up to 1.5 mi.)

For the **Bolinas Lagoon hike**, look for a County Parks trailhead sign on the left, about a mile in on Olema-Bolinas Road—just before the road makes a sharp right. Start out on the Bob Stewart Trail, beside a small creek among vines and under a leafy ceiling of alder and elms. You pop out to a big view of the lagoon, looking across a mile of open water toward the Bolinas Ridge. Veer right, skirting the water and crossing a foot-bridge. You'll come around to a view south of Kent Island, where the lagoon's harbor seals haul out to rest, breed, and molt. In recent years, sedimentation has adversely affected the lagoon's tidal flows, a problem being addressed by the Bolinas Lagoon Foundation. *Additional Access:* A second trailhead is just beyond the Bolinas School.

To stroll **Agate Beach**, and the renowned tide pools of Duxbury Reef, you need to drive up to the Mesa from Bolinas. Turn right on Brighton Avenue as you drop into town, veer right on Park Avenue behind the tennis courts, and keep right on Terrace Avenue. As Terrace becomes Ocean Avenue on the mesa, turn right on Overlook Drive, and then immediately left on Elm Road. Follow Elm to its end, at Agate Beach parking. Offshore is the Gulf of the Farallones National Marine Sanctuary. Then take the short road down to the beach. Stroll the shell-and-rock beach, or, during low tides, head left out to the tide pools of the reef. A dozen or more ships have run aground here, including the *Duxbury* in 1849. *Be Aware:* Surging tide and waves present hazards, as does venturing too close to unstable cliffs. Do not remove or collect anything from this marine study area. *Note:* You can also get to Agate Beach, by turning right on Mesa Road, before Bolinas, and then turning left on Overlook Avenue.

ST: Bolinas town and beach loop (1.75 mi.)

In 1850, two-thirds of Marin's 325 residents lived in this bawdy logging town, where lumber was shipped to build booming San Francisco. Prior to that, this most southern tip of the Point Reyes Peninsula was part of *Rancho las Baulenes*, a cattle ranch granted to two brothers, former Mexican soldiers. In the late 1800s, the stagecoach brought summer home builders, followed by the first funky subdivisions in the early 1900s. In Bolinas, dogs sleep on sidewalks and sandy-footed people walk the middle of the street— a bohemian Cannery Row where fishermen, surfers, New Age entrepreneurs, neo-Hippies, and tourists mingle amid breezes wafting espresso, salt air, and patchouli.

For the **Bolinas loop stroll**, begin at the corner of Brighton Avenue and head down Wharf Road—which Bolinas Road becomes. You'll pass a favorite watering hole on your left—Smiley's, formerly the Schooner Saloon built in 1852, the one remaining among nine former bars. Rounding the corner, you'll see galleries, including the Bolinas Museum—with several must-stops for those interested in local history and artwork. Down from the museum is the College of Marin's Marine Station—where for years biologist Gordy Chan was the Bolinas version of John Steinbeck's Doc. Wharf Road narrows and ends at a concrete ramp—where you begin a .5-mile beach walk that should not be attempted at high tide. To your left, across the mouth of the lagoon is the end of the sand spit at Stinson Beach, TH62. With cliffs and bulkheads to your right, walk the tide-washed sand until reaching Brighton, where you walk another concrete ramp up between houses. You'll pass Bolinas Park on your left, and several old Victorians made into boutiques, bookshops, and antique stores, before coming back to the parking spot.

MB: Get a feeling of the local character by taking a ride on the seriously potholed, unpaved alleyways on the **Bolinas Mesa**; head up there via the directions to Agate Beach. The streets on the mesa are laid out in a grid, so it's hard to get too lost. Then head down Overlook and turn left to ride the pavement of scenic **Mesa Road to Palomarin** trailhead parking. You go through open dairylands with ocean views.

Burton Wilderness, Bolinas Beach

For a country ride—of about 15 miles round-trip—pedal to **Five Brooks**, TH66, via the **Olema Valley Trail**. Head out of town on Olema-Bolinas Road and stay left past the school on Horseshoe Hill Road. This road will take you to the highway and the trailhead on your left—opposite a trailhead for the McCurdy Trail. You then ride the bumpy, pastoral Olema Valley Trail for about 5.5 miles to Five Brooks.

Special Interest: Surfing: An offshore break at the mouth of Bolinas Lagoon, as well as a little farther north up the beach, makes Bolinas one of the more popular spots in Marin. *Kayaks:* The Bolinas Lagoon is a tranquil paddle, with lots of open water, but it is shallow, so be aware of tides. The lagoon is also a wildlife sanctuary with special status. Contact the Point Reyes Visitors Center before venturing out.

65.   PALOMARIN   H, J

> **Best for:**   Coastal wilderness, with rugged beaches, a bird observatory, forested slopes pocketed with lakes, and a waterfall that empties into the sea.
>
> **Parking:**   *From southern Marin:* Take Hwy. 1-Stinson Beach exit from north of Sausalito and follow to north of Stinson Beach. Turn left on Olema-Bolinas Rd. *From central Marin:* Take Sir Francis Drake Blvd.-San Anselmo exit and follow through Fairfax to Hwy. 1 at Olema. Go south on Hwy. 1 for about 7.5 mi., and turn right on Olema-Bolinas Rd. *From Bolinas Rd:* Go left at Horseshoe Rd. stop sign, toward Bolinas. Turn right at Mesa Rd. stop sign and follow for about 4 mi. to Palomarin parking at road's end.
>
> **Agency:**   Point Reyes National Seashore; *Special Interest: Backpacking, Kids

H: **Point Reyes Bird Observatory loop (1 mi.); Palomarin Beach (up to 1.25 mi.); Palomarin Trailhead to: Abalone Point view (1.75 mi.), or Crystal Lake (7 mi.), or Alamere Falls (8 mi.)**

The **Point Reyes Bird Observatory** is on your left about .75-miles after passing the seashore boundary on the way in to Palomarin parking. At the modest office of this nonprofit research and conservation organization is an interesting interpretive display. From the observatory's parking lot, the Fern Canyon Nature Trail dips down into a mossy Arroyo Hondo Creek canyon and loops back through dry woodland.

Palomarin Beach is rock-strewn, gravelly, and set against crumbling cliffs. You'll find access about .5-mile beyond the bird observatory, before the parking lot at road's end. Interpretive signs on the eroded road down explain the beach's ecology.

For all Palomarin Trailhead hikes, head up the stairs from the parking area and go left on the Coast Trail. You start out among massive eucalyptus trees. Very soon you'll pass a road on the left that leads to **Palomarin Beach**. After that, the trail emerges from the grove to open hills, with dwarf vegetation and big Pacific views. The trail enters the Philip Burton Wilderness Area—named for a congressman who, along with his brother then-Assemblyman John Burton, and many others, helped establish the GGNRA. Less than a mile from the trailhead, on an outside bend in the trail, you have a view of **Abalone Point** down to your left.

After crossing a bridge at the creek and heading inland about .75-mile, you pass the Lake Ranch Trail on your right—keep left. For a mile-long stretch the trail stays away from ocean views, beginning up a rocky ramp and then burrowing through a forest with Douglas fir growing up from a jungly undergrowth. A series of lakelets, and then big Bass Lake will appear on your left, set well below the trail in a conifer forest. **Crystal Lake** is off-trail between two steep, forested ridges. Take the Crystal Lake Trail to your right, after passing Bass Lake but before reaching Pelican Lake.

To continue to **Alamere Falls**—best seen in late winter—bear left, passing Pelican Lake, which sits in open lands next to sea cliffs. Immediately after dropping down from the saddle at Pelican Lake, look to your left for a spur trail—and don't be confused by a preceding erosion ditch. The trail goes down the ravine above Alamere Creek. You come in above Alamere Falls, where several cascades fall into pools, before the runoff takes a three-story drop to meet salt water at the beach. Only goat trails lead down to cascades and the beach; the last one is way to the right as you face the water. The big rock offshore is called Stormy Stack. *Be Aware:* The cliff edge at the falls is extremely unstable, as are the trails leading to the beach. *Additional Access:* The Coast Trail, 2 miles from Alamere, reaches Wildcat Camp. A second, well-marked trail to Wildcat provides for a loop around two lakes—Ocean and Wildcat—on the way. From the camp, you can walk south on long Wildcat Beach to reach the falls.

J: Cross-country runners won't find a better training track than the Coast Trail going north out of Palomarin trailhead. The trail dips and dives 150 feet or more, but in general you maintain a contour about 400 feet above sea level. Wildcat Camp is almost 11 miles, round trip.

*Special Interest: *Backpacking:* The GGNRA operates two campgrounds on the shore-line, the Coast and Wildcat camps. Call Bear Valley Visitors Center for permits and other information. *Kids:* Any child interested in birds will like the Point Reyes Bird Observatory, which has educated and entertained school kids since 1965. The steps down to the creek on Fern Canyon Nature Trail will also enchant kids.

66. FIVE BROOKS   H, MB, J, R

Best for: Long hiking routes through forest to the coast, or treks up either of two parallel ridges—close together as the hawk flies, but geologically speaking a continental plate apart.

Parking: *From southern Marin:* Take Hwy. 1-Stinson Beach exit from north of Sausalito and follow Hwy. 1 north of Stinson Beach about 5.5 mi. Turn left to signed parking. *From central Marin:* Take Sir Francis Drake Blvd.-San Anselmo exit and follow through Fairfax to Hwy. 1 at Olema. Go south on Hwy. 1 for about 3.5 mi. *Note:* Additional parking described in hiking section. *Bus:* GGT weekend route 63

Agency: Point Reyes National Seashore; *Special Interest: Horses, Backpacking

H: Five Brooks to: **Pond loop** (.75-mi.), or **Bolema-Stewart Trail Ridge loop** (5.25 mi.), or **Greenpicker Trail to Firtop summit** (6 mi.), or **Rift Zone Trail to Olema** (8.5 mi.); **Randall Trail to Bolinas Ridge** (3.5 mi.); **McCurdy Trail to Bolinas Ridge** (3.5 mi.)

Highway 1 though the Olema Valley runs atop the San Andreas Fault. The Point Reyes Peninsula is part of the Pacific Plate, which is moving northward, while lands to the east of the road are on the North American Plate, which is moving south. If you hike both sides, you'll note different geology and flora, with denser pine and fir forests on the peninsula, contrasted on the east with grassy hillsides with pockets of oaks and redwoods—with plant overlap that has occurred with time.

For the **Five Brooks Pond loop**, walk straight through the gate on the wide Stewart Trail road, with the pond at your left. The pond is a bird watcher's special: Look for ring-necked ducks, mergansers, grebes, and green-back heron. At the far end of the pond, which is fringed by Douglas fir, oaks and several other trees, go left on the Olema Valley Trail and then go left again on a trail that leads back along the shore, passing the stables.

The **Bolema-Stewart Trail Ridge loop** is a moderately strenuous jaunt through mixed forest to a 1,000-foot-high ridge with ocean views. Start on Stewart Trail, the main road from the parking area. Go left at the far end of the pond on the Olema Valley Trail, along a creek under a leafy canopy, to reach the Bolema Trail after about 1.25 miles. Go right, making a climb of about 800 feet in a little more than a mile, coming to the Ridge Trail. Two trails go south on the ridge, but you want to go north, for .75-miles—fairly level with tree-filtered views—to the Stewart Trail, on which you go right. You'll pass mammoth Douglas firs on the upper part of a winding, 3-mile return to the parking area.

For the **Greenpicker Trail to Firtop summit**, which is just 83 feet shy of the highest point in the seashore, start out on the Stewart Trail. Bear right at the far shore and continue .75-mile to a trailhead on your right on an outside bend. You'll pass a trail spur to Stewart Horse Camp along the way. The Greenpicker is a steep sucker, making a climb of nearly 1,000 feet through a tangle of forest and vines in about 2 miles, approaching Firtop from its north face. Near the top of the 1,324-foot rounded summit, you'll see the Stewart Trail, which leads back to trailhead parking. Don't expect sweeping views on this tree-lover's hike. *Additional Access:* Trails lead east from the Firtop summit to the rocky coastline. One good path is to continue on Stewart Trail. You'll wind and drop to the southwest to Wildcat Camp and its beach; this route is some 13 miles round-trip from Five Brooks.

The Randall and McCurdy trails climb east from the Olema Valley up to Bolinas Ridge. The **Randall Trail** is on your left, 2.25 miles south, just north of the Pacific Coast Learning Center. It is a graded road, rising about 800 feet, through shaggy Douglas fire, laurel, and mossy oaks, to the Bolinas Ridge Trail. A spur trail near the trailhead leads to pretty Hagmaier Pond. The **McCurdy Trail** is on your left about 4.5 miles south of Five Brooks, just north of Dogtown. This trail also ascends about 800 feet to the ridge trail, but on more of a trail, and through a drier habitat. You'll have Bolinas Lagoon and Stinson Beach views at your back. *Additional Access:* You can make a Randall-McCurdy loop, of about 8 miles, by walking up the Randall Trail and taking the Bolinas Ridge Trail south 1.25 miles to connect with the McCurdy. At the bottom, cross Highway 1 and go north on the Olema Valley Trail, which connects after 3.25 miles with the Randall Trail parking.

MB: Fit cyclists will like the **Stewart Trail to Wildcat Beach**, a 13-mile ride. You climb on a sane grade up 800 feet over 3.75 miles, and then drop, very steeply at times, some 1,300 feet down to sea level. For an easier go of it, try an 11-mile round-trip ride south on the **Olema Valley Trail**, coming out on Highway 1 at Dogtown. You'll encounter a dip of 250 feet not far south of Five Brooks, as the road leaves Olema Creek. You then follow Pine Gulch Creek through a bucolic valley.

J: The Five Brooks Pond loop is a jogging path Thoreau would enjoy. Adventure runners can take off west on the nicely graded Stewart Trail, to Firtop and continue to Wildcat Camp on the coast.

R: **Strollers and Wheelchairs:** The Five Brooks Pond loop has pleasant viewing areas of the water, as well as good looks at the Point Reyes forest and the Bolinas Ridge. Strollers will also be able to navigate the Stewart Trail, as well as the first mile or more of the Olema Valley Trail. A variety of birds provide company.

*Special Interest: *Horse rides:* Rentals available at Five Brooks and at Stewart Horse camp, which is just north. Five Brooks is a popular riding trailhead. *Backpacking:* The coastal Wildcat Camp and the mountainous Glen Camp are accessible from this trailhead; contact PRNS Visitors Center in Bear Valley for permits.

67.   BEAR VALLEY HEADQUARTERS   H, MB, J, R

Best for: Attractions on the beautiful grounds of park headquarters keep families coming back for more, and coastal ridges lure adventurous hikers.

Parking: *From southern Marin:* Take Hwy. 1-Stinson Beach exit from north of Sausalito and follow Hwy. 1 past Stinson to Olema. Just north of Olema, go left on Bear Valley Rd. and watch for signs to visitors center. *From central Marin:* Take Sir Francis Drake Blvd.-San Anselmo exit and follow through Fairfax to Hwy. 1 at Olema. Jog north and make an immediate left on Bear Valley Rd. *Bus:* GGT weekend route 65

Agency: Point Reyes National Seashore *Special Interest;: Kids, Backpacking

H: Earthquake Trail (.75-mi.); Morgan Horse Ranch (.5-mi.); Woodpecker Nature Trail (.75-mi.); Kule Loklo Miwok Village (1 mi.); Mt. Wittenberg (4.5 mi.); Divide Meadow (3.25 mi.); Sculptured Beach (10.25 mi.); Coast at Arch Rock (8.25 mi.)

The open-beamed **Bear Valley Visitors Center and Park Headquarters**, with displays, photos, and dioramas, is a destination unto itself. The center is also the first stop to learn about trail conditions, obtain permits, and become acquainted with the history and ecology of the seashore. From 1890 through the early 1930s, Bear Valley was a private hunting club. In September 1962, John F. Kennedy signed a bill authorizing the national seashore, one of his last official acts as president.

Several short hikes are near the visitor center grounds. The most popular may be the **Earthquake Trail**, beginning in the towering oaks and picnic area, off the parking lot to the left as you pass the main building. The San Andreas Fault runs under foot—the epicenter of the great quake of '06. Here, poor Matilda the cow was swallowed as the fault shifted. Staggered fence posts demonstrate the 20-foot shift that took place that morning.

The **Morgan Horse Ranch** is where the rangers' mounts for the National Park Service are bred and trained. Go right up the road at the beginning of the Bear Valley trailhead that is south of the visitors center. Working exhibits and displays tell you all about America's first native breed. The **Woodpecker Trail**, a riparian self-guided nature walk, will impart a deep-forest experience without having to go far. Beginning to the right at the Bear Valley Trail, the Woodpecker Trail circles through the habitat of woodland creatures and passes the horse ranch on the way back.

Kule Loklo—which is Miwok for "bear valley," named in the days when grizzlies ruled—is now a replica of a Coast Miwok village, replete with a bark dwelling, an earthen sweatlodge, sunshade and other structures, made using traditional methods and tools, and native materials. The trail begins to the right, or north as you drive in toward the visitors center.

For the hike up to **Mt. Wittenberg**, which at 1,407 feet is the highest point on the peninsula, start south on the Bear Valley Trail. Go right at the trail junction .25-mile from the trailhead gate. This steepest of trails to the ridge takes you up some 1,300 feet over 1.75 miles, through a sampling of the peninsula's wide variety of flora. Once at the ridge, take a spur trail to your right, .25-mile, to the summit and its grand view of Drakes Bay and northern Marin. *Additional Access:* From Mt. Wittenberg you have several loop options, all of which involve heading south to the Sky Trail, which runs the ridgeline, taking a connector trail left down to the Bear Valley Trail, and going left on this main trail back to visitors center. A Meadow Trail loop is 5.75-miles. A loop using the Old Pine Trail is 7.5 miles. Finally, you can come down the Sky Trail for 2.5 miles and go left on the Baldy Trail, which makes for a loop of almost 10 miles.

To **Divide Meadow**, a pleasant bird watcher's hike, head down the Bear Valley Trail. In the shade of a mixed Douglas fir forest, you walk beside Bear Valley Creek. The trail features several benches to sit and enjoy a woodland habitat rich with birds, including owls, thrushes, woodpeckers, and wrens. After climbing a rise, you come to the grassy meadow with sunny picnic areas, unless it happens to be raining.

For the strenuous hike to the battered coastline at **Sculptured Beach**, take the Bear Valley Trail south from the parking area for 1.5 miles and go right on Old Pine Trail. This forested grade takes you on a 2-mile trek up to the ridge, gaining about 400 feet on the way. From the ridge—with its east-west views—go right on the Sky Trail for about .25-mile and then drop off to the west on the Woodward Valley Trail. This trail snakes 2 miles down to the coast. To Sculptured Beach you need to go south, or left, on the Coast Trail. In less than .5-mile you'll see a spur trail from the bluff. *Note:* Woodward Valley is shown as "Woodworth" on some maps. To get to **Arch Rock**, a landmark on a craggy coast, head south on the Bear Valley Trail for 3 miles, all the way to its end. The Arch Rock Trail will be straight ahead, the middle of three options. You hike the next mile alongside Coast Creek, and reach the Coast Trail. A short spur leads west from this junction to the formation.

MB: No through trails lead west from park headquarters, but the **Bear Valley Trail** presents a great opportunity for a hike 'n' bike: Ride in the 3 miles through lush forest, lock your bike at racks provided by the Park Service, and take a hike to the coast. One hiking option from the end of the Bear Valley Trail is to walk to Arch Rock, and head on north on the **Coast Trail** for 2.5 miles, passing Kelham Beach, Secret Beach, and coming to Sculptured Beach. This option is 7.75 miles of hiking, plus a 6.25-mile bike ride.

For a **Baldy Trail loop** of 4 miles, head down the trail to Arch Rock and go north on the Coast Trail for .5-mile. Then head up the ridge on the Sky Trail. You climb about 600 feet for 1.5 miles, before joining the Baldy Trail, where you hang a right and travel a rough contour through mostly chaparral back to the bike rack.

J: The 6-plus-mile round-trip jog on the Bear Valley Trail, through pleasant and varied forest, is fairly flat overall, although you make a 250-foot climb midway, through Divide Meadow. Runners will also like the pastoral Rift Zone Trail, so long as an earthquake does not take place; take the trail that is off to the left from near the start of the Bear Valley Trail. The route, covering 4.75-miles to Five Brooks, skirts the tranquil Vedanta Retreat and then follows a fairly level course.

R: **Wheelchairs and Strollers:** The Earthquake Trail is paved, and features a pleasant streamside and oak knoll route. Kule Loklo and the Morgan Horse Ranch are also doable for rollers. You'll have a full day rolling around the visitors center.

*Special Interest: *Kids:* The Earthquake, Morgan Ranch, Kule Loklo, and Woodpecker trails are, as they say, fun for the whole family. Combined with the visitors center itself, a family with young kids can make several trips here. *Backpacking:* Permits for all the primitive campgrounds in the seashore are issued here.

68. LIMANTOUR HIGH TRAILS   H, MB, J

Best for: Fit the pieces of the Point Reyes puzzle together with bird's-eye views from its ridge tops—by starting out at high-elevation trailheads.

Parking: *From Olema:* Jog north on Hwy. 1 and turn left on Bear Valley Rd. Pass visitors center and turn left on Limantour Rd. *From Pt. Reyes Station:* Go south on Hwy. 1, turn right on Sir Francis Drake Blvd., left on Bear Valley Rd. and then right on Limantour Rd. *For Sky Trail:* Look for turnout on left at top, after about 3.5 mi. on Limantour Rd. *For Bayview Trail:* Look for turnout on right after about 4.5 mi. on Limantour Rd.

Agency: Point Reyes National Seashore

H: Sky Trail to: Sky Camp (2.5 mi.), or Mt. Wittenberg (4.25 mi.), or Coast Trail via Woodward Valley (9.5 mi.); Bayview Trailhead to: Point Reyes Hill (5.5 mi.), or Mt. Vision (7.25 mi.), or Bayview-Drakes View loop (4.75 mi.)

Sky Trail hikes: **Sky Camp**, one of the seashore's backpacking sites, is set near a spring and a grove of eucalyptus, a few hundred feet in elevation up from the trailhead. Stay on the road all the way. To get to **Mt. Wittenberg**, some 700 feet above trailhead parking, go left on the Horse Trail after .75-mile, before reaching the camp. After a short distance, go right on the Z Ranch Trail, which after .75-mile connects with a spur trail to the 1,407-foot summit. To make a short loop on the way back, you can go south from Mt. Wittenberg on the Z Ranch Trail, for almost .5-mile, and connect with the Sky Trail; then go right about .5-mile to Sky Camp and continue back to trailhead parking.

For the longer walk to the **Coast Trail via Woodward Valley**, stride through Sky Camp—after which the road becomes a trail—and in another 1.5 miles you'll see the Woodward Valley trail to the right. The next 1,000-foot drop through the valley is a study in flora transition, from mixed conifers, through woodland and chaparral, and finally to coastal grasslands. Near the bottom you can see the whole coast, from Palomarin to Drakes Bay. *Note:* Woodward Valley is shown as "Woodworth" in some publications.

Bayview Trail hikes: **Pt. Reyes Hill**—called a "hill" even though, at 1,336 feet, it is the peninsula's second-highest summit—is up Inverness Ridge Road from Bayview parking. After a mile on the dirt road, veer left at a fork that leads to Drakes View Drive. About .75-mile after that, the road becomes more of a trail during the last, steeper walk to the top of the hill. You'll have climbed some 700 feet above trailhead parking. **Mt Vision**, accessible by car from the north, via TH72, is about .5-mile north on the ridge road from Pt. Reyes Hill. You drop down to Mt. Vision's 1,282-foot top, which is a wide-open parking area with views both of Tomales Bay and the Pacific.

The **Bayview-Drakes View loop** runs through an area reviving after a wildfire. Start on the Bayview Trail from the parking area. With of Pt. Reyes Head, you'll descend for 1.5 miles, and then cut inland up a creek to join the Drakes View Trail. Go right, up a spur ridge for 2 miles, veering right near the top, to join the Inverness Ridge Road. This junction is a mile north of Bayview parking. *Additional Access:* At the junction with Drakes View Trail, you can also go left on the Muddy Hollow Trail, which drops to the coast over a 2-mile course; this works best if some nice person has a car parked below at Limantour.

MB: From **Inverness Ridge Road**, going north from the Bayview Trail, you can make a downhill loop ride to Sir Francis Drake Boulevard in Inverness. For this **Drakes View-Drakes Summit loop**—covering some 5.5 miles and requiring about 800 feet of climb—head up the ridge road for a mile and veer right at a fork. After less than .5-

mile you connect with the gate at the top of Drakes View Drive. Take this twisty paved road down, passing other funky roads, coming out between Inverness and Inverness Park. Go right for a mile on Drake Boulevard and then right again on Balboa Avenue, which is just north of Bear Valley Road. Balboa connects with Drakes Summit Road. You'll come to a gate after a long ride up, and pop out on Limantour Road. Go right for about .5-mile to the Bayview trailhead.

J: The Sky Trail is steep in places, but the cool choice for adventure runners looking for a grind. Another option is to take the Inverness Ridge Road north from Bayview parking, which is also a workout with big views.

69. LIMANTOUR BEACH   H, MB, J, R

Best for: Miles of beachcombing, estuaries teeming with birdlife, and coastal hiking trails along sculpted bluffs—landscape that swallows a parking lot full of nature-loving visitors.

Parking: *From Olema:* Jog north on Hwy. 1 and turn left on Bear Valley Rd. Pass visitors center and turn left on Limantour Rd. *From Pt. Reyes Station:* Go south on Hwy. 1, turn right on Sir Francis Drake Blvd., left on Bear Valley Rd., and then right on Limantour Rd. Follow Limantour Rd., some 8 mi. to parking at coast. *Note:* Additional parking in hiking descriptions.

Agency: Point Reyes National Seashore

H: Limantour Spit (up to 5 mi.); Limantour Spit-Estero loop (2 mi.);
     Limantour to Sculptured Beach (4.25 mi.); Youth Hostel-Coast Camp loop
     (4.75 mi.)

Limantour Spit is named for a French commander on his day of ignominy in 1841, when he ran aground a Mexican trading ship. Take the paved path down from the parking area and go right on the beach. You'll have more than 2 miles of open sand. Look for harbor seals, or the larger sea lions, to bob their sleek heads from the surf. Squadrons of pelicans often soar above the swells. The spit ends at the opening to Drakes Estero, across from Drakes Beach, TH74. For the **Limantour Spit-Estero loop**—a bird-watcher's special—go right from the paved path, just before you cross the beach dunes. Along this inland path's mile-long route, you'll see narrow inlets at Muddy Hollow and Glenbrook Creek, before viewing the larger Estero de Limantour near trail's end. A connector path leads left at isoltated trees, through dunes to the beach. Walk the sand back to complete the loop.

For the **Limantour to Sculptured Beach** hike—along which the dunes rise and bluffs begin—go left at the beach after taking the .25-mile path. About .5-mile down the beach, you'll see a creek gully to your left, where the Coast Trail comes down from the Point Reyes Hostel. At 1.5 miles down the beach, a second creek comes in, this one usually crossing the sand to the sea; from here a short trail leads to the Coast Camp and joins the Coast Trail. About .25-mile farther—now on Santa Maria Beach—you come to Santa Maria Creek, with the most flow of all.

Beyond the beach, you can walk trails over low bluffs to Sculptured Beach, where tidal action has artistically eroded bluffs and created tide pools. Cliffs and tides soon make the route impossible. To go farther south, take a feeder trail up to the Coast Trail. *Be Aware:* Don't let tides or sleeper waves catch you off guard in little coves. Also, the cliffs here are unstable and present a hazard for every level of hiker.

The **Youth Hostel-Coast Camp loop** is a gentle hike through scrub and grassland, with superlative ocean views. Drive to the trailhead near the Clem Miller Environmental Education Center-Pt. Reyes Youth Hostel. The trailhead is a short drive from Limantour Road, to your left about a mile before reaching the beach. Beginning on a slight uphill on the Laguna Trail, you then descend on a 1.75-mile route to join the Coast Trail at Santa Maria Beach—joining the Fire Lane Trail about halfway down. At the coast, go right on the Coast Trail, on low bluffs for a mile. Then the trail hooks inland and follows a stream back up to the hostel.

MB: The **Coast Trail** from the Point Reyes Hostel is bike-friendly for 2.75-miles, to Coast Camp. Once at the camp, you can walk south. Hiking the bluffs over the next 3.5 miles, you'll pass Secret Beach, Point Resistance, Kelham Beach, and then arrive at Arch Rock.

J: The sands of Limantour, though not flat and hard, even at low tide, are still a good choice for beach runners. One excellent course for cross-country jogging is to take the Coast Trail down from the Point Reyes Hostel, jog right up the beach to the main parking area. Then run up the Muddy Hollow Trail along the creek, through willows, vines, and alder. You then connect back on the Muddy Hollow Road, crossing Limantour Road, and hoofing it back to the hostel. This varied loop is about 5.5 miles, with about .75-mile on sand.

R: **Wheelchairs and Strollers:** The road down to the beach is paved, although the gate may be difficult for wheelchairs to get around, and you need to be prepared for a fairly steep grade down. Just before reaching the beach, a level paved path goes left along a bird-viewing marsh, with ocean views through the dunes.

70.   TOMALES BAY STATE PARK   H

Best for: Sheltered evergreen and leafy forests overlooking sunny, sandy coves— if located anywhere but West Marin this park would be the main event.

Hearts Desire Beach,
Indian Beach

Parking: From Hwy. 1 between Pt. Reyes Station and Olema, turn west on Sir Francis Drake Blvd. Continue through Inverness and veer right on Pierce Point Rd. Look for sign on right after about 1 mi. *Note:* Parking fee at Hearts Desire Beach. Additional parking in hiking description.

Agency: Tomales Bay State Park; *Special Interest: Kayaks; Hike and Bike Camping, Swimming

H: Hearts Desire Beach (up to .5-mi.); Indian Beach via Nature Trail (1 mi.); Pebble Beach (1 mi.); Jepson Memorial Grove loop (3 mi.); Shell Beach (.75-mi.)

Tomales Bay State Park was established in 1952 through the joint efforts of the Marin Conservation League and several other groups. **Hearts Desire Beach**, the darling of the park, is readily accessed from the large parking area. A broad swath of sand, bordered by lawns, leads down to gently lapping waters. Fir, pine, oak and madrone forests—with an undergrowth of toyon, huckleberry and a host of other shrubs—provide a backdrop in many shades of green. Hearts Desire is developed, with restrooms, picnic areas and barbecues.

To **Indian Beach via Nature Trail**, go left as you face the water at Hearts Desire. You hug the coast and cross a footbridge as you reach the small beach. Interpretive signs along the way tell of the plants and animals vital to the Coast Miwok, who made their home here for some 3,500 years. A service road provides a loop route back, but not one as scenic. To **Pebble Beach**, popular among clams and those who eat them, take the Johnstone Trail to the right from Hearts Desire. The trail leads up and over a rounded point and down to the rock-pocked shoreline. When tides permit, you can walk south from Pebble Beach to Shallow Beach, a depression in the forested coastline.

The **Jepson Memorial Grove loop** goes through one of the only virgin stands of the rare Bishop pine. Continue past the Pebble Beach spur on the Johnstone Trail. You'll weave up through mixed forest for 1.5 miles. Go right at the top, and then take the Jepson Trail down through the ancient, craggy pines. This trail leads through the grove to the bike campground in the upper parking area. The grove's name honors Willis Linn Jepson, a botanist from the University of California at Berkeley. *Additional Access:* The Jepson Trail also can be accessed from its high point, at Pierce Point Road, .25-mile before the park entrance.

Lovely **Shell Beach** was made public in 1945, seven years before the rest of the park. To get there, turn right off Sir Francis Drake less than 2 miles north of Inverness—on Camino del Mar. Follow for less than a mile to the ample parking area. Walking down the Johnstone Trail, follow switchbacks along a split-rail fence bordered by sword ferns, under a luscious canopy of oaks, madrone, and redwoods. The sandy beach may remind some of a sunny day on a secluded nook in the Puget Sound.

*Special Interest: *Hike and Bike Camping:* The park features a 6-site, walk-in campground, with no required reservations. *Swimming:* Though Tomales is not the tropics, it is warmer than the ocean, and free of shorebreak and riptides. This is the best saltwater swimming in Marin. *Kayaks:* Put-in at Chicken Ranch Beach—not part of the state park—located 1.5-miles north of Inverness, where the road makes a sweeping left turn away from the water. The beach is across from Pine Hill Drive.

71. MARSHALL BEACH   H, MB, J

> **Best for:**   Sweeping view trails on the pastoral uplands of the north peninsula—"Cow Heaven"—that lead down to a forested, sandy beach on the bay.

> **Parking:**   From Hwy. 1 between Pt. Reyes Station and Olema, turn west on Sir Francis Drake Blvd. Continue through Inverness and veer right on Pierce Point Rd. Immediately past entrance to the Tomales State Park, veer right on Duck Cove-Marshall Beach Rd. Follow about 2.5 mi. to parking at road's end.

> **Agency:**   Point Reyes National Seashore; *Special Interest: Boat Camping

H: Marshall Beach (2.75 mi.); Lairds Landing (2.25 mi.)

To **Marshall Beach**, head straight from the gate, up and over a rise through a dairyland vista. Cross a second gate to your right. The ranches of the peninsula are all historic, dating from the 1800s. The road then curves right, making gentle switchbacks down 300 feet to the beach. Nicely spaced cypress and pine trees buffer a sandy shore. When tides permit, you can walk north toward Tomales Beach, about .75-miles away. For **Lairds Landing**, a more active locale during pre-auto days when dairy products were shipped out Tomales Bay, take the road to the right from the trailhead gate. You contour around the other side of the head, dropping down to a coastal nook on the south side of Marshall Beach.

MB: The roads to both **Marshall Beach** and **Lairds Landing** make excellent, if short, rides. A better option is to park at Pierce Point Road and pedal all the way on **Duck Cove-Marshall Road**, through the heart of Cow Heaven. Although you share the dirt road with cars, traffic is seldom an issue. After about 1.25 miles, just past L Ranch, you can veer right toward **Sacramento Landing** on another swerving slope down to a pine-framed cove on the bay. A right fork near the bottom heads towards Ducks Cove, while the left fork goes to the landing.

J: All of the above described for hiking and biking goes double for runners. Indeed, you may feel like Julie Andrews in Spandex jogging Sound-of-Music landscapes.

Special Interest: Boat Camping: Although you cannot launch a craft from this trailhead, you can paddle to a shoreside camp at Marshall Beach. Contact PRNS for permit information.

72.   MOUNT VISION   H, MB, R

Best for: A sky-high look at all the beaches and hiking routes of the north Point Reyes Peninsula, fit together in one panorama; or a roll down Inverness Ridge on a bicycle.

Parking: From Hwy. 1 between Pt. Reyes Station and Olema, turn west on Sir Francis Drake Blvd. Continue through Inverness and veer left toward lighthouse, past Pierce Point Rd. In less than 1 mi., go left on Mt. Vision Rd. Continue up 4 mi. to parking at top.

Agency: Point Reyes National Seashore

H: **Mount Vision (0 mi.); Point Reyes Hill (1 mi.); Pt. Reyes Hill to Limantour Beach car-shuttle (6 mi.)**

You can drive to the 1,282-foot summit of aptly named **Mt. Vision**, a place to see where you've been and where you'd like to go next. The road up is steep but well-paved. The best vista point is about 2.5 miles from Drake Boulevard, where an outside bend in the road and hillside trail combine for a great lunch spot. On **Point Reyes Hill** are views of Mt. Tam, Barnabe Peak, and the north Marin hills are added to the sea-scapes. Walk past the cable gate on the paved road and make the dogleg up. On the summit is a fenced FAA installation. Walk around it to achieve views in all directions.

To descend 1,336 feet to **Limantour Beach**, on a one-way route, continue south from Point Reyes Hill on the Inverness Ridge Trail. After about 1.5 miles, go right on the Drakes View Trail. After coming down a side-hill for 2 miles, you'll join the Bayview Trail. After another .5-mile, you get to the Muddy Hollow Trail—where you continue to follow the creek, through the willows, alder and other riparian flora for an additional 2 miles, until your westward progress is thwarted by the Pacific Ocean.

MB: Several gated roads lead up to Mt. Vision and the Inverness Ridge, providing cyclists with long downhill runs for a car-shuttle, or several knarly down-and-up loop rides. For a one-way ticket, ride the **Inverness Ridge Road south** from Mt. Vision, over Point Reyes Hill, and drop down Limantour Road at Bayview Trailhead. From there you can ride down to Limantour Beach. Or, before reaching the road, hang a left at Drakes View Drive and come up Drakes Summit Road, a loop described in TH68.

For another loop ride, take the road that heads toward the bay from the **Mt. Vision parking area**. This horsemen's route connects with **Perth Way** that you follow down, via Forrest Way, and come out in Inverness at Park Avenue. You then go left on Drake Boulevard for almost .75-mile. Across from the yacht club, turn left on Vision Road. Follow Vision to the top; it is unpaved for a mile near the end. You'll come out on Mt. Vision Road almost 2 miles down from the summit, where you turn left and ride to the top. This is a 6-mile loop, with 1,300-foot climb.

R: **Wheelchairs and Strollers:** Although the drive up to the Mt. Vision parking area provides ample view spots, the paved road up to Point Reyes Hill is worth the push. The hill is the highest peak reasonably attained by wheelchair in Marin County.

73.   THE ESTEROS   H, ST, MB, J

Best for: The peninsula's unexpected bonus: A huge estuary, with four bays, surrounded by pastoral slopes that lead to a dramatic opening to the Pacific.

Parking: From Hwy. 1 between Pt. Reyes Station and Olema, turn west on Sir Francis Drake Blvd. Continue through Inverness and veer left toward the lighthouse, past Pierce Point Rd. Continue on Drake Blvd. for another 2 mi. and turn left on signed road to Estero. Park after 1 mi. at large lot. *Note:* Additional parking in hiking and stroll descriptions.

Agency: Point Reyes National Seashore; *Special Interest: Kayaks, Kids

H: Home Bay (2.75 mi.); Sunset Beach (7.75 mi.); Drakes Head (9 mi.); Estero de Limantour (7.5 mi.); Bull Point (3.75 mi.)

Between Drakes Beach and Limantour Spit is a .25-mile wide opening where the ocean mixes with the fresh water of a half-dozen streams in a large shallow bay—called an estuary since the fresh water content is high and the tidal flow is low. Radiating off the main body of Drakes Estero, like fingers from a hand, are four bays, plus Estero de Limantour, as the thumb. At places, stretches of open water are 4 miles in from the coast, and almost 2 miles across from shore to shore.

For all hikes but Bull Point, head to the right from the parking area on the Estero Trail. At .75-mile you drop down through a grand grove of Bishop pine and come to the footbridge across the upper tentacle of **Home Bay**. This spot is an 11 on a 10-scale of scenic beauty. Continue on Estero Trail, traversing a few hundred feet up the bluff, passing an open view of the esteros. You come to a trail junction. For **Sunset Beach**— and a big look out the mouth of Drakes—veer right on the trail junction. The trail drops to the shore over a run of about 1.5 miles. Then the going gets rocky. But when the tide is right you can work your way farther toward the Pacific.

For **Drakes Head** and **Estero de Limantour**, continue left on the Estero Trail at the Sunset Beach junction. After almost .75-mile, a trail leads to the right for 1.5 miles out to Drakes Head, a walk you are likely to share with cows. You reach a bluff that looks over Limantour Spit to the sea, at the mouth of Estero de Limantour. To get to the outer reaches of Estero de Limantour, continue past the spur trail to Drakes Head, and you'll be down to the marshy northern tip of the estuary in less than .5-mile.

Bull Point is reached via a different trailhead: Drive past the Estero turnoff for about 3 miles, to parking on your left. Veering to your left from the trailhead, you walk

Cow Heaven dairy ranch

through pasture often in close contact with your bovine brothers and sisters. The path continues onto a bluff between narrow Creamery Bay, which is to your right, and larger Schooner Bay to the left. During the late 1800s and early 1900s, schooners sailed with the tides into Drakes Estero, picking up boxes of butter for transport back to San Francisco. *Be Aware:* Bull Point's cliffs are unstable.

ST: Johnsons Oyster Company

To **Johnsons Oyster Company**—with its weatherworn docks and silvery hillocks of spent shells—drive about a mile past the Estero turnoff. Then go left on a signed road for about .75-mile. Oysters have been farmed here since the 1930s, now on about 1,000 acres of leased tidelands at Schooner Landing, the north tip of the bay. Jars of the big mollusks are for sale, prepared before your eyes in the shucking shack. Johnson's main appeal as a tourist attraction is that it is not touristy.

MB: **All the trails** described in the hiking section are open to bikes, as is the 2-mile run out to Bull Point. You can't make any loop rides, but this is a fabulous place to visit on a mountain bike—about 20 miles of riding to cover all the destinations.

J: Drakes Head is the choice for joggers. You'll be going up and down a few hundred feet on reasonable grades, but these are great scenic training trails.

Special Interest: Kayaks: Put in at Schooner Landing, at Johnsons Oyster Company. Low tide can leave you stranded in Drakes Estero, and breaking surf can be an issue near the mouth. Inquire at PRNS Headquarters for restrictions and information. *Kids:* Johnsons Oyster Farm will be fun for curious kids, a glimpse back in time. For an up-close cow encounter, try the Bull Point hike, and for a fun place to hang around with the family, take the hike to the footbridge at Home Bay.

74.   DRAKES BEACH   H, R

Best for: A long curving swath of sand set below pale cliffs and sheltered from the prevailing winds—with a informative visitors center and beachside café.

Parking: From Hwy. 1 between Pt. Reyes Station and Olema, turn west on Sir Francis Drake Blvd. Continue through Inverness and veer left toward lighthouse, past Pierce Point Rd. Continue on Drake Blvd. for another 7 mi., passing North Beach, and turn left on signed road to Drakes Beach. Park after 1.5 mile at lot.

Agency: Point Reyes National Seashore

H: Drakes Beach toward: Chimney Rock (up to 3 mi.), or Drakes Estero (2.25 mi.), or Peter Behr Overlook (.5-mi.)

Inverness

In 1579, most historians believe, the sailing vessel *Golden Hind* sprung a leak off the coast of Northern California—two years gone from England on a journey around the world—and its captain Francis Drake doubled-back to find safe harbor inside the mouth of Drakes Estero. He careened the ship—laid her on its side in the mudflats—and took some six weeks to do repairs. While there, Drake and his men enjoyed the hospitality of Coast Miwok, and claimed all their lands for Queen Elizabeth I. But 16 years later the Spanish galleon *San Agustin* foreshadowed the empire to come, when it became California's first known shipwreck—and its crew was forced to row a launch back to Mexico. Not long after, in 1603, a second Spanish vessel, the *Capitana*, found safe harbor here and its captain gave the peninsula its name: *La Punta de Los Tres Reyes*, Point of the Kings. Almost two centuries passed, however, before the land-based Spanish Empire set up camp in the Presidio.

The **Ken Patrick Visitors Center** features exhibits on these and other maritime explorations, a gift shop, marine exhibits, and a 150-gallon salt-water aquarium. The center is open weekends and holidays. A café next door is open all week during the summer, but usually only weekends the rest of the year. The **Drakes Beach** hike **toward Chimney Rock**, to your right as you face the water, ends when cliffs encroach on the beach. Going left, toward the mouth of **Drakes Estero**, is a shorter walk. Drakes is a sheltered swimming beach, however, you should avoid shorebreak conditions. *Be Aware:* The pale cliffs that ring Drakes Beach are unstable to walk on or sit beneath.

For the **Peter Behr Overlook**, go right along the front of the parking lot and take the short, but fairly steep path to the top. You can wander farther on trails along the bluff. You'll get a good perspective not only on the beach, but inland of a wildlife pond that you would not otherwise see.

R: **Strollers and Wheelchairs:** The Patrick Visitors Center is accessible, and when the center is closed, you can enter its foyer and take a look at several displays. The Peter Behr Overlook, although somewhat steep, is one of the better viewpoints to push the wheels along the entire coast.

75.   POINT REYES HEAD   H, MB, J, R

Best for: A historic lighthouse, wildflowers, migrating whales, birthing elephant seals, and postcard views—all attract a pilgrimage of admirers to these high cliffs at the western reaches of the seashore.

Parking: From Hwy. 1 between Pt. Reyes Station and Olema, turn west on Sir Francis Drake Blvd. Continue through Inverness and veer left toward lighthouse, past Pierce Point Rd. Continue on Drake Blvd. for about 12 mi. to parking at road's end. *Note:* Additional parking in hiking description. *Be Aware:* On weekends and holidays, from January through early April, the road may be closed past the entrance to South Beach. Visitors are directed to a shuttle bus at Drakes Bay; ticket fee for adults, children are free.

Agency: Point Reyes National Seashore

H: **Point Reyes Lighthouse (1.25 mi.); Chimney Rock (1.25 mi.); Lifeboat Station tide pools and seal viewing (up to 1.75 mi.)**

Point Reyes, jutting 10 miles out to sea, is the windiest place on the Pacific Coast and the second-foggiest. Since the *Agustin* wrecked here in 1595, some 37 other ships have met a similar fate. Balmy, sunny days occur more frequently in the fall and winter. From the **Point Reyes Lighthouse** parking lot, head down the cliff-side road to your right. After passing through a cypress tree tunnel, you'll come to the Lighthouse Visitors Center and adjacent historic buildings. Behind the center is an observation deck, 600 feet above sea level. The deck is a popular spot to observe migrating gray whales, which head south beginning mid-December and return in March and early April.

The lighthouse is below, down more than 300 concrete steps, set on a point that was blasted away in order to put the beacon under the fog line when it was constructed in 1870. The lighthouse's 6000-pound French Fresnel lens was shipped around the Horn to San Francisco and then carted out here by oxen. The beacon warned mariners until 1975, when automated lights were installed by the Coast Guard. During the morning of 1906, when the lighthouse and entire peninsula moved 20 feet northward during an earthquake, the lighthouse was out of service for 13 minutes. *Note:* Lighthouse stairs are normally open from 10 a.m. to 4:30 p.m., Thursday through Monday, but may close during high winds.

For **Chimney Rock** and the **Life Boat Station** tide pools, you need to drive to a different parking area: Veer left on a narrow paved road, where the lighthouse road forks right. Continue for a mile through pasturelands to the trailhead. **Chimney Rock** is a now-fallen arch that is the eastern end of the hammer-head point. The trail begins to the right. You curve atop an open hill, which in late winter and spring boasts a plethora of coastal wildflowers. During winter rains and the foggy days of summer, the same path may evoke the Scottish moors at their most forlorn—a different kind of drama. Staying left, the trail meanders to the point, where you can view Chimney Rock, as well as the entire sweep of coastline from Drakes Bay around to Duxbury Point at Bolinas. On your return, you can make a partial loop using a path that contours the Pacific-side. *Be Aware:* Cliffs are sheer and unstable; stay back.

The historic **Life Boat Station** is set in a protected cove on the Drakes Bay side of the point. From the parking area go down the road that points to the seal-viewing area, and keep right. The wood-frame station building was built in 1927, although lifesaving boats have been at work near the lighthouse since 1890. This station was active until 1968. At low tide, the rocky beach beyond the station features the best tide pools on the northern peninsula.

Just down from the Chimney Rock trailhead is the **seal-viewing area.** The massive elephant seals, numbering some 1,500 in these waters, have made a comeback since being hunted to near extinction. They haul out to breed from December through March. Mature bulls can tip the scales at 5,000 pounds, but, lovesick, they do not eat during the breeding period and lose up to 30 percent of their fat. Seal pups start out at around 65 pounds, but during the first month, fortified by mother's milk that is 55 percent fat, they pork up to 300 pounds. *Be Aware:* Elephant seals are protected by federal law; obey posted closure areas and keep 100 yards away from beached seals.

MB: The short roads to the **Lighthouse Visitors Center** and **Life Boat Station** and **Chimney Rock Trail** are all open to bicycles. The best bet for cyclists, however, may be to come out on winter and spring weekends during the peak times when the road out to the lighthouse is closed at South Beach. You can jump on the pedals and ride out to the point. About 3.5 miles from the road closure you come to a fork: The right fork goes 1.5 miles to the lighthouse, and the left goes the same distance to Chimney Rock. Rolling pasturelands with blue-water vistas border the roads.

J: Though not a great distance, Chimney Rock Trail is a top-of-the-world jogging path. You can add distance with a run down the road to the Life Boat Station.

R: **Strollers and Wheelchairs:** Handicapped parking is about .25-mile past the lighthouse parking area. The path is wheel-ready all the way, and the visitors center and observation deck are accessible—great whale watching and lighthouse views. A paved road leads down the Lifeboat Station, a smooth surface for wheels, but it is steep in places and the gates are not designed for wheelchairs.

76. POINT REYES BEACHES   H, J

Best for: Miles of sand and big waves, beachcombers' beaches with piles of driftwood and junk treasures washed ashore.

Parking: From Hwy. 1 between Pt. Reyes Station and Olema, turn west on Sir Francis Drake Blvd. Continue through Inverness and veer left toward lighthouse, past Pierce Point Rd. Continue on Drake Blvd. *For North Beach:* Turn right about 4.5 mi. past Pierce Point Rd., just after G Ranch. *For South Beach:* Turn right about 2.5 miles past North Beach, past E Ranch.

Agency: Point Reyes National Seashore

H: **North Beach to: Abbotts Lagoon (5.5 mi.), or Point Reyes Beach walk (3.5 mi.); South Beach to Point Reyes cliffs (6.25 mi.)**

Along the western face of the Point Reyes Peninsula is some 11 miles of beach, stretching straight as a string between the 600-foot cliffs of Point Reyes on the south to Elephant Rock of McClures Beach to the north. The wide margin of sand takes a pounding from high surf and prevailing winds. Bordering the inland are sea-grass dunes and coastal hillocks that in turn give way to the pasturelands of the north peninsula's historic dairy ranches. If you're seeking a solitary beach experience, these vast beaches are a sure thing.

From **North Beach to Abbotts Lagoon**, head to the right as you face the water. After about .75-mile, on the bluffs is the AT&T Radio Station, looking like a techno-art installation, which has received airwaves since 1931 from faraway locales. After almost 3 miles, you'll have to climb the sand dunes of Great Beach to see Abbotts Lagoon, set just offshore between beach bluffs and hills. Going the other way from North Beach, left as you face the water, you'll reach the parking lot at South Beach after about 1.5 miles. The area between the two parking lots is called **Point Reyes Beach**.

From **South Beach to Point Reyes cliffs**, head left as you face the water. You should be able to see the Coast Guard light flashing some 300 feet above the water at the tip of the point. This beach walk is a classic example of dunes giving way to big cliffs. How close you get to the rock wall will depend on surf and tides. *Be Aware:* Point Reyes beaches are notoriously treacherous swimming beaches, due to high surf, wave-borne debris, riptides, and, for a special bonus, the presence of great white sharks. The most-common hazard, however, are rogue waves that can snatch a hiker from the shore.

J: Sloping sand makes for tough sledding, so time it for low-tide. These long stretches of sand will run the legs out from under even the most-ardent among joggers.

77. ABBOTTS LAGOON   H, R

Best for: Migratory waterfowl and shorebirds flourish around these two large lakes, set so close to the ocean that surf spray rises above the sand dunes at their western shore.

Parking: From Hwy. 1 between Pt. Reyes Station and Olema, turn west on Sir Francis Drake Blvd. Continue through Inverness and veer right on Pierce Point Rd. Continue 3 mi. to trailhead parking on left.

Agency: Point Reyes National Seashore

H: Hunter Browbach Bench-North Wing view (.75-mi.); Lagoon Bluff (2.75 mi.); Abbotts Lagoon-Great Beach (3 mi.)

Except after heavy storms, when the dunes open and salt water mixes with fresh run-off, Abbotts Lagoon is comprised of two large lakes, the biggest nearly a mile long, that are joined together by a short stream. Between the North Wing of the lagoon, which can be seen from trailhead parking, and the South Wing, which is the larger, is a low-lying bluff. Grebes, terns, black-shouldered kites, ducks, several kinds of raptors, and the endangered snowy plover are some of the winged creatures to be seen soaring about or bobbing on the water.

For all hikes, start down the hard-packed, unpaved path from the parking area. After a little more than .25-mile, you'll get to the **Browbach Bench**, set among the cattails. After the bench, the going becomes sandy, as the trail curves left toward the bluff. After a mile you reach the footbridge that crosses the stream that joins the lagoon's two wings. For the **Lagoon Bluff**, go left at the bridge on a trail that winds about 200 feet up to the top of the bluff. You'll be surprised at the size of South Wing, upon first sight.

For **Abbotts Lagoon and Great Beach**, continue straight across the footbridge, as the broad waters of South Wing come into view. With typical onshore wind gusts, you may get sand blasted as you walk the .5-mile west along the shore. You cross a huge dune to the beach. The margins of the lagoon blush with wildflowers in the spring-time. *Be Aware:* Plovers and other birds nest in the dune grasses during the spring and early summer; watch where you step.

R: **Wheelchairs and Strollers:** The first part of the Lagoon Trail, to Hunter Browbach Bench, is packed hard to accommodate visitors sitting on wheels. Even going this short distance affords a good look at the wildlife and ecology of the North Wing of Abbotts Lagoon.

78.   KEHOE BEACH   H, J

Best for: A family beach with many facets—big dunes, a marsh trail, and waves that duel with cliffs and rocky islands.

Parking: From Hwy. 1 between Pt. Reyes Station and Olema, turn west on Sir Francis Drake Blvd. Continue through Inverness and veer right on Pierce Point Rd. Continue some 5 mi. to trailhead parking on left, about 2 mi. beyond Abbotts Lagoon.

Agency: Point Reyes National Seashore

H: **Kehoe Marsh to Beach (1.25 mi.); Kehoe Beach Walks (2.75 mi. to 5.75 mi.)**

The trail from roadside parking goes along a stream through **Kehoe Marsh**, reaching the beach dunes at a small lagoon. Keep your eyes peeled for birds flitting about, and for rabbits and bobcats, uneasy bedfellows who may venture down to the fresh water from the coastal scrub hillsides. Cresting the beach dune, you can go right on **Kehoe Beach** toward Elephant Rock, the landmark offshore of McClures Beach. But high surf, rocks, and an intervening point usually will prevent you from going much farther than .75-mile in that direction. *Be Aware:* Swimming is dangerous here.

Going left, or south, on Kehoe Beach you can walk all day. One worthy destination is the Great Beach at Abbotts Lagoon, TH77, which is about 2.25 miles away. Set your sights on the major hill rising out of the dunes that you can see from the beginning of the hike. Southern Kehoe is a deep beach, with a high-water mark scattered with driftwood, boat parts, and possibly anything else that floats. After passing Abbotts Lagoon, the next trail inland is another 2 miles, at North Beach. *Note:* Campfires are allowed by permit on Kehoe, adding atmosphere to a family picnic on blustery days.

J: With the marsh, the dunes, and different kinds of beach runs north and south, Kehoe Beach is a good choice for off-road runners—especially those who want to bring the dog along.

Kehoe Beach

79. TOMALES POINT

Best for: A narrow, pastoral peninsula separating the bay from the ocean—roamed by elk and carpeted with flowers—that ends at a wild seascape; or a big beach walled in by cliffs that greet monster waves.

Parking: From Hwy. 1 between Pt. Reyes Station and Olema, turn west on Sir Francis Drake Blvd. Continue through Inverness and veer right on Pierce Point Rd. Continue about 8 mi. to road's end, about 3 mi. beyond Kehoe Beach.

Agency: Point Reyes National Seashore

H: Tomales Point Trail to: Tule Elk Range (2.25 mi.), or Tomales Bluff (9.5 mi.); McClures Beach (1.25 mi.); Elephant Rock (2 mi.)

Tomales Point is the peninsula's northernmost finger of land, ever-narrowing and descending toward sea level. You start out on grasslands about 1.5 miles across and 400-feet high, and wind up at Tomales Bluff, a pointed land's end that is just above the surf spray. To the west is the Pacific and to the east is Tomales Bay, with the San Andreas Fault running under its shallow, 12-mile long waters—separating two continental plates. If an earthquake like the '06 happens when you're on the bluff, then the Pacific plate upon which you stand will become the prow of a tectonic ship, motoring forward perhaps 20 feet up the shoreline.

For the **Tomales Point Trail** hikes, start out just to the left of white-washed Pierce Point Ranch, contouring left around the highest hills of the point. At the outset, views of Driftwood Beach will be down to your left. The trail then descends into Windy Gap, a deep crease in the peninsula hosting a cypress grove. Heading inland at the gap, White Gulch leads to an inlet on the bay, where offshore you'll see little Hog Island. All around this area is the **Tule Elk Range**—supporting a healthy herd of these large animals, thousands of whom once roamed Point Reyes.

The trail winds up from Windy Gap, and then descends again for another 2-plus miles to **Tomales Bluff**. This northern tip is where you'll find some of the 860 species of wildflowers that grow in the park. One sandy portion of the trail goes through a field of lupine, bushlike and over knee-high. Offshore of the Pacific side, about .75-mile from trail's end, is guano-hued Bird Rock. Overhead, keep an eye out, mostly during fall and winter, for owls, peregrine falcons, and hawks. At Tomales Bluff, the trail drops down to sandstone perches, and you're most likely to see pelicans and other shorebirds. In the frothing, clear water you may spot a harbor seal or sea lion. Offshore, in the winter and spring, look for spouting whales.

PT. REYES TRAILHEADS | 217

Pierce Point Ranch

The trail to **McClures Beach** and **Elephant Rock** begins to the left, downhill from the parking area, dropping 300 feet through a ravine. McClures is a former county park, donated in 1942 by Margaret McClure. After a little more than .5-mile, you reach the wide cove, framed by tall cliffs. To the right, or north of McClures, an unsafe trail leads over a point to wild Driftwood Beach. To the left, where the sand gives way to cliffs, a trail leads up a rocky spur to a view of Elephant Rock, where wave-foam erupts with the cannon-shots of big combers hitting rocks. *Be Aware*: Watch your footing on the spur trail, narrow at times.

ST: Pierce Point Ranch

Right next to trailhead parking are the whitewashed barn, cottages, and former milking stations of historic **Pierce Point Ranch**—spread out over grassy acres in the shade of cypress and eucalyptus trees. The ranch gives you a close-up of dairy life that began with the Spanish in the early 1800s and extends to today. Andrew Randall purchased most of the ranches on Point Reyes in 1852, but a creditor shot him four years later. The lands went into litigation, eventually winding up in the hands of attorneys, the Shafter brothers—no kidding—who divided the lands into tenant farms which they colorfully named Ranches A through Z. Point Reyes butter, carrying its "PR" stamp, was highly prized in early years of San Francisco, so much so that it was forged into inferior products, some of which were shipped from Chile and the East Coast. Some of today's ranching families date back to the 1800s, including the folks at B Ranch, out near the lighthouse, in the hands of the Mendoza family.

J: The Tomales Point Trail to the bluff at land's end—almost 10 miles round-trip— should be on the "A" list for cross country runners. You'll encounter a few hundred feet of elevation change on the run, over trails with footing good enough to allow looking up to take in spectacular scenery.

80. POINT REYES STATION   H, ST, MB, J

Best for: Bird watcher's walks along a creek or marshland with bay views; or a stroll in a coastal town that is both historic and outdoorsy-chic.

Parking: *From central and southern Marin:* Take Sir Francis Drake Blvd. or Hwy. 1 to Olema and go north on Hwy. 1 for a little more than 2 mi. *From northern Marin:* Take Lucas Valley Rd. or Novato Blvd. to Point Reyes-Petaluma Rd.; continue west to Hwy. 1 and jog south .5-mile. *Note:* Additional parking in hiking descriptions. *Bus:* GGT weekend route 65

Agency: Marin County Parks; Golden Gate National Recreation Area

H: Tomales Bay Trail (3.75 mi.); White House Pool (.75 mi.)

The **Tomales Bay Trail** takes you over pasturelands at the bottom of Tomales Bay and onto a levee. Begin about 1.5 miles north of Point Reyes Station on Highway 1, at a signed GGNRA trailhead. Veer left through the pasture and keep left as the trail drops down to a gully and comes up the other side. You then walk right, over a treed point. The .5-mile-plus levee path extends almost to the shore, but allows water flow to create a large lagoon on the south side. To your left—the shallow flats that are the bottom of Tomales Bay—is the Audubon's William P. Shields Salt Marsh Study Area, which is accessible just south of Inverness Park.

White House Pool is a 24-acre county park featuring benches on a path alongside Lagunitas Creek. To get there, drive south of Point Reyes Station a short distance, turn right across the bridge on Drake Boulevard. Continue .5-mile to signed parking on your right. Go right on the trail over a footbridge and through a tunnel of vines and oak trees. Lagunitas Creek was used in the old days to ship rags inland on flat-bottomed boats for pulping at Samuel P. Taylor's Pioneer Pulp Mill; see TH85.

Additional Access: Just south of Point Reyes Station is another spot to enjoy the bay marshlands: Just before you cross the steel bridge, on your right is a Tomales Bay State Park trail that runs along Lagunitas Creek. Blackberry pickers will like this one in season, as will birders. But even those hikers fond of a whiff of fresh manure may be overwhelmed by the aroma wafting down from the dairy.

ST: Point Reyes Station

When the North Pacific Coast Railway laid tracks to the bottom lands of Tomales Bay in 1875, the stop was called Olema Station. In 1883, a prominent dentist and land-owner from Novato named Galen Burdell bought up land, laid out a town site and changed the name to Point Reyes Station. Those who purchased lots from Burdell were prohibited from selling liquor—he reserved that opportunity for himself—until 1902 when hotelier Salvatore Grandi sued Burdell and won. The large brick building in town, dating from 1906, is one of Grandi's properties.

The railroad stopped running in 1933, and Point Reyes Station became a quieter dairy town. The popularity of Point Reyes National Seashore has brought B&Bs, cafés and restaurants, galleries, specialty gift shops to join the town's venerable bars and feed store. Start your **Point Reyes Station** stroll at either end of A Street, which is the old railway easement. You can then peel off to B and C streets, the only others, to see the large dairy, Point Reyes Dance Palace, and shops that are springing up on back streets. Sort of a Mendocino in coveralls and garden clogs, Point Reyes Station has retained its farming community roots, while becoming the place to be for West Marin's active visitors.

MB: **Tomales Bay Trail** is open to bikes—not a cycling destination, but you can see this scenic spot on a day when you don't have time to hike it.

J: Watch for gopher holes and uneven footing on the cow path that is the Tomales Bay Trail, but this is definitely a good run to combine with a brunch or whatever in Point Reyes Station. You go over hill and dale, perhaps dropping 250 feet when cross-ing the gully, and end up on the flat levee. The trail described in *Additional Access* is also a good running track, cow poop notwithstanding.

81.   EAST TOMALES BAY   H, J

Best for: A scenic, alternative way home from West Marin, via the historic railway line along the east shore of Tomales Bay.

Parking: From Hwy 101, take Lucas Valley Rd. or Novato Blvd. to Pt. Reyes-Petaluma Rd. and turn left, or west, to Point Reyes Station. Go north on Hwy. 1. *Note:* Although several walks are included, this trailhead is more of a driving tour, with distances given going north from the Pt. Reyes-Petaluma Rd.

Agency: Tomales Bay State Park; GGNRA; Marin County Parks *Special Interest: Kayaks, Kids

H: **Millerton Point to: Sieroty Beach (up to .75-mi.), or Millerton Point loop (1.25 mi.); Marconi Conference Center (up to .75-mi.); Audubon Cypress Grove-Sealy Trail (.75-mi.); Miller Park Boat Launch (.25-mi.)**

In 1875 the North Pacific Coast Railway laid narrow-gauge tracks for 15 miles down the east shore of Tomales Bay, making it possible to roll the tonnage of dairy products to burgeoning San Francisco—rather than haul goods via stagecoach or risk the precious cargo on the seas. The line served West Marin until 1930. The highway pavement now covers the track bed, but the shoreline scenery remains the same: open water, boatworks, fishing docks, cottages, and parklands.

Millerton Point—part of Tomales Bay State Park—features a pastoral head facing the bay's open waters and a sheltered beach. It is located about 4 miles north of Point Reyes Station. **Alan Sieroty Beach**, an underrated sunning spot, is just down from the parking area, with a long strip of sand facing toward Inverness. For the **Millerton Point loop**, veer right from the fence line, heading north across the grassland and reaching the north-facing bluff in a little more than .25-mile. The trail then curves around the point. *Additional Access:* Tomales Bay Oyster Company is on state park lands, about 1.5 miles north of the Millerton Point parking. Also, lands east of the highway are part of the state park.

The **Marconi Conference Center** is a State Historic Park, located up the hill to your right about 3 miles north of Millerton Point. Many of its buildings date from 1913, when the American Marconi Company used this site as a link in its "wireless girdle around the world." The center's 62 hillside acres, with stately Bishop pines overlooking the bay, may have you thinking of Monterey.

About 3 miles up the coast from the historic park, and a mile north of quaint Marshall, is the privately held **Audubon Canyon Cypress Grove Preserve**. The preserve is bordered on the north by a parcel of State Park land, and on the south by a small parcel of the GGNRA. The Carolyn Sealy Livermore Trail, which commemorates the founder of the Marin Conservation League, leads northward from the preserve. Contact Audubon Canyon Ranch for access information.

Miller Park Boat Launch is a 6-acre county park at the north end of Tomales Bay. It's right next to Nick's Cove, a salty bar and restaurant known for its barbecued oysters. You can also walk the eucalyptus-shaded bluff above the boat park, along a .5-mile stretch of GGNRA lands.

J: Millerton Point loop is an excellent jogging path, a natural track with bluff and beach view. Marconi Conference Center also has a jogging path.

Special Interest: Kids: Children may not be fond of eating oysters, but they may enjoy seeing how they're grown and harvested at Tomales Bay Oyster Company. Nearby Millerton Point serves nicely for a family beach picnic. *Kayaks:* Paddlers can put in at Alan Sieroty Beach at Millerton Point or at the Miller Park Boat Launch.

Miwok Woodlands

Olompali

The Coast Miwok inhabited Marin County for some forty centuries, harvesting plants and animals from the woodlands and tidelands as if the place were a garden that was perpetually planted. Village and camp remnants have been discovered throughout Marin. But the Miwok were particularly fond of the northern valleys that were sheltered from extremes of weather, were close to both game and the fruits of the sea, and were located to allow passage to both the ocean and bay coasts without arduous travel through the steep valleys of Tamalpais.

With lands nearly surrounded by water—the bay and ocean on three sides, and rivers cutting nearly across the northern boundary of the peninsula—it is not surprising that these people sustained their culture in a way similar to the island cultures of other native peoples. With knowledge passed on through storytelling and dance from generation to generation, the Miwok developed an intimate knowledge of the plants, animals, and all other aspects of their geographic surroundings. They were able to prosper. They were expert weavers, making baskets that could hold water and, on a larger scale, constructing bark-and-branch roofs that kept Pacific rainstorms at bay. Their houses were partially dug into the earth, providing coolness in the summer and insulation in the winter. Miwok culture achieved a state of balance with nature that was designed to last forever.

But sixty years after the Spanish arrival in Marin and San Francisco, ninety percent of the Coast Miwok had died from diseases, such as smallpox and measles, and from emotional bankruptcy resulting from slavelike conditions of the missionary and ranchero systems. The last full-blooded Miwok, Tom Smith, died in 1932.

Nicasio Reservoir

Olema Valley, Terra Linda acacia, Pt. Reyes-Petaluma Road

Miwok Park in Novato is a good place to start to learn the details of the Miwok way of life. Walking the hills of north Marin—which range from pleasant strolls just above suburban neighborhoods, to full-fledged hikes to ridges largely unchanged since antiquity—is a way to get a more subjective grasp on the culture. These hills have an appeal that many hikers will find most alluring of all Golden Gate scenery. Spring green in the winter and golden blond in the summer, the hills roll and mound sensually together inviting a hiker to roam without care. Up close, the downy carpet reveals its stickers, poison oak, scrabbled outcrops, and steep faces scorched by the sun.

The Miwok Woodlands section begins at Lagunitas Creek and San Geronimo Valley, at the north slope of the Tamalpais watershed. Here, the mixed conifer forests and chaparral make an abrupt transition to the oak savanna and woodland hills. This transition is most evident in Samuel P. Taylor State Park, which is cleaved by Lagunitas Creek with redwoods and mixed-pine forest above its south banks and steep grasslands of Barnabe Peak to the north. The transition is just as evident on San Geronimo Ridge, where the chaparral and conifers to the south of the ridge are markedly different from high grasslands of Loma Alta, White Hill and Nicasio Hill to the north.

Most of the public trails in the north Marin hills have been preserved due to the efforts of the Marin County Open Space District, which has worked with landowners and citizen groups to create preserves. The district was formed by voter approval in 1972, and has continuously expanded since then. Although several of the open space preserves stand alone, most are linked by shared trails and boundaries with other public lands. Each preserve features multiple access points, allowing residents of neighboring communities places to walk without getting in the car. Several large, new preserves are currently in the works, which will complete a system of trails, linking various public lands and allowing hikers to walk the length and breadth of Marin.

At Big Rock Ridge and Indian Tree Hills, hikers are able to see to the most remote parts of the county: the ranchlands of the northwest which remain in large, private parcels much the same as they were at the time of the Mexican land grants in the early 1800s. Although access to these lands is limited, they nonetheless provide an open view.

The northernmost trailhead in this section, Olompali State Park, was also the northern boundary for the Coast Miwok, where the hills drop into the broader drainages of San Antonio Creek and the Petaluma River. This is also the present-day boundary between Marin and Sonoma counties. In the late 1800s, early settlers recognized this boundary as well, building a railroad to link the commerce of West Marin to the lines that ran north and south through the county.

Roys Redwoods, Lucas Valley, Samuel P. Taylor Park

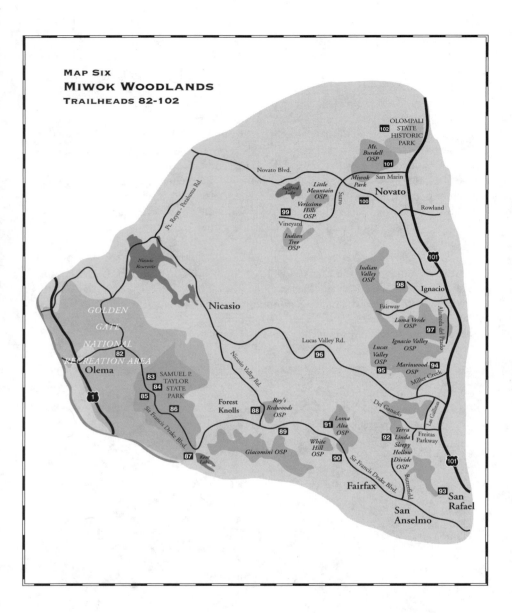

MAP SIX
MIWOK WOODLANDS
TRAILHEADS 82-102

OLOMPALI STATE HISTORIC PARK
102

Mt. Burdell OSP
101

Novato Blvd.

Stafford Lake

Little Mountain OSP

Miwok Park

San Marin

Novato

Sutro

100

Rowland

Verissimo Hills OSP
99

Vineyard

Indian Tree OSP

Pt. Reyes - Petaluma Rd.

Nicasio Reservoir

Indian Valley OSP

98

Ignacio

101

Fairway

GOLDEN GATE NATIONAL RECREATION AREA

Nicasio

Lucas Valley Rd.

Loma Verde OSP

97

Alameda del Prado

82

Olema

Nicasio Valley Rd.

96

Ignacio Valley OSP

Lucas Valley OSP
95

Marinwood OSP
94

Miller Creek

83
84

SAMUEL P. TAYLOR STATE PARK

Del Ganado

La Gallinas

85

86

Forest Knolls

Roy's Redwoods OSP
88

89

Loma Alta OSP
91

Terra Linda Sleepy Hollow Divide OSP
92

Freitas Parkway

101

1

87 Kent Lake

Giacomini OSP

White Hill OSP

90

Sir Francis Drake Blvd.

Sir Francis Drake Blvd.

Fairfax

Butterfield

93 San Rafael

San Anselmo

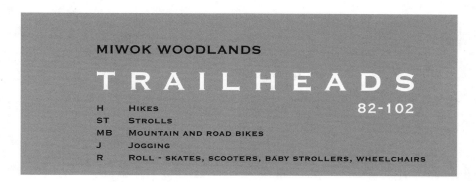

All hike and stroll distances are ROUND TRIP except as noted for shuttles.
Please contact Agency to obtain current rules and regulations. See Resource Links for all telephone numbers.
See also special Doggie Trails section.

82. BOLINAS RIDGE   H, MB, J

Best for: This old stagecoach route offers superlative outings for hikers, runners and bikers—extending 12 miles, from the grazing highlands above Tomales
Bay to the forested ridges of Mount Tam.

Parking: *From Hwy. 101:* Take Sir Francis Drake Blvd. past Samuel P. Taylor
Park's western boundary. Park on left at top of hill, up from Platform Bridge Rd.
From Olema on Hwy. 1: Drive about 1.5 mi. east on Drake Blvd. *Note:* Limited
roadside parking on weekends; watch for high-speed traffic.

Agency: GGNRA-administered by Point Reyes National Seashore

H: Bolinas Ridge Trail (up to 23 mi.); Samuel P. Taylor car-shuttle (4.25 mi.);
Kent Lake car-shuttle (7.5 mi.); Randall Trail car-shuttle (8 mi.)

Beginning amid a dairy cow hangout at 400 feet, the **Bolinas Ridge Trail** undulates
over hillock and saddle, but maintains a steady ascent for 11.5 miles, reaching an
elevation of 1,500 feet. It ends at the saddle of Fairfax-Bolinas Road, coming up from
Alpine Lake, TH42. The trail's end is also where Ridgecrest Boulevard, TH61, curves
down from Mount Tam. The long road is a garden of West Marin trees—starting out
in grasslands with pockets of oak and laurels, entering forests of fir and madrone, and
winding up in redwoods. It's also a history tour, since the tourist stages from the Tam
railroad junctions came along here en route to Olema and Taylorville.

The road offers no convenient loops, but several very good car-shuttles are possible.
For a **Samuel P. Taylor car-shuttle**, go almost 1.5 miles, gaining around 200 feet, on
the ridge trail. Then take a left down the Jewell Trail. The Jewell Trail drops 400 feet,

coming to the paved Cross Marin Trail which runs along Papermill Creek. From there you go right, leaving oak woodlands and entering the big redwoods and other conifers, over another 2 miles to park headquarters—where you had the foresight to leave a second car on the way to trailhead parking.

For the **Kent Lake car-shuttle**, leave a car near the gated entrance to Kent Lake, TH87, which is less than 2 miles east of the Samuel P. Taylor Park main entrance. On the ridge trail, walk 3.75 miles south of the Jewell Trail junction, leaving behind the grasslands and entering mixed conifer forest—humping up more than 700 feet in the process. You reach Shafter Road. Go left down this steep road, dropping 1,200 feet through dense forest for almost 2 miles, with filtered views of Kent Lake. You eventually come to the concrete bridge near the parking at Drake Boulevard. *Note:* From December through February, trailhead parking is available at dam road; other months park on shoulders .25-mile west of dam road.

For the **Randall Trail car-shuttle**, which takes you west into the Olema Valley, continue another mile beyond the Shafter Road junction. The Randall Trail, a graded road, drops steeply down a spur ridge and reaches Highway 1, about 2 miles south of Five Brooks, TH66. Large Douglas fir are in abundance, although this side of the ridge is more open than the Taylor Park side—or the ridge of the Point Reyes Peninsula, that looms to the west above Olema Valley. *Additional Access:* Another car-shuttle into the Olema Valley is available: The McCurdy Trail, beginning about 1.5 miles south of the Randall, drops 1,200 feet. This hike is almost 10 miles, reaching Highway 1 about .5-mile north of the turnoff to Bolinas.

MB: All the car-shuttle hikes are accessible to cyclists—with a home leg on Highway 1 or a short stretch of Drake Boulevard—making **Bolinas Ridge Trail** a first-class mountain bike area. Or forget about a loop and do the out-and-back to Fairfax-Bolinas Road, a round-trip ride of 23 miles with some 1,200 feet of overall elevation gain.

The **Samuel P. Taylor loop**, via the Jewell Trail, is about 4.5 miles. At the bottom of the Jewell Trail, go left on the Cross Marin Trail for 1.5 miles to the Platform Bridge on Drake Boulevard. From there it's .75-mile up a fairly steep grade back to trailhead parking. For the **Kent Lake loop**—a great ride of 13.5 miles—you need to turn left on Drake Boulevard after dropping down from Shafter Road. After 1.25 miles, turn right into Irving Picnic Area, where you go left, crossing over Drake Boulevard on a footbridge, now on the Cross Marin Trail. The trail continues through the state park to the Platform Bridge.

Doing the **Randall Trail loop** on a bike involves riding Highway 1 north through Olema Valley for about 6 miles, and then riding up several hundred feet on Drake Boulevard for another 1.5 miles. You probably don't want to ride these roads on a busy weekend. But on other days, this 15.5-mile ride can be just the ticket. The same traffic conflicts apply to the McCurdy Trail loop and the granddaddy loop—riding Bolinas

Ridge Trail to its end, coming down the Fairfax-Bolinas Road, and coming back up through the Olema Valley on Highway 1.

J: The Bolinas Ridge Trail is tailor-made for adventure runners in training. Curves and undulations, plus big views and great scenery, take the monotony from a long-distance run. Marathon trainers will get their fill running the road's course—20-plus miles with a roller-coaster net gain of 1,200 feet. Of course, you don't have to eat the whole thing—runs suited to any workout regimen are available.

83. DEVILS GULCH   H, MB, J, R

Best for: A misnamed lush creek valley, sporting wildflowers, a fern-and-red-wood creek, and fruit trees surviving from the Taylorville dairy days.

Parking: From Hwy. 101, take Sir Francis Drake Blvd. west of Fairfax and continue to Samuel P. Taylor State Park. Park on left, about 1 mi. beyond main park entrance, opposite sign for Devils Gulch. *Bus:* GGT weekend route 65

Agency: Samuel P. Taylor State Park

H: Devils Gulch Creek loop (3.25 mi.); Devils Gulch Road (up to 5 mi.); Bills Trail to: Stairstep Falls (1.5 mi.), or Barnabe Peak (8.75 mi.)

For the **Devils Gulch Creek loop**, come up the road a short distance and veer right on a signed trail that runs upstream alongside the creek. You enter a fern forest, under a ceiling of oak and laurel trees. Just over .25-mile up the creek, you'll pass the bridge to Bills Trail, and another .5-mile after that, the trail hooks up left and meets the road. Go left on the open road back to trailhead parking.

Devils Gulch Road follows part of an ancient trans-Marin route used by Miwok. The gulch connects the shaded recesses of Lagunitas Creek with the grassland hills near what is now Nicasio Reservoir, less than 3 miles north as the owl flies. You pass the horse camps in .5-mile, ascend a grassy slope and then drop down to creek level, entering a woodland riparian zone. Still following the creek, the road reaches the state park boundary in less than 1.5-mile, entering GGNRA lands. After another .75-mile, public lands end at a gate, a net 300 feet up from the trailhead. *Note:* Some of the place names in the park derive from Samuel P. Taylor's children's play-time imaginations.

The **Bills Trail** hikes are excellent. Walk to your right off the road to the creek, less than .5-mile from the trailhead gate—after horse Camp 2 and just before Camp 3. This clearing is the site of the Taylorville dairy and home sites for Taylor's son and camp workers. You cross a bridge beside a huge redwood, and go left on the trail. After less than .5-mile, going steadily up on Bills Trail, you'll see a spur trail veering left that leads to **Stairstep Falls**. When the runoff conditions are right, water cascades over mossy rocks and then collects to a stream that continues on its merry way down to join Devils Gulch Creek. Bills Trail continues to **Barnabe Peak**, up some easy-grade switchbacks, joining the Barnabe Peak Road about .25-mile away from the fire look-out at the 1,466-foot summit. *Additional Access:* By crossing the bridge to Bills Trail and going right, you can take a trail through Deadmans Gulch to Barnabe Trail. This option is an alternative loop hike to Barnabe Peak, using Bills Trail as a return route to Devils Gulch.

MB: **Devils Gulch Road** is a fun, intermediate bike ride. For a longer **loop ride to Irving Picnic Area**, go right toward Deadmans Gulch, as described in the preceding paragraph. Then take a contour trail through Madrone Group area to Irving Picnic Area. From Irving, take the bridge to your right, the Cross Marin Trail, through the campground. A bridge to the right, just past the historic mill site, pops you out to Drake Boulevard, where you need to turn right and ride a short distance to Devils Gulch trailhead. This 5 mile loop gives you a good look at Taylor Park's many faces.

J: Devils Gulch Trail is an A-ticket for recreational joggers, while Bills Trail will challenge the most hardcore of adventure runners. The Irving Picnic Area loop, as described in the bike section, is also a good route for runners in training.

R: **Wheelchairs and Strollers:** The gate may cause difficulty for wheelchairs, but Devils Gulch Road into the horse camps takes in some of the prettiest country for this trailhead. The going gets steeper after that, but the surface is still okay—although potentially muddy and debris-strewn—for those adventuring by chair and stroller.

Samuel Taylor's grave site

84. BARNABE PEAK   H, MB

Best for: This high ridge is a slice of Taylor family history and a place to visually connect the forested watershed of Mount Tam with the grassy ridges of the northern rancheros.

Parking: From Hwy. 101, take Sir Francis Drake Blvd. west, through Fairfax. Park at Madrone Group Area, on right, less than .5-mi. west of the main entrance to Samuel P. Taylor Park. *Note:* Hiking distances assume gate is closed at main road; if not, drive up and subtract .25-mi. from each hike. *Bus:* GGT weekend route 65

Agency: Samuel P. Taylor State Park; *Special Interest: Group Picnics and Camping

H: **Taylor's Grave Site (1.25 mi.); Barnabe Peak (4.5 mi.)**

Barnabe Peak, a sentinel of north Marin at 1,466-feet, has been a fire lookout station since 1940. You can see the top from the ranger office at the main park entrance. Barnabe was a white mule, a good animal by all reports, who came across the country with Captain John C. Fremont and Kit Carson during the Expedition of the Western Territories in the early 1840s. His last days were as a beloved pet for Sam and Sarah Taylor's boys, who named the peak for him since it was his favorite place to roam.

For **both hikes**, follow the road up through the oak groves to the trailhead, which is at the back left of the parking lot above the picnic area. Start up the gravel fire road, and veer left after the first little climb. You can look up the draw northward and see Barnabe, with mixed forests in the creases of its knuckled, grassy top. The road to the right at this first junction goes to Irving Picnic Area, TH86. You'll contour left, and come to a trail junction, some .75-miles from the trailhead. To **Taylor's Grave Site**, a modest memorial to the honest, enterprising pioneer, go left at this junction. Then bear left as another trail goes right, on the way to Devils Gulch. Taylor died of a heart attack in 1885; the family businesses, run by wife Sarah and their seven sons, went into default in the depression of 1893, and the lands were foreclosed. New landowners refused Sarah's wish to be buried with her husband. She died in Oakland several years later.

For **Barnabe Peak**, go right at the junction, beginning a 900-foot climb over the next 1.5 miles. Bring water and a good hat on sunny days, as open spaces are the rule on this south-facing trail. You walk above the tree line, contouring above mixed forests that spread up the Barnabe Creek drainage and other ravines. The ridge top has views of almost everywhere—private property to the north blocks access to one small area. To the south, Mount Tam pokes above the San Geronimo Ridge and you'll see Kent Lake nestled in the conifer forest.

Additional Access: One loop option is through Devils Gulch via Bills Trail, which is 7.5 miles. You'll pass Bills Trail on your left going up the Barnabe Trail, about .25-mile from the top. Take this trail on the way back, switchbacking down through lovely forest to Devils Gulch Creek. You'll be back at Madrone Group Area in another mile. A second loop option, this one almost 7 miles, is to continue easterly over the peak on the Barnabe Ridge Trail. You drop to the Cross Marin Trail on Papermill Creek. Go right on the trail, coming to Irving Picnic Area after almost .75-mile. Continue for 1.75 miles to the Madrone Group Area—not across the footbridge.

MB: The second **Barnabe loop option**, as described in the above paragraph, is an excellent outing for fit cyclists. The rest of us need to push the wheels on sections on the way up. A slight variation on this ride is to take the Cross Marin Trail across the bridge at Irving Picnic Area instead of heading toward the Madrone Group Area. This route takes you through the cool redwoods of the park, and along the bike path beside Papermill Creek. Just beyond the Old Mill Site, cross a bridge out to Drake Boulevard and ride back about a mile to the Madrone. Going through the park makes the loop about 8 miles.

*Special Interest: *Group Picnics and Camping:* The Madrone Group Area is available for picnics and group camping.

85. SAMUEL P. TAYLOR PARK   H, MB, J, R

Best for: Since 1875, nature lovers have enjoyed these redwood-and-fern streamside trails, which impart a sense of history along with serene beauty.

Parking: From Hwy. 101, take Sir Francis Drake Blvd. to park headquarters, about 10 mi. west of Fairfax. *Note:* Parking fee required inside park gates; some on-street parking available. *Bus:* GGT weekend route 65

Agency: Samuel P. Taylor State Park; *Special Interest: Camping and Group Picnics

H: **Papermill Creek to Old Mill Site loop (2.5 mi.); Ox Trail-Papermill Creek loop (2 mi.); Pioneer Tree Trail loop (2.75 mi.)**

After several years of effort by the Marin Conservation League, Samuel P. Taylor State Park was established in 1945. The park now covers 2,613 acres of redwoods and woodlands on either side of Lagunitas—or Papermill—Creek, stretching 4 miles along Sir Francis Drake Boulevard. See also TH83, TH84, and TH86.

The park honors Samuel Penfield Taylor who, at age 21, came around the Horn to San Francisco, opened a snack stand on the Barbary Coast. He parlayed his meager earn-

Samuel P. Taylor Park

ings into a grubstake that, in turn, netted him a small sack of gold from the Mother Lode. He used that money to buy 100 acres along the creek in 1852, then roadless. Rather than cut down virgin timber for lumber-starved San Francisco, he—along with wife Sarah and a growing family—constructed Pioneer Paper Mill, powered by the creek flow and using imported rags and jute to make pulp. In operation for 40 years, the mill was the first on the Pacific Coast. In this digital-cable era a little over 100 years later, it's hard to believe that, in the late 1800s, if Taylor's paper rolls weren't hauled by oxen and then shipped to daily papers in San Francisco, that city of 300,000 was without news. In 1875, when a railway was constructed down the east shore of Tomales Bay, Taylor opened a resort hotel and campground—Camp Taylor or Taylorville. It was one of the first parks in America to offer camping as a recreational pursuit.

For the **Papermill Creek to Old Mill Site loop**, head through the campground on the paved road, keeping right on the road. The Cross Marin Trail continues alongside the creek bank, while a rustic trail runs closer to the water. Within a mile you'll come to the remains of the paper mill, and then a plaque marking the mill site itself. Downstream from this bridge is the park's swimming hole, a must on hot days. Cross the wide bridge beyond the historic sites, go right along Drake Boulevard, and drop down toward the creek to pick up the North Creek Trail.

The **Ox Trail-Papermill Creek loop** takes in a portion of the first road that was used to cart paper to San Francisco and bring pulping rags back to the mill. Veer left from the park road, up toward Upper Campground. The Ox Trail follows a rough contour about 200 feet above the creek and then drops down to creek level near the swimming hole and the gate for the Cross Marin Trail. Turn right on the road, passing the Old Mill Site and dam remains. Walk the trail along the creek or stay on the broad path.

To take the **Pioneer Tree Trail loop**, walk through the main picnic area at the rangers station and go left toward the Redwood Grove Picnic Area. This trail does a squiggly contour, climbing about 200 feet, crossing Wildcat Canyon Creek, and coming down the drainage of Irving Creek. About halfway you pass the Pioneer Tree, an old-growth redwood, hollowed by a lightening fire, but still standing—a metaphor for Taylor, his family, and their workers, who worked hard in these forests but left them unharmed.

MB: The **Cross Marin Trail** runs for more than 5 miles. It begins across the creek at the road to Kent Lake. Ford the stream there and continue through the state park campground to Platform Bridge. This is a car-free and highly scenic way to get through the creek canyon. To avoid parking issues, drive to Platform Bridge Road and pick up the path heading upstream toward the park—a wonderful family ride. Big-time pedal pushers can also use the Cross Marin Trail as part of loop rides that involve climbing to Bolinas Ridge Trail; see the **Samuel P Taylor loop** and the **Kent Lake loop**, described in TH82. You can start these loops lower and climb up to the ridge trail.

J: The Cross Marin Trail, toward Platform Bridge, is a flat run of about 7 miles, round-trip—one of the better in Marin, or anywhere else.

R: **Skates and Scooters:** The paved Cross Marin Trail runs for more than 3 miles along the creek, reaching Drake Boulevard at Platform Bridge Road. This is a very scenic roll, from redwoods to woodlands, always near the creek. **Strollers and Wheelchairs:** The Cross Marin Trail, in addition to the above stretch, also runs .5-mile the other way, to Irving Picnic Area through the lush recesses of the park.

Special Interest: Camping and Picnicking: Samuel P. Taylor State Park, including Madrone Group Area and Irving Picnic Area.

86. IRVING PICNIC AREA   H, MB, J

Best for: Firs, ferns, and redwoods along a wide creek path; or a high grassy ridge with views from Tomales Bay to Tamalpais.

Parking: From Hwy. 101, take Sir Francis Drake Blvd. to about 9 mi. west of Fairfax, and about 1.25 miles west of state park boundary and Shafter Bridge. Park without blocking gate at Irving Picnic Area.

Agency: Samuel P. Taylor State Park

H: Papermill Creek to Shafter Bridge (2.5 mi.); Barnabe Peak (5.5 mi.); Pioneer Tree Trail loop (3 mi.)

Irving Picnic Area is named for Sarah Taylor's uncle, Washington Irving, author of *Legend of Sleepy Hollow*, *Rip Van Winkle* and other nineteenth century classics. Indeed, on foggy days as you start down the trail from **Papermill Creek to Shafter Bridge**, you may feel like Ichabod Crane, making your way through a misty tree tunnel under leafy trees and towering evergreens. The level trail—which is the western-most segment of the Cross Marin Trail, that does not completely cross Marin—ends at Papermill Creek, which is also Lagunitas Creek. When the water is low, you can cross the creek and then Drake Boulevard, to continue walking up to Kent Lake, TH87.

To **Barnabe Peak**—also accessed via a shorter route from TH84—start to your right on the Cross Marin Trail along the creek. About .75-mile later, as you pop out of the redwoods and enter a fir and laurel woodland, you'll see the Barnabe Peak Trail going up to your left. Over the next 1.75 miles the trail climbs some 1,300 feet, breaking out to an open ridge. You can make a semi-loop out of the hike by veering left on a trail—after you've curved back to your left on a steep ascent. This trail parallels the road to the top. You can then take the road all the way back down.

For the **Pioneer Tree Trail loop**—which is also described from a different starting point in TH85—go left at the Irving Picnic Area and cross over the road on the footbridge. You'll see the Pioneer Tree Trail on your left. The trail goes up the Irving Creek drainage, passes the venerable old growth redwood, and drops into the Redwood Picnic Area. Go right at the picnic area, passing through the visitor area and coming back to Irving Picnic Area on the Cross Marin Trail.

MB: Several park loops and Bolinas Ridge rides go by the Irving Picnic Area—any one of which can begin here as well. See TH82, Bolinas Ridge, for the Kent Lake loop. Also see Devils Gulch, TH83, and Barnabe Peak, TH84 for in-park loops.

J: Take the Cross Marin Trail upstream to Shafter Bridge, cross the creek and the road, and run up Peters Dam Road to Kent Lake. This run, of about 6 miles up-and-back, gives you a nice flat stretch along the creek and an uphill of almost 200 feet on pavement. Or, take the Cross Marin Trail the other way, over the bridge and through the park. It continues for about 4 miles before coming out at Drake Boulevard. You cover a varied terrain from fern rainforest to moist woodlands. Irving is a two-thumbs-up joggers' trailhead.

87. KENT LAKE   H, ST, MB, R

Best for: A deep creek with spawning salmon and steelhead; or trails to Marin's biggest lake, fringed by thick evergreen forests and steep ridges.

Parking: From Hwy. 101, take Sir Francis Drake Blvd. about 8 mi. west of Fairfax, to east boundary of Taylor State Park at Shafter Bridge; two gated roads on left. *Note:* During winter and early spring, the right side gate is open to a parking area; at other times roadside parking is available about .25-mi. beyond the bridge, adding about .5-mile to hiking distances.

Agency: Marin Municipal Water District

H: Shafter Road to: Peters Dam loop (2.5 mi.), or Bolinas Ridge (4 mi.); Peters Dam Road to: Continental Cove (5.75 mi.), or San Geronimo Ridge loop (4.5 mi.)

Built in 1953, Kent Lake is named to honor conservationist and Congressman William Kent, who donated Muir Woods for a park in 1905. The reservoir, which is more than double the capacity of the four others in the Mount Tam watershed, is wishbone-shaped. One arm collects the waters of Big Carson Creek, coming down from the San Geronimo Ridge, and the other, the waters of Lagunitas Creek, coming down from Tamalpais and Alpine Lake.

For the **Shafter Road hikes**, head up the road on the right as you face upstream. For the **Peters Dam loop**, veer left on the unpaved path that follows the creek through maples and fir. After less than .5-mile, turn right at a switchback that takes you back up to Shafter Road—but before you do, you may want to continue on the creek trail, which peters out at pools below Peters Spillway. Back on Shafter Road, you pass the right-junction to Bolinas Ridge and continue up, passing a tempting left option that dead-ends at a log landing. You top out about 100 feet above the lake. Go left, down to water level, and then left again on Peters Dam Road, which follows the other side of Lagunitas Creek back to the trailhead.

For **Bolinas Ridge**, keep right on Shafter Road and take a signed right turn—you'll see the spillway but not the lake. The inviting road, with a surface cushioned by orange redwood and fir needles, leads up for 1.5-miles. It's very steep, with more than 1,000-feet in elevation gain. You reach the Bolinas Ridge Trail about 5 miles south of TH82.

For the **Peters Dam Road hikes**, start up the paved road going upstream to the left. You follow the creek for a short distance and then veer away on a rising grade that makes a couple sweeps before reaching the top of the dam. Continue to your left, passing view spurs and piles of big logs that are routinely fished out of the lake. You'll go up several hundred feet, with views through trees of the lake down to your right. Almost a mile from the dam you top out at a junction. To **Continental Cove**, go straight, losing all the elevation through fir and mixed woodland forest—passing a left-bearing option after .25-mile—and coming to road's end at the cove, about .5-mile from the junction. The cove is on the Kent Lake branch that is fed by the Big Carson Creek.

For the **San Geronimo Ridge loop**, go left at the Continental Road junction, on a steep uphill road that enters drier flora. The road reaches a junction with San Geronimo Ridge Road after gaining several hundred feet in little more than .5-mile. Go left at this saddle—and avoid a right-bearing road shortly thereafter—as you head around a wooded knoll. You then make a 1.25-mile downhill run back to Peters Dam Road. Turn right and walk the last .25-mile back to the main road.

ST: Leo T. Cronin Fish Viewing Area

Usually from November through February, the Shafter Road gate is open at Drake Boulevard, creating a zone—the **Leo T. Cronin Fish Viewing Area**—to observe the silver salmon and steelhead that spawn in Papermill Creek. Although fishing is no longer permitted in the lower portion of the creek, in 1959 the largest silver salmon ever caught in California—22 pounds—came from these waters. The salmon spawn is usually over in early January; look for brick-red males and bronze females. The pink-stripped spawning steelhead usually appear later, in February and early March. The creek is also habitat for the threatened coho salmon. Near Papermill Dam in the state park, the west coast's first spawning fish ladder was constructed in 1881.

MB: The two rides out of steep-ridged Kent Lake require strong thighs and a steady will. The less difficult, but longer of the two, is a **Bolinas Ridge loop**, covering some 10 miles. Ford the creek across Drake Boulevard, and get on the Cross Marin Trail; or you can ride down the Drake for 1.25 miles and pick up the path at Irving Picnic Area. Continue on the Cross Marin Trail to about 2 miles beyond the campground and make a left on the Jewell Trail. You climb a few hundred feet over a mile to the Bolinas Ridge Trail. Turn left on the ridge trail, and pump the rising roller coaster for almost 4 miles, gaining 600 feet and coming to Shafter Road. Hang a left and hang on down Shafter, rolling a steep 2 miles past Kent Lake to trailhead parking.

For a short but steep **San Geronimo Ridge loop**, head up Peters Dam Road and bear left, going toward Continental Cove. Pass a left option at the first plateau above the dam, and continue, dropping toward the cove. Just before the spur trail goes to the cove, take a steep uphill on your left. Ride up just over .5-mile to the San Geronimo Ridge Road in a saddle at the Marin Open Space District boundary. Bear left here, and keep left, dropping back down to the trailhead over a 1.5-mile run. This loop is some 5 miles, with about 1,000-feet of upping.

R: **Wheelchairs Strollers:** Off-road Moms & Dads will like the Peters Dam loop hike to immerse the young one in nature. It's fairly steep, but big-wheel strollers are often seen making the trip. For an easier time of it, keep left on Shafter Road, staying on the creek all the way to the bottom on the spillway, about .5-mile in. The spillway roll is also a good one for wheelchairs.

88. ROYS REDWOODS   H

Best for: Old growth redwoods, a meadow, and a grassland hill that offers a view from the Mount Tam watershed to the north Marin hills.

Parking: From Hwy. 101, take Sir Francis Drake Blvd. west of Fairfax. Past Woodacre, turn right at golf course clubhouse on Nicasio Valley Rd. Park after .5-mi. at MCOSD gate. *Note:* Additional access, including to Maurice Thorner Memorial Open Space, in hiking descriptions. *Bus:* GGT routes 23, 24

Agency: Marin County Open Space District

H: Meadow Trail (.5-mi.); Nature Trail to Nicasio Hill (2.5 mi.); Moon Hill (.25-mi.); Maurice Thorner Memorial Open Space (up to 1.5 mi.)

In 1978, the county purchased initial lands of the 377-acre preserve above the San Geronimo Valley from descendants of the Roy brothers, Thomas and James, who had come by the land in 1877 as a debt repayment from Napoleon Bonaparte's nephew, Adolph Malliard, who, in the late 1840s, had purchased the land from Paul Revere's grandson, Joseph Warren Revere. A pop quiz follows.

For the **Meadow Trail**, a level stroll alongside redwoods that rival some of the Muir Woods giants, go left from the gate on a trail. You soon reach a glade, by veering right where a sign directs equestrians to the left. At the far edge of the meadow, look for the Council Tree—a circle of redwoods, one almost 250-feet high, that sprouted from an ancestral tree that once was at the center. Other mammoth trees are in the neighborhood, where some of George Lucas' *Star Wars* was filmed in the mid-1980s.

To continue on **Roys Nature Trail to Nicasio Hill**, the nearly 789-foot-high open summit above the valley, continue north, climbing about 150 feet up from the meadow and reaching a trail junction. *Note:* To the left at this junction, .5-mile away, is Nicasio Road and a MCOSD gate for the Dickson Fire Road-Roys Redwoods Loop Trail; this gate is just up the road from the primary parking area. Continue, and, after another .25-mile, go right at a junction with the Roys Nature Trail, which takes you up the hill, through open laurel and madrone woodlands. After another .25-mile the trail forks— take your pick because this fork is a .25-mile loop that takes in the top of Nicasio Hill. *Be Aware:* Poison oak thrives along the margins of this trail.

Additional Access: Instead of going right on Roys Nature Trail to the top, you can continue on a trail that makes a 2.5-mile loop around the preserve. Also, as noted above, a gate for Dickson Fire Road is on the right, a short distance from the first MCOSD gate. Dickson is a steep ramp, climbing 1,000-feet in under a mile to reaching the preserve's northern boundary.

Moon Hill, more of a stroll and picnic area, is the portion of the preserve on the left as you head up Nicasio Valley Road. *Additional Access:* The Marin Open Space District plans a new preserve, to be called French Ranch, that probably will be accessed via the fire road to the left up the hill from the present Roys Redwoods' gates, and also from Drake Boulevard just past Lagunitas School Road.

Maurice Thorner Memorial is a stand-alone, 33-acre woodland ridge that was made an Open Space Preserve in 1981. You can access the 500-foot-high ridge from either end. On Nicasio Valley Road, park on west side of the golf cart overpass, and take an unsigned side-hill trail that connects with the ridge trail. Or, continue past Nicasio Valley Road on Drake Boulevard and turn right on Lagunitas School Road; circle around behind the school and look for a MCOSD marker on your left. From either access, you climb about 200 feet to the ridge.

Additional Access: To Nicasio Reservoir, an MMWD lake with shoreline trails, continue north on Nicasio Valley Road. You'll pass pastoral Nicasio with its Old West buildings including its red schoolhouse and church. The reservoir offers strolls for bird-watchers and is a back way to get to the coast via Pt. Reyes Station; see TH80.

89.   SAN GERONIMO RIDGE   H, MB

> **Best for:**   The wooly hinterlands of Marin, a long and high ridge that separates the Tamalpais watershed from the grassland hills of north Marin.
>
> **Parking:**   From Hwy. 101, take Sir Francis Drake Blvd. west of Fairfax. Turn left on San Geronimo Valley Dr., continue, and go left on Park St. in Woodacre. From Park go left on Railroad Ave., right on Carson Rd., and left on Redwood Dr. at stop sign. Follow Redwood to Buckeye Circle, go right, and park on right after 10 Redwood at MCOSD gate. *Note:* This preserve has multiple trailheads, described below.
>
> **Agency:**   Marin County Open Space District

H: **Buckeye access to: White Hill (2.5 mi.), or Sargent cypress grove (4.25 mi.); Conifer access to: Carson Meadow (2 mi.), or Green Hill (5 mi.); Bates Canyon Trail (1.5 mi.)**

The north slopes of the 1,400-foot high San Geronimo Ridge, which is about 6.5 miles long, are part of the Gary Giacomini Open Space Preserve. The 1,549 acres are named in honor of the Marin County Supervisor who worked diligently during his 24-year career to make these lands public. The north slopes of the ridge are MMWD lands—accessible via Alpine Lake, TH42, and Cascade Canyon, TH44.

Loma Alta, Nicasio

For both **Buckeye hikes**, head up the easement road, Summit Fire Road, through oaks and Douglas fir, coming to the MCOSD border. The road gets steep, breaks into the open, and reaches the White Hill Fire Road, less than .5-mile from the trailhead. For **White Hill**, a 1,430-foot virgin ridge top, pale with blonde grass most of the year, go left on the fire road. You drop into a saddle and over a false summit—avoid a left-bearing road, which is actually White Hill road—and continue right on Blue Ridge Road to the top of cashew-shaped White Hill. You'll have a view northward to sister peak Loma Alta, as well as the San Francisco skyline and the bay. Blue Ridge Road continues down to Cascade Canyon.

To see the **Sargent cypress grove,** go right on White Hill Fire Road when you reach the top of Summit Fire Road. These dwarf trees, unique to California, grow in the stingy serpentine soils of the ridge. You'll enter a Douglas fir and scrub forest, and then drop through a rocky ravine. You then make a steep but short climb and come to San Geronimo Ridge Fire Road—at a point almost as high as White Hill. Go left, or south, on this popular biking road, climbing another 150 feet before coming to the small but century-old conifers that manage to thrive here. The grove extends for nearly .5-mile.

The **Conifer Fire Road** hikes are on a less-traveled trail because of difficult access roads. Drive straight through Woodacre on Park Street, go left on Conifer Way and follow to Carson Road. Turn right, negotiating a hairpin, and follow funky Carson until you hit Conifer again—go left on Conifer, all the way to the end, where you are rewarded with an open parking area under oaks at an MCOSD gate. Conifer Fire Road climbs steeply, through Douglas fire and mixed woodland forest, gaining 600 feet over a .75-mile route to meet San Geronimo Ridge Fire Road; take a right fork, at **Carson Meadows**, as the Conifer Road splits near its terminus.

To **Green Hill**, go right on the ridge road from Carson Meadows. Over the next 1.5 miles, you climb slightly and then begin a slow descent; keep left where Hunt Camp

Fire Road comes in from the right. From there, with Green Hill in plain view, you climb several hundred feet over a short distance to its summit. You'll get big view down to a long arm of Kent Lake, curving through the uniform mixed-fir forests up the canyon of Big Carson Creek.

The **Bates Canyon Trail** begins in a shaded redwood grove, easily accessed from San Geronimo Valley Road: Continue west past Park Street in Woodacre and park on left at Redwood Canyon Drive, which is .5-mile west of Railroad Avenue. The trail is fairly level near the bottom, meandering through redwoods—and the stumps of their ancestors—on a trail made muddy in places by horses. The Bates Canyon Trail, after climbing 350 feet, comes out on Conifer Way.

Additional Access: The Sylvestris Fire Road connects with the San Geronimo Road, near Green Hill. Going west on San Geronimo Valley Road, veer left on Meadow Way and immediately go left on E. Sylvestris Drive, until you see a MCOSD gate.

MB: The **Summit Fire Road**, which connects with White Hill Fire Road from Buckeye Circle, is a good access option. After making the short, steep climb of White Hill, described in the hiking section, you can take **Blue Ridge Road into Cascade Canyon** and hump back up Repack Road.

You can also go right on White Hill Fire Road and connect with San Geronimo Ridge Road. Then go south, or left, to Pine Mountain Road—where you turn right to make an ambitious **loop toward Kent Lake**. This tough route through Marin's wildest country takes you over the top of Pine Mountain, and through the Big Carson Creek Canyon. You then come to San Geronimo Ridge Road. Turn right and head east along the roller coaster ridge—passing a number of roads on the left—until you return to White Hill Road. This loop is about 13 hard miles.

90.   WHITE HILL   H

> **Best for:**   Trails less traveled—through woodland, redwoods, and grasslands—leading to valley views and a back way to White Hill.
>
> **Parking:**   From Hwy. 101, take Sir Francis Drake Blvd. west of Fairfax to Bothin Rd. on left at 3125 Drake Blvd. *Note:* Additional parking described in hiking section.
>
> **Agency:**   Marin County Open Space District

H: White Hill Fire Road to San Geronimo Valley overlook (1.75 mi.); Martha McCormack Trail to overlook (1.5 mi.)

The 390-acre White Hill Open Space Preserve is on the eastern end of the San Geronimo Ridge, a narrow greenbelt that connects Loma Alta on the north to Cascade Canyon on the south. A short road, marked by a MCOSD sign, leads to the right, at the entrance to Bothin Youth Center, to the **White Hill Fire Road**. You begin on switchbacks and then walk a ridgeline, at first through dry scrub and then denser woodland trees. At the upper lip of a redwood and fir forest, bear left at a road junction, and ascend the last of the 600-foot climb. You pop out on open grassland with the verdant San Geronimo Valley spread out below. The preserve boundary ends at a locked gate. Down to your left is Bothin Youth Center—at the upper end of which is the eastern portal of a now-blocked North Pacific Coast Railroad tunnel, a passage under the mountain from 1904 to 1933. Lofted above that is the curving, steep top of 1,430-foot White Hill.

Additional Access: When you reach the boundary gate, a narrow strip of the White Hill Open Space extends to the south, your left. An unofficial trail skirts the fence line through this preserve segment to White Hill Fire Road. You can take this route to the summit.

The sleeper hike for this preserve is the **Martha McCormack Trail**, which leads steeply up through a mossy redwood-and-fern ravine to connect with the White Hill Fire Road. Access is just up Drake Boulevard from Bothin Camp, on your left near where the short passing lane ends. You'll see a MCOSD sign on a chain link fence beside a large turnout. Not many take this route, so you may have to step over a few branches. The upper part of the trail contours through laurels and other woodland trees, coming to the fire road. Go right to the overlook at the preserve boundary, about .5-mile distant. *Be Aware:* Take notice of where the McCormack Trail reaches the fire road, as it may be difficult to spot coming back.

91. LOMA ALTA   H, MB, J

Best for: A massive grassland mountain with several, easily reached trailheads leading to views of everywhere—from Tam to San Francisco to Point Reyes National Seashore.

Parking: From Hwy. 101, take Sir Francis Drake Blvd. west of Fairfax. Park at right at top of hill past Bothin Youth Camp at MCOSD gate. *Note:* Additional parking in hiking descriptions.

Agency: Marin County Open Space District; *Special Interests: Kids

H: Gunshot Road to Loma Alta (5.75 mi.); Smith Fire Road Loma Alta (6.75 mi.); Fox Hollow loop (1 mi.)

The broad, sloping shoulders of Loma Alta—Tall Hill—can be seen to the northwest from much of central Marin. Once the landmark where three Mexican rancheros met, the 1,560-foot-high peak is now the boundary between the urban, evergreen watershed of Tam and the sprawling, tawny ranchlands of the north hills. The preserve's 379-acres were acquired by the MCOSD over a 13-year period. *Note:* The open space boundary stops just short of the summit, which is on private property.

To hike the **Gunshot Road to Loma Alta**, head through the gate, dipping around the upper part of a ravine, and veer left on a road that goes up within .25-mile. Gunshot Fire Road contours right and then hairpins back left up a ridgeline on a relentless 700-foot ascent over .75-mile, a south-facing and almost treeless portion of the Bay Area Ridge Trail. Coming back down, with big views in your face and gravity as a friend, you'll have greater appreciation for the trail. Gunshot tops out at the Smith Fire Road, on which you go left, coming to its end after almost .5-mile and 200-feet of elevation. From there an unofficial trail, within the preserve boundary, leads a mile to the northeast, up another 150 feet to the open space boundary, just shy of the top of Loma Alta. *Additional Access:* The straight-ahead route, to the right at the start of Gunshot Fire Road, is a continuation of the Old Railroad Grade. This old North Pacific Coast Railroad route, which ran from 1874 to 1904, contours around the base of Loma Alta and connects with other access points described below.

The **Smith Fire Road to Loma Alta** hikes starts from a less used access that delivers big views from the get-go. Turn right on Oak Manor Drive, at the last traffic signal after Fairfax. Park at the top, near an unmarked fire road on the left. Walk up this short connector road, a rutted scar, coming to a MCOSD gate in less than .25-mile. Proceed on the road, the short Oak Manor Fire Road, with a San Francisco view already at your back. The road dips into an oak-choked ravine and then up to a saddle, where two water tanks mark the beginning of Smith Fire Road. Over a course of 1.75 miles, Smith Fire road climbs some 800 feet at a reasonable grade, at first up a shoulder, and then under Loma Alta across the top of a ravine that is the headwaters of Fairfax Creek.

The **Fox Hollow loop** is a down-low nature stroll, although you can use this access to connect with the Old Railroad Grade for monster loop hikes. From Drake Boulevard west of Fairfax, turn right on Glen Drive, which is past Oak Manor. Drive past the school to an MCOSD gate at road's end. Take the Fox Hollow Trail to the left, dropping into a shaded creek that the kids will like. The short Fox Hollow Trail leaves the creek and reaches the Old Railroad Grade. After .5-mile on this woodland tree tunnel, drop down to your left at a spur trail that comes out behind White Hill School; from there walk Glen Drive to trailhead parking.

MB: For an ambitious, but not long view ride—about 1,500 feet of gain, over less than 5 miles—try the **Loma Alta loop**. Begin at the primary parking on Sir Francis Drake. Just down from the trailhead, keep right on Old Railroad Grade. You'll curve around the base of Loma Alta, encounter a steep dip above Baywood Canyon, and then round the toe of the mountain on a gradual decline into the woodlands of Fox Hollow. From there, go left up the ravine on Glen Fire Road, connecting with Smith Fire Road on its steady ascent toward Loma Alta. You can hang a left down Gunshot Road before the end, saving 200 feet of climb and about .75-mile. Otherwise, take the remaining segment to the end, and then backtrack to Gunshot. Then hang on for dear life on the way down to trailhead parking.

J: Runners in training looking for a top-of-the world workout will like Smith Fire Road from Oak Manor. For a gentler run, through a canopy of woodland trees, take Fox Hollow Trail or the Glen Fire Road from Glen Drive, and go left on Old Railroad Grade. You can do an out-and-back on the grade, around to Baywood Canyon, which covers about 2.5 miles round trip.

*Special Interest: *Kids:* The Fox Hollow loop, along the oak forest creek bed and then a woodland tree tunnel, may get young kids playing Peter Pan, or Crouching Tiger.

92.   SLEEPY HOLLOW DIVIDE   H, MB, J, R

Best for: A mounded, grassy ridge, rising above suburbia, with oak-fringed view roads for hikers, joggers, and cyclists.

Parking: *From south or central Marin:* Take Sir Francis Drake exit from Hwy. 101. Continue west of San Anselmo and turn right on Butterfield Rd. Enter Sleepy Hollow, turn right on Fawn Dr. and follow to on-street parking at MCOSD gate near 390 Fawn. *From northern Marin:* Take Freitas Pkwy. exit in Terra Linda and follow to end. Park on-street at MCOSD gate. *Note:* Additional parking in hiking descriptions. Other access to this open space is included in San Rafael Ridge, TH93, and Lucas Valley, TH95.

Agency: Marin County Open Space District; *Special Interest: Kids

H: Fawn-Freitas to: **Terra Linda Ridge (3.25 mi.), or Luiz Ranch Fire Road high point (3.75 mi.), or Irving loop (2 mi.); Santa Margarita Valley Park to: Terra Linda Ridge (3.75 mi.), or Luiz Ranch Fire Road high point (2.5 mi.)**

Making a dozen separate acquisitions over a 19-year period beginning in 1974, the MCOSD has managed to patch together 1,169 acres of pleasant, rolling-ridge open space that curls above neighborhoods of San Anselmo, San Rafael, and Terra Linda. *Be Aware:* This is poison oak country, and don't be surprised if the pooch picks up a tick.

For all **Fawn-Freitas hikes**, take the paved Mission Pass Road up the short, but steep incline to the saddle. Go north on the Terra Linda Ridge Fire Road, coming quickly to a view knoll—cabin site for a young priest who once communed with nature here,

Sleepy Hollow Divide

giving Mission Pass its name. Proceed south along the curving road. You'll enter mounded grassy hills, with oaks and laurels tucked into their creases. For **Terra Linda Ridge**, pass three roads on the left, beginning at .5-mile with the next two .25-mile apart; these lead down to Sleepy Hollow. As the Terra Linda Ridge Road curves to your right, you pass the Luiz Ranch Fire Road on the left. Continue almost another .5-mile, reaching a trail junction: A road from the right comes up from Santa Margarita Park, and one to the left from Lucas Valley. Turn around here.

To walk up the scenic spur of the **Luiz Ranch Fire Road**, keep left at the junction as described above. After a little more than .5-mile, and 350-feet of upping, you reach the preserve boundary and its high point—at nearly 900 feet. The Luiz Ranch Fire Road continues, on private property, to Loma Alta. This road was once planned as part of a freeway extension. Today, it is where the neighborhoods end and the nature of the hills becomes dominant.

For the **Irving loop**, pass the Sleepy Hollow Fire Road on your left at .5-mile and go to the right of Lang Hill—named for kindly Harold Lang who lived nearby and helped create the open space. On the other side of the wooded knoll, you reach the Irving Fire Road. Go left on Irving, and keep left all the way. Circle back around Lang Hill, coming up the short Sleepy Hollow Road to the Terra Linda Fire Road. *Additional Access:* The middle of the Terra Linda Ridge can be accessed via Sleepy Hollow and

Irving drives, both of which are right turns farther up Butterfield. Also, at the Mission Pass, you can take Fox Lane Trail south, over a knoll, coming out on a cul-de-sac which leads to upper Fawn Drive. Fawn ends at an access point for San Rafael Ridge, TH93.

The **Santa Margarita Valley Park** hikes begin on the Terra Linda side of the divide: As you drive up Freitas Parkway, veer right on Del Ganado Way and follow it to its end, at a MCOSD gate. Take the Del Ganado Road up from the pleasant park, heading up a grassy ravine. Bear left at a junction, hardly .25-mile from the trailhead, taking the Terra Linda Ridge Road as it begins its route around the top of Santa Margarita Valley. In less than .5-mile, you'll see the **Luiz Ranch Fire Road** going to the right. To continue along the **Terra Linda Ridge**, follow the road as it curves around to your left—and avoid all right-bearing options. In another 1.25-miles, you reach Mission Pass above the Fawn-Freitas trailheads.

MB: **Mission Pass Road** is a godsend for anyone trying to ride between San Anselmo-Fairfax and Terra Linda-Marinwood. You also have the option of two loop rides, beginning at the Fawn-Freitas trailhead, which takes in the ridge and return via suburban streets. For the longer of the two, a **Lucas Valley loop** of some 6.5 miles, head north on the Terra Linda Ridge Road, as described in the first hike above. At about .5-mile past the Luiz Ranch Fire Road, veer left, around a knoll and down to Lucas Valley—.5-mile away. Go right on Lucas Valley Road. Across from Lassen Drive, veer right on Old Lucas Valley Road. This sweet stretch of car-free pedaling follows the creek for about a mile and pops back out on the Lucas Valley Road. Not long afterward, go right on Las Gallinas Avenue for 1.5 miles and right again on Freitas Parkway.

For a shorter **Santa Margarita Valley loop**, of almost 4 miles, begin as described above, only go right down the ravine on the Del Ganado Fire Road, which is almost .5-mile from the Luiz Ranch Fire Road. This short spur drops you down to Del Ganado Way, which you pedal for 1.25 miles and hang a right on Freitas.

J: The Terra Linda Ridge—accessed from either Fawn-Freitas or Santa Margarita Valley Park—will score high marks for off-pavement runners seeking an after-work run. The route undulates a hundred feet or more in places, but it's not a grind.

R: **Wheelchairs and Strollers**: The paved connection between Freitas and Fawn, although steep, can be navigated by strollers and wheelchairs, perhaps needing a little help. You can then roll up to the viewpoint at the beginning of Terra Linda Ridge Road. Wheelchair riders may find it rough beyond that during the rainy season.

*Special Interest: *Kids:* Santa Margarita Valley Park, which is at the end of Del Ganado, has a big playground, set below the hills. You can combine playtime with a short walk.

93. SAN RAFAEL RIDGE

Best for: A tree-lined path, offering a quick weekday getaway and a primer on central Marin geography.

Parking: From Hwy. 101 take Central San Rafael exit and go west on Third St. Turn right on A Street and then left on Fifth Ave. Continue, then go right on H St., left on Forbes Ave. and right on Elizabeth Wy. Follow Elizabeth up, go left on Ridgewood Dr. and follow to its end, at MCOSD gate. *Note:* Additional parking in hiking descriptions.

Agency: Marin County Open Space District; San Anselmo Parks Department

H: **San Rafael Ridge (2 mi.); Sorich Park loop (2.5 mi.); Tomahawk Road to San Rafael Ridge (2.75 mi.)**

The **San Rafael Ridge** hike, part of the Terra Linda-Sleepy Hollow Open Space, begins on the inviting Ridgewood Fire Road, through a large grove of eucalyptus. At the outset, you'll pass road junctions on your left, leading up from Crestwood and then the Cemetery Road. After that, you may choose to take a spur trail on the right, leading the ridge's high point. About a mile from the trailhead, the Tomahawk Fire Road leads up from San Anselmo on your left. You'll have views of Mount Tam in that direction. The road then drops to its end, at the top of Fawn Drive coming up from Sleepy Hollow. You can connect with the Terra Linda Ridge Road, TH92, by walking down Fawn, going right on Fox Lane and taking the Fox Lane Trail for about .25-mile. *Additional Access:* Lower access is via Cemetery Fire Road: Take the Fifth all the way to its end, entering the Mt. Tamalpais Cemetery; go right, circling around to the top of the grounds.

The **Sorich Park loop** goes up a sunny ravine to the ridge. Continue driving west from San Rafael to Sir Francis Drake Boulevard. Past a shopping center, go right on San Francisco Boulevard, to its end at Sorich Park. Walk up the trail to your right—leading from the former So-Rich Dairy. You cross a footbridge and join the Cemetery Fire Road. At the top, having gained nearly 400 feet in elevation, go left on Ridgewood Fire Road. Just beyond the knoll, take Tomahawk Fire Road on your left. After less than .25-mile, take the Sorich Park Road down to your left.

To walk the ridge from **Tomahawk Fire Road**, a pleasing access with bay vistas, you need to connect via some confusing surface streets. From San Francisco Boulevard, as described above, go left on Santa Cruz, right on Santa Barbara, and left on Pasadena. From Pasadena, go left on Miwok, left on Blackhawk, and then right on Tomahawk. Congratulations. Now, walk through a MCOSD gate on the Tomahawk Fire Road. The road climbs about 250 feet and reaches the ridge in less than .5-mile.

MB: The **Ridgewood Fire Road** is an excellent ride to connect with the Fawn-Freitas trailhead and then continue along the **Terra Linda Ridge**. To do that, ride to the end of the fire road at Fawn Drive and drop down to the MCOSD gate near 390 Fawn; see TH92 for loop rides you can make from there. If you're pedaling up to the Ridgewood trailhead, you may wish to use **Cemetery Road**, as described above.

J: • The San Rafael Ridge is a prime-cut jogging path. Try Ridgewood Fire Road for a 2-mile spin, or continue down Fawn, to Fox Lane and the Fox Lane Trail for a workout along the Terra Linda Ridge.

R: **Wheelchairs and Strollers:** Although mud puddles and eucalyptus berries make for a less-than-smooth surface, the Ridgewood Fire Road is level at the beginning, with a parklike feel and a great view. You'll encounter some undulation beyond the trees, but not drastic.

94. MARINWOOD   H, MB, J, R

Best for: Less-traveled, rugged routes through thick woodland forest to Big Rock Ridge; or a quiet creek-side stroll of a large neighborhood park

Parking: From Hwy. 101, take St. Vincents-Marinwood exit and go west on Miller Creek Rd. Pass Las Gallinas Ave. and turn right on Queenstone Dr. Park at gate at end of cul-de-sac. *Bus:* GGT route 1

Agency: Marinwood Community Open Space District; *Special Interest: Kids

H: **Queenstone to Big Rock Ridge (3.5 mi.); Ridge Ravine Trail (2.25 mi.); Quietwood Park-Miller Creek (up to 1 mi.)**

The Marinwood Community Open Space is on the east end of Big Rock Ridge, where it borders Lucas Valley Open Space Preserve. Other county preserves are at its northern boundary. Marinwood's trails, less publicized than those of neighboring parklands, lead steeply up deep oak woodland and are some of the best places to spot critters and birds.

The hike up rugged **Queenstone Fire Road to Big Rock Ridge** gains 1,200 feet, taking you atop a 1,444-foot viewing knoll looking to the San Pablo Bay. Although there are plenty of trees, this can be a hot hike, best not pursued on a summer afternoon. Queenstone is sometimes called Big Cat Road, since the remote woodlands it cuts through support a food chain ending at the mountain lions. Watch your dog. About 1.5 miles up, Queenstone ends, where Chicken Shack Fire Road comes in from the right and Big Rock Ridge Fire Road begins its tortuous journey to the west. Go left on Big Rock Ridge Road, to the vista point. Continuing west on Big Rock takes you immediately down a saddle; see Lucas Valley, TH95, for other access to the ridge.

The **Ridge Ravine Trail** goes up a rich woodland ravine along an ephemeral stream. You need to drive Miller Creek Road from the freeway and turn right on Las Galinas Avenue, before you get to Queenstone. Then go left on Blackstone Drive and veer left on short Valleystone Drive. Park at entrance gate. This is one of the better woodland walks. The trail meanders on an easy grade at first, but as the ridge's shoulders squeeze from either side, the going gets steep. Eventually, you can connect with Chicken Shack Fire Road, but this steep, brushy route is used infrequently. *Be Aware:* Poison oak grows trailside.

To get to **Quietwood Park**, take Miller Creek Road and park on your left near the community center, just before you reach Lucas Valley Road. The park features rolling lawns shaded by large oaks and laurels, curving around a nearly .5-mile stretch of Miller Creek. The creek, with water flowing over bedrock pools, is one of the larger in Marin, taking the runoff from Lucas Valley.

MB: **Queenstone Fire Road** is a masochist's dream, steep and rugged, going straight up to Big Rock Ridge. You can then ride west along the ridge and come down Luiz Fire Road, making a loop ride by coming back on Lucas Valley Road—7.5 tough miles in all.

To ride to **San Rafael**, TH31, from Marinwood, take Las Galinas Avenue, which turns into Los Ranchitos Road. You pump over Puerto Suello Hill and drop down to Lincoln Avenue. To ride north from Marinwood toward **Indian Valley**, TH98, or Novato, take the bike path that begins at the on-ramp at Clay Court, which takes you to Alameda del Prado, and on to Ignacio Boulevard.

J: Adventure runners might like a road that runs westward from Marinwood along the foot of Big Rock Ridge, through the oak grasslands above quiet suburban neighborhoods. To access the easternmost part of the road, head up Idylberry Road, which is off Miller Creek Road across from Quietwood Park. Turn immediately right on Juniperberry Drive, to its end. The road curves and dips for about 2.5 miles— accessed along the way from Lucas Valley, TH95—before ending at Bridgegate Drive.

R: **Wheelchairs and Strollers:** Quietwood Park's paved riparian paths are a recommended respite in this part of Marin.

*Special Interest: *Kids:* Take the family for a picnic stroll of Miller Creek—a place for one spouse to hang with the kids while the more energetic of the pair takes a hike up Queenstone to Big Rock Ridge.

95. LUCAS VALLEY   H, MB, J, R

Best for: Only Tam is higher than this grassy wall of a ridge, whose steep, sunny face challenges hikers; or, opt for a shaded creek with a trail leading to a more pastoral peak.

Parking: From Hwy. 101 take Smith Ranch-Lucas Valley Rd. exit. Go west on Lucas Valley Rd. for about 4 mi. and turn right on Westgate Dr. From Westgate, turn right on Creekside Dr. Park at MCOSD gate opposite tennis courts and children's park. *Note:* Several different access points described in hiking section.

Agency: Marin County Open Space District; San Rafael Parks *Special Interest: Kids

H: **Luiz Road to Big Rock Ridge (4 mi.); Goat Trail to Big Rock Ridge (3 mi.); Old Lucas Valley-Miller Creek (up to 1.25 mi.); Mont Marin (2 mi.)**

The sweeping, steep turns of **Luiz Fire Road to Big Rock Ridge**—gaining 1,300 feet in little more than 1.5 miles—take you from a pastoral woodland valley to a King-Kong view from the top of the North Bay world. You may wish to avoid this south-facing hump in mid-summer. But on a spring or winter day, flowers popping from green grass will add arm's length beauty to the splashy panoramas. From the top—now at almost 1,500 feet—you can go left for a little more than .25-mile, up another 150 feet, to the preserve's western boundary and its higher point, at 1,640 feet. The high point of Big Rock Ridge—at 1,895 feet and marked by a telecommunications installation—is on private property another mile west of the boundary gate.

The **Goat Trail to Big Rock Ridge** switchbacks up 1,000 feet, coming to a saddle on the ridge. Turn right off Lucas Valley on Mt. McKinley Drive—which is east of the Westgate parking area. Then go left on Idylberry and right on Red Mt. Court. Enter through a MCOSD rough-hewn gate and go left. The Goat Trail at first follows an ephemeral streambed up a ravine. After less than .5-mile, you cut right, leaving the ravine, and begin switchbacks cut through chaparral to the 1,240-foot low-point on the ridge. Once there, you can go to the right, just over .25-mile, to the 1,400-plus-foot viewpoint of east Big Rock Ridge; or left, almost .5-mile and 250 feet up to the junction with the Luiz Fire Road. On the other hand, you can just sit down and contemplate infinity. *Additional Access:* A fire road runs along the base of the ridge. One access is to turn right on Lassen Drive and drive to the top, where you turn right on Mt. Dana Drive, a cul-de-sac.

Old Lucas Valley Road is a delightfully decrepit paved road running along Miller Creek—take Lucas Valley Road west, past Huckleberry Drive, and park on left at MCOSD sign opposite Lassen Drive. Under the boughs of bay, oak, and madrone, Old Lucas Valley curves eastward on a level stretch for over .75-mile, coming to a gate at Canyon Oaks Drive. To your right as you walk is a part of the Terra Linda-Sleepy Hollow Divide Open Space, and, as you approach Canon Oaks, to the right is San Rafael's large Russom Memorial Park, a rustic greenbelt.

To hike the rolling low ridge that separates Lucas Valley from Terra Linda—**Mont Marin**—take a road that curves up about midway along on Old Lucas Valley Road— a little more than .25-mile from both east and west gates. A .5-mile trail snakes up to the soft ridge, passing a water tank and gaining about 350 feet along the way. Once at the top, you can go right on Park Ridge Road about .25-mile to Mont Marin's high point, some 490 feet. Or, go left a similar distance to another hump, which has a view toward the Marin Civic Center and the San Pablo Bay wetlands.

MB: Only the fittest and most-whacked cyclists will want to try pedaling up **Luiz Fire Road to Big Rock Ridge**—it's a toughie. You can make a loop by riding the ridge road—through a saddle that dips steeply almost 300 feet over a hellish mile-long stretch—and come down **Queenstone Fire Road**. At the bottom of Queenstone, go right on Miller Creek Road, and then right on Lucas Valley Road, which you take back to the trailhead on Creekside off Westgate. This loop is about 8.5 miles.

A saner ride, headed the other direction, is a **Terra Linda Ridge loop**, of about 4.5 miles. Use the Terra Linda Ridge access on Lucas Valley Road opposite Muir Court. This will take you up and around Terra Linda to the Sleepy Hollow Divide, coming to the Fawn-Freitas trailhead in less than 2 miles. You then go left to Freitas Parkway. Roll

Lucas Valley Preserve

down and go left on Del Ganado, riding 1.2 miles up to the MCOSD gate at Santa Margarita Park. Take the road up from the park, connecting again with the Terra Linda Ridge Road, where you turn right for the last .5-mile.

J: Old Lucas Valley Road is an easy, pleasant run to which you can add a workout by heading up Mont Marin. For adventure running, try the trailhead off Mt. Dana described in *Additional Access*, above. Going to your right is the undulating road that curves along the foot of Big Rock Ridge for several miles to Marinwood.

R: Skates: The going is not all smooth, but Old Lucas Valley Road is a find for skaters looking for wooded privacy. **Strollers and Wheelchairs:** Old Lucas Valley Road, along Miller Creek under leafy branches, is an easy pleasant roll. Midway on the journey, Russom Park offers a bucolic resting place, under the slopes of Mont Marin. Picnic tables sit beside a meadow, near the creek.

Special Interest: Kids: Westgate Park is next to tennis courts on Creekside, right across from the Luiz Road route to Big Rock Ridge. With play sets sitting amidst oaks and a nearby trail along a woodsy creek, the park is just right for some people in the party to hang with the kids while others take on the ridge hike.

96. BIG ROCK H

Best for: Marin's newest preserve will be the crown jewel of the north hills, linking Big Rock Ridge with the slopes of Loma Alta. Its first trails expected to open by late 2001.

Parking: From Hwy. 101 take Smith Ranch Rd.-Lucas Valley Rd. exit north of Terra Linda. Go west on Lucas Valley Rd. about 6 mi., to where the road has climbed out of the valley. Park at gate near the big rock. *Note:* Call MCOSD for current trail information.

Agency: Marin County Open Space District

H: Big Rock

With trails scheduled to lead north and south from this central trailhead, the Big Rock Open Space Preserve provides a missing link in Marin's Bay Area Ridge Trail. Marin County Supervisors, MCOSD planners and landowner George Lucas, Marin's famous filmmaker, have put their heads together toward making this hiker's dream a reality. The *Star Wars* maker has built a new Lucasfilm-Skywalker Ranch facility near the Big Rock trailhead. Lucas' surname is coincidental to that of the valley, which refers to John Lucas, who ranched 7,600 hundred acres here in the mid-1800s when movies were yet to be invented.

The **northern trail, from Lucas Valley Road to Big Rock Ridge**, requires construction of a 2-mile, switchbacking trail to connect with Big Rock Ridge. The ridge, on which is Marin's second-highest point at 1,895 feet, rises above the wetlands east of Marinwood and runs northeasterly for nearly 10 miles, before dying into the dairyland valleys that send their waters to the southern end of Tomales Bay. The southern and eastern faces of the ridge can be accessed from Lucas Valley, TH66, Marinwood, TH94, and Village Valleys, TH97. Below its northeastern flanks are the trails of Indian Valley, TH98, and Indian Tree Hills, TH99.

A **southern trail section**, using an existing fire road, will connect with **Loma Alta**, TH91, over a 4-plus-mile run that rises a net of some 800 feet along a circuitous undulating route. From Loma Alta, public lands—those of open space, Mount Tam watershed, state park, and national recreation area—are contiguous to the Golden Gate.

97.   VILLAGE VALLEYS   H, MB

> **Best for:**   Native woodlands on the wild, north face of Big Rock Ridge, with trails visited more by wildlife than people.
>
> **Parking:**   *Two access options,* depending on hike selected, both north of Marinwood and south of Hwy. 37 on Hwy. 101: *Take Alameda de Prado exit* just north of Marinwood. Or take the *Bel Marin Keys-Ignacio Blvd. exit* and go west on Ignacio Blvd. *Note:* Further directions in hiking section. *Bus:* GGT route 1
>
> **Agency:**   Marin County Open Space District

H: **Alameda del Prado access hikes: Chicken Shack Fire Road to Big Rock Ridge (6.5 mi.); Pacheco Creek Trail (.75-mi.); Ponti Fire Road to Big Rock Ridge (4.25 mi.) Ignacio Boulevard access hikes: Halloween Trail (1.75 mi.); Pebble Beach Road (2 mi.)**

Three adjacent Open Space Preserves—Pacheco Valle, Loma Verde, and Ignacio Valley, totaling 1,618 acres—provide access to shoulders and ravines on the shady side of Big Rock Ridge. These steep woodlands and creek meadows that give way to bay wetlands were for 3,000 years the locales of thriving Coast Miwok villages. Coast Miwok lived all over what is now Marin County, but these temperate bay-woodland environs were particularly desirable—set on fresh streams in open valleys, with a backdoor entrance to the hills and a front door facing tidelands. Pacheco Valle is most southerly, a narrow indent in the eastern end of Big Rock Ridge. Ignacio Valley lies over a shoulder to Pacheco's north, and over a ridge from Ignacio is Indian Valley.

Alameda del Prado hikes: To walk the length of **Chicken Shack Fire Road** to its 1,300-foot-high terminus at Big Rock Ridge, begin at Clay Court, which is right across from the freeway on-ramp for Alameda del Prado. The first part of the walk is up a paved easement that passes by a tennis club. You then walk up a fairly steep grade through sparsely growing oaks, reaching a first rise, where the road bends norhtward. Via Escondida Road joins from the right. Spaced at .25- to .5-mile intervals from the Via Escondida junction, you pass, in succession: Little Cat Road on your left; Pebble Beach Road on the right; Halloween Trail, also on the right; and, finally Ponti Road coming up from the left. You'll have to drop through a saddle to reach the end of Chicken Shack, another .5-mile away. *Be Aware:* This hike can be a scorcher in the summer.

To stroll with the deer in oak woodlands to a waterfall on **Pacheco Creek Trail**, go left from the freeway exit on Alameda del Prado. Then go right on Pacheco Creek Drive. Heading into the narrowing valley, look for the trailhead at the end of the drive. You take an inviting trail amid stately oaks, crossing the creek several times. The going gets sketchy as the trail starts to climb, but you'll want to continue a short distance to a waterfall, a good one to visit after rains. You can continue up the steep ravine—deer do—but it becomes very steep and overgrown, and you are not a deer.

For the **Ponti Fire Road**, a woodland arboretum with great views, turn left from the freeway exit on Alameda del Prado. Follow it into the quiet condos as the road curves, passing Pacheco Creek Drive. Then, on your right, look for Curlew Way, off which is the beginning of Curlew Trail. This .25-mile connector is steep and rocky. You then veer right on Ponti Fire Road, which rises 1,100 feet through a series of ramps and benches along a 1.5-mile journey that ends at Chicken Shack Fire Road. *Additional Alameda del Prado Access:* The Little Cat Fire Road, is .5-mile long and follows beautiful oak woodland up a shoulder to reach Chicken Shack Fire Road about midway along that ridge. It begins off Alameda del Prado near Hummingbird Way.

Ignacio Boulevard hikes: The **Halloween Trail** is a steep and sometimes rugged ascent toward a view ridge through a woodland garden. Turn left from Ignacio Boulevard on Carnoustie Drive. Then go right on Burning Tree Drive. Park on-street at Obertz Lane, at the MCOSD sign. The trail begins along the property line of a trophy home, gaining elevation from the get-go and quickly entering a grove of wavy, deep-maroon manzanita—"burning trees." Overall, the trail makes its 600-foot climb in several steep pitches, reaching flatter grasslands in between where you might spot wildflowers.

For the hike up **Pebble Beach Fire Road**, through mixed woodland trees to a view spot on the ridge, turn left off Ignacio on Fairway Drive. Then make your first left on Alameda de la Loma and your first right, on Pebble Beach Drive, which you take to the top to a MCOSD gate. The road climbs at a reasonable grade through mixed oaks, offering tree-filtered views of the baylands. After less than .5-mile, the Winged Foot Road comes in from the right, which is accessed from the paved road of the same name off Fairway Drive. Keep left, dropping through a saddle, and then making the final steep push up to Chicken Shack Fire Road—having gained a net 400 feet during the mile-long hike. You can go right up Chicken Shack for a steep .5-mile and come down the Halloween Trail to make a loop—requiring a mile-plus connection via neighborhood streets.

MB: For a meaty woodland ride, try the **Ponti-Pebble Beach loop**, which takes you on 5 different roads on a 7-mile swing through the Loma Verde and Pacheco Valle open spaces. Start at Pebble Beach Fire Road as per hiking description. After the first 1.25 miles and 400-foot climb, go right on Chicken Shack Fire Road, grinding up 700 feet over a mile-long stretch. Then hang a left down Ponti Fire Road, reaching Pacheco Creek Road after 1.5 miles. Ride surface streets out Pacheco Creek and continue on Alameda del Prado. Turn left across from the freeway on-ramp, near Clay Court, heading up past the tennis club to get on Chicken Shack Fire Road. Take Chicken Shack up for 1.25 mile—climbing 500 feet—to where you veer right and come down Via Escondida Fire Road. Keep left on the way down, and then go left on Alameda de la Loma, which you ride back to the Pebble Beach trailhead.

The heftiest ride here is the **Chicken Shack-Big Cat loop**, which covers 6.5 miles, taking in the eastern tip of Big Rock Ridge. Starting from the bottom of Chicken Shack Fire Road, as per hiking directions, ride 3.25 miles, all the way to the top. Veer left down Big Cat, or Queenstone Fire Road, and ride the steep scar 1.5-plus-miles to the bottom. Coast to your right to Miller Creek Road, toward the freeway. Hang a left on a bike path that follows the freeway 1.25 miles back to the Clay Court parking area.

98.   INDIAN VALLEY   H, MB, J, R

Best for: A number of pleasant trails, meandering along creeks and woodland knolls, create loop options on these former lands of the Coast Miwok.

Parking: From Hwy. 101, take the Bel Marin Keys-Ignacio Valley Blvd. exit north of Terra Linda and go west about 3 mi. to the College of Marin, Indian Valley Campus. Keep right and park at Lot 8, in front of Campus Police. *Note:* Parking fee may be required at campus; bring quarters. *Bus:* GGT route 1

Agency: Marin County Open Space District; *Special Interest: Kids

H: **Waterfall Trail-Pacheco Pond loop** (2.5 mi.); **Hill Ranch-Wildcat Trail loop** (3.25 mi.); **Indian Valley loop** (4.75 mi.)

The 654-acre Indian Valley Open Space Preserve provides popular neighborhood nature trails, meandering about the woodland ravines that ripple down from the towering wall of Big Rock Ridge. For **all hikes**, take the .25-mile connector path to your left along the border of athletic fields, reaching the MCOSD gate.

The **Waterfall Trail-Pacheco Pond loop** crisscrosses a small stream in a pretty wood-land forest. Proceed from the gate, dipping down Indian Valley Fire Road. Turn left after about .25-mile, crossing a footbridge. You'll reach the 20-foot falls—with a vol-ume that varies dramatically with rainfall—after .25-mile of gentle climbing. Above the falls, you pass the Alexander Trail on your right and then curve left through bay-and-oak birdland, cresting the ravine some 400 feet above the trailhead. Follow the Waterfall Trail on its squiggly descent to Pacheco Pond—a duck's dream with willows and cattails. Veer right around its eastern shore and meet the Pacheco Pond Fire Road.

The **Hill Ranch-Wildcat Trail loop** takes you through big cat country past a historic upper ranch site. Take the Indian Valley Fire Road and go left at the second footbridge, about .5-mile from the MCOSD gate. The trail veers left, ascending the creek ravine on switchbacks amid large laurel trees. You break out to a view clearing after about .5-mile—some 400 feet higher than the bridge. Go right, now on the Wildcat Trail; a spur of the Hill Ranch Trail goes up the hillside. The ranch here was the upper portion of a late 1800s dairy operation. The Wildcat Trail curves its way through frizzy manza-nita and madrone, and then becomes the Buzzard Burn Fire Road, which drops back down to the Indian Fire Road. *Be Aware:* Mountain lions have been spotted in this preserve.

For the longest hike in the preserve, the **Indian Valley loop**, go left on Pacheco Pond Road as you enter the gate. After passing the pond, continue up on the Waterfall Trail, heading above the ravine and dropping along the stream course. Partway down, go left on the Alexander Trail. This trail, a little over .5-mile long, contours around a deeply wooded hillside and joins the Hill Ranch Trail. Go left on Hill Ranch, through the old ranch clearings, and join the Wildcat Trail, which hooks back down the Indian Valley Fire Road—becoming the Buzzard Burn Road on the way down. You complete the loop on the road, the preserve's centerpiece hike.

MB: Most trails are closed to bikes, but **Indian Valley Fire Road** provides a key through route **from central Marin to Novato**. Take Ignacio Boulevard through the campus and then ride the unpaved road through the preserve. You come out on Indian Valley Road, where you can ride left to Wilson Way and hang a right, which takes you into west Novato near Miwok Park, TH100.

J: Indian Valley Fire Road is a pleasant but short run, and all the trails noted above are good courses for adventure runners—although you'll have plenty of com-pany at peak times. The college's athletes train in these hills: Look for a trail on the right, opposite the Waterfall Trail, that curves back toward the athletic fields.

R: **Strollers and Wheelchairs:** Indian Valley Fire Road curves and undulates gently, passing all the preserve's trailheads and the two main creeks that wash down form the high ridge.

*Special Interest: *Kids:* Indian Valley has some level stretches that invite kids into the woods. Also check out the playground at Hoog Community Park, which is on Montura Way, off Ignacio Boulevard. It has lots of rolling lawn.

99. INDIAN TREE HILLS   H, MB, J, R

Best for: Three open space preserves and a lakeside county park combine for a diverse system of trails—ranging from a short nature loop, to rolling deer-and-raccoon hills, to a 1,400-foot ridge top covered with a mystical grove of virgin coast redwoods.

Parking: From Hwy. 101, take the DeLong Ave. exit, continue through traffic signal on Diablo Ave., and turn right on Novato Blvd. Pass Miwok Park on the west end of Novato. *For Indian Tree hikes:* Go left on Sutro Ave. and then right on Vineyard Rd. *For Verissimo Hills and Little Mountain hikes:* Go left on Sutro Ave. and right on Center Rd. *For Stafford Lake Park:* Continue on Novato Blvd another 2 mi. and turn left into park; day use fee required. *Note:* Additional directions in hiking descriptions.

Agency: Marin County Open Space District; Marin County Parks

H: Indian Trees hikes: Rebelo to Indian Trees (4.25 mi.); Big Trees Trail to Indian Trees (6 mi.); Verissimo Hills-Little Mountain hikes: Verissimo Hills (up to 2.75 mi.), Doe Hill Fire Road (1.5 mi.); Stafford Lake: Terwilliger Nature Trail (1 mi.)

Indian Trees hikes: For the **Rebelo to Indian Trees** walk—the pick for this trailhead—turn left on Rebelo Lane off Vineyard, past Verissimo Drive. Take Rebelo up past new homes and continue on a paved lane that looks like a driveway in a cul-de-sac. Park at an MCOSD gate. Hiking up Indian Tree Fire Road, you'll hit a second gate after the road dips. After about .75-mile, keep left on a side-hill trail that follows a fence line to avoid a major dip in the road's course. You rejoin the road about 600 feet above the trailhead. A few redwoods here preview those that await. Ramping up another .75-mile, to the road's highpoint, you then come to the redwood grove that can be seen from far below. The biggest diameter tree is almost hidden in the grove to your left as you go up the knoll. Big Trees Trail joins the road in the glade below the redwood knoll. West of Big Trees, the road reaches the preserve boundary in less than .25-mile.

The **Big Trees Trail** is a longer route than the fire road, and requires 300 feet more climbing. Park on left after the pavement ends on Vineyard. Begin on the Upper Meadow Trail as it veers off to the right, and then take the Big Trees Trail as it departs to the left. You take easy-graded, switchbacks through bay and laurel woodlands over the next 2 miles. The Deer Camp Trail joins from the right, and, .5-mile later, the Ships Mast

Trail comes in from the left. Above these junctions, your route becomes more direct, amid Douglas fir as large as some of their redwood neighbors. The Indian Tree, in the middle of the knoll at the top, is partially hollowed by a lightning fire long ago. According to local lore, this tree was once the home of a Coast Miwok, and now touching its bark is said to bring good fortune to all who have made the pilgrimage.

Verissimo Hills-Little Mountain hikes: The rolling **Verissimo Hills** provide a good view of Stafford lake, as well as habitat for a number of woodland critters. Go left across the gully from the Center Road parking. You cross a short section of North Marin Water District lands, and then begin a gentle switchback up the Stafford Lake Trail through nicely spaced oaks. After about .75-mile, you'll be able to see over to Indian Tree Open Space—to where the trail continues. But you go left at a junction with the Verissimo Hills Trail, up to the first, and highest of the ridge's four grassy mounds.

The **Doe Hill Fire Road**, to the right from the parking at the end of Center Road, runs along the south base of 806-foot high Little Mountain. Only deer trails and neighborhood routes lead to the top. For such a small open space, Little Mountain has a wealth of access: You'll see four spots if you turn right off Center Road on Trish Drive and continue on Taurus Drive.

Stafford Lake: The easy-walking **Terwilliger Nature Trail**—named after Marin's grandame of conservation, Elizabeth—begins along the lakeshore to the right of the parking area inside Stafford Lake Park. Interpretive signs explain marshland ecology. You'll find room to roam on the lawns of this 139-acre park that is the setting for family picnics and group outings—featuring playgrounds, athletic fields, volleyball courts, and barbecue facilities.

MB: The 4-mile round-trip ride from Rebelo up **Indian Tree Fire Road**—gaining 1,200 feet, but not insanely steep—is one of the better view rides in north Marin. The **Stafford Lake bike path** is a pleasant 3.25 stretch for cyclists taking the ride from Novato toward the coast.

J: The Verissimo Hills are ideal for cross-county runners who want some undulation without grueling climbs. From the Center Road access, you can do the ridge hills and then double-back to continue on the Stafford Lake Trail to Indian Tree Preserve. To continue from there—or if you want to start a run at Indian Tree—go up to the stables and head up the Deer Camp Trail and contour across the ravine on the Upper Meadow Trail.

R: **Skates and Scooters:** The Stafford Lake bike path, beginning just east of the park entrance, is perhaps the best track in north Marin. It's fairly flat through pastoral scenery and, although used, not often crowded. **Wheelchairs and Strollers:** Ditto the skate verbiage above. The path continues inside Stafford Lake Park, which is the more tranquil place to push the wheels—along the water and a nature trail.

100. MIWOK PARK
H, ST, MB, R

Best for: All the ingredients for a family outing: American Indian Museum, nature walks, rustic picnic area and an easy bike path.

Parking: From Hwy. 101 in Novato, take either the Rowland Ave. or DeLong Ave. exit and go west to Novato Blvd. Continue on Novato Blvd., past Wilson Ave., to signs on right for Miwok Park. *Bus:* GGT route 50

Agency: City of Novato; *Special Interest: Kids

H: **Rueger Nature Trail (.75-mi.)**

For the **Rueger Nature Trail**, an oak island in the backyard of Miwok Park, head up the path through the park away from the museum. You'll come to San Miguel Way, where the path curves right and you'll see a footbridge leading across Novato Creek. Jays and squirrels may join you on a circular path of the rocky woodland knoll. Spur routes lead out to different streets. You'll want to circle back around to the footbridge.

ST: **Miwok Park-Marin Museum of the American Indian**

Miwok Park's spacious grounds—lawns and natural areas under spreading oak trees, along the banks of Novato Creek—feature picnic and barbecue areas for families big and small, as well as horseshoe pits, play sets, and places to get away and just sit quietly. Central in the park is the **Marin Museum of the American Indian**, a modest, wood-frame structure. The museum's smallish quarters belie a wealth of exhibits, artifacts and artwork inside. When the museum opened its doors 25 years ago, Miwok culture was emphasized, but the years have seen a broadening of scope to include all American Indian cultures, as part of a new movement to retrieve and teach values that were lost.

MB: **The Stafford Lake bike path** runs for a little more than 3 miles to the county park at Stafford Lake, along the way passing greenbelts of O'Hair Park and Little Mountain Open Space Preserve. About .5-mile from Miwok Park, at Sutro Avenue, you need to cross to the other side of Novato Boulevard. The path is close to the boulevard at times, while at others it loops inward closer to Novato Creek.

R: **Skates and Scooters:** The paved 3-mile bike path to Stafford Lake is an invitation to get out and roll. **Wheelchairs and Strollers:** The bike path provides a roller's exercise route, while the path within the park is a place to enjoy nature at a slower pace.

*Special Interest: *Kids:* Miwok Park is a trailhead for families.

101. MOUNT BURDELL   H, MB, J

Best for: The high outpost of north Marin, with a system of trails leading to a panorama from the Bolinas Ridge and Sonoma hills to Tamalpais and the Parking. From Hwy. 101 in Novato, go north of DeLong Ave. and take the San Marin Dr.-Atherton Ave. exit and go west on San Marin. Turn right on San Andreas Ave. Follow to top to on-street parking at MCOSD gate. *Note:* Additional parking in hiking descriptions. *Bus:* GGT route 50

Agency: Marin County Open Space District

H: San Andreas to: Deer Camp loop (4 mi.), or Cobblestone route to Mt Burdell (5.25 mi.), or Hidden Lake loop (3 mi.); Fieldstone Trail to Mt. Burdell (4.75 mi.)

Mt. Burdell, 1,558-feet high, is appreciated now as north Marin's most popular hiking getaway, a preserve of 1,558 acres. (Yes, the elevation and area are the same number.) The mountain is named for Galen Burdell, a Gold-Rush era dentist who married Mary Augustina Black, the daughter of Judge James Black—who had purchased large parcels of former Mexican land grants. In the mid-1800s, Black owned more Marin land than anyone except for the Shafters in West Marin. Mary Augustina inherited her father's properties, but only after a series of lawsuits; Judge Black tried to disown Mary after Galen, during routine dental care, overdosed his mother-in-law.

For **all San Andreas trailhead hikes**, start up the appealing trail, the San Andrea Fire Road, to your left. Ascending gradually, you'll pass the Dwarf Oak Trail on the left. Then bear right at Middle Burdell Fire Road as the San Andreas Road continues left to the preserve boundary. For the **Deer Camp loop**, through a classic oak forest, go left at the trail junction about .25-mile from the start of Middle Burdell Road. The Deer Camp Fire Road takes a 1.5-mile swing out to the preserve's northwestern boundary—passing a serene oak grove named in honor of Pierre Joske, a former MCOSD general manager—and climbing gradually about 400 feet. The route doubles back to your right and reaches the Cobblestone Fire Road. Here you go right and drop back down to Middle Burdell Fire Road.

For the **Cobblestone route to Mt. Burdell**, pass the Deer Camp Road on Middle Burdell Road. Walk another .5-mile to Hidden Lake, where you go left on Cobblestone. Over a mile-long course, Cobblestone takes you up almost 700 feet to the Burdell Ridge Fire Road, passing the Deer Camp Road on the left about one-third of the way up. Stone from this route provided the cobbles for many of San Francisco's early streets. From the top of the trail, the summit of Burdell is to your left. The paved ridge road, adorned with telecommunications installations, is about .5-mile long; to your left it ends in short order and to the right a trail leads down the peak's north side to Olompali State Park. Bring binoculars to enjoy Burdell's extensive vista.

For the **Hidden Lake loop**, continue straight on Middle Burdell Road, passing the Cobblestone junction. The lake is at best a pond, and most often a marshy bog that can dry out altogether in August. Continue for .75-mile, passing a stream ravine and then Old Quarry Road before coming to San Carlos Fire Road. Head down San Carlos for .75-mile, while dropping 400 feet and leaving behind woodlands for open grassy slopes. Go right on the Michako Trail which takes you on a .5-mile contour to rejoin the San Andreas Fire Road.

For the **Fieldstone Trail up the east face of Mt. Burdell**, you need to begin at different parking: Immediately west of the freeway on San Marin Drive, turn right on Redwood Boulevard, and then left on Wood Hollow Drive. Drive to the top, go left on Fieldstone Drive, and look for parking on the right at 473 Fieldstone. The Fieldstone Trail takes you on a 1.25-mile, 400-foot switchbacking ascent to meet Middle Burdell Fire Road. You cross the jumbled remains of an old quarry that helped build San Francisco in the gold and silver booms of the late 1870s. Go left on Middle Burdell, climbing a dignified 200 feet over .75-mile before reaching the Old Quarry Road, where you climb like a goat—up 650 feet over about .75-mile. You hit the Burdell Ridge Road, where the Cobblestone Trail also joins. *Additional Access:* A direct and shorter route to the Burdell Ridge is via the San Carlos Fire Road; turn right on San Carlos Way and veer right on Verdad.

MB: Burdell has two kinds of trails—steep and too steep. For a 7.25 mile **Burdell Preserve loop**, which makes a circle within the mountain's south-facing folds, head

Mount Burdell

up the San Andreas Road and go left on the Deer Camp Road, as described in the loop hike above. You ride Deer Camp around and up for 1.5-miles, joining the Cobblestone Road—where you have an option of going up .6-mile to the ridge. Then drop down Cobblestone to Middle Burdell Road, where you go left, at the bog of Hidden Lake. In .75-mile you pass San Carlos Road—where you could drop down—and continue another .5-mile to Salt Lick Road, a sharp right-hand turn. After dropping .5-mile on Salt Lick, hang a left on San Marin Road. San Marin comes down the side of a ravine and then contours along the base of the preserve, connecting back with the San Andreas trailhead after 2 miles.

J: The Hidden Lake loop or Deer Camp loop both are good runs, but not for beginners, since elevation changes are pronounced. But the routes are not so steep as to blow out knees, and buff runners will enjoy these cross-country jogs. You can combine both loops for a run of about 6.5 miles by taking the Deer Camp loop and going left on Middle Burdell Road when you drop down from Cobblestone. The San Marin Fire Road is also a good runner's trail; see *Additional Access* and use Sereno Way. You can run San Marin Road over to San Andreas, and take the Michako Trail back for a semi-loop.

102. OLOMPALI   H, ST

Best for: A short walk through a park that reveals layers of Marin's history—from Sir Francis Drake to the Summer of Love; or a longer walk to Mount Burdell to view almost all of the region's topography.

Parking: Go north of Novato on Hwy. 101, passing Olompali State Historic Park, and turn around after 2.25 mi. at San Antonio Rd. Return southbound to park. *Notes:* Park is accessible only to southbound traffic. Parking fee may be required.

Agency: Olompali State Historic Park; *Special Interest: Kids

H: Olompali loop (3.25 mi.); Mt. Burdell (9.25 mi.)

For **both hikes**, walk up through the Burdell complex and continue past the dairy toward the Miwok Village. Go left at the village and bear right on a trail that leads up one of Mt. Burdell's shoulders. You gain about 250 feet over a short distance and come to a trail junction. For the **Olompali loop**, go straight on the trail that will take you across the stream ravine and then down switchbacks over a 2-mile route to the parking area.

To summit 1,558-foot **Mt. Burdell**, turn right at the trail junction. In widely looping switchbacks, the trail covers 3.5-miles to Burdell Ridge Road. The peak is to the right when you reach the ridge. You'll be able to see from the San Francisco Bay and Mount Tam in the south to the sparsely populated ranchlands and beginnings of the remote California coast to the north. *Notes:* Rock walls you may see on Olompali's trails were built in the 1870s by Chinese workers; the walls mark ranchero boundaries. *Additional Access:* You can reach both the loop trail and Burdell trail from the upper end of the parking area. Mt. Burdell also can be accessed via TH101.

ST: Olompali State Historic Park

Olompali—thought to mean "southern people"—tells the history of Marin, from antiquity to the present. For centuries the grounds were a trading village—a transition border between the Coast Miwok of Marin and other Miwok people. Olompali's last leader, Camilo Ynitia, was the only Miwok to receive a Mexican land grant—in 1843 from General Mariano Vallejo. Unlike most people of Miwok descent, who perished under the Mexicans and later the Americans, Ynitia adapted. He was able to trade wheat with the Russian colonials on the coast and livestock with the Mexicans in Sonoma. Ynitia sold his properties to big landowner and politico James Black, whose son-in-law was Galen Burdell—a dentist who prospered in post-Gold Rush California. The Burdell family kept the extensive property until the 1940s, prospering in ranching, quarries, and land development.

The University of San Francisco became the new owners of Olompali, hoping to establish a Jesuit retreat, but those plans fell through and the buildings fell into disrepair. In the 1960s, the Grateful Dead moved in as renters, and fellow rock legends like Janis Joplin and the Jefferson Airplane's Grace Slick jammed here. When the Dead moved out, the grounds became a hippie commune known as "The Chosen Family," with numbers swelling to 100 on special occasions. Alas, the amplified music proved too much for the old electrical wiring, and one of the Burdell buildings was partially destroyed by fire. But the fire turned out to be a blessing, as it revealed the adobe walls of Camilo Ynitia's dwelling, which had been framed over, and prompted efforts to turn the grounds into a 700-acre state park, which took place in 1977. The final impetus for the creation of the park came in 1974: Archeologists found an Elizabethan silver sixpence dated 1567—thought to have been left by Sir Francis Drake during his soiree in West Marin in 1579.

To stroll the historic ruins and recreated Coast Miwok village of **Olompali State Historic Park**, head across the bridge from the parking area. On the lower grounds are the Burdell Mansion, which envelopes the adobe ruins, the ranch house and barns, and remains of Mary Augustina Black-Burdell's extensive Victorian garden. Near the original barn is Kitchen Rock, where Coast Miwok would gather around, generation after generation, to grind acorns. The recreated Coast Miwok village, an interpretive site begun in 1994, is a short walk up the road from the Burdell estate.

*Special Interest: Bring the family; docents lead history tours.

Doggie Trails

In almost all cases dogs must be on leash. You must also clean up after your pet. Public policy may change, so observe all signs when hiking.

Bijou

SAN FRANCISCO

Dogs allowed on city streets and most city parks including Golden Gate Park, TH3 and TH4. Dogs are not permitted in some areas of Golden Gate Park, such as gardens and arboretums. Corona Heights dog park, TH2, has a great view. Pine Lake Park, TH5, is a doggie oasis in the city. For a complete city listing for off and on leash zones, check out the "Run Wild" section at www.sfdog.org.

GOLDEN GATE NATIONAL RECREATION AREA-SAN FRANCISCO

Fort Funston, TH6, is a popular dog walking area, as is Ocean Beach, TH7, which is immediately north. Baker Beach, TH9, also welcomes the pooch, on the north side of the beach. Dogs are allowed at Sutro Baths and Sutro Heights Park, TH9. The trails of the Presidio, TH10, are open to dogs, as is the Golden Gate Promenade at Crissy Field, TH13. The east end of the beach at Crissy Field is also dog city. You may also walk Spot along the waterfront toward Fort Mason, TH12, and Aquatic Park.

GOLDEN GATE NATIONAL RECREATION AREA-MARIN HEADLANDS

Dogs generally are not allowed on Headlands trails, but there are a number of exceptions: In TH16, dogs are allowed on the Coastal Trail all the way to Muir Beach, the Rodeo Lagoon Trail, Miwok Trail to Wolf Ridge Trail, and the westbound portion of the Wolf Ridge Trail. They are also allowed on Rodeo Beach. Stop by the Headlands Vistiors Center for a free map, which shows these trails.

You can escort the dog around Horseshoe Bay at Fort Baker, TH17. Dogs are also permitted on the first part of the Alta Trail, described in TH19. In TH20, Tennessee Valley, dogs are allowed to walk through on the Coastal Trail, but you cannot access that trail from here. You can take the canine on the Oakwood Valley loop, as well as the Miwok Trail heading north from the Tennessee Valley parking area. Dogs are permitted at Muir Beach, TH55.

GOLDEN GATE NATIONAL RECREATION AREA-MARIN

Although "No Dogs" is the rule, you'll find notable exceptions. The north end on Stinson Beach, TH62, beyond the GGRNA boundary, is a dog-friendly beach. From Five Brooks Trailhead, TH66, you can take dogs up the Randall and McCurdy trails. The Bolinas Ridge Trail is a nice long dog walk. You can access it from either end of its 11-mile run, at TH83, or TH61. Palomarin Beach, accessed from TH65, is also a dog beach, although the trail is subject to closure. In Bolinas, TH64, dogs are given almost full citizenship—Bolinas is not in the GGNRA.

POINT REYES NATIONAL SEASHORE
Dogs are not allowed on trails at the seashore, but you will find several great dog beaches: The south end of Limantour Beach, TH69, Point Reyes Beaches, TH76, and Kehoe Beach, TH78.

CALIFORNIA STATE PARKS
Although dogs are not allowed on trails at state parks, the north side of Samuel P. Taylor Park offers some pleasing exceptions. Dogs are permitted in Devils Gulch, TH83, with the exception of Bills Trail; in Barnabe Peak, TH84; and in Irving Picnic Area, TH86. You can also have the pooch in picnic areas and roads of all parks, and in China Camp Village in TH33.

OTHER STATE AGENCIES
State Fish and Game administers some of the areas in the Bay Wetlands section. See Shorebird Marsh, TH27, Bel Marin Keys, TH38, and Black Point, TH39. Leashed pets are permitted.

MULTI-USE PATHS
Multi-use paths almost always allow dogs. These include Blackies Pasture, TH22, and Richardson Bayfront to Bothin Marsh, TH21. Try Corte Madera Creek, TH28, and at Larkspur Landing, TH29, which can include a side-trip to the nice little beach at San Quentin Point. Shoreline Park, TH30, is also a keeper for pets, including the extended loop around Pickleweed Park. You'll find a dog park at Piper Park, TH50. The Stafford Lake path can be accessed from TH100 and TH101.

MARIN COUNTY OPEN SPACE PRESERVES AND PARKS
Dogs are allowed in preserves, although a few trails have restrictions. In general, the MCOSD lands area among the best places to take dogs. Most of the trailheads in the Miwok Woodlands are opens space preserve: See Trailheads 88 through 101. You'll also find a number of preserves in Bay Wetlands, including San Pedro Mountain, TH34, and the marshes near the Marin Civic Center, TH35. Farther north are Deer Island, TH40, and Rush Creek, TH41.

The Mount Tamalpais section also has some open space preserve walks, mostly forested. Check out Cascade Canyon, TH44, Mt. Baldy in San Anselmo, TH46, Phoenix Lake, TH47, Baltimore Canyon, TH48, and King Mountain, TH49. You'll find three preserves in Corte Madera Ridge, TH51, and plenty of dog access in Blithedale Summit, TH52. And don't forget Ring Mountain, TH26, and Old St. Hilarys, TH25. Most county parks don't allow dogs, but the trails in McInnis Park, TH36, area an exception.

MARIN DOG PARKS
You'll also find Martin Luther King Dog Park in TH19, across from Gate 5 Road, and an excellent running park at TH21, Richardson Bayfront. Marin Civic Center, TH35, has a dog run near the lagoon. For a current park listing, consult www.marin-humane.org/html/dogpark.html.

MARIN MUNICIPAL WATER DISTRICT
MMWD trails allow dogs in almost all cases. On the north side of Tamalpais, you'll find access to these lands in Alpine Lake, TH42, Sky Oaks Lakes, TH43, and out of Deer Park, in Fairfax, TH45. Other trailheads with access to MMWD are to be found in Mill Valley, TH53, Mountain Home Inn, TH56, and from the Rock Springs area of TH59. Also see the east side of Ridgecrest Boulevard, TH61. Kent Lake, TH88, is an excellent dog walk, and TH82, Nicasio Reservoir, is additional water district lands where dogs are allowed. *Be Aware:* Don't let the dogs in the water anywhere on MMWD trails.

MARIN CITIES AND TOWNS
The dog might enjoy the strolls in Tiburon, TH23, and Sausalito, TH18. Most often, city parks allow dogs on leash. San Rafael has some of the best, including San Rafael Hill in TH31, and Barbier Park, which is accessed best from Marin Drive in Peacock Gap, TH32, or Gold Hill Grade in TH34.

GOLDEN GATE BRIDGE
Facts and Lore

"High overhead its lights shall gleam,
Far, far below life's restless stream,
Unceasingly shall flow;
For this was spun its lithe line form,
To fear not war, nor time, nor storm,
For fate had meant it so."

—Last stanza of *The Mighty Task is Done*
By Chief Engineer, Joseph Baermann Strauss

The original plans for the bridge were not for an art-deco suspension, but for a hybrid cantilever-suspension structure.

During the foggy season, from July through October, the bridge's baritone horns sound for five hours a day.

The bridge opened on May 28, 1937, after just over four years of construction.

The bridge has never been gold, but its vermilion-orange color was selected over carbon black and the choice of the U.S. Navy, which was black with yellow stripes.

Golden Gate refers to the mile-wide strait, and was named in 1846 by Captain John C. Fremont—several years before the discovery of gold in California.

The bridge has been closed three times due to high winds.

Eleven men died building the bridge, ten of them when a scaffold gave way just three months short of completion. A safety net saved nineteen lives during construction. These men made up the "Halfway-to-Hell Club."

Most car traffic, one day: 162,414 vehicles, after an earthquake damaged the Bay Bridge, October, 1989. **Fewest:** 3,921, in 1981 when storms closed nearby roads. **Yearly average:** 42 million.

Length: Including approaches, 1.7 miles; total suspended, 1.2 miles; suspended between towers, .8-mile

Width: Total, 90 feet; sidewalks, 10 feet each.

Height: Tower above water, 746 feet; between roadway and water, 220 feet; deepest foundation below water, 110 feet.

The concrete poured to construct the bridge is enough for a driveway 20 feet wide, one foot thick and 100 miles long.

Toll per round trip: 1937: $1, with 5 cents additional for more than three passengers; 1973: 50 cents; 2001: $3, or free of charge if more than three passengers, 5 a.m. to 9 a.m. and 4 p.m. to 6 p.m.

Non-vehicular access:
Pedestrians, strollers, wheelchairs: East sidewalk from 5 a.m. to 9 p.m.
Bicycles: East sidewalk, daily from 9 p.m. to 5 a.m., and Monday through Friday from 5 a.m. to 3:30 p.m.; West sidewalk, Saturday and Sunday from 5 a.m. to 9 p.m., and Monday through Friday from 3:30 p.m. to 9 p.m.
Skates, Scooters, Skateboards: Never

Non-vehicular visits per year: 10 million
Load capacity: 4,000 pounds per lineal foot

Length of one main cable: 1.45 miles; length of wire per cable: 80,000 miles.

Rivets per tower: 600,000; Size of tower base: 33 X 54 feet.

Original construction cost: $35 million; Cost of late 1990s seismic retrofit: $313.8 million

upper right: The Muir Woods group as they arrive at the bridge site on Febuary 24, 1934
Fort Point photo collection, Golden Gate National Recreation Area, National Park Service

Free Advice and Opinion

DISCLAIMER

Think of this book as you would any other piece of outdoor gear. It will help you do what you want to do, but it depends solely upon you to supply responsible judgment and common sense. The publisher and authors are not responsible for injury, damage, or legal violations that occur when someone is using our guidebooks. Please contact the appropriate public agencies to familiarize yourself with rules and regulations. All posted signs and changes in trail status determined by public agencies supersede any recommendations in this book. Okay, now go out there and have fun.

RULES, GOLDEN & OTHER

Rules, unfortunately, are written for people who are less likely to read them … When in doubt, trust your gut feeling when safety is concerned … Be here now … Rules are made to be changed: If you have a problem with one, make phone calls and let the right people know … Be nice … Public parks are off-limits at night unless you have a camping permit … No swimming in Marin lakes … Litter karma incarnate: Pick up stray garbage; you will later be rewarded by finding something valuable … Share … Roads close on Mount Tam after sunset.

ROAD BLISS

People always drive slower on the way home from a hike ... What goes around, comes around: Let someone turn or merge and they will do the same for someone else ... Proposed name change for The City: Sans Parkingspasco, Carifornia ... If you want to go fast at rush hour, ride a bicycle ... Traffic Jams: Southbound on 101 weekday mornings and Friday evenings; northbound on 101 weekday afternoons ... Or anytime else ... Look both ways before crossing the street, and then run like hell ... We are how we drive ... Lying fallow in plain sight: the railroad easement-mass transit corridor through the center of Marin ... Those bicyclists are reducing traffic; give them space ... Also avoid, eastbound on Sir Francis Drake Boulevard, mornings, and westbound in the evenings ... And watch out for jams northbound on 19th Avenue on weekends.

PEDALING POINTERS

Bikes on streets need to obey traffic laws ... Back to the future transportation system: bike paths ... Emergency flat repair: stuff the tire with grass and leaves ... Use hand signals for turns ... Watch for opening doors of parked cars ... Remember: cars weigh two tons, so don't assume they see you ... And while you're at it, watch out for pedestrians ... Carry a spare tube ... For all-day cool drinks, freeze a half-full water bottle and then top off with water before the ride ...

Have a rear reflector in place for night travel ... On corners, keep your outside pedal down and your weight on it ... Bicyclists under 18 must wear a helmet, and so should everyone but the terminally hard-headed ... When facing obstacles on the trail, focus on the line where you want your bike to go ... Use orange juice from your lunch to clean greasy hands ... Keep tire pressure up to prevent flats.

WEATHER & HAZARDS

The coldest winter Mark Twain ever spent was a summer in San Francisco ... Prepare for coastal summer fog ... 'Bad' weather means fewer people on the trail ... The hard way to identify poison oak: catch a rash and you'll never forget it ... Try a forest hike in the fog ... Stay away from cliffs at the beach ... And never turn your back on a wave ... Dr. Jeff Schneider's sunscreen tips: buy twice the spf rating you want because people normally apply half what they should; for ingredients, look for zinc oxide and Parsol 1789 ...

Best for winter and spring: Miwok Woodlands, Bay Wetlands ... You are more likely to get sunburned on a windy day; chill factor makes you less aware ... Venturing off-trail is likely to hurt you as well as the terrain ... Riptides and strong currents exists at all beaches ... Before long hikes, tell someone where you're going ... Mountain lions can eat dogs ... Lyme disease ticks are tiny ... Twist a tick counterclockwise from your dog ... Drink plenty of water, whether the day is hot or not ... Beachcombers and kayakers need to know the tides … Standing under a cliff is not safe … Yet another reason to keep dogs on leash: They don't get poison oak, but you will from petting oily fur … Try Tamalpais in the summer, or cool off at Point Reyes.

HAPPY TRAILS

Never walk downhill with your hands in your pockets … There are no "secret" trails in Marin and San Francisco … Stay on established trails … For quiet walks, try weekdays or mornings … Never use a cell phone on a trail, except for emergency … Ordering pizza is not an emergency … Walkers stay to the right on multi-use paths … Remember: Someone might be afraid of your horse, dog, or bike, so pass with care … Never jog at night holding a television: you might look suspicious …

If you get lost, backtrack … Trail Zen: You can never walk the same trail twice … How to teach a dog to follow: Put your puppy in a safe place outdoors and hide from it when it loses track of you … This rarely works among couples … Friendly factor: You know you're in the wilds when people say hello on the trail … Always turn back on a hike before you're half exhausted … Splat! Never trust a passing gull … Canine Credo: If you keep your dog happy, you are getting enough exercise and nature for yourself, too.

NATURE & HEALTH

The environment can take care of itself; it's human habitat that needs saving … Tao of Environmentalism: Do nothing and nothing is left undone … Call to find out how you can volunteer to help preserve out parks … Coast Miwok Public Utilities: Sun, Rain, Trees … Noise won't kill anyone, but songbirds who can no longer communicate … Universal free cure for everything: Drink water and walk outdoors …

All science and art comes from nature … Any technology that cannot be sustained forever is already outmoded … You own your phone and TV, not the other way around … Really, you can stop anytime you want … Among the contests humans lose against other mammals: running, swimming, jumping, seeing, smelling, hearing … If you want to know what's important in life ask someone older than 80.

Resource Links

PUBLIC AGENCIES

Area code is 415 unless otherwise noted.

**GOLDEN GATE NATIONAL
RECREATION AREA**
Recorded information
    lines, 331-1422, 556-0561
Fort Mason-Park Headquarters, 556-0560
Alcatraz Island Visitors Center, 705-1092
Camping, 331-1540
Cliff House Visitors Center, 556-8642
Fort Funston, 239-2366
Fort Point National Historic Site, 556-1693
Golden Gate National Parks
    Association, 561-3000
Marin Headlands Visitors Center 331-1540
    Camping, 561-4304, 331-1540
    Nike Missile Museum, 331-1453
Muir Woods National Monument, 388-2595
    Bookstore, 388-7368
    Gift Shop, 388-7059
Planning information
    (Crissy Field, Fort Baker), 561-4844

Presidio, Mott Visitors Center, 561-4323
    Presidio Trust, 561-5300
    Park Archives and Records, 561-4807
    Park Stewards, 668-9765
    Public Affairs Division, 561-5418
    Special Park Uses, 561-4300
Ocean District, 556-8371
Stinson Beach, 868-0734, weather 868-1922
Volunteer job line, 561-4755

POINT REYES NATIONAL SEASHORE
Bear Valley Visitors Center, 464-5100
Camping reservations, 663-8054
Field Seminars, 663-1200
Indian Skills Classes, 479-3281
Elephant Seal Docent
    Program, 663-8522, ext. 285
Lighthouse Visitors Center, 669-1534
Morgan Horse Ranch, 663-1763
Natural History Explorations, 663-1363
National Seashore Association, 663-1155
Ken Patrick Visitors Center, 669-1250
Recorded weather, 663-1092

*Ranger Buttons,
Kule Loklo,
Bear Valley Headquarters*

CALIFORNIA STATE PARKS

Marin District Office, 893-1580
Public Affairs, Sacramento, 916-653-6995
California State Parks Association, 258-9975
Camping Reservations, 800-444-7275
Angel Island 435-1915, 897-0715
    Tours & Events, 897-0715
China Camp, 456-0766
Marconi Conference Center, 663-9020
Mount Tamalpais, 388-2070, 800-444-7275
Roads within park are closed from sunset to sunrise.
    Pantoll, Camp Alice Eastwood,
    Steep Ravine
Mt. Tamalpais Interpretive
    Association, 258-2410
Olompali, 892-3383
Samuel P. Taylor, 488-9897
Tomales Bay, 669-1140

OTHER CALIFORNIA AGENCIES

Department of Fish and Game, 892-0460,
    707-944-5500
Coastal Conservancy, 510-286-1015
Wildlife Conservation Board, 916-445-8448

MARIN MUNICIPAL WATER
DISTRICT, 945-1195
Watershed lands are closed from sunset to sunrise.

Sky Oaks Ranger Station, 459-5267
Conservation Assistance
    Program, 924-2600, ext. 347
Friends of the Watershed, 461-3386
Tamalpais Watershed Volunteer
    Program, 945-1180

MARIN COUNTY PARKS & OPEN
SPACE DISTRICT, 499-6387
*Oversees 32 open space
preserves and county parks.*

MCOSD Volunteer Program, 499-3778
District Rangers, 499-6405
MCOSD Naturalist Walks, 499-3647
MCOSD Board Office, 499-7331
McInnis Park, 499-3646
McNears Beach, 446-4424
Paradise Beach Park, 435-9212
Stafford Lake, 897-0618
Las Galinas Sanitary District, 472-1734

CITY PARKS

Belvedere-Tiburon Recreation
    Department, 435-4355
Corte Madera Recreation Department, 927-5072
Golden Gate Park,
    McLaren Lodge Headquarters, 831-2700
    Beach Chalet Visitors Center, 751-2766
    AIDS Memorial Grove, 750-8340
    Adopt-a-Monument, 252-2593
    Band Concerts, 831-2790
    Fly Casting, 386-2630
    Picnicking, 666-7035
    Senior Center, 666-7015
    Stables, 668-7360
    Stow Lake Boating, 752-0347
    Volunteer Guides, 750-5105
    Walking Tours, 263-0991, 221-1310
    Weddings, 666-7027, 666-7035
Larkspur Recreation, 927-5110
Marinwood Community Services, 479-0775
Mill Valley Parks & Recreation, 383-1370
Novato Parks & Recreation, 897-4323
Ross Recreation Department, 892-5098
San Anselmo Parks & Recreation, 459-2477
San Francisco Recreation and Park
    Department, 831-2700, 800-990-9777
    Friends of San Francisco Parks, 750-5105
    Permits and Reservations, 831-5500
    Volunteer Office, 753-7265
San Rafael Community Services, 485-3333
Sausalito Parks & Recreation, 289-4100
Tiburon Town Hall, 435-7373, 435-7399

Japanese Tea Garden

SUPPLEMENTAL MAPS

Trailblazer's parking directions, trail descriptions and maps are all you need. But supplemental maps are available, many of which are free. No one trail map covers the area. You should most probably get a street map, since the most difficult part about recreating in Marin and San Francisco is finding where to leave the car.

Overall

Thomas Guides, 800-899-6227: Street maps in spiral booklets, one for Marin and one for San Francisco. Show fire roads not on other maps.

AAA, 472-6700: Automobile Association maps cover San Francisco and Marin, with the exception of West Marin. These maps also show fire roads, public lands and park boundaries. Compass Maps publishes a fold-up street map that covers all of Marin; call 800-441-6277.

A very good overall map for Marin is the *Marin Bicycle Map*, published by the Marin Bicycle Coalition, 456-3469. It is available free to members or may be purchased at book or bike stores. It shows surface streets as well as hiking roads on public lands. Likewise for the city, the San Francisco Bike Coalition, 431-2453, produces *San Francisco Bike Map & Walking Guide*, which shows surface streets, many trails and numbered bike routes.

For other San Francisco and Marin maps, which show the area but not trails, you can also contact the visitors bureaus listed below under *Visitor Information and Services*.

Golden Gate National Recreation Area

A free park brochure, showing trails in Marin and San Francisco is available at all GGNRA visitors centers. In addition, the Presidio and Headlands visitors centers have more detailed trail maps for their portions of the park.

Point Reyes National Seashore

A very good and free trail map is available at the Bear Valley Visitors Center. An excellent supplement is *Point Reyes National Seashore Trail Map*, by Tom Harrison Maps, 800-265-9090, 456-7940. It has more detail than the park map, and also shows a portion of Taylor State Park.

California State Parks

Each state park offers a trail map, but you have to be there when the office is open. Do yourself a favor and contact the regional office in Ignacio, 893-1580, and pick up a complete set—Samuel P. Taylor, Mt. Tamalpais, China Camp, Olompali, Angel Island and Tomales Bay. A nominal fee is charged. Many of these trails are only shown on these maps.

Mount Tamalpais-Marin Municipal Water District

MMWD offers a free map as well as another trail map available for a nominal fee. These maps, which are adequate, are available at the district office in Corte Madera, 945-1195, and at the Sky Oaks Ranger Station, 459-5267. The best map for this region is *Trails of Mt. Tamalpais and the Marin Headlands*, by Olmstead & Bros., 510-658-6534. Also available in bookstores.

Marin Open Space District Preserves

The MCOSD office at the Marin Civic Center publishes maps that are only so-so; call 499-6387. If you use them in conjunction with a street map, you can figure things out. The preserves are shown in a very good set of maps in a trail book, *Open Spaces* by Barry Spitz, which is available at the district and bookstores.

The *Marin Bicycle Map*, available in bookstores, also shows open space fire roads. The preserves for much of Marin are also shown on *Trails of Northeast Marin County* by Pease Press, 387-1437, a very good map for its region.

San Francisco-Golden Gate Park

The San Francisco Recreation and Park Department publishes *A Guide to San Francisco Recreation and Parks*, which serves as a street map and park locator, with a decent map of Golden Gate Park. The department also published the excellent *Map & Guide to Golden Gate Park*. Call, 831-2700.

Bicycles

Maps published by the bike coalitions, as mentioned above, are good overall maps as well as excellent cycling guides: Marin, 456-3469; San Francisco, 431-2453. The *Trails of Northeast Marin County*, 387-1437, is good for its more limited region.

MUSEUMS, HISTORIC SITES & ATTRACTIONS

Also see Public Agencies

Ansel Adams Center, 495-7000
Asian Art Museum, 379-8801
Bay Area Discovery Museum, 487-4398
Bay Model, 332-3871, 332-3870
Bolinas Museum, 868-0330
California Academy of Sciences, 750-7145
California Historical Society, 357-1848
California Palace of the Legion of
    Honor, 750-3600, 863-3330
China Camp Village, Friends of, 454-8954
Chinese Culture Center, 986-1822
Chinese Historical Society, 391-1188
Coit Tower, 362-0808
M. H. de Young Museum, 750-3600,
Exploratorium, 563-7337, 561-0360
Falkirk Cultural Center, 485-3328
Golden Gate Theological Seminary, 380-1340
Golden Gate Bridge, 921-5858
Headlands Center for the Arts, 331-3853
Hyde Street Pier, 556-6435, 556-0859
Marin County Civic Center, 499-6646
Marin County Museum
    (Historical Society), 454-8538
Marin Museum of the
    American Indian, 897-4064
Marinship, 332-3871
Maritime Museum, Aquatic
    Park, 556-3002, 561-7100
Mission San Rafael Archangel, 454-8141
Morrison Planetarium, 750-7141
Musee Mecanique, 386-1170
North Beach Museum, 626-7070
Novato History Museum, 897-4320
Pacific Bell Park, 972-2000
Randall Museum, 554-9600
San Anselmo Historical Museum, 258-4659
San Francisco Museum of
    Modern Art, 357-4000
San Francisco National Cemetery, 589-7737
San Francisco Zoo, 753-7061, 753-7080
Sausalito Historical Society, 289-4117
Steinhart Aquarium, 750-7145
Tomales Regional History
    Center, 707-878-9443
Transamerica Pyramid, 775-1943
Yerba Buena Center for the
    Arts, 978-2710, 978-2787

Transamerica Pyramid

GROUPS & ORGANIZATIONS

CONSERVATION & PRESERVATION

Angel Island Association, 435-3522
Audubon Canyon Ranch, 868-9244
Audubon Society, Marin, 383-1770
Bay Audubon Center & Sanctuary, 388-2524
The Bay Institute, 721-7680
Belvedere-Tiburon Landmarks
    Society, 435-1853
Bolinas Lagoon Foundation, Box 444,
    Stinson Beach, 94970
California Alpine Club, 388-9940
California Indian Museum and
    Cultural Center, 561-3991
Clem Miller Environmental Center, 663-1200
Coastal Commission
    Adopt-a-Beach, 800-262-7848
Coastal Conservancy, 510-286-1015
Common Earth, 455-0646

Environmental Forum of Marin, 479-7814
Environmental Science Center
    Fort Funston, 469-4763
Friends of Corte Madera Creek, 457-6045
Friend of San Francisco Parks, 750-5105
Golden Gate Raptor Observatory, 331-0730
Gulf of the Farallones Marine
    Sanctuary, 561-6622, 561-6625
Headlands Institute, 332-5771
Marin Agricultural Land Trust, 663-1158
Marin Environmental Alliance, 472-6170
Marin Conservation Corps, 454-4554
Marin Conservation League, 472-6170
Marin Mammal Center, Headlands, 289-7325
North Bay Riparian Station, 332-1941
Pacific Environment and Resources
    Center, 332-8200
Pioneer Park Project, Coit Tower, 398-5112
Point Reyes Bird Observatory, 868-0655
Resource Renewal Institute
    Fort Mason, 928-3774
Romberg Tiburon Center, 338-6063
S.F. Zoological Society,
    Adopt-an-Animal, 753-7117
Sausalito Historical Society, 289-4117
Slide Ranch, 381-6155
Tamalpais Interpretive Association, 388-2070
Trust for Public Land, 495-4014
WildCare, San Rafael, 453-1000

Point Bonita Lighthouse

RECREATION

American Discovery Trail, 800-663-2387
Bay Area Ridge Trail Council, 391-9300
Blue Waters Kayaking, 669-2600
Club Nautique (sailing), 332-8001
Coastwalk, 800-550-6854
The Dipsea Race, 331-3550
Five Brooks Horse Ranch, 663-1570
Heritage Trails Fund, 510-937-7661
Marin Athletic Foundation, 454-2247
Marin YMCA, 492-9622
Miwok Stables, 383-8048
Novato Youth Center, 892-1643
NIA Exercise Program, 800-762-5762
Oceanic Society Farallon Cruises, 474-3385
Osher Marin Jewish Community
    Center, 479-2000
San Francisco Bay Trail, 510-464-7900
Sausalito Bay Adventures, 331-0444
Strawberry Recreation Center, 383-6494
Tamalpa Runners, 721-3791
Tamalpais Conservation Club, 391-8021
Tiburon Adventure Camp, 435-4366
YMCA Point Bonita Center, 331-9622

BICYCYLE

Bicycle Safety Education, 454-2309
Bicycle Trails Council of Marin, 456-7512
Camp Tamarancho (Boy Scouts), 454-1081
California Bicycle Coalition, 916-446-7558
Marin Bicycle Coalition, marinbike.org,
    456-3469, 457-8687
Marin Cyclists, 721-4337
San Francisco Bicycle Coalition, 431-2453
San Francisco Bicycle Program, 585-2453
Transportation Alternatives for
    Marin, 383-4826
Trips for Kids, 458-2968

PLANTS & GARDENS

California Native Plant Society, 647-5300
Conservatory of Flowers, Save the, 750-5443
Fort Mason Community Garden, 776-8616
Friends of the Urban Forest, 561-6890
Golden Gate Rose Society, 436-0497
Green Gulch, 383-3134
Japanese Tea Garden, 752-1171
Larkspur Community Garden, 927-5110
Marin Art & Garden Center, 454-5597
Marin County Farmers Market, 456-3276
Presidio Native Plant Nursery, 561-4380
Strybing Arboretum, 661-1316

groups and organizations, continued—

COMMUNITY SERVICE

Bread & Roses, 945-7120
Bicycle Community Project, 561-6488
Coalition for San Francisco
    Neighborhoods, 346-5525
Dance Palace Community Center, 663-1075
Guide Dogs for the Blind, 499-4000
Marin Community Foundation, 461-3333
San Francisco Family Fest, 239-0161
Spirit Rock Meditation Center, 488-0164
Volunteer Center of Marin, 479-5660

ART & PERFOMANCE

American Conservatory Theater, 834-3200
Downtown Art Center, San Rafael, 451-8119
Film Institute of Northern
    California, 383-5256
Headlands Center for the Arts, 331-2787
Marin Center, 472-3500
Marin Arts Council, 499-8350
Marin Society of Artists, 454-9561
Mill Valley Film Festival, 383-5266
Mountain Theater Play, 383-1100
Rafael Film Center, 454-1222
Ross Valley Players, 456-9555
San Francisco Ballet, 865-2000
San Francisco Opera, 864-3330
Shakespeare at Stinson, 868-1115
Stern Grove Music Festival, 252-6253
Wildlife Gallery, Bolinas, 868-0402
Yerba Buena Center for the Arts, 978-2700

PUBLICATIONS

Bay Area Naturally
    (organic living), 800-486-4794
Bay Guardian, 552-5222
Cycle California Magazine, 650-961-2663
Marin Independent Journal
    (daily newspaper), 883-8600
Marin Visitor (free tourist), 897-1658
Pacific Sun (Marin weekly), 383-4500
Point Reyes Light, 663-8404
San Francisco Chronicle, 777-1111
San Francisco Magazine, 777-2691
Sierra Club Yodeler, 510-848-0800
SF Weekly, 541-0700
S. F. Bay Area Gallery Guide, 921-1600

VISITOR INFORMATION & SERVICES

Also see Public Agencies

Corte Madera Chamber of
    Commerce, 924-0441
Fairfax Chamber of Commerce, 453-5928
Larkspur Chamber of Commerce, 412-8192
Marin County Convention &
    Visitors Bureau, 499-5000
Mill Valley Chamber of Commerce, 388-9700
Novato Chamber of Commerce, 800-897-1164
San Anselmo Chamber of
    Commerce, 454-2510
San Francisco Chamber of
    Commerce, 392-4511
San Francisco Convention & Visitors
    Bureau, 974-6900
San Francisco Visitor Information
    Center, 391-2000
San Francisco Welcome Center, 956-3493
San Francisco history walks, 557-4266
San Rafael Chamber of
    Commerce, 800-454-4163
Sausalito Chamber of Commerce, 331-7262
Tiburon Peninsula Chamber of
    Commerce, 435-5633
Sausalito Chamber of
    Commerce, 332-0505, 331-7262
Sausalito Downtown Visitors Center, 332-0532
West Marin Chamber of Commerce, 663-9232
West Marin Visitors Bureau, 669-2684

TRANSPORTATION

Angel Island-Tiburon Ferry, 435-2131
Blue & Gold Fleet, 705-5555, 773-1188
California Road Conditions, 800-427-ROAD
Golden Gate Transit
    Marin, 455-2000
    San Francisco, 923-2000
Golden Gate-Larkspur Ferry, 925-5567
Marin Airport, 461-4222
Red and White Fleet
    (ferry), 447-0597, 800-229-2784
San Francisco Muni, 673-6864
SFO Ground Transportation, 800-736-2008
Travinfo, 817-1717
Wheelchair Accessible Van
    Rentals, 800-638-1912

Where to Stay

SAN FRANCISCO HOTELS

SWANK

Mark Hopkins, 392-3434
S.F. Marriott Hotel, 800-228-9290
W San Francisco, 777-5300
Westin St. Francis Hotel, Powell, 397-7000

BOUTIQUE & BUDGET HOTELS

Alisa Hotel, 956-3232
Beresford Hotel, 673-9900
Cartwright Hotel, 421-2865
Commodore Hotel, 923-6800
Cornell Hotel, 421-3154
Foley's Inn, 397-7800
Galleria Park Hotel, 781-3060
Grant Plaza, Grant Ave., 434-3883
Herbert Hotel, 362-1600
Hotel Monaco, 292-0100
Hotel Palomar, 348-1111
Hotel Triton, 781-3566
Juliana Hotel, 392-2540
Monticello Inn, 392-8800
Mosser Victorian Hotel, 986-4400
Prescott Hotel, 563-0303
Serrano Hotel, 885-2500
Stratford Hotel, 397-7080
Prescott Hotel, 563-0303
Villa Florence Hotel, 397-7700

B&B'S

SAN FRANCISCO

Albion House, Gough St., 621-0896
Amsterdam Hotel, Taylor St., 673-3277
Archbishop's Mansion, Fulton St., 563-7872
Dockside Boat and Bed, Pier 39, 392-5526
Golden Gate Hotel, Bush St., 392-3702
Mansions Hotel, Sacramento St., 929-9444
The Slack Mansion, Sacramento St., 447-7600
Victorian Inn, Lyon St., 800-435-1967
White Swann Inn, Bush St., 775-1755

MARIN

Carriage House, Point Reyes, 663-8627
Case Del Mar, Stinson Beach, 868-2124
Fairfax Inn, 455-8702
Gables Inn, Sausalito, 800-966-1554
Glen Park House, San Rafael, 258-0714
Hotel Inverness, 669-7393
B&B Exchange of Marin, 485-1971
Point Reyes Vineyard Inn, 663-1011

RUSTIC LODGINGS, HOSTELS

SAN FRANCISCO & MARIN

California Alpine Club, 381-4975
Coastal Lodging of West Marin, 663-1351
Green Tortoise Hostel, S.F., 834-1000
Marin Headlands Hostel, 331-2777
New Central Hostel, Market St., 703-9986
Northern California Hostels, 863-1444
Olema Ranch Campground, 800-655-2267
Pacific Tradewinds, Sacramento St., 433-7970
Point Reyes Hostel, 663-8811
San Francisco Hostel, Downtown, 788-5604
Fort Mason Hostel, 771-7277
Tourist Club, Mt. Tam, 331-9622
West Point Inn, 388-9955, 646-0702
YMCA, Golden Gate Ave, S.F., 885-5439

MARIN HOTELS

Alta Mira Hotel, Sausalito, 332-1350
Casa Madrona Hotel, 332-0502
Courtyard by Marriott, 800-321-2211
Embassy Suites, San Rafael, 499-9222
Gerstle Park Inn, San Rafael, 800-726-7611
Hotel Sausalito, 888-442-0700
Inn Marin, Novato, 883-5952
Manka's Inverness Lodge, 669-1034
Mill Valley Inn, 800-595-2100
Olema Inn, 663-9559
Panama Hotel, San Rafael, 457-3993
San Anselmo Inn, 800-598-9771
Tiburon Lodge, 435-3133

SAN FRANCISCO RESTAURANTS

Where to Eat

VERY ESS EFF

Aqua, California St., 956-9662
Boulevard, Mission St., 543-6084
Buena Vista, Hyde St., 474-5044
Cafe Claude, Claude Lane, 392-3505
Delfina, 18th St., 773-6198
Dine, Mission St., 538-3463
Globe, Pacific Ave., 391-4132
La Folie, Polk St., 776-5577
Lulu's, Folsom St., 495-5775
Masa's, Bush St., 989-7154
Postrio, Post St., 776-7825
Splendido, California St. 986-3222
Tadich Grill, California St., 391-1849
Tosca Cafe, Columbus Ave., 986-9651
Yabbie's Coastal Kitchen, Polk St., 474-4088
XYZ, W Hotel, Third St., 817-7836
Zuni Cafe, Market St., 552-2522

WHERE LOCALS GO

2223 Restaurant, Market St., 431-0692
Akiko's Sushi, Mason St., 989-8218
Angkor Wat, Geary St., 221-7887
Aux Delices Vietnamese, Polk St., 928-4977
Axum Cafe, Haight St., 252-7912
B44 Catalan Bistro, Beldon Pl., 986-6287
Boogaloos, 22nd St., 824-3211
Bow Hon, Grant Ave., 362-0601
Cafe Elena, Market St., 543-8933
Cha Cha Cha, Haight St., 386-5758
Country Station Sushi, Mission St., 861-0972
Ella's, Presidio Ave., 441-5669
Frankie's Bohemian Cafe, Divisadero, 921-4725
Georgiou Pizza, Brannan St., 558-8012
Gold Mirror Italian, Taraval St., 564-0401
Kate's Kitchen, Haight St., 626-3984
Khan Toke Thai, Geary St., 668-6654
King of Thai, Clement St., 752-5198
Mel's Diner, Geary St., 387-2244
Magnolia, Haight St., 864-7468
Moose's, Stockton St., 989-7800
Nagano Sushi, Geary St., 221-9811
Park Chow's, 9th Ave., 221-9811
South Park Cafe, Park St., 495-7275
Thirsty Bear Brewing, Howard St. 974-0905
Ti Couz Creperie, 16th St., 252-7373
Tommy's Mexican, Geary St., 387-4747
Ton Kiang, Geary St., 387-8273
Tu Lan Vietnamese, 6th St., 626-0927

MARIN RESTAURANTS

Amici's Pizzeria, San Rafael, 455-9777
Bubba's Diner, San Anselmo, 459-6862
Buckeye Road House, Mill Valley, 331-2600
Cactus Cafe, Mill Valley, 388-8226
Cafe Amsterdam, Fairfax, 256-8020
Chalet Basque, San Rafael, 479-1070
Coast Cafe, Bolinas, 868-2224
Deer Park Villa, Fairfax, 456-8084
Dipsea Cafe, Mill Valley, 381-0298
Insalata's, San Anselmo, 457-7700
Lark Creek Inn, 924-7766
Las Camelias, San Rafael, 453-5850
Manka's, Inverness, 669-1034
Marin Brewing Co., Larkspur, 461-4677
Marin Joe's, Corte Madera, 924-2081
Nick's Cove, Marshall, 663-1033
Pacific Cafe, Kentfield, 456-3898
Paradise Vegetarian, San Rafael, 456-3572
Pelican Inn, Muir Beach, 383-6000
Phyllis' Giant Burgers, San Rafael, 456-0866
Royal Thai, San Rafael, 485-1074
Station House Cafe, Pt. Reyes, 663-1515
Sushi Ran, Sausalito, 332-3620
Taqueria San Jose, San Rafael, 455-0999
Vladimir's, Inverness, 669-1021
Wild Fox, Novato, 883-9125

Restaurants With A View

SAN FRANCISCO
Alioto's, Fisherman's Wharf, 673-0183
Crab House, Pier 39, 434-2722
Beach Chalet, Golden Gate Park, 386-8439
Burger King, The Presidio, 673-1856
Carnelian Room, California St., 433-8500
Cityscape, S.F. Hilton, O'Farrell St., 923-5002
Cliff House, Ocean Beach, 386-3330
Equinox, Hyatt Regency, Drumm St., 788-1234
Gaylord, Ghiradelli Square, 771-8822
Grand Views, Hyatt Union Square, 403-4847
Greens, Fort Mason, 771-6222
Julius' Castle, Montgomery St., 392-2222
Marriott Hotel, Mission St., 896-1600
Mark Hopkins, Nob Hill, 392-3434
Night Kitchen, Metreon, 369-6000
Palomino, Spear St., 512-7400
Pasqua Coffee Bar, Sansome St., 986-4206
Waterfront, The Embarcadero, 391-2696

MARIN
Alta Mira, Sausalito, 332-6849
Caprice, Tiburon, 435-3400
Casa Madrona, Sausalito, 331-5888
Guaymas, Tiburon, 435-6300
Horizons, Sausalito, 331-3232
Sam's Anchor Cafe, Tiburon, 435-4527
Mountain Home Inn, Mill Valley, 381-9000
Spinnaker, Sausalito, 332-1500

Websites

What's Goin' On

VISITOR INFO:
www.sfguide.com	www.sanfran.com\
www.sfvisitor.org	www.travinfo.org
www.marinweb.org	www.craigslist.com
www.goldengate.org	www. exploratorium.edu.
www.sfmuni.com	www.angelislandferry.com
www.bart.org	www.blueandwhitefleet.com
www.angelisland.org	www.bayarea.citysearch.com
www.citypass.net	www.sfdowntown.com
www.zpub.com	www.bayareabackroads.com
www.millvalley.org	www.trailblazertravelbooks.com
www.marinairporter.com	www.ridgetrail.org

EVENTS:
www.calacademy.org	www.kfog.com
www.sfopera.com	www.bayguardian.com
www.sfballet.org	www.yerbabuenaarts.org
www.thinker.org	www.act-sfbay.org
www.sfmoma.org	www.marinsymphony.org
www.badm.org	www.finc.org
www.baydance.com	www.marinij.com
www.marinarts.org	www.marincenter.org
www.sfweekly.com	www.sweetwatersaloon.com
www.sfbg.com	www.bookpassage.com
www.sfgate.com.	www.baytv.com

AGENCIES:
Golden Gate National Recreation Area
www.nps.gov./goga
Point Reyes National Seashore
www.nps.gov./pore
Marin County Department of Parks
www.marin.org
Muir Woods National Monument
www.nps.gov./muwo
City of San Francisco
www.sfgov.org
California State Parks
www.cal-parks.ca.gov/

Index

See Resource Links for telephone numbers and listings of agencies, organizations, campgrounds, accommodations, and restaurants.

For individual copies or booktrade orders, please contact:

DIAMOND VALLEY COMPANY
89 Lower Manzanita Drive
Markleeville, CA   96120

Phone/fax: 530-694-2740

www.trailblazertravelbooks.com
email: trailblazer@gbis.com

All titles also available through major book distributors, stores and websites. Please notify the publisher with comments and suggestions. We value your readership.

Diamond Valley Company's
Trailblazer Travel Book Series:

ALPINE TRAILBLAZER
WHERE TO HIKE, SKI, BIKE, PACK,
PADDLE, FISH IN THE ALPINE SIERRA
FROM TAHOE TO YOSEMITE
ISBN 0-9670072-3-2

KAUAI TRAILBLAZER
WHERE TO HIKE, SNORKEL, BIKE,
PADDLE, SURF
ISBN 0-9670072-1-6

GOLDEN GATE TRAILBLAZER
WHERE TO HIKE, STROLL, BIKE, JOG, ROLL
IN SAN FRANCISCO AND MARIN
ISBN 0-9670072-2-4

*"It's an odd thing, but anyone who disappears
is said to have been seen in San Francisco."*
—Oscar Wilde